EVERYMAN'S LIBRARY
EDITED BY ERNEST RHYS

CLASSICAL

LIVY'S
HISTORY OF ROME · TRANS-
LATED WITH INTRODUCTION
BY REV. CANON ROBERTS
VOL. THREE

The Sages of Old Live Again in Us

GLANVILL

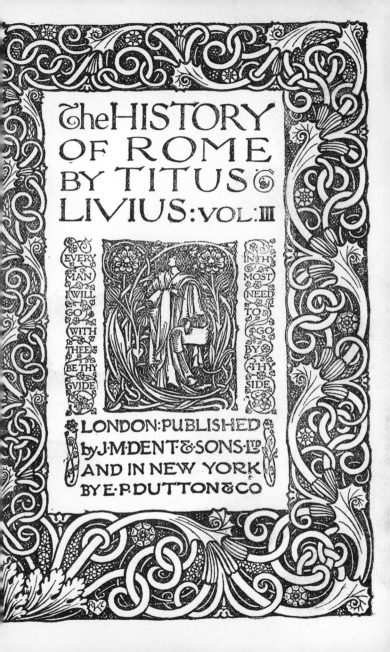

The HISTORY OF ROME BY TITUS LIVIUS: VOL. III

EVERY MAN I WILL GO WITH THEE BE THY GUIDE IN THY MOST NEED TO GO BY THY SIDE

LONDON: PUBLISHED by J. M. DENT & SONS L?? AND IN NEW YORK BY E. P. DUTTON & CO

SUMMARY

BOOK XXI

THE origin of the Second Punic War, pp. 1, 2. The Carthaginian general Hannibal crossed the Ebro in defiance of treaty obligations, pp. 4-6. The city of Saguntum, in alliance with Rome, besieged for eight months, pp. 6-14. Envoys sent to Carthage to demand redress, p. 16. Declaration of war on the part of Rome, pp. 17, 18. Commencement of Hannibal's march to Rome, pp. 19-22. After surmounting the passes of the Pyrenees he proceeded through Gaul and routed the Volcae who tried to oppose him, pp. 22-29. He reached the Alps and after a wearisome and trying journey over them, in the course of which he frequently repulsed the attacks of the natives, he descended into Italy, pp. 30-35. Defeat of the Romans in a cavalry action at the Ticinus; Publius Cornelius Scipio was wounded in the action and saved by his son, who was afterwards known as " Africanus," pp. 36-43. Second defeat of the Romans at the Trebia, pp. 48-53. Attempt of Hannibal to cross the Apennines; the men suffered terrible hardships owing to the violent storms, pp. 54-55. Success of Cn. Scipio in Spain, Mago, the Carthaginian general, taken prisoner, pp. 56-58.

BOOK XXII

Hannibal led his army through the marshes of the Arno, where he lost the sight of one eye, and after a march of four days and three nights without sleep or rest he entered Etruria, pp. 63-64. The consul Flaminius, a rash and headstrong man, advanced to meet him in defiance of the auspices. He was thrown from his horse and as the military standards could not be lifted out of the grounds he ordered them to be dug out, pp. 64-65. Circumvented by the tactics of Hannibal he and his army were destroyed at Lake Trasumennus, pp. 65-68. Six thousand men who had surrendered on terms to Maharbal were afterwards, through Hannibal's perfidy, thrown into chains, p. 68. Great grief in Rome at the reception of the news; two mothers died from excess of joy at the unhoped-for return of their sons, pp. 68-69. In consequence of this disaster a sacred spring was vowed in accordance with the directions of the Sacred Books, pp. 71-72. Quintus Fabius Maximus was nominated Dictator to oppose Hannibal and refused to risk a general engagement as he would not expose his troops, dispirited by their defeats, to an enemy whose confidence was raised by so many victories, pp. 73-75. M. Minucius, Master of the Horse, an impetuous and reckless man, accused the Dictator of lack of courage and enterprise and succeeded in persuading the people to place him in joint command with the Dictator, p. 76; pp. 88-91. The army was divided between them and they occupied separate camps, pp. 90-91. Minucius engaged the enemy in an unfavourable position, p. 92. His legions were in the greatest danger and were only saved by Fabius Maximus coming up with his troops, p. 93. Overcome by this generous act, he joined camp with the Dictator, saluted him as "Father," and ordered his men to do the same, pp. 93-94. After devastating Campania, Hannibal was shut in by Fabius between Casilinum and Mt. Callicula. Fastening bundles of hay on the heads of oxen and setting them on fire he put the Roman detachment stationed on Callicula to flight, and so emerged from the pass, pp. 78-80. Whilst setting fire to the surrounding country he spared the Dictator's land in the hope of casting suspicion on him, p. 86. After this, Æmilius Paulus and Terentius Varro, the new consuls, fought against Hannibal at Cannae and sustained a crushing defeat, pp. 108-111. The number of those killed amounted to 45,000 men; amongst them were ninety senators and thirty who had been either consuls or praetors or ædiles, p. 112. A plot was formed by the young nobles who despaired of their country to abandon Italy. Publius Cornelius Scipio surprised them in the midst of their deliberations and, holding his drawn sword over them, swore that he would treat as an enemy any man who refused to take an oath not to quit his country. They all took the oath, p. 115. Owing to the scarcity of fighting men 8000 slaves were furnished with arms, p. 119. Those who had been taken prisoners at Cannae asked permission to ransom themselves, but were not allowed to do so, pp. 119-125. Successful operations in Spain, pp. 81-86. Two Vestal virgins, Opimia and Florentia, were convicted of unchastity, p. 118. Varro was met on his return to the City and formally thanked for not having despaired of the republic, p. 126.]

BOOK XXIII

Capua revolted to Hannibal, pp. 128-133. Mago went to Carthage to announce the victory of Cannae and produced in the vestibule of the Senate-house a quantity of golden rings taken from the bodies of the slain, which were said to amount to more than a *modius*. Hanno thereupon urged the senate to make peace with Rome, but failed owing to the opposition of the Barcine party, pp. 138-140. The praetor C. Marcellus gained a success over Hannibal at Nola by making a sortie from the town, pp. 144, 145. Casilinum was invested by the Carthaginians and reduced to such extremities that the besieged ate mice and the leather straps and coverings of their shields; nuts were floated down the Vulturnus by the Romans for their support, p. 148. The number of senators was made up by electing 177 from the equestrian order, p. 154. The praetor L. Postumius and his army were destroyed by the Gauls, pp. 153, 154. The two Scipios—Cnaeus and Publius—defeated Hasdrubal and made themselves masters of Spain, pp. 158, 159. The remains of the army of Cannae were sent to Sicily, not to return till the war was over, p. 161. The praetor C. Marcellus defeated and routed Hannibal at Nola, and was thus the first to raise the hopes of the Romans after their many defeats, pp. 177, 178. An alliance was formed between Hannibal and Philip, King of Macedon, pp. 164, 165. The two Scipios were successful in Spain, pp. 181, 182, and T. Manlius in Sardinia, where he captured Hasdrubal, the Carthaginian commander, and also Mago and Hanno, pp. 171-173. Hannibal's army was in such luxurious winter quarters that it became completely enervated in both mind and body, p. 147.

BOOK XXIV

Carthaginian operations in Bruttium, pp. 183-186. Hieronymus, whose father Hiero had been a steady friend to Rome, went over to the Carthaginians, pp. 186-189, and was murdered by his subjects for his tyranny, pp. 189, 190. Tiberius Gracchus defeated Hanno in a great battle at Beneventum and the slaves who formed the majority of his army received their freedom after the victory, pp. 197-200. Marcellus fought an action with Hannibal at Nola, pp. 200, 201. Capture of Casilinum, pp. 203, 204. Revolution in Sicily, pp. 205-214. Capture of Leontini by Marcellus, p. 215. Syracuse hostile to Rome, pp. 217, 218. Marcellus began the siege of Syracuse, p. 218. War declared against Philip of Macedon, who was routed and retreated to his own country, pp. 226, 227. Scipio's successes in Spain and recapture of Saguntum, pp. 227-229. Fabius recovered Arpi in Apulia, pp. 231-234. Syphax, king of Numidia, became an ally of Rome, pp. 235, 236; defeated and put to flight by Masinissa, p. 236. The Celtiberians enlisted in the service of Rome as the first mercenary troops the Romans ever employed, p. 236.

BOOK XXV

Foreign superstitions in Rome, pp. 237, 238. Publius Cornelius Scipio elected ædile before attaining the legal age, p. 239. Fraudulent public contractors prosecuted, pp. 240-242. Unsuccessful appeal of the survivors of Cannae, pp. 242-245. Surrender of Tarentum, with the exception of the citadel, to Hannibal, pp. 245-249. The prophecies of Marcius, pp. 251-253. Hanno's army defeated by the two consuls, pp. 254-256. Revolt of Metapontum and Thurii to Hannibal, pp. 256, 257. Betrayal and death of Tiberius Gracchus, pp. 258-260. Centenius Paenula, formerly a centurion, was entrusted by the senate with 8000 men, and after augmenting his force, engaged Hannibal, who almost annihilated his army, p. 263. Fulvius defeated by Hannibal with a loss of 10,000 men, pp. 264, 265. Capua invested, p. 266. Capture of Syracuse by Marcellus after a two years' siege, pp. 267-277. Death of Archimedes, pp. 277, 278. Defeat and death of the two Scipios in Spain, pp. 278-285. Lucius Marcius, a Roman knight, rallied the defeated troops and ultimately vanquished the enemy and captured both their camps, pp. 283-288. Settlement of Sicily by Marcellus, pp. 289-291.

CONTENTS

CONTENTS

LIVY

BOOK XXI

FROM SAGUNTUM TO THE TREBIA

I. *Importance of the Second Punic War.*—I consider myself at liberty to commence what is only a section of my history with a prefatory remark such as most writers have placed at the very beginning of their works, namely, that the war I am about to describe is the most memorable of any that have ever been waged, I mean the war which the Carthaginians, under Hannibal's leadership, waged with Rome. No states, no nations ever met in arms greater in strength or richer in resources; these Powers themselves had never before been in so high a state of efficiency or better prepared to stand the strain of a long war; they were no strangers to each other's tactics after their experience in the first Punic War; and so variable were the fortunes and so doubtful the issue of the war that those who were ultimately victorious were in the earlier stages brought nearest to ruin. And yet, great as was their strength, the hatred they felt towards each other was almost greater. The Romans were furious with indignation because the vanquished had dared to take the offensive against their conquerors; the Carthaginians bitterly resented what they regarded as the tyrannical and rapacious conduct of Rome.

The prime author of the war was Hamilcar. There was a story widely current that when, after bringing the African War to a close, he was offering sacrifices before transporting his army to Spain, the boy Hannibal, nine years old, was coaxing his father to take him with him, and his father led him up to the altar and made him swear with his hand laid on the victim that as soon as he possibly could he would show himself the enemy of Rome. The loss of Sicily and Sardinia vexed the proud spirit of the man, for he felt that the cession of Sicily had been made hastily in a spirit of despair, and that Sardinia had been filched by the Romans during the troubles in

Africa, who, not content with seizing it, had imposed an indemnity as well.

II. Smarting under these wrongs, he made it quite clear from
his conduct of the African War which followed immediately
upon the conclusion of peace with Rome, and from the way in
which he strengthened and extended the rule of Carthage during
the nine years' war with Spain, that he was meditating a far
greater war than any he was actually engaged in, and that had
he lived longer it would have been under his command that the
Carthaginians effected the invasion of Italy, which they actually
carried out under Hannibal.

Death of Hamilcar.—The death of Hamilcar, occurring as it
did most opportunely, and the tender years of Hannibal delayed
the war. Hasdrubal, coming between father and son, held the
supreme power for eight years. He is said to have become a
favourite of Hamilcar's owing to his personal beauty as a boy;
afterwards he displayed talents of a very different order, and
became his son-in-law. Through this connection he was placed
in power by the influence of the Barcine party, which was unduly
preponderant with the soldiers and the common people, but
his elevation was utterly against the wishes of the nobles.
Trusting to policy rather than to arms, he did more to extend
the empire of Carthage by forming connections with the petty
chieftains and winning over new tribes by making friends of
their leading men than by force of arms or by war. But peace
brought him no security. A barbarian whose master he had
put to death murdered him in broad daylight, and when seized
by the bystanders he looked as happy as though he had escaped.
Even when put to the torture, his delight at the success of
his attempt mastered his pain and his face wore a smiling
expression.

Owing to the marvellous tact he had shown in winning over
the tribes and incorporating them into his dominions, the
Romans had renewed the treaty with Hasdrubal. Under its
terms, the River Ebro was to form the boundary between the
two empires, and Saguntum, occupying an intermediate position
between them, was to be a free city.

III. *Hannibal made Commander-in-Chief.*—There was no
hesitation shown in filling his place. The soldiers led the way
by bringing the young Hannibal forthwith to the palace and
proclaiming him their commander-in-chief amidst universal
applause. Their action was followed by the plebs.

Whilst little more than a boy, Hasdrubal had written to

invite Hannibal to come to him in Spain, and the matter had actually been discussed in the senate. The Barcines wanted Hannibal to become familiar with military service; Hanno, the leader of the opposite party, resisted this. " Hasdrubal's request," he said, " appears a reasonable one, and yet I do not think we ought to grant it." This paradoxical utterance aroused the attention of the whole senate. He continued: " The youthful beauty which Hasdrubal surrendered to Hannibal's father he considers he has a fair claim to ask for in return from the son. It ill becomes us, however, to habituate our youths to the lust of our commanders, by way of military training. Are we afraid that it will be too long before Hamilcar's son surveys the extravagant power and the pageant of royalty which his father assumed, and that there will be undue delay in our becoming the slaves of the despot to whose son-in-law our armies have been bequeathed as though they were his patrimony? I, for my part, consider that this youth ought to be kept at home and taught to live in obedience to the laws and the magistrates on an equality with his fellow-citizens; if not, this small fire will some day or other kindle a vast conflagration."

IV. Hanno's proposal received but slight support, though almost all the best men in the council were with him, but as usual, numbers carried the day against reason.

Character of Hannibal.—No sooner had Hannibal landed in Spain than he became a favourite with the whole army. The veterans thought they saw Hamilcar restored to them as he was in his youth; they saw the same determined expression, the same piercing eyes, the same cast of features. He soon showed, however, that it was not his father's memory that helped him most to win the affections of the army. Never was there a character more capable of the two tasks so opposed to each other of commanding and obeying; you could not easily make out whether the army or its general were more attached to him. Whenever courage and resolution were needed Hasdrubal never cared to entrust the command to any one else; and there was no leader in whom the soldiers placed more confidence or under whom they showed more daring. He was fearless in exposing himself to danger and perfectly self-possessed in the presence of danger. No amount of exertion could cause him either bodily or mental fatigue; he was equally indifferent to heat and cold; his eating and drinking were measured by the needs of nature, not by appetite; his hours of sleep were not determined by day or night, whatever time was not taken up with active duties was given to sleep and rest, but that rest was not wooed on a soft couch or in silence, men often saw him lying on the ground amongst the sentinels and outposts, wrapped in his military cloak. His dress was in no way superior to that of his comrades; what did make him conspicuous were his arms and horses. He was by far the foremost both of the cavalry and the infantry, the first to enter the fight and the last to leave the field.

But these great merits were matched by great vices—inhuman cruelty, a perfidy worse than Punic, an utter absence of truthfulness, reverence, fear of the gods, respect for oaths, sense of religion. Such was his character, a compound of virtues and vices. For three years he served under Hasdrubal, and during the whole time he never lost an opportunity of gaining by practice or observation the experience necessary for one who was to be a great leader of men.

V. *Preparations for attacking Saguntum.* — From the day when he was proclaimed commander-in-chief, he seemed to regard Italy as his assigned field of action, and war with Rome as a duty imposed upon him. Feeling that he ought not to delay operations, lest some accident should overtake him as in the case of his father and afterwards of Hasdrubal, he decided to attack the Saguntines. As an attack on them would inevitably set the arms of Rome in motion, he began by invading the Olcades, a tribe who were within the boundaries but not under the dominion of Carthage. He wished to make it appear that Saguntum was not his immediate object, but that he was drawn into a war with her by the force of circumstances, by the conquest, that is, of all her neighbours and the annexation of their territory. Cartala, a wealthy city and the capital of the tribe, was taken by storm and sacked; the smaller cities, fearing a similar fate, capitulated and agreed to pay an indemnity.

His victorious army enriched with plunder was marched into winter quarters in New Carthage. Here, by a lavish distribution of the spoils and the punctual discharge of all arrears of pay, he secured the allegiance of his own people and of the allied contingents.

At the beginning of spring he extended his operations to the Vaccaei, and two of their cities, Arbocala and Hermandica, were taken by assault. Arbocala held out for a considerable time, owing to the courage and numbers of its defenders; the fugitives from Hermandica joined hands with those of the Olcades who had abandoned their country—this tribe had been subjugated the previous year—and together they stirred up the Carpetani to war. Not far from the Tagus an attack was made upon Hannibal as he was returning from his expedition against the Vaccaei, and his army, laden as it was with plunder, was thrown into some confusion. Hannibal declined battle and fixed his camp by the side of the river; as soon as there was quiet and silence amongst the enemy, he forded the stream. His entrenchments had been carried just far enough to allow room for the enemy to cross over, and he decided to attack them during their passage of the river. He instructed his cavalry to wait until they had actually entered the water and then to attack them; his forty elephants he stationed on the bank. The Carpetani together with the contingents of the Olcades and Vaccaei numbered altogether 100,000 men, an irresistible force had they been fighting on level ground. Their innate fearlessness, the confidence inspired by their numbers, their belief that the enemy's retreat was due to fear, all made them look on victory as certain, and the river as the only obstacle to it. Without any word of command having been given, they raised a universal shout and plunged, each man straight in front of him, into the river. A huge force of cavalry descended from the opposite bank, and the two bodies met in mid-stream. The struggle was anything but an equal one. The infantry, feeling their footing insecure, even where the river was fordable, could have been ridden down even by unarmed horsemen, whereas the cavalry, with their bodies and weapons free and their horses steady even in the midst of the current, could fight at close quarters or not, as they chose. A large proportion were swept down the river, some were carried by cross currents to the other side where the enemy were, and were trampled to death by the elephants. Those in the rear thought it safest to return to their own side, and began to collect together as well as their fears allowed them, but before they had time to recover themselves Hannibal entered the river with his infantry in battle order and drove them in flight from the bank.

He followed up his victory by laying waste their fields, and in a few days was able to receive the submission of the Carpetani.

There was no part of the country beyond the Ebro which did not now belong to the Carthaginians, with the exception of Saguntum.

VI. War had not been formally declared against this city, but there were already grounds for war. The seeds of quarrel were being sown amongst her neighbours, especially amongst the Turdetani. When the man who had sown the seed showed himself

ready to aid and abet the quarrel, and his object plainly was
not to refer the question to arbitration, but to appeal to force,
the Saguntines sent a deputation to Rome to beg for help in a
war which was inevitably approaching. The consuls for the
time being were P. Cornelius Scipio and Tiberius Sempronius
Longus. After introducing the envoys they invited the senate
to declare its opinion as to what policy should be adopted. It
was decided that commissioners should be sent to Spain to
investigate the circumstances, and if they considered it necessary
they were to warn Hannibal not to interfere with the Saguntines,
who were allies of Rome; then they were to cross over to Africa
and lay before the Carthaginian council the complaints which they
had made. But before the commission was despatched news
came that the siege of Saguntum had, to every one's surprise,
actually commenced. The whole position of affairs required to
be reconsidered by the senate; some were for assigning Spain
and Africa as separate fields of action for the two consuls, and
thought that the war ought to be prosecuted by land and sea;
others were for confining the war solely to Hannibal in Spain;
others again were of opinion that such an immense task ought
not to be entered upon hastily, and that they ought to await the
return of the commission from Spain. This latter view seemed
the safest and was adopted, and the commissioners, P. Valerius
Flaccus and Q. Baebius Tamphilus, were despatched without
further delay to Hannibal. If he refused to abandon hostilities
they were to proceed to Carthage to demand the surrender of the
general to answer for his breach of treaty.

VII. *The Siege of Saguntum.*—During these proceedings in
Rome the siege of Saguntum was being pressed with the utmost
vigour. That city was by far the most wealthy of all beyond
the Ebro; it was situated about a mile from the sea. It is said
to have been founded by settlers from the island of Zacynthus,
with an admixture of Rutulians from Ardea. In a short time,
however, it had attained to great prosperity, partly through its
land and sea-borne commerce, partly through the rapid increase
of its population, and also through the maintenance of a high
standard of political integrity which led it to act with a loyalty
towards its allies that brought about its ruin.

After carrying his ravages everywhere throughout the territory,
Hannibal attacked the city from three separate points. There
was an angle of the fortifications which looked down on a more
open and level descent than the rest of the ground surrounding
the city, and here he decided to bring up his *vineae* to allow the

battering rams to be placed against the walls. But although the ground to a considerable distance from the walls was sufficiently level to admit of the *vineae* being brought up, they found when they had succeeded in doing this that they made no progress. A huge tower overlooked the place, and the wall, being here more open to attack, had been carried to a greater height than the rest of the fortifications. As the position was one of especial danger, so the resistance offered by a picked body of defenders was of the most resolute character. At first they confined themselves to keeping the enemy back by the discharge of missiles and making it impossible for them to continue their operations in safety. As time went on, however, their weapons no longer flashed on the walls or from the tower, they ventured on a sortie and attacked the outposts and siege works of the enemy. In these irregular encounters the Carthaginians lost nearly as many men as the Saguntines. Hannibal himself, approaching the wall somewhat incautiously, fell with a severe wound in his thigh from a javelin, and such was the confusion and dismay that ensued that the *vineae* and siege works were all but abandoned.

VIII. For a few days, until the general's wound was healed, there was a blockade rather than an active siege, and during this interval, though there was a respite from fighting, the construction of siege works and approaches went on uninterruptedly. When the fighting was resumed it was fiercer than ever. In spite of the difficulties of the ground the *vineae* were advanced and the battering rams placed against the walls. The Carthaginians had the superiority in numbers—there were said to have been 150,000 fighting men—whilst the defenders, obliged to keep watch and ward everywhere, were dissipating their strength and finding their numbers unequal to the task. The walls were now being pounded by the rams, and in many places had been shaken down. One part where a continuous fall had taken place laid the city open; three towers in succession, and the whole of the wall between them fell with a tremendous crash. The Carthaginians looked upon the town as already captured after that fall, and both sides rushed through the breach as though the wall had only served to protect them from each other. There was nothing of the desultory fighting which goes on when cities are stormed, as each side gets an opportunity of attacking the other. The two bodies of combatants confronted one another in the space between the ruined wall and the houses of the city in as regular formation as though they had been in an open field.

On the one side there was the courage of hope, on the other the courage of despair. The Carthaginians believed that with a little effort on their part the city would be theirs; the Saguntines opposed their bodies as a shield for their fatherland now stripped of its walls; not a man relaxed his foothold for fear of letting an enemy in through the spot which he had left open. So the hotter and closer the fighting became the greater grew the number of wounded, for no missile fell ineffectively amongst the crowded ranks.

The missile used by the Saguntines was the *phalarica*, a javelin with a shaft smooth and round up to the head, which, as in the *pilum*, was an iron point of square section. The shaft was wrapped in tow and then smeared with pitch; the iron head was three feet long and capable of penetrating armour and body alike. Even if it only stuck in the shield and did not reach the body it was a most formidable weapon, for when it was discharged with the tow set on fire the flame was fanned to a fiercer heat by its passage through the air, and it forced the soldier to throw away his shield and left him defenceless against the sword thrusts which followed.

IX. The conflict had now gone on for a considerable time without any advantage to either side; the courage of the Saguntines was rising as they found themselves keeping up an unhoped-for resistance, whilst the Carthaginians, unable to conquer, were beginning to look upon themselves as defeated. Suddenly the defenders, raising their battle-shout, forced the enemy back to the débris of the ruined wall; there, stumbling and in disorder, they were forced still further back and finally driven in rout and flight to their camp.

The Envoys land in Spain.—Meantime it was announced that envoys had arrived from Rome. Hannibal sent messengers down to the harbour to meet them and inform them that it would be unsafe for them to advance any further through so many wild tribes now in arms, and also that Hannibal in the present critical position of affairs had no time to receive embassies. It was quite certain that if they were not admitted they would go to Carthage. He therefore forestalled them by sending messengers with a letter addressed to the heads of the Barcine party, to warn his supporters and prevent the other side from making any concessions to Rome.

X. *Their Arrival in Carthage.*—The result was that, beyond being received and heard by the Carthaginian senate, the embassy found its mission a failure. Hanno alone, against the whole senate, spoke in favour of observing the treaty, and his speech was listened to in silence out of respect to his personal authority, not because his hearers approved of his sentiments.

He appealed to them in the name of the gods, who are the witnesses and arbiters of treaties, not to provoke a war with Rome in addition to the one with Saguntum. "I urged you," he said, "and warned you not to send Hamilcar's son to the army. That man's spirit, that man's offspring cannot rest; as long as any single representative of the blood and name of Barca survives our treaty with Rome will never remain unimperilled. You have sent to the army, as though supplying fuel to the fire, a young man who is consumed with a passion for sovereign power, and who recognises that the only way to it lies in passing his life surrounded by armed legions and perpetually stirring up fresh wars. It is you, therefore, who have fed this fire which is now scorching you. Your armies are investing Saguntum, which by the terms of the treaty they are forbidden to approach; before long the legions of Rome will invest Carthage, led by the same generals under the same divine guidance under which they avenged our breach of treaty obligations in the late war. Are you strangers to the enemy, to yourselves, to the fortunes of each nation? That worthy commander of yours refused to allow ambassadors who came from allies, on behalf of allies, to enter his camp, and set at naught the law of nations. Those men, repulsed from a place to which even an enemy's envoys are not refused access, have come to us; they ask for the satisfaction which the treaty prescribes; they demand the surrender of the guilty party in order that the State may clear itself from all taint of guilt. The slower they are to take action, the longer they are in commencing war, so much the more persistence and determination, I fear, will they show when war has begun. Remember the Ægates and Eryx, and all you had to go through for four-and-twenty years. This boy was not commanding then, but his father, Hamilcar—a second Mars as his friends would have us believe. But we broke the treaty then as we are breaking it now; we did not keep our hands off Tarentum or, which is the same thing, off Italy then any more than we are keeping our hands off Saguntum now, and so gods and men combined to defeat us, and the question in dispute, namely, which nation had broken the treaty, was settled by the issue of the war, which, like an impartial judge, left the victory on the side which was in the right. It is against Carthage that Hannibal is now bringing up his *vineae* and

towers, it is Carthage whose walls he is shaking with his battering rams. The ruins of Saguntum—would that I might prove
a false prophet—will fall on our heads, and the war which
was begun with Saguntum will have to be carried on with
Rome.

" ' Shall we then surrender Hannibal? ' some one will say. I
am quite aware that as regards him my advice will have little
weight, owing to my differences with his father, but whilst I
was glad to hear of Hamilcar's death, for if he were alive we
should already be involved in war with Rome, I feel nothing but
loathing and detestation for this youth, the mad firebrand who
is kindling this war. Not only do I hold that he ought to be
surrendered as an atonement for the broken treaty, but even
if no demand for his surrender were made I consider that he
ought to be deported to the farthest corner of the earth, exiled
to some spot from which no tidings of him, no mention of his
name, could reach us, and where it would be impossible for him
to disturb the welfare and tranquillity of our State.

" This then is what I propose: ' That a commission be at once
despatched to Rome to inform the senate of our compliance with
their demands, and a second to Hannibal ordering him to withdraw his army from Saguntum and then surrendering him to
the Romans in accordance with the terms of the treaty, and I
also propose that a third body of commissioners be sent to
make reparation to the Saguntines.' "

XI. When Hanno sat down no one deemed it necessary to
make any reply, so completely was the senate, as a body, on
the side of Hannibal. They accused Hanno of speaking in a
tone of more uncompromising hostility than Flaccus Valerius,
the Roman envoy, had assumed.

The reply which it was decided to make to the Roman
demands was that the war was started by the Saguntines not
by Hannibal, and that the Roman people would commit an act
of injustice if they took the part of the Saguntines against
their ancient allies, the Carthaginians.

Final Assault on Saguntum.—Whilst the Romans were wasting time in despatching commissioners, things were quiet round
Saguntum. Hannibal's men were worn out with the fighting
and the labours of the siege, and after placing detachments on
guard over the *vineae* and other military engines, he gave his
army a few days' rest. He employed this interval in stimulat-
ing the courage of his men by exasperating them against the
enemy, and firing them by the prospect of rewards. After he

had given out in the presence of his assembled troops that the plunder of the city would go to them, they were all in such a state of excitement that had the signal been given then and there it seemed impossible for anything to withstand them. As for the Saguntines, though they had a respite from fighting for some days, neither meeting attacks nor making any, they worked at their defences so continuously by day and night that they completed a fresh wall at the place where the fall of the former wall had laid the town open.

The assault was recommenced with greater vigour than ever. In every direction confused shouts and clamour resounded, so that it was difficult to ascertain where to render assistance most promptly or where it was most needed. Hannibal was present in person to encourage his men, who were bringing up a tower on rollers which overtopped all the fortifications of the city. Catapults and *ballistae* had been put in position on each of the storeys, and after it had been brought up to the walls it swept them clear of the defenders. Seizing his opportunity, Hannibal told off about 500 African troops to undermine the wall with pick-axes, an easy task, as the stones were not fixed with cement but with layers of mud between the courses in the ancient fashion of construction. More of it consequently fell than had been dug away, and through the gaping ruin the columns of armed warriors marched into the city. They seized some high ground, and after massing their catapults and *ballistae* there they enclosed it with a wall so as to have a fortified position actually within the city which could dominate it like a citadel. The Saguntines on their side carried an inside wall round the portion of the city not yet captured. Both sides kept up their fortifying and fighting with the utmost energy, but by having to defend the interior portion of the city the Saguntines were continually reducing its dimensions. In addition to this there was a growing scarcity of everything as the siege was prolonged, and the anticipations of outside help were becoming fainter; the Romans, their one hope, were so far away, whilst all immediately round them was in the hands of the enemy.

For a few days their drooping spirits were revived by the sudden departure of Hannibal on an expedition against the Oretani and the Carpetani. The rigorous way in which troops were being levied in these two tribes had created great excitement, and they had kept the officers who were superintending the levy practically prisoners. A general revolt was feared, but the unexpected swiftness of Hannibal's movements took them by surprise and they abandoned their hostile attitude.

XII. The attack on Saguntum was not slackened; Maharbal, the son of Himilco, whom Hannibal had left in command, carried on operations with such energy that the general's absence was not felt by either friends or foes. He fought several successful actions, and with the aid of three battering rams brought down a considerable portion of the wall, and on Hannibal's return showed him the place all strewn with the newly-fallen wall. The army was at once led to an assault on the citadel; a desperate fight began, with heavy losses on both sides, and a part of the citadel was captured.

Attempts were now made in the direction of peace, though with but faint hopes of success. Two men undertook the task, Alco, a Saguntine, and Alorcus, a Spaniard. Alco, thinking that his prayers might have some effect, crossed over without the knowledge of the Saguntines to Hannibal at night. When he found that he gained nothing by his tears, and that the conditions offered were such as a victor exasperated by resistance would insist upon, harsh and severe, he laid aside the character of a pleader and remained with the enemy as a deserter, alleging that any one who advocated peace on such terms would be put to death. The conditions were that restitution should be made to the Turdetani, all the gold and silver should be delivered up, and the inhabitants should depart with one garment each and take up their abode wherever the Carthaginians should order them.

As Alco insisted that the Saguntines would not accept peace on these terms, Alorcus, convinced, as he said, that when everything else has gone courage also goes, undertook to mediate a peace on those conditions. At that time he was one of Hannibal's soldiers, but he was recognised as a guest friend by the city of Saguntum. He started on his mission, gave up his weapon openly to the guard, crossed the lines, and was at his request conducted to the praetor of Saguntum. A crowd, drawn from all classes of society, soon gathered, and after a way had been cleared through the press, Alorcus was admitted to an audience of the senate. He addressed them in the following terms:

XIII. " If your fellow-townsman, Alco, had shown the same courage in bringing back to you the terms on which Hannibal will grant peace that he showed in going to Hannibal to beg for peace, this journey of mine would have been unnecessary. I have not come to you either as an advocate for Hannibal or as a deserter. But as he has remained with the enemy either through your fault or his own—his own if his fears were only feigned, yours if those who report what is true have to answer for their lives—I have come to you out of regard to the old ties of hospitality which have so long subsisted between us, that you may not be left in ignorance of the fact that there do exist terms on which you can secure peace and the safety of your lives. Now, that it is for your sake alone and not on behalf of any one else that I say what I am saying before you is proved by the fact that as long as you had the strength to maintain a successful resistance, and as long as you had any hopes of help from Rome, I never breathed a word about making peace. But now that you have no longer anything to hope for from Rome, now that neither your arms nor your walls suffice to protect you, I bring you a peace forced upon you by necessity rather than recommended by the fairness of its conditions. But the hopes, faint as they are, of peace rest upon your accepting as conquered men the terms which Hannibal as conqueror imposes and not looking upon what is taken from you as a positive loss, since everything is at the victor's mercy, but regarding what is left to you as a free gift from him. The city, most of which he has laid in ruins, the whole of which he has all but captured, he takes from you; your fields and lands he leaves you; and he will assign you a site where you can build a new town. He orders all the gold and silver, both that belonging to the State and that owned by private individuals, to be brought to him; your persons and those of your wives and children he preserves inviolate on condition that you consent to leave Saguntum with only two garments apiece and without arms. These are the demands of your victorious enemy, and heavy and bitter as they are, your miserable plight urges you to accept them. I am not without hope that when everything has passed into his power he will relax some of these conditions, but I consider that even as they are you ought to submit to them rather than permit yourselves to be butchered and your wives and children seized and carried off before your eyes."

XIV. A large crowd had gradually collected to listen to the speaker, and the popular Assembly had become mingled with the senate, when without a moment's warning the leading citizens withdrew before any reply was given. They collected all the gold and silver from public and private sources and brought it into the forum, where a fire had already been kindled, and flung it into the flames, and most of them thereupon leaped

into the fire themselves. The terror and confusion which this
occasioned throughout the city was heightened by the noise of
a tumult in the direction of the citadel. A tower after much
battering had fallen, and through the breach created by its fall
a Carthaginian cohort advanced to the attack and signalled to
their commander that the customary outposts and guards had
disappeared and the city was unprotected. Hannibal thought
that he ought to seize the opportunity and act promptly.
Attacking it with his full strength, he took the place in a
moment. Orders had been given that all the adult males were
to be put to death; a cruel order, but under the circumstances
inevitable, for whom would it have been possible to spare when
they either shut themselves up with their wives and children
and burnt their houses over their heads, or if they fought,
would not cease fighting till they were killed?

XV. An enormous amount of booty was found in the captured city. Although most of it had been deliberately destroyed by the owners, and the enraged soldiers had observed
hardly any distinctions of age in the universal slaughter, whilst
all the prisoners that were taken were assigned to them, still,
it is certain that a considerable sum was realised by the sale
of the goods that were seized, and much valuable furniture
and apparel was sent to Carthage.

Some writers assert that Saguntum was taken in the eighth
month of the siege, and that Hannibal led his force from there
to New Carthage for the winter, his arrival in Italy occurring
five months later. In this case it is impossible for P. Cornelius
and Ti. Sempronius to have been the consuls to whom the
Saguntine envoys were sent at the beginning of the siege and
who afterwards, whilst still in office, fought with Hannibal,
one of them at the Ticinus, both shortly afterwards at the
Trebia. Either all the incidents occurred within a much
shorter period or else it was the capture of Saguntum, not the
beginning of the siege, which occurred when those two entered
upon office. For the battle of the Trebia cannot have fallen so
late as the year when Cn. Servilius and C. Flaminius were in
office, because C. Flaminius entered upon his consulship at
Ariminum, his election taking place under the consul Tiberius
Sempronius, who came to Rome after the battle of the Trebia
to hold the consular elections, and, after they were over, returned
to his army in winter quarters.

XVI. *Preparations in Rome for War.*—The commissioners
who had been sent to Carthage, on their return to Rome, reported

that everything breathed a hostile spirit. Almost on the very day they returned the news arrived of the fall of Saguntum, and such was the distress of the senate at the cruel fate of their allies, such was their feeling of shame at not having sent help to them, such their exasperation against the Carthaginians and their alarm for the safety of the State—for it seemed as though the enemy were already at their gates—that they were in no mood for deliberating, shaken as they were by so many conflicting emotions. There were sufficient grounds for alarm. Never had they met a more active or a more warlike enemy, and never had the Roman republic been so lacking in energy or so unprepared for war. The operations against the Sardinians, Corsicans, and Histrians, as well as those against the Illyrians, had been more of an annoyance than a training for the soldiers of Rome; whilst with the Gauls there had been desultory fighting rather than regular warfare. But the Carthaginians, a veteran enemy which for three-and-twenty years had seen hard and rough service amongst the Spanish tribes, and had always been victorious, trained under a general of exceptional ability, were now crossing the Ebro fresh from the sack of a most wealthy city, and were bringing with them all those Spanish tribes, eager for the fray. They would rouse the various Gaulish tribes, who were always ready to take up arms; there would be the whole world to fight against; the battle-ground would be Italy; the struggle would take place before the walls of Rome.

XVII. The seat of the campaigns had already been decided; the consuls were now ordered to draw lots. Spain fell to Cornelius, Africa to Sempronius. It was resolved that six legions should be raised for that year, the allies were to furnish such contingents as the consuls should deem necessary, and as large a fleet as possible was to be fitted out; 24,000 Roman infantry were called up and 1800 cavalry; the allies contributed 40,000 infantry and 4400 cavalry, and a fleet of 220 ships of war and 20 light galleys was launched.

The question was then formally submitted to the Assembly, Was it their will and pleasure that war should be declared against the people of Carthage? When this was decided, a special service of intercession was conducted; the procession marched through the streets of the city offering prayers at the various temples that the gods would grant a happy and prosperous issue to the war which the people of Rome had now ordered.

The forces were divided between the consuls in the following way: To Sempronius two legions were assigned, each consisting of 4000 infantry and 300 cavalry, and 16,000 infantry and 1800 cavalry from the allied contingents. He was also provided with 160 warships and 12 light galleys. With this combined land and sea force he was sent to Sicily, with instructions to cross over to Africa if the other consul succeeded in preventing the Carthaginian from invading Italy. Cornelius, on the other hand, was provided with a smaller force, as L. Manlius, the praetor, was himself being despatched to Gaul with a fairly strong detachment. Cornelius was weakest in his ships; he had only 60 warships, for it was never supposed that the enemy would come by sea or use his navy for offensive purposes. His land force was made up of two Roman legions, with their complement of cavalry, and 14,000 infantry from the allies with 1600 cavalry. The province of Gaul[1] was held by two Roman legions and 10,000 allied infantry with 600 Roman and 1000 allied cavalry. This force was ultimately employed in the Punic War.

XVIII. *War Declared.*—When these preparations were completed, the formalities necessary before entering upon war required that a commission should be despatched to Carthage. Those selected were men of age and experience—Q. Fabius, M. Livius, L. Æmilius, C. Licinius, and Q. Baebius. They were instructed to inquire whether it was with the sanction of the government that Hannibal had attacked Saguntum, and if, as seemed most probable, the Carthaginians should admit that it was so and proceed to defend their action, then the Roman envoys were to formally declare war upon Carthage.

As soon as they had arrived in Carthage they appeared before the senate. Q. Fabius had, in accordance with his instructions, simply put the question as to the responsibility of the government, when one of the members present said: "The language of your previous deputation was peremptory enough when you demanded the surrender of Hannibal on the assumption that he was attacking Saguntum on his own authority, but your language now, so far at least, is less provocative, though in effect more overbearing. For on that occasion it was Hannibal whose action you denounced and whose surrender you demanded, now you are seeking to extort from us a confession of guilt and insist upon obtaining instant satisfaction, as from men who admit they are in the wrong. I do not, however, consider that

the question is whether the attack on Saguntum was an act of
public policy or only that of a private citizen, but whether it
was justified by circumstances or not. It is for us to inquire
and take proceedings against a citizen when he has done anything on his own authority; the only point for you to discuss
is whether his action was compatible with the terms of the
treaty. Now, as you wish us to draw a distinction between
what our generals do with the sanction of the State and what
they do on their own initiative, you must remember that the
treaty with us was made by your consul, C. Lutatius,[2] and
whilst it contained provisions guarding the interests of the
allies of both nations, there was no such provision for the
Saguntines, for they were not your allies at the time. But,
you will say, by the treaty concluded with Hasdrubal, the
Saguntines are exempted from attack. I shall meet that with
your own arguments. You told us that you refused to be
bound by the treaty which your consul, C. Lutatius, concluded
with us, because it did not receive the authorisation of either
the senate or the Assembly. A fresh treaty was accordingly
made by your government. Now, if no treaties have any binding force for you unless they have been made with the authority
of your senate or by order of your Assembly, we, on our side,
cannot possibly be bound by Hasdrubal's treaty, which he made
without our knowledge. Drop all allusions to Saguntum and
the Ebro, and speak out plainly what has long been secretly
hatching in your minds."

Then the Roman, gathering up his toga, said, "Here we
bring you war and peace, take which you please." He was met
by a defiant shout bidding him give whichever he preferred,
and when, letting the folds of his toga fall, he said that he gave
them war, they replied that they accepted war and would carry
it on in the same spirit in which they accepted it.

XIX. *Its Justification.*—This straightforward question and
threat of war seemed to be more consonant with the dignity of
Rome than a wordy argument about treaties; it seemed so
previous to the destruction of Saguntum, and still more so
afterwards. For had it been a matter for argument, what
ground was there for comparing Hasdrubal's treaty with the
earlier one of Lutatius? In the latter it was expressly stated
that it would only be of force if the people approved it, whereas
in Hasdrubal's treaty there was no such saving clause. Besides,
his treaty had been silently observed for many years during his
lifetime, and was so generally approved that, even after its

author's death, none of its articles were altered. But even if they took their stand upon the earlier treaty—that of Lutatius— the Saguntines were sufficiently safeguarded by the allies of both parties being exempted from hostile treatment, for nothing was said about "the allies for the time being" or anything to exclude "any who should be hereafter taken into alliance." And since it was open to both parties to form fresh alliances, who would think it a fair arrangement that none should be received into alliance whatever their merits, or that when they had been received they should not be loyally protected, on the understanding that the allies of the Carthaginians should not be induced to revolt, or if they deserted their allies on their own accord were not to be received into alliance by the others?

The Roman envoys in accordance with their instructions went on to Spain for the purpose of visiting the different tribes and drawing them into alliance with Rome, or at least detaching them from the Carthaginians. The first they came to were the Borgusii, who were tired of Punic domination and gave them a favourable reception, and their success here excited a desire for change amongst many of the tribes beyond the Ebro. They came next to the Volciani, and the response they met with became widely known throughout Spain and determined the rest of the tribes against an alliance with Rome. This answer was given by the senior member of their national council in the following terms:

" Are you not ashamed, Romans, to ask us to form friendship with you in preference to the Carthaginians, seeing how those who have done so have suffered more through you, their allies, cruelly deserting them than through any injury inflicted on them by the Carthaginians? I advise you to look for allies where the fall of Saguntum has never been heard of; the nations of Spain see in the ruins of Saguntum a sad and emphatic warning against putting any trust in alliances with Rome." They were then peremptorily ordered to quit the territory of the Volciani, and from that time none of the councils throughout Spain gave them a more favourable reply.

After this fruitless mission in Spain they crossed over into Gaul.

XX. Here a strange and appalling sight met their eyes; the men attended the council fully armed, such was the custom of the country. When the Romans, after extolling the renown and courage of the Roman people and the greatness of their dominion, asked the Gauls not to allow the Carthaginian

invaders a passage through their fields and cities, such interruption and laughter broke out that the younger men were with
difficulty kept quiet by the magistrates and senior members
of the council. They thought it a most stupid and impudent
demand to make, that the Gauls, in order to prevent the war
from spreading into Italy, should turn it against themselves
and expose their own lands to be ravaged instead of other
people's. After quiet was restored the envoys were informed
that the Romans had rendered them no service, nor had the
Carthaginians done them any injury to make them take up
arms either on behalf of the Romans or against the Carthaginians. On the other hand, they heard that men of their race
were being expelled from Italy, and made to pay tribute to
Rome, and subjected to every other indignity.

Their experience was the same in all the other councils of Gaul,
nowhere did they hear a kindly or even a tolerably peaceable
word till they reached Massilia. There all the facts which their
allies had carefully and honestly collected were laid before
them; they were informed that the interest of the Gauls had
already been secured by Hannibal, but even he would not find
them very tractable, with their wild and untamable nature,
unless the chiefs were also won over with gold, a thing which as
a nation they were most eager to procure.

After thus traversing Spain and the tribes of Gaul the envoys
returned to Rome not long after the consuls had left for their
respective commands. They found the whole City in a state of
excitement; definite news had been received that the Carthaginians had crossed the Ebro, and every one was looking forward
to war.

XXI. *Hannibal prepares to invade Italy*.—After the capture of
Saguntum, Hannibal withdrew into winter quarters at New
Carthage. Information reached him there of the proceedings
at Rome and Carthage, and he learnt that he was not only the
general who was to conduct the war, but also the sole person who
was responsible for its outbreak. As further delay would be
most inexpedient, he sold and distributed the rest of the plunder,
and calling together those of his soldiers who were of Spanish
blood, he addressed them as follows: " I think, soldiers, that you
yourselves recognise that now that we have reduced all the tribes
in Spain we shall either have to bring our campaigns to an end
and disband our armies or else we must transfer our wars to other
lands. If we seek to win plunder and glory from other nations,
then these tribes will enjoy not only the blessings of peace, but

also the fruits of victory. Since, therefore, there await us campaigns far from home, and it is uncertain when you will again see your homes and all that is dear to you, I grant a furlough to every one who wishes to visit his friends. You must reassemble at the commencement of spring, so that we may, with the kindly help of the gods, enter upon a war which will bring us immense plunder and cover us with glory." They all welcomed the opportunity, so spontaneously offered, of visiting their homes after so long an absence, and in view of a still longer absence in the future. The winter's rest, coming after their past exertions, and soon to be followed by greater ones, restored their faculties of mind and body and strengthened them for fresh trials of endurance.

In the early days of spring they reassembled according to orders. After reviewing the whole of the native contingents, Hannibal left for Gades, where he discharged his vows to Hercules, and bound himself by fresh obligations to that deity in case his enterprise should succeed. As Africa would be open to attack from the side of Sicily during his land march through Spain and the two Gauls into Italy, he decided to secure that country with a strong garrison. To supply their place he requisitioned troops from Africa, a light-armed force consisting mainly of slingers. By thus transferring Africans to Spain and Spaniards to Africa, the soldiers of each nationality would be expected to render more efficient service, as being practically under reciprocal obligations. The force he despatched to Africa consisted of 13,850 Spanish infantry furnished with ox-hide bucklers, and 870 Balearic slingers, with a composite body of 1200 cavalry drawn from numerous tribes. This force was destined partly for the defence of Carthage, partly to hold the African territory. At the same time recruiting officers were sent to various communities;[3] some 4000 men of good family were called up who were under orders to be conveyed to Carthage to strengthen its defence, and also to serve as hostages for the loyalty of their people.

XXII. Spain also had to be provided for, all the more so as Hannibal was fully aware that Roman commissioners had been going all about the country to win over the leading men of the various tribes. He placed it in charge of his energetic and able brother, Hasdrubal, and assigned him an army mainly composed of African troops—11,850 native infantry, 300 Ligurians, and 500 Balearics. In addition to this body of infantry there were 450 Libyphoenician cavalry—these are a mixed race of Punic and aboriginal African descent—some 1800 Numidians and Moors, dwellers on the shore of the Mediterranean, and a small mounted contingent of 300 Ilergetes raised in Spain. Finally, that his land force might be complete in all its parts, there were twenty-one elephants.

The protection of the coast required a fleet, and as it was natural to suppose that the Romans would again make use of that arm in which they had been victorious before, Hasdrubal had assigned to him a fleet of 57 warships, including 50 quinqueremes, 2 quadriremes, and 5 triremes, but only 32 quinqueremes and the 5 triremes were ready for sea.

Commences his Long March.—From Gades he returned to the winter quarters of his army at New Carthage, and from New Carthage he commenced his march on Italy. Passing by the city of Onusa,[4] he marched along the coast to the Ebro. The story runs that whilst halting there he saw in a dream a youth of god-like appearance who said that he had been sent by Jupiter to act as guide to Hannibal on his march to Italy. He was accordingly to follow him and not to lose sight of him or let his eyes wander. At first, filled with awe, he followed him without glancing round him or looking back, but as instinctive curiosity impelled him to wonder what it was that he was forbidden to gaze at behind him, he could no longer command his eyes. He saw behind him a serpent of vast and marvellous bulk, and as it moved along trees and bushes crashed down everywhere before it, whilst in its wake there rolled a thunder-storm. He asked what the monstrous portent meant, and was told that it was the devastation of Italy; he was to go forward without further question and allow his destiny to remain hidden.

XXIII. Gladdened by this vision he proceeded to cross the Ebro, with his army in three divisions, after sending men on in advance to secure by bribes the good-will of the Gauls dwelling about his crossing-place, and also to reconnoitre the passes of the Alps. He brought 90,000 infantry and 12,000 cavalry over the Ebro.

His next step was to reduce to submission the Ilergetes, the Bargusii, and the Ausetani, and also the district of Lacetania, which lies at the foot of the Pyrenees. He placed Hanno in charge of the whole coast-line to secure the passes which connect Spain with Gaul, and furnished him with an army of 10,000 infantry to hold the district, and 1000 cavalry. When his army commenced the passage of the Pyrenees and the barbarians found that there was truth in the rumour that they were being led

against Rome, 3000 of the Carpetani deserted. It was understood that they were induced to desert not so much by the
prospect of the war as by the length of the march and the im-
possibility of crossing the Alps. As it would have been hazardous
to recall them, or to attempt to detain them by force, in case the
quick passions of the rest of the army should be roused, Hannibal
sent back to their homes more than 7000 men who, he had
personally discovered, were getting tired of the campaign, and
at the same time he gave out that the Carpetani had also been
sent back by him.

Then, to prevent his men from being demoralised by further
delay and inactivity, he crossed the Pyrenees with the remainder
of his force and fixed his camp at the town of Iliberri. The
Gauls were told that it was against Italy that war was being
made, but as they had heard that the Spaniards beyond the
Pyrenees had been subjugated by force of arms, and strong
garrisons placed in their towns, several tribes, fearing for their
liberty, were roused to arms and mustered at Ruscino. On
receiving the announcement of this movement, Hannibal, fearing
delay more than hostilities, sent spokesmen to their chiefs to
say that he was anxious for a conference with them, and either
they might come nearer to Iliberri, or he would approach
Ruscino to facilitate their meeting, for he would gladly receive
them in his camp or would himself go to them without loss of
time. He had come into Gaul as a friend not a foe, and unless
the Gauls compelled him he would not draw his sword till he
reached Italy. This was the proposal made through the envoys,
but when the Gauls had, without any hesitation, moved their
camp up to Iliberri, they were effectually secured by bribes and
allowed the army a free and unmolested passage through their
territory under the very walls of Ruscino.

XXV. *Trouble in Cisalpine Gaul.*—No intelligence, meanwhile, had reached Rome beyond the fact reported by the
Massilian envoys, namely that Hannibal had crossed the Ebro.
No sooner was this known than the Boii, who had been tamper-
ing with the Insubres, rose in revolt, just as though he had
already crossed the Alps, not so much in consequence of their
old standing enmity against Rome as of her recent aggressions.
Bodies of colonists were being settled on Gaulish territory in the
valley of the Po, at Placentia and Cremona, and intense irritation
was produced. Seizing their arms they made an attack on the
land, which was being actually surveyed at the time, and created
such terror and confusion that not only the agricultural popula-

tion, but even the three Roman commissioners who were engaged in marking out the holdings, fled to Mutina, not feeling themselves safe behind the walls of Placentia. The commissioners were C. Lutatius, C. Servilius, and M. Annius. There is no doubt as to the name Lutatius, but instead of Annius and Servilius some annalists have Manlius Acilius and C. Herennius, whilst others give P. Cornelius Asina and C. Papirius Maso. There is also doubt as to whether it was the envoys who had been sent to the Boii to remonstrate with them that were maltreated, or the commissioners upon whom an attack was made whilst surveying the ground.

The Gauls invested Mutina, but as they were strangers to the art of conducting sieges, and far too indolent to set about the construction of military works, they contented themselves with blockading the town without inflicting any injury on the walls. At last they pretended that they were ready to discuss terms of peace, and the envoys were invited by the Gaulish chieftains to a conference. Here they were arrested, in direct violation not only of international law but of the safe-conduct which had been granted for the occasion. Having made them prisoners the Gauls declared that they would not release them until their hostages were restored to them.

When news came that the envoys were prisoners and Mutina and its garrison in jeopardy, L. Manlius, the praetor, burning with anger, led his army in separate divisions to Mutina. Most of the country was uncultivated at that time and the road went through a forest. He advanced without throwing out scouting parties and fell into an ambush, out of which, after sustaining considerable loss, he made his way with difficulty on to more open ground. Here he entrenched himself, and as the Gauls felt it would be hopeless to attack him there, the courage of his men revived, though it was tolerably certain that as many as 500 had fallen. They recommenced their march, and as long as they were going through open country there was no enemy in view; when they re-entered the forest their rear was attacked and great confusion and panic created. They lost 700 men and six standards. When they at last got out of the trackless and entangled forest there was an end to the terrifying tactics of the Gauls and the wild alarm of the Romans. There was no difficulty in repelling attacks when they reached the open country and made their way to Tannetum, a place near the Po. Here they hastily entrenched themselves, and, helped by the windings of the river and assisted by the Brixian Gauls, they

held their ground against an enemy whose numbers were daily
increasing.

XXVI. When the intelligence of this sudden outbreak
reached Rome and the senate became aware that they had a
Gaulish war to face in addition to the war with Carthage, they
ordered C. Atilius, the praetor, to go to the relief of Manlius
with a Roman legion and 5000 men who had been recently
enlisted by the consul from among the allies. As the enemy,
afraid to meet these reinforcements, had retired, Atilius reached
Tannetum without any fighting.

After raising a fresh legion in place of the one which had
been sent away with the praetor, P. Cornelius Scipio set sail
with sixty warships and coasted along by the shores of Etruria
and Liguria, and from there past the mountains of the Salyes
until he reached Marseilles. Here he disembarked his troops
at the first mouth of the Rhone to which he came—the river
flows into the sea through several mouths—and formed his
entrenched camp, hardly able yet to believe that Hannibal
had surmounted the obstacle of the Pyrenees. When, however, he understood that he was already contemplating crossing
the Rhone, feeling uncertain as to where he would meet him
and anxious to give his men time to recover from the effects
of the voyage, he sent forward a picked force of 300 cavalry
accompanied by Massilian guides and friendly Gauls to explore
the country in all directions and if possible to discover the
enemy.

Hannibal crosses the Rhone.—Hannibal had overcome the
opposition of the native tribes by either fear or bribes and had
now reached the territory of the Volcae. They were a powerful tribe, inhabiting the country on both sides of the Rhone, but
distrusting their ability to stop Hannibal on the side of the
river nearest to him, they determined to make the river a
barrier and transported nearly all the population to the other
side, on which they prepared to offer armed resistance. The
rest of the river population and those of the Volcae even, who
still remained in their homes, were induced by presents to collect
boats from all sides and to help in constructing others, and
their efforts were stimulated by the desire to get rid as soon as
possible of the burdensome presence of such a vast host of men.
So an enormous number of boats and vessels of every kind,
such as they used in their journeys up and down the river, was
got together; new ones were made by the Gauls by hollowing
out the trunks of trees, then the soldiers themselves, seeing the

abundance of timber and how easily they were made, took to fashioning uncouth canoes, quite content if only they would float and carry burdens and serve to transport themselves and their belongings.

Everything was now ready for the crossing, but the whole of the opposite bank was held by mounted and unmounted men prepared to dispute the passage. In order to dislodge them Hannibal sent Hanno, the son of Bomilcar, with a division, consisting mainly of Spaniards, a day's march up the river. He was to seize the first chance of crossing without being observed, and then lead his men by a circuitous route behind the enemy and at the right moment attack them in the rear. The Gauls who were taken as guides informed Hanno that about 25 miles up-stream a small island divided the river in two, and the channel was of less depth in consequence. When they reached the spot they hastily cut down the timber and constructed rafts on which men and horses and other burdens could be ferried across. The Spaniards had no trouble; they threw their clothes on to skins and placing their leather shields on the top they rested on these and so swam across. The rest of the army was ferried over on rafts, and after making a camp near the river they took a day's rest after their labours of boat-making and the nocturnal passage, their general in the meantime waiting anxiously for an opportunity of putting his plan into execution.

The next day they set out on their march, and lighting a fire on some rising ground they signalled by the column of smoke that they had crossed the river and were not very far away. As soon as Hannibal received the signal he seized the occasion and at once gave the order to cross the river. The infantry had prepared rafts and boats, the cavalry mostly barges on account of the horses. A line of large boats was moored across the river a short distance up-stream to break the force of the current, and consequently the men in the smaller boats crossed over in smooth water. Most of the horses were towed astern and swam over, others were carried in barges, ready saddled and bridled so as to be available for the cavalry the moment they landed. The Gauls flocked together on the bank with their customary whoops and war songs, waving their shields over their heads and brandishing their javelins. They were somewhat dismayed when they saw what was going on in front of them; the enormous number of large and small boats, the roar of the river, the confused shouts of the soldiers and boatmen, some of whom were trying to force their way against the current, whilst others on the bank were cheering their comrades who were crossing. Whilst they were watching all this movement with sinking hearts, still more alarming shouts were heard behind them; Hanno had captured their camp. Soon he appeared on the scene, and they were now confronted by danger from opposite quarters—the host of armed men landing from the boats and the sudden attack which was being made on their rear. For a time the Gauls endeavoured to maintain the conflict in both directions, but finding themselves losing ground they forced their way through where there seemed to be least resistance and dispersed to their various villages. Hannibal brought over the rest of his force undisturbed, and, without troubling himself any further about the Gauls, formed his camp.

In the transport of the elephants I believe different plans were adopted; at all events, the accounts of what took place vary considerably. Some say that after they had all been collected on the bank the worst-tempered beast amongst them was teased by his driver, and when he ran away from it into the water the elephant followed him and drew the whole herd after it, and as they got out of their depth they were carried by the current to the opposite bank. The more general account, however, is that they were transported on rafts; as this method would have appeared the safest beforehand so it is most probable that it was the one adopted. They pushed out into the river a raft 200 feet long and 50 feet broad, and to prevent it from being carried down-stream, one end was secured by several stout hawsers to the bank. It was covered with earth like a bridge in order that the animals, taking it for solid ground, would not be afraid to venture on it. A second raft, of the same breadth but only 100 feet long and capable of crossing the river, was made fast to the former. The elephants led by the females were driven along the fixed raft, as if along a road, until they came on to the smaller one. As soon as they were safely on this it was cast off and towed by light boats to the other side of the river. When the first lot were landed others were brought over in the same way. They showed no fear whilst they were being driven along the fixed raft; their fright began when they were being carried into mid-channel on the other raft which had been cast loose. They crowded together, those on the outside backing away from the water, and showed considerable alarm until their very fears at the sight of the water made them quiet. Some in their excitement fell overboard and threw their drivers, but their mere weight kept them steady, and as they felt their way into shallow water they succeeded in getting safely to land.

XXIX. While the elephants were being ferried across, Hannibal sent 500 Numidian horse towards the Romans to ascertain their numbers and their intentions. This troop of horse encountered the 300 Roman cavalry who, as I have already stated, had been sent forward from the mouth of the Rhone. It was a much more severe fight than might have been expected from the number of combatants. Not only were there many wounded but each side lost about the same number of killed, and the Romans, who were at last completely exhausted, owed their victory to a panic among the Numidians and their consequent flight. Of the victors as many as 160 fell, not all Romans, some were Gauls; whilst the vanquished lost more than 200. This action with which the war commenced was an omen of its final result, but though it portended the final victory of Rome it showed that the victory would not be attained without much bloodshed and repeated defeats.

The forces drew off from the field and returned to their respective commanders. Scipio found himself unable to form any definite plans beyond what were suggested to him by the movements of the enemy. Hannibal was undecided whether to resume his march to Italy or to engage the Romans, the first army to oppose him. He was dissuaded from the latter course by the arrival of envoys from the Boii and their chief, Magalus. They came to assure Hannibal of their readiness to act as guides and take their share in the dangers of the expedition, and they gave it as their opinion that he ought to reserve all his strength for the invasion of Italy and not fritter any of it away beforehand. The bulk of his army had not forgotten the previous war and looked forward with dismay to meeting their old enemy, but what appalled them much more was the prospect of an endless journey over the Alps, which rumour said was, to those at all events who had never tried it, a thing to be dreaded.

XXX. *From the Rhone to the Alps.*—When Hannibal had made up his mind to go forward and lose no time in reaching Italy, his goal, he ordered a muster of his troops and addressed them in tones of mingled rebuke and encouragement. " I am astonished," he said, " to see how hearts that have been always dauntless have now suddenly become a prey to fear. Think of the many victorious campaigns you have gone through, and remember that you did not leave Spain before you had added to the Carthaginian empire all the tribes in the country washed by two widely remote seas. The Roman people made a demand for all who had taken part in the siege of Saguntum to be given up to them, and you, to avenge the insult, have crossed the Ebro to wipe out the name of Rome and bring freedom to the world. When you commenced your march, from the setting to the rising sun, none of you thought it too much for you, but now when you see that by far the greater part of the way has been accomplished; the passes of the Pyrenees, which were held by most warlike tribes, surmounted; the Rhone, that mighty stream, crossed in the face of so many thousand Gauls, and the rush of its waters checked—now that you are within sight of the Alps, on the other side of which lies Italy, you have become weary and are arresting your march in the very gates of the enemy. What do you imagine the Alps to be other than lofty mountains? Suppose them to be higher than the peaks of the Pyrenees, surely no region in the world can touch the sky or be impassable to man. Even the Alps are inhabited and cultivated, animals are bred and reared there, their gorges and ravines can be traversed by armies. Why, even the envoys whom you see here did not cross the Alps by flying through the air, nor were their ancestors native to the soil. They came into Italy as emigrants looking for a land to settle in, and they crossed the Alps often in immense bodies with their wives and children and all their belongings. What can be inaccessible or insuperable to the soldier who carries nothing with him but his weapons of war? What toils and perils you went through for eight months to effect the capture of Saguntum! And now that Rome, the capital of the world, is your goal, can you deem anything so difficult or so arduous that it should prevent you from reaching it? Many years ago the Gauls captured the place which Carthaginians despair of approaching; either you must confess yourselves inferior in courage and enterprise to a people whom you have conquered again and again, or else you must look forward to finishing your march on the ground between the Tiber and the walls of Rome." [5]

XXXI. After this rousing appeal he dismissed them with orders to prepare themselves by food and rest for the march. The next day they advanced up the left bank of the Rhone towards the central districts of Gaul, not because this was the most direct route to the Alps, but because he thought that there would be less likelihood of the Romans meeting him, for he had no desire to engage them before he arrived in Italy.

Four days' marching brought him to the " Island." Here

the Isère and the Rhone, flowing down from different points in the Alps, enclose a considerable extent of land and then unite their channels; the district thus enclosed is called the " Island." The adjacent country was inhabited by the Allobroges, a tribe who even in those days were second to none in Gaul in power and reputation. At the time of Hannibal's visit a quarrel had broken out between two brothers who were each aspiring to the sovereignty. The elder brother, whose name was Brancus, had hitherto been the chief, but was now expelled by a party of the younger men, headed by his brother, who found an appeal to violence more successful than an appeal to right. Hannibal's timely appearance on the scene led to the question being referred to him; he was to decide who was the legitimate claimant to the kingship. He pronounced in favour of the elder brother, who had the support of the senate and the leading men. In return for this service he received assistance in provisions and supplies of all kinds, especially of clothing, a pressing necessity in view of the notorious cold of the Alps.

After settling the feud amongst the Allobroges, Hannibal resumed his march. He did not take the direct course to the Alps, but turned to the left towards the Tricastini; then, skirting the territory of the Vocontii, he marched in the direction of the Tricorii. Nowhere did he meet with any difficulty until he arrived at the Durance. This river, which also takes its rise in the Alps, is of all the rivers of Gaul the most difficult to cross. Though carrying down a great volume of water, it does not lend itself to navigation, for it is not kept in by banks, but flows in many separate channels. As it is constantly shifting its bottom and the direction of its currents, the task of fording it is a most hazardous one, whilst the shingle and boulders carried down make the foothold insecure and treacherous. It happened to be swollen by rain at the time, and the men were thrown into much disorder whilst crossing it, whilst their fears and confused shouting added considerably to their difficulties.[6]

XXXII. Three days after Hannibal had left the banks of the Rhone, P. Cornelius Scipio arrived at the deserted camp with his army in battle order, ready to engage at once. When, however, he saw the abandoned lines and realised that it would be no easy matter to overtake his opponent after he had got such a long start, he returned to his ships. He considered that the easier and safer course would be to meet Hannibal as he came down from the Alps. Spain was the province allotted to him, and to prevent its being entirely denuded of Roman troops he sent his brother Cneius Scipio with the greater part of his army to act against Hasdrubal, not only to keep the old allies and win new ones, but to drive Hasdrubal out of Spain. He himself sailed for Genoa with a very small force, intending to defend Italy with the army lying in the valley of the Po.[7]

The Passage of the Alps.—From the Durance Hannibal's route lay mostly through open level country, and he reached the Alps without meeting with any opposition from the Gauls who inhabited the district. But the sight of the Alps revived the terrors in the minds of his men. Although rumour, which generally magnifies untried dangers, had filled them with gloomy forebodings, the nearer view proved much more fearful. The height of the mountains now so close, the snow which was almost lost in the sky, the wretched huts perched on the rocks, the flocks and herds shrivelled and stunted with the cold, the men wild and unkempt, everything animate and inanimate stiff with frost, together with other sights dreadful beyond description—all helped to increase their alarm.

As the head of the column began to climb the nearest slopes, the natives appeared on the heights above; had they concealed themselves in the ravines and then rushed down they would have caused frightful panic and bloodshed. Hannibal called a halt and sent on some Gauls to examine the ground, and when he learnt that advance was impossible in that direction he formed his camp in the widest part of the valley that he could find; everywhere around the ground was broken and precipitous. The Gauls who had been sent to reconnoitre got into conversation with the natives, as there was little difference between their speech or their manners, and they brought back word to Hannibal that the pass was only occupied in the daytime, at nightfall the natives all dispersed to their homes.

Accordingly, at early dawn he began the ascent as though determined to force the pass in broad daylight, and spent the day in movements designed to conceal his real intentions and in fortifying the camp on the spot where they had halted. As soon as he observed that the natives had left the heights and were no longer watching his movements, he gave orders, with the view of deceiving the enemy, for a large number of fires to be lighted, larger in fact than would be required by those remaining in camp. Then, leaving the baggage with the cavalry and the greater part of the infantry in camp, he himself with a specially selected body of troops in light marching order rapidly moved

out of the defile and occupied the heights which the enemy
had held.

XXXIII. The following day the rest of the army broke camp
in the grey dawn and commenced its march. The natives
were beginning to assemble at their customary post of observation when they suddenly became aware that some of the enemy
were in possession of their stronghold right over their heads,
whilst others were advancing on the path beneath. The
double impression made on their eyes and imagination kept
them for a few moments motionless, but when they saw the
column falling into disorder mainly through the horses becoming frightened, they thought that if they increased the
confusion and panic it would be sufficient to destroy it. So
they charged down from rock to rock, careless as to whether
there were paths or not, for they were familiar with the ground.
The Carthaginians had to meet this attack at the same time
that they were struggling with the difficulties of the way, and
as each man was doing his best for himself to get out of the
reach of danger, they were fighting more amongst themselves
than against the natives. The horses did the most mischief;
they were terrified at the wild shouts, which the echoing woods
and valleys made all the louder, and when they happened to be
struck or wounded they created terrible havoc amongst the
men and the different baggage animals. The road was flanked
by sheer precipices on each side, and in the crowding together
many were pushed over the edge and fell an immense depth.
Amongst these were some of the soldiers; the heavily-laden
baggage animals rolled over like falling houses. Horrible as
the sight was, Hannibal remained quiet and kept his men back
for some time, for fear of increasing the alarm and confusion,
but when he saw that the column was broken and that the army
was in danger of losing all its baggage,[8] in which case he would
have brought them safely through to no purpose, he ran down
from his higher ground and at once scattered the enemy. At
the same time, however, he threw his own men into still greater
disorder for the moment, but it was very quickly allayed now
that the passage was cleared by the flight of the natives. In a
short time the whole army had traversed the pass, not only
without any further disturbance, but almost in silence.

He then seized a fortified village, the head place of the district, together with some adjacent hamlets, and from the food
and cattle thus secured he provided his army with rations for
three days. As the natives, after their first defeat, no longer

impeded their march, whilst the road presented little difficulty, they made considerable progress during those three days.

XXXIV. They now came to another canton which, considering that it was a mountain district, had a considerable population. Here he narrowly escaped destruction, not in fair and open fighting, but by the practices which he himself employed —falsehood and treachery. The head men from the fortified villages, men of advanced age, came as a deputation to the Carthaginian and told him that they had been taught by the salutary example of other people's misfortunes to seek the friendship of the Carthaginians rather than to feel their strength. They were accordingly prepared to carry out his orders; he would receive provisions and guides, and hostages as a guarantee of good faith. Hannibal felt that he ought not to trust them blindly nor to meet their offer with a flat refusal, in case they should become hostile. So he replied in friendly terms, accepted the hostages whom they placed in his hands, made use of the provisions with which they supplied him on the march, but followed their guides with his army prepared for action, not at all as though he were going through a peaceable or friendly country. The elephants and cavalry were in front, he himself followed with the main body of the infantry, keeping a sharp and anxious look-out in all directions.

Just as they reached a part of the pass where it narrowed and was overhung on one side by a wall of rock, the barbarians sprang up from ambush on all sides and assailed the column in front and rear, at close quarters, and at a distance by rolling huge stones down on it. The heaviest attack was made in the rear, and as the infantry faced round to meet it, it became quite obvious that if the rear of the column had not been made exceptionally strong, a terrible disaster must have occurred in that pass. As it was, they were in the greatest danger, and within an ace of total destruction. For whilst Hannibal was hesitating whether to send his infantry on into the narrow part of the pass —for whilst protecting the rear of the cavalry they had no reserves to protect their own rear—the mountaineers, making a flank charge, burst through the middle of the column and held the pass so that Hannibal had to spend that one night without his cavalry or his baggage.

XXXV. The next day, as the savages attacked with less vigour, the column closed up, and the pass was surmounted, not without loss, more, however, of baggage animals than of men. From that time the natives made their appearance in smaller numbers and behaved more like banditti than regular soldiers; they attacked either front or rear just as the ground gave them opportunity, or as the advance or halt of the column presented a chance of surprise. The elephants caused considerable delay, owing to the difficulty of getting them through narrow or precipitous places; on the other hand, they rendered that part of the column safe from attack where they were, for the natives were unaccustomed to the sight of them and had a great dread of going too near them.

Nine days from their commencing the ascent they arrived at the highest point of the Alps, after traversing a region mostly without roads and frequently losing their way either through the treachery of their guides or through their own mistakes in trying to find the way for themselves. For two days they remained in camp on the summit, whilst the troops enjoyed a respite from fatigue and fighting. Some of the baggage animals which had fallen amongst the rocks and had afterwards followed the track of the column came into camp. To add to the misfortunes of the worn-out troops, there was a heavy fall of snow —the Pleiads were near their setting—and this new experience created considerable alarm.

In the early morning of the third day the army recommenced its heavy march over ground everywhere deep in snow. Hannibal saw in all faces an expression of listlessness and despondency. He rode on in front to a height from which there was a wide and extensive view, and halting his men, he pointed out to them the land of Italy and the rich valley of the Po lying at the foot of the Alps. "You are now," he said, "crossing the barriers not only of Italy, but of Rome itself. Henceforth all will be smooth and easy for you; in one or, at the most, two battles, you will be masters of the capital and stronghold of Italy."

Then the army resumed its advance with no annoyance from the enemy beyond occasional attempts at plunder. The remainder of the march, however, was attended with much greater difficulty than they had experienced in the ascent, for the distance to the plains on the Italian side is shorter, and therefore the descent is necessarily steeper. Almost the whole of the way was precipitous, narrow, and slippery, so that they were unable to keep their footing, and if they slipped they could not recover themselves; they kept falling over each other, and the baggage animals rolled over on their drivers.

XXXVI. At length they came to a much narrower pass which

descended over such sheer cliffs that a light-armed soldier could
hardly get down it even by hanging on to projecting roots and
branches. The place had always been precipitous, and a land-
slip had recently carried away the road for 1000 feet. The
cavalry came to a halt here as though they had arrived at their
journey's end, and whilst Hannibal was wondering what could
be causing the delay he was informed that there was no passage.
Then he went forward to examine the place and saw that there
was nothing for it but to lead the army by a long circuitous
route over pathless and untrodden snow. But this, too, soon
proved to be impracticable. The old snow had been covered to
a moderate depth by a fresh fall, and the first comers planted
their feet firmly on the new snow, but when it had become
melted under the tread of so many men and beasts there was
nothing to walk on but ice covered with slush. Their progress
now became one incessant and miserable struggle. The smooth
ice allowed no foothold, and as they were going down a steep
incline they were still less able to keep on their legs, whilst, once
down, they tried in vain to rise, as their hands and knees were
continually slipping. There were no stumps or roots about for
them to get hold of and support themselves by, so they rolled
about helplessly on the glassy ice and slushy snow. The baggage
animals as they toiled along cut through occasionally into the
lowest layer of snow, and when they stumbled they struck out
their hoofs in their struggles to recover themselves and broke
through into the hard and congealed ice below, where most of
them stuck as though caught in a gin.

XXXVII. At last, when men and beasts alike were worn out
by their fruitless exertions, a camp was formed on the summit,
after the place had been cleared with immense difficulty owing
to the quantity of snow that had to be removed. The next
thing was to level the rock through which alone a road was
practicable. The soldiers were told off to cut through it. They
built up against it an enormous pile of tall trees which they had
felled and lopped, and when the wind was strong enough to blow
up the fire they set light to the pile. When the rock was red
hot they poured vinegar upon it to disintegrate it.[9] After thus
treating it by fire they opened a way through it with their tools,
and eased the steep slope by winding tracks of moderate gradient,
so that not only the baggage animals but even the elephants
could be led down.

Four days were spent over the rock, and the animals were
almost starved to death, for the heights are mostly bare of

vegetation and what herbage there is is buried beneath the snow. In the lower levels there were sunny valleys and streams flowing through woods, and spots more deserving of human inhabitants. Here the beasts were turned loose to graze, and the troops, worn out with their engineering, were allowed to rest. In three days more they reached the open plains and found a pleasanter country and pleasanter people living in it.

XXXVIII. Such, in the main, was the way in which they reached Italy, five months, according to some authorities, after leaving New Carthage, fifteen days of which were spent in overcoming the difficulties of the Alps. The authorities are hopelessly at variance as to the number of the troops with which Hannibal entered Italy. The highest estimate assigns him 100,000 infantry and 20,000 cavalry; the lowest puts his strength at 20,000 infantry and 6000 cavalry.[10] L. Cincius Alimentus tells us that he was taken prisoner by Hannibal, and I should be most inclined to accept his authority if he had not confused the numbers by adding in the Gauls and Ligurians; if these are included there were 80,000 infantry and 10,000 cavalry. It is, however, more probable that these joined Hannibal in Italy, and some authorities actually assert this. Cincius also states that he had heard Hannibal say that subsequently to his passage of the Rhone he lost 36,000 men, besides an immense number of horses and other animals.

Hannibal in Italy.—The first people he came to were the Taurini, a semi-Gallic tribe.[11] As tradition is unanimous on this point I am the more surprised that a question should be raised as to what route Hannibal took over the Alps, and that it should be generally supposed that he crossed over the Poenine range, which is said to have derived its name from that circumstance. Coelius asserts that he crossed by the Cremonian range.[12] These two passes, however, would not have brought him to the Taurini but through the Salassi, a mountain tribe, to the Libuan Gauls. It is highly improbable that those routes to Gaul were available at that time, and in any case the Poenine route [13] would have been closed by the semi-German tribes who inhabited the district. And it is perfectly certain, if we accept their authority, that the Seduni and Veragri, who inhabit that range, say that the name of Poenine was not given to it from any passage of the Carthaginians over it but from the deity Poeninus, whose shrine stands on the highest point of the range.

XXXIX. It was a very fortunate circumstance for Hannibal at the outset of his campaign that the Taurini, the first people he came to, were at war with the Insubres. But he was unable to bring his army into the field to assist either side, for it was whilst they were recovering from the ills and misfortunes which had gathered upon them that they felt them most. Rest and idleness instead of toil, plenty following upon starvation, cleanliness and comfort after squalor and emaciation, affected their filthy and well-nigh bestialised bodies in various ways. It was this state of things which induced P. Cornelius Scipio, the consul, after he had arrived with his ships at Pisa and taken over from Manlius and Atilius an army of raw levies disheartened by their recent humiliating defeats, to push on with all speed to the Po that he might engage the enemy before he had recovered his strength. But when he reached Placentia Hannibal had already left his encampment and taken by storm one of the cities of the Taurini, their capital, in fact, because they would not voluntarily maintain friendly relations with him. He would have secured the adhesion of the Gauls in the valley of the Po, not by fear but by their own choice, if the sudden arrival of the consul had not taken them by surprise whilst they were waiting for a favourable moment to revolt. Just at the time of Scipio's arrival, Hannibal moved out of the country of the Taurini, for, seeing how undecided the Gauls were as to whose side they should take, he thought that if he were on the spot they would follow him.

The Skirmish at the Ticinus.—The two armies were now almost within sight of one another, and the commanders who were confronting each other, though not sufficiently acquainted with each other's military skill, were even then imbued with mutual respect and admiration. Even before the fall of Saguntum the name of Hannibal was on all men's lips in Rome, and in Scipio Hannibal recognised a great leader, seeing that he had been chosen beyond all others to oppose him. This mutual esteem was enhanced by their recent achievements; Scipio, after Hannibal had left him in Gaul, was in time to meet him on his descent from the Alps; Hannibal had not only dared to attempt but had actually accomplished the passage of the Alps. Scipio, however, made the first move by crossing the Po and shifting his camp to the Ticinus. Before leading his men into battle he addressed them in a speech full of encouragement, in the following terms:

XL. "If, soldiers, I were leading into battle the army which I had with me in Gaul, there would have been no need for me to address you. For what encouragement would those cavalry need who had won such a brilliant victory over the enemy's cavalry at the Rhone or those legions of infantry with whom I pursued this same enemy, who by his running away and shirking an engagement acknowledged that I was his conqueror? That army, raised for service in Spain, is campaigning under my brother, Cn. Scipio, who is acting as my deputy in the country which the senate and people of Rome have assigned to it. In order, therefore, that you might have a consul to lead you against Hannibal and the Carthaginians, I have volunteered to command in this battle, and as I am new to you and you to me I must say a few words to you.

"Now as to the character of the enemy and the kind of warfare which awaits you. You have to fight, soldiers, with the men whom you defeated in the former war by land and sea, from whom you have exacted a war indemnity for the last twenty years, and from whom you wrested Sicily and Sardinia as the prizes of war. You, therefore, will go into this battle with the exultation of victors, they with the despondency of the vanquished. They are not going to fight now because they are impelled by courage but through sheer necessity; unless indeed you suppose that, after shirking a contest when their army was at its full strength, they have gained more confidence now that they have lost two-thirds of their infantry and cavalry in their passage over the Alps, now that those who survive are fewer than those who have perished.

" 'Yes,' it may be said, 'they are few in number, but they are strong in courage and physique, and possess a power of endurance and vigour in attack which very few can withstand.' No, they are only semblances or rather ghosts of men, worn out with starvation, cold, filth, and squalor, bruised and enfeebled amongst the rocks and precipices, and, what is more, their limbs are frost-bitten, their thews and sinews cramped with cold, their frames shrunk and shrivelled with frost, their weapons battered and shivered, their horses lame and out of condition. This is the cavalry, this the infantry with whom you are going to fight; you will not have an enemy but only the last vestiges of an enemy to meet. My only fear is that when you have fought it will appear to be the Alps that have conquered Hannibal. But perhaps it was right that it should be so, and that the gods, without any human aid, should begin and all but finish this war with a people and their general who have broken treaties, and that to us, who next to the gods have been sinned against, it should be left to complete what they began.

XLI. " I am not afraid of any one thinking that I am saying this in a spirit of bravado for the sake of putting you in good heart, whilst my real feelings and convictions are far otherwise. I was at perfect liberty to go with my army to Spain, for which country I had actually started, and which was my assigned province. There I should have had my brother to share my plans and dangers; I should have had Hasdrubal rather than Hannibal as my foe, and undoubtedly a less serious war on my hands. But as I was sailing along the coast of Gaul I heard tidings of this enemy, and at once landed, and after sending on cavalry in advance moved up to the Rhone. A cavalry action was fought—that was the only arm I had the opportunity of employing—and I defeated the enemy. His infantry were hurrying away like an army in flight, and as I could not come up with them overland, I returned to my ships with all possible speed, and after making a wide circuit by sea and land have met this dreaded foe almost at the foot of the Alps. Does it seem to you that I have unexpectedly fallen in with him whilst I was anxious to decline a contest and not rather that I am meeting him actually on his track and challenging and dragging him into action? I shall be glad to learn whether the earth has suddenly within the last twenty years produced a different breed of Carthaginans, or whether they are the same as those who fought at the Ægates, and whom you allowed to depart from Eryx on payment of eighteen *denarii* a head, and whether this Hannibal is, as he gives out, the rival of Hercules in his journeys, or whether he has been left by his father to pay tax and tribute and to be the slave of the Roman people. If his crime at Saguntum were not driving him on, he would surely have some regard, if not for his conquered country, at all events for his house and his father, and the treaties signed by that Hamilcar who at the order of our consul withdrew his garrison from Eryx, who with sighs and groans accepted the hard conditions imposed on the conquered Carthaginians, and who agreed to evacuate Sicily and pay a war indemnity to Rome. And so I would have you, soldiers, fight not merely in the spirit which you are wont to show against other foes, but with feelings of indignant anger as though you saw your own slaves bearing arms against you. When they were shut up in Eryx we might have inflicted the most terrible of human punishments and starved them to death; we might have taken our victorious fleet across to Africa, and in a few days destroyed Carthage without a battle. We granted pardon to their prayers, we allowed them to escape from the blockade, we agreed to terms of peace with those whom we had conquered, and afterwards when they were in dire straits through the African war we took them under our protection. To requite us for these acts of kindness they are following the lead of a young madman and coming to attack our fatherland. I only wish this struggle were for honour alone and not for safety. It is not about the possession of Sicily and Sardinia, the old subjects of dispute, but for Italy that you have to fight. There is no second army at our back to oppose the enemy if we fail to win, there are no more Alps to delay his advance while a fresh army can be raised for defence. Here it is, soldiers, that we have to resist, just as though we were fighting before the walls of Rome. Every one of you must remember that he is using his arms to protect not himself only but also his wife and little children; nor must his anxiety be confined to his home, he must realise, too, that the senate and people of Rome are watching our exploits to-day. What our strength and courage are now here, such will be the fortune of our City yonder and of the empire of Rome."

XLII. Such was the language which the consul used towards the Romans. Hannibal thought that the courage of his men ought to be roused by deeds first rather than by words. After forming his army into a circle to view the spectacle, he placed in the centre some Alpine prisoners in chains, and when some Gaulish arms had been thrown down at their feet he ordered an interpreter to ask if any one of them was willing to fight if he were freed from his chains and received arms and a horse as the reward of victory. All to a man demanded arms and battle, and when the lot was cast to decide who should fight, each wished that he might be the one whom Fortune should select for the combat. As each man's lot fell, he hastily seized his arms full of eagerness and exultant delight, amidst the congratulations of his comrades and danced after the custom of his country. But when they began to fight, such was the state of feeling not only amongst the men who had accepted this condition, but amongst the spectators generally that the good fortune of those who died bravely was lauded quite as much as that of those who were victorious.

XLIII. After his men had been impressed by watching several pairs of combatants Hannibal dismissed them, and afterwards summoned them round him, when he is reported to have made the following speech:

" Soldiers, you have seen in the fate of others an example how to conquer or to die. If the feelings with which you watched them lead you to form a similar estimate of your own fortunes, we are victors. That was no idle spectacle but a picture, as it were, of your own condition. Fortune, I am inclined to think, has bound you in heavier chains and imposed upon you a sterner necessity than on your captives. You are shut in on the right hand and on the left by two seas, and you have not a single ship in which to make your escape; around you flows the Po, a greater river than the Rhone and a more rapid one; the barrier of the Alps frowns upon you behind, those Alps which you could hardly cross when your strength and vigour were unimpaired. Here, soldiers, on this spot where you have for the first time encountered the enemy you must either conquer or die. The same Fortune which has imposed upon you the necessity of fighting also holds out rewards of victory, rewards as great as any which men are wont to solicit from the immortal gods. Even if we were only going to recover Sicily and Sardinia, possessions which were wrested from our fathers, they would be prizes ample enough to satisfy us. Everything that the Romans now possess, which they have won through so many triumphs, all that they have amassed, will become yours, together with those who own it. Come then, seize your arms and with the help of heaven win this splendid reward. You have spent time enough in hunting cattle on the barren mountains of Lusitania and Celtiberia, and finding no recompense for all your toils and dangers; now the hour has come for you to enter upon rich and lucrative campaigns and to earn rewards which are worth the earning, after your long march over all those mountains and rivers, and through all those nations in arms. Here Fortune has vouchsafed an end to your toils, here she will vouchsafe a reward worthy of all your past services.

" Do not think because the war, being against Rome, bears a great name, that therefore victory will be correspondingly difficult. Many a despised enemy has fought a long and costly fight; nations and kings of high renown have been beaten with a very slight effort. For, setting aside the glory which surrounds the name of Rome, what point is there in which they can be compared to you? To say nothing of your twenty years' campaigning carried on with all your courage, all your good fortune, from the pillars of Hercules, from the shores of the ocean, from the furthest corners of the earth, through the midst of all the most warlike peoples of Spain and Gaul, you have arrived here as victors. The army with which you will fight is made up of raw levies who were beaten, conquered, and hemmed in by the

Gauls this very summer, who are strangers to their general, and he a stranger to them. I, reared as I was, almost born, in the headquarters tent of my father, a most distinguished general, I, who have subjugated Spain and Gaul, who have conquered not only the Alpine tribes, but, what is a much greater task, the Alps themselves—am I to compare myself with this six months' general who has deserted his own army, who, if any one were to point out to him the Romans and the Carthaginians after their standards were removed, would, I am quite certain, not know which army he was in command of as consul? I do not count it a small matter, soldiers, that there is not a man amongst you before whose eyes I have not done many a soldierly deed, or to whom I, who have witnessed and attested his courage, could not recount his own gallant exploits and the time and place where they were performed. I was your pupil before I was your commander, and I shall go into battle surrounded by men whom I have commended and rewarded thousands of times against those who know nothing of each other, who are mutual strangers.

XLIV. " Wherever I turn my eyes I see nothing but courage and strength, a veteran infantry, a cavalry, regular and irregular alike, drawn from the noblest tribes, you, our most faithful and brave allies, you, Carthaginians, who are going to fight for your country, inspired by a most righteous indignation. We are taking the aggressive, we are descending in hostile array into Italy, prepared to fight more bravely and more fearlessly than our foe because he who attacks is animated by stronger hopes and greater courage than he who meets the attack. Besides, we are smarting from a sense of injustice and humiliation. First they demanded me, your general, as their victim, then they insisted that all of you who had taken part in the siege of Saguntum should be surrendered; had you been given up they would have inflicted upon you the most exquisite tortures. That outrageously cruel and tyrannical nation claims everything for itself, makes everything dependent on its will and pleasure; they think it right to dictate with whom we are to make war or peace. They confine and enclose us within mountains and rivers as boundaries, but they do not observe the limits which they themselves have fixed. ' Do not cross the Ebro, see that you have nothing to do with the Saguntines.' ' But Saguntum is not on the Ebro.' ' You must not move a step anywhere.' ' Is it a small matter, your taking from me my oldest provinces, Sicily and Sardinia? Will you cross over into Spain as well, and if I withdraw from there, will you cross over into Africa? Do I say, *will* cross over? You *have* crossed over.' They have sent the two consuls for this year, one to Africa, the other to Spain. There is nothing left to us anywhere except what we claim by force of arms. Those may be allowed to be cowards and dastards who have something to fall back upon, whom their own land, their own territory will receive as they flee through its safe and peaceful roads; you must of necessity be brave men, every alternative between victory and death has been broken off by the resolve of despair, and you are compelled either to conquer, or if Fortune wavers, to meet death in battle rather than in flight. If you have all made up your minds to this, I say again you are victors, no keener weapon has been put into men's hands by the immortal gods than a contempt for death."

XLV. After the fighting spirit of both armies had been roused by these harangues, the Romans threw a bridge over the Ticinus and constructed a blockhouse for its defence. Whilst they were thus occupied, the Carthaginian sent Maharbal with a troop of 500 Numidian horse to ravage the lands of the allies of Rome, but with orders to spare those of the Gauls as far as possible, and to win over their chiefs to his side. When the bridge was completed the Roman army crossed over in the territory of the Insubres and took up a position five miles from Ictumuli, where Hannibal had his camp. As soon as he saw that a battle was imminent, he hastily recalled Maharbal and his troopers. Feeling that he could never say enough by way of admonition and encouragement to his soldiers, he ordered an assembly, and before the whole army offered definite rewards in the hope of which they were to fight. He said that he would give them land wherever they wished, in Italy, Africa, or Spain, which would be free from all taxation for the recipient and for his children; if any preferred money to land, he would satisfy his desires; if any of the allies wished to become Carthaginian citizens he would give them the opportunity; if any preferred to return to their homes he would take care that their circumstances should be such that they would never wish to exchange them with any of their countrymen. He even promised freedom to the slaves who followed their masters, and to the masters, for every slave freed, two more as compensation. To convince them of his determination to carry out these promises, he held a lamb with his left hand and a flint knife in his right and prayed to Jupiter and the other gods, that, if he broke his word and forswore himself they would slay him as he had slain the lamb. He then crushed the animal's head with the flint. They all felt then that the gods themselves would guarantee the fulfilment of their hopes, and looked upon the delay in bringing on an action as delay in gaining their desires; with one mind and one voice they clamoured to be led into battle.

XLVI. The Romans were far from showing this alacrity. Amongst other causes of alarm they had been unnerved by some portents which had happened lately. A wolf had entered the camp and after worrying all it met had got away unhurt. A swarm of bees, too, had settled on a tree which overhung the headquarters tent. After the necessary propitiation had been made Scipio moved out with a force of cavalry and light-armed javelin men towards the enemy's camp to get a nearer view and to ascertain the number and nature of his force. He fell in with Hannibal who was also advancing with his cavalry to explore the neighbourhood. Neither body at first saw the other; the first indication of a hostile approach was given by the unusually dense cloud of dust which was raised by the tramp of so many men and horses. Each party halted and made ready for battle. Scipio placed the javelin men and the Gaulish cavalry in the front, the Roman horse and the heavy cavalry of the allies as reserves. Hannibal formed his centre with his regular cavalry, and posted the Numidians on the flanks. Scarcely had the battle shout been raised before the javelin men retired to the second line amongst the reserves. For some time the cavalry kept up an equal fight, but as the foot-soldiers became mixed up with the mounted men they made their horses unmanageable, many were thrown or else dismounted where they saw their comrades in difficulty, until the battle was mainly fought on foot. Then the Numidians on the flanks wheeled round and appeared on the rear of the Romans, creating dismay and panic amongst them. To make matters worse the consul was wounded and in danger; he was rescued by the intervention of his son who was just approaching manhood.[14] This was the youth who afterwards won the glory of bringing this war to a close, and gained the *soubriquet* of Africanus for his splendid victory over Hannibal and the Carthaginians. The javelin men were the first to be attacked by the Numidians and they fled in disorder, the rest of the force, the cavalry, closed round the consul, shielding him as much by their persons as by their arms, and returned to camp in orderly retirement.

Caelius assigns the honour of saving the consul to a Ligurian slave, but I would rather believe that it was his son; the majority of authors assert this and the tradition is generally accepted.

XLVII. This was the first battle with Hannibal, and the result made it quite clear that the Carthaginian was superior in his cavalry, and consequently that the open plains which stretch from the Po to the Alps were not a suitable battlefield for the Romans. The next night accordingly, the soldiers were ordered to collect their baggage in silence, the army moved away from the Ticinus and marched rapidly to the Po, which they crossed by the pontoon bridge which was still intact, in perfect order and without any molestation by the enemy. They reached Placentia before Hannibal knew for certain that they had left the Ticinus; however, he succeeded in capturing some 600, who were loitering on his side of the Po, and were slowly unfastening the end of the bridge. He was unable to use the bridge for crossing, as the ends had been unfastened and the whole was floating down-stream. According to Caelius, Mago with the cavalry and Spanish infantry at once swam across, whilst Hannibal himself took his army across higher up the river where it was fordable, the elephants being stationed in a row from bank to bank to break the force of the current. Those who know the river will hardly believe this, for it is highly improbable that the cavalry could have stood against so violent a river without damage to their horses and arms, even supposing that the Spaniards had been carried across by their inflated skins, and it would have required a march of many days to find a ford in the Po where an army loaded with baggage could be taken across. I attach greater weight to those authorities who state that it took them at least two days to find a spot where they could throw a bridge over the river, and that it was there that Mago's cavalry and the Spanish light infantry crossed. Whilst Hannibal was waiting near the river to give audience to deputations from the Gauls, he sent his heavy infantry across, and during this interval Mago and his cavalry advanced a day's march from the river in the direction of the enemy at Placentia. A few days later Hannibal entrenched himself in a position six miles from Placentia, and the next day he drew out his army in battle order in full view of the enemy and gave him the opportunity of fighting.

XLVIII. *The Romans withdraw to the Trebia.*—The following night a murderous outbreak took place amongst the Gaulish auxiliaries in the Roman camp; there was, however, more excitement and confusion than actual loss of life. About 2000 infantry and 200 horsemen massacred the sentinels and deserted to Hannibal. The Carthaginian gave them a kind reception and sent them to their homes with the promise of great rewards if they would enlist the sympathies of their countrymen on his behalf. Scipio saw in this outrage a signal of revolt for all the Gauls, who, infected by the madness of this crime, would at once fly to arms, and though still suffering severely from his wound, he left his position in the fourth watch of the following night, his army marching in perfect silence, and shifted his camp close to the Trebia on to higher ground where the hills were impracticable for cavalry. He was less successful in escaping the notice of the enemy than he had been at the Ticinus, Hannibal sent first the Numidians, then afterwards the whole of his cavalry in pursuit and would have inflicted disaster upon the rear of the column at all events, had not the Numidians been tempted by their desire for plunder to turn aside to the deserted Roman camp. Whilst they were wasting their time in prying into every corner of the camp, without finding anything worth waiting for, the enemy slipped out of their hands, and when they caught sight of the Romans they had already crossed the Trebia and were measuring out the site for their camp. A few stragglers whom they caught on their side the river were killed.

Unable any longer to endure the irritation of his wound, which had been aggravated during the march, and also thinking that he ought to wait for his colleague—he had already heard that he had been recalled from Sicily—Scipio selected what seemed the safest position near the river, and formed a standing camp which was strongly entrenched. Hannibal had encamped not far from there, and in spite of his elation at his successful cavalry action he felt considerable anxiety at the shortness of supplies which, owing to his marching through hostile territory where no stores were provided, became more serious day by day. He sent a detachment to the town of Clastidium where the Romans had accumulated large quantities of corn. Whilst they were preparing to attack the place they were led to hope that it would be betrayed to them. Dasius, a Brundisian, was commandant of the garrison, and he was induced by a moderate bribe of 400 gold pieces to betray Clastidium to Hannibal. The place was the granary of the Carthaginians while they were at the Trebia. No cruelty was practised on the garrison, as Hannibal was anxious to win a reputation for clemency at the outset.

XLIX. *Operations in Sicily.*—The war on the Trebia had for the time being come to a standstill, but military and naval actions were taking place around Sicily and the islands fringing Italy, both under the conduct of Sempronius and also before his arrival. Twenty quinqueremes with a thousand soldiers on board had been despatched by the Carthaginians to Italy, nine of them to Liparae, eight to the island of Vulcanus, and three had been carried by the currents into the Straits of Messana. These were sighted from Messana, and Hiero, the King of Syracuse, who happened to be there at the time waiting for the consul, despatched twelve ships against them, and they were taken without any opposition and brought into the harbour of Messana. It was ascertained from the prisoners, that besides the fleet of twenty ships to which they belonged which had sailed for Italy thirty-five quinqueremes were also on the way to Sicily with the object of stirring up the old allies of Carthage. Their main anxiety was to secure Lilybaeum, and the prisoners were of opinion that the storm which had separated them from the rest had also driven that fleet up to the Ægates.

The king communicated this information just as he had received it to M. Æmilius, the praetor, whose province Sicily was, and advised him to throw a strong garrison into Lilybaeum. The praetor at once sent envoys and military tribunes to the neighbouring states to urge them to take measures for self-defence. Lilybaeum especially was engrossed in preparations for war; orders were issued for the seamen to carry ten days' rations on board that there might be no delay in setting sail when the signal was given; and men were despatched along the coast to look out for the approach of the hostile fleet. So it came to pass that although the Carthaginians had purposely lessened the speed of their vessels, so that they might approach Lilybaeum before daylight, they were descried in the offing owing to there being a moon all night, and also because they were coming with their sails set. Instantly the signal was given by the look-out men; in the town there was the cry, " To arms," and the ships were manned. Some of the soldiers were on the walls and guarding the gates, others were on board the ships. As the Carthaginians saw that they would have to deal with people who were anything but unprepared, they stood out from the harbour till daylight, and spent the time in lowering their masts and preparing for action. When it grew light they put out to sea that they might have sufficient room for fighting, and that the enemy's ships might be free to issue from the harbour. The Romans did not decline battle, encouraged as they were by the recollection of their former conflicts in this very place, and full of confidence in the numbers and courage of their men.

L. When they had sailed out to sea the Romans were eager to come to close quarters and make a hand-to-hand fight of it; the

Carthaginians, on the other hand, sought to avoid this and to succeed by manœuvring and not by direct attack; they preferred to make it a battle of ships rather than of soldiers.[15] For their fleet was amply provided with seamen, but only scantily manned by soldiers, and whenever a ship was laid alongside one of the enemy's they were very unequally matched in fighting men. When this became generally known, the spirits of the Romans rose as they realised how many of their military were on board, whilst the Carthaginians lost heart when they remembered how few they had. Seven of their ships were captured in a very short time, the rest took to flight. In the seven ships there were 1700 soldiers and sailors, amongst them three members of the Carthaginian nobility. The Roman fleet returned undamaged into port, with the exception of one which had been rammed, but even that was brought in.

Immediately after this battle Tiberius Sempronius, the consul, arrived at Messana before those in the town had heard of it. King Hiero went to meet him at the entrance of the Straits with his fleet fully equipped and manned, and went on board the consul's vessel to congratulate him on having safely arrived with his fleet and his army, and to wish him a prosperous and successful passage to Sicily. He then described the condition of the island and the movements of the Carthaginians, and promised to assist the Romans now in his old age with the same readiness which he had shown as a young man in the former war; he should supply the seamen and soldiers with corn and clothing gratis. He also told the consul that Lilybaeum and the cities on the coast were in great danger, some were anxious to effect a revolution. The consul saw that there must be no delay in his sailing for Lilybaeum; he started at once and the king accompanied him with his fleet.

LI. At Lilybaeum Hiero and his fleet bade him farewell, and the consul, after leaving the praetor to see to the defence of the coast of Sicily, crossed over to Malta which was held by the Carthaginians. Hamilcar, the son of Gisgo, who was in command of the garrison, surrendered the island and his men, a little under 2000 in number. A few days later he returned to Lilybaeum, and the prisoners, with the exception of the three nobles, were sold by auction.

After satisfying himself as to the security of that part of Sicily, the consul sailed to the Insulae Vulcani,[16] as he heard that the Carthaginian fleet was anchored there. No enemy, however, was found in the neighbourhood, for they had left for

Italy to ravage the coastal districts, and after laying waste the territory of Vibo they were threatening the city. Whilst he was returning to Sicily the news of these depredations reached the consul, and at the same time a despatch was handed to him from the senate informing him of Hannibal's presence in Italy and ordering him to come to his colleague's assistance as soon as possible.

With all these causes for anxiety weighing upon him, the consul at once embarked his army and despatched it up the Adriatic to Ariminum. He furnished Sex. Pomponius, his legate, with twenty-five ships of war, and entrusted to him the protection of the Italian coast and the territory of Vibo, and made up the fleet of M. Æmilius, the praetor, to fifty vessels. After making these arrangements for Sicily, he started for Italy with ten ships, and cruising along the coast reached Ariminum. From there he marched to the Trebia and effected a junction with his colleague.

LII. *The Battle of the Trebia.*—The fact that both consuls and all the available strength that Rome possessed were now brought up to oppose Hannibal, was a pretty clear proof that either that force was adequate for the defence of Rome or that all hope of its defence must be abandoned. Nevertheless, one consul, depressed after his cavalry defeat, and also by his wound, would rather that battle should be deferred. The other, whose courage had suffered no check and was therefore all the more eager to fight, was impatient of any delay. The country between the Trebia and the Po was inhabited by Gauls who in this struggle between two mighty peoples showed impartial goodwill to either side, with the view, undoubtedly, of winning the victor's gratitude. The Romans were quite satisfied with this neutrality if only it was maintained and the Gauls kept quiet, but Hannibal was extremely indignant, as he was constantly giving out that he had been invited by the Gauls to win their freedom. Feelings of resentment and, at the same time, a desire to enrich his soldiers with plunder prompted him to send 2000 infantry and 1000 cavalry, made up of Gauls and Numidians, mostly the latter, with orders to ravage the whole country, district after district, right up to the banks of the Po. Though the Gauls had hitherto maintained an impartial attitude, they were compelled in their need of help to turn from those who had inflicted these outrages to those who they hoped would avenge them. They sent envoys to the consuls to beg the Romans to come to the rescue of a land which was suffering because its people had been too loyal to Rome. Cornelius Scipio did not consider that either the grounds alleged or the circumstances justified his taking action. He regarded that nation with suspicion on account of their many acts of treachery, and even if their past faithlessness could have been forgotten through lapse of time, he could not forget the recent treachery of the Boii. Sempronius, on the other hand, was of opinion that the most effective means of preserving the fidelity of their allies was to defend those who first asked for their help. As his colleague still hesitated, he sent his own cavalry supported by about a thousand javelin men to protect the territory of the Gauls on the other side of the Trebia. They attacked the enemy suddenly whilst they were scattered and in disorder, most of them loaded with plunder, and after creating a great panic amongst them, and inflicting severe losses upon them, they drove them in flight to their camp. The fugitives were driven back by their comrades who poured in great numbers out of the camp, and thus reinforced they renewed the fighting. The battle wavered as each side retired or pursued, and up to the last the action was undecided. The enemy lost more men; the Romans claimed the victory.

LIII. To no one in the whole army did the victory appear more important or more decisive than to the consul himself. What gave him especial pleasure was that he had proved superior in that arm in which his colleague had been worsted. He saw that the spirits of his men were restored, and that there was no one but his colleague who wished to delay battle; he believed that Scipio was more sick in mind than in body, and that the thought of his wound made him shrink from the dangers of the battlefield. " But we must not be infected by a sick man's lethargy. What will be gained by further delay, or rather, by wasting time? Whom are we expecting as our third consul; what fresh army are we looking for? The camp of the Carthaginians is in Italy, almost in sight of the City. They are not aiming at Sicily and Sardinia, which they lost after their defeats, nor the Spain which lies on this side the Ebro; their sole object is to drive the Romans away from their ancestral soil, from the land on which they were born. What groans our fathers would utter, accustomed as they were to warring round the walls of Carthage, if they could see us, their descendants, with two consuls and two consular armies, cowering in our camp in the very heart of Italy, whilst the Carthaginian is annexing to his empire all between the Alps and the Apennines." This was the way he spoke when sitting by his incapacitated colleague, this the language he used before his soldiers as though he were haranguing the Assembly. He was urged on, too, by the near approach of the time for the elections, and the fear that the war, if delayed, might pass into the hands of the new consuls, as well as by the chance he had of monopolising all the glory of it while his colleague was on the sick list. In spite, therefore, of the opposition of Cornelius he ordered the soldiers to get ready for the coming battle.

Hannibal saw clearly what was the best course for the enemy to adopt, and had very little hope that the consuls would do anything rash or ill-advised. When, however, he found that what he had previously learnt by hearsay was actually the case, namely, that one of the consuls was a man of impetuous and headstrong character, and that he had become still more so since the recent cavalry action, he had very little doubt in his own mind that he would have a favourable opportunity of giving battle. He was anxious not to lose a moment, in order that he might fight whilst the hostile army was still raw and the better of the two generals was incapacitated by his wound, and also whilst the Gauls were still in a warlike mood, for he knew that most of them would follow him with less alacrity the further they were dragged from their homes. These and similar considerations led him to hope that a battle was imminent, and made him desirous of forcing an engagement if there was any holding back on the other side. He sent out some Gauls to reconnoitre—as Gauls were serving in both armies they could be most safely trusted to find out what he wanted—and when they reported that the Romans had prepared for battle, the Carthaginian began to look out for ground which would admit of an ambuscade.

LIV. Between the two armies there was a stream with very high banks which were overgrown with marshy grass and the brambles and brushwood which are generally found on waste ground. After riding round the place and satisfying himself from personal observation that it was capable of concealing even cavalry, Hannibal, turning to his brother Mago, said, "This will be the place for you to occupy. Pick out of our whole force of cavalry and infantry a hundred men from each arm, and bring them to me at the first watch, now it is time for food and rest." He then dismissed his staff. Presently Mago appeared with his 200 picked men. "I see here," said Hannibal, "the very flower of my army, but you must be strong in numbers as well as in courage. Each of you therefore go and choose nine others like himself, from the squadrons and the maniples. Mago will show you the place where you are to lie in ambuscade, you have an enemy who are blindly ignorant of these practices in war."

After sending Mago with his 1000 infantry and 1000 cavalry to take up his position, Hannibal gave orders for the Numidian cavalry to cross the Trebia in the early dawn and ride up to the gates of the Roman camp; then they were to discharge their missiles on the outposts and so goad the enemy on to battle. When the fighting had once started they were gradually to give ground and draw their pursuers to their own side of the river. These were the instructions to the Numidians; the other commanders, both infantry and cavalry, were ordered to see that all their men had breakfast, after which they were to wait for the signal, the men fully armed, the horses saddled and ready.

Eager for battle, and having already made up his mind to fight, Sempronius led out the whole of his cavalry to meet the Numidian attack, for it was in his cavalry that he placed most confidence; these were followed by 6000 infantry and at last the whole of his force marched on to the field. It happened to be the season of winter, a snowstorm was raging, and the district, situated between the Alps and the Apennines, was rendered especially cold by the vicinity of rivers and marshes. To make matters worse, men and horses alike had been hurriedly sent forward, without any food, without any protection against the cold, so they had no heat in them and the chilling blasts from the river made the cold still more severe as they approached it in their pursuit of the Numidians. But when they entered the water which had been swollen by the night's rain and was then breast high, their limbs became stiff with cold, and when they emerged on the other side they had hardly strength to hold their weapons; they began to grow faint from fatigue and as the day wore on, from hunger.

LV. Hannibal's men, meanwhile, had made fires in front of their tents, oil had been distributed amongst the maniples for them to make their joints and limbs supple and they had time for an ample repast. When it was announced that the enemy had crossed the river they took their arms, feeling alert and active in mind and body, and marched to battle.

The Balearic and light-armed infantry were posted in front of the standards; they numbered about 8000; behind them the heavy-armed infantry, the mainstay and backbone of the army;

on the flanks Hannibal distributed the cavalry, and outside
them, again, the elephants.

When the consul saw his cavalry, who had lost their order in
the pursuit, suddenly meeting with an unsuspected resistance
from the Numidians, he recalled them by signal and received
them within his infantry. There were 18,000 Romans, 20,000
Latin allies, and an auxiliary force of Cenomani, the only Gallic
tribe which had remained faithful. These were the forces engaged.

The Balearics and light infantry opened the battle, but on
being met by the heavier legions they were rapidly withdrawn
to the wings, an evolution which at once threw the Roman
horse into difficulties, for the 4000 wearied troopers had been
unable to offer an effective resistance to 10,000 who were fresh
and vigorous, and now in addition they were overwhelmed by
what seemed a cloud of missiles from the light infantry. Moreover, the elephants, towering aloft at the ends of the line, terrified
the horses not only by their appearance but by their unaccustomed smell, and created widespread panic. The infantry
battle, as far as the Romans were concerned, was maintained
more by courage than by physical strength, for the Carthaginians,
who had shortly before been getting themselves into trim,
brought their powers fresh and unimpaired into action, whilst
the Romans were fatigued and hungry and stiff with cold.
Still, their courage would have kept them up had it been only
infantry that they were fighting against. But the light infantry, after repulsing the cavalry, were hurling their missiles
on the flanks of the legions; the elephants had now come up
against the centre of the Roman line, and Mago and his Numidians, as soon as it had passed their ambuscade, rose up in the
rear and created a terrible disorder and panic. Yet in spite
of all the dangers which surrounded them, the ranks stood firm
and immovable for some time, even, contrary to all expectation, against the elephants. Some skirmishers who had been
placed where they could attack these animals flung darts at
them and drove them off, and rushed after them, stabbing them
under their tails, where the skin is soft and easily penetrated.

LVI. Maddened with pain and terror, they were beginning
to rush wildly on their own men, when Hannibal ordered them
to be driven away to the left wing against the auxiliary Gauls
on the Roman right. There they instantly produced unmis-
takable panic and flight, and the Romans had fresh cause for
alarm when they saw their auxiliaries routed. They now stood
fighting in a square, and about 10,000 of them, unable to escape

in any other direction, forced their way through the centre of
the African troops and the auxiliary Gauls who supported them
and inflicted an immense loss on the enemy. They were prevented by the river from returning to their camp, and the rain
made it impossible for them to judge where they could best
go to the assistance of their comrades, so they marched away
straight to Placentia. Then desperate attempts to escape were
made on all sides; some who made for the river were swept
away by the current or caught by the enemy while hesitating
to cross; others, scattered over the fields in flight, followed the
track of the main retreat and sought Placentia; others, fearing
the enemy more than the river, crossed it and reached their
camp. The driving sleet and the intolerable cold caused the
death of many men and baggage animals, and nearly all the
elephants perished. The Carthaginians stopped their pursuit
at the banks of the Trebia and returned to their camp so benumbed with cold that they hardly felt any joy in their victory.

In the night the men who had guarded the camp, and the
rest of the soldiers, mostly wounded, crossed the Trebia on
rafts without any interference from the Carthaginians, either
because the roaring of the storm prevented them from hearing
or because they were unable to move through weariness and
wounds and pretended that they heard nothing. Whilst the
Carthaginians were keeping quiet, Scipio led his army to Placentia and thence across the Po to Cremona, in order that one
colony might not be burdened with providing winter quarters
for the two armies.

LVII. *Hannibal's Winter Operations.*—This defeat so unnerved people in Rome that they believed the enemy was
already advancing to attack the City, and that there was no
help to be looked for, no hope of repelling him from their walls
and gates. After one consul had been beaten at the Ticinus
the other was recalled from Sicily, and now both consuls and
both consular armies had been worsted. What fresh generals,
men asked, what fresh legions could be brought to the rescue?
Amidst this universal panic Sempronius arrived. He had
slipped through the enemy's cavalry at immense risk while
they were dispersed in quest of plunder, and owed his escape
rather to sheer audacity than to cleverness, for he had little hope
of eluding them or of successful resistance if he failed to do so.
After conducting the elections, which was the pressing need for
the moment, he returned to winter quarters. The consuls
elected were Cneius Servilius and C. Flaminius.

Even in their winter quarters the Romans were not allowed much quiet; the Numidian horse were roaming in all directions, or where the ground was too rough for them, the Celtiberians and Lusitanians. They were, therefore, cut off from supplies on every side, except what were brought in ships on the Po. Near Placentia there was a place called Emporium, which had been carefully fortified and occupied by a strong garrison. In the hope of capturing the place, Hannibal approached with cavalry and light-armed troops, and as he trusted mainly to secrecy for success, he marched thither by night. But he did not escape the observation of the sentinels, and such a shouting suddenly arose that it was actually heard at Placentia. By daybreak the consul was on the spot with his cavalry, having given orders for the legions of infantry to follow in battle formation. A cavalry action followed in which Hannibal was wounded, and his retirement from the field discomfited the enemy; the position was admirably defended.

After taking only a few days' rest, before his wound was thoroughly healed Hannibal proceeded to attack Victumviae. During the Gaulish war this place had served as an emporium for the Romans; subsequently, as it was a fortified place, a mixed population from the surrounding country had settled there in considerable numbers, and now the terror created by the constant depredations had driven most of the people from the fields into the town. This motley population, excited by the news of the energetic defence of Placentia, flew to arms and went out to meet Hannibal. More like a crowd than an army they met him on his march, and as on the one side there was nothing but an undisciplined mob, and on the other a general and soldiers who had perfect confidence in each other, a small body routed as many as 35,000 men. The next day they surrendered and admitted a Carthaginian garrison within their walls. They had just completed the surrender of their arms in obedience to orders, when instructions were suddenly given to the victors to treat the city as though it had been carried by storm, and no deed of blood, which on such occasions historians are wont to mention, was left undone, so awful was the example set of every form of licentiousness and cruelty and brutal tyranny towards the wretched inhabitants.

Such were the winter operations of Hannibal.

LVIII. *Unsuccessful Attempt to cross the Apennines.*—The soldiers rested whilst the intolerable cold lasted; it did not, however, last long, and at the first doubtful indications of spring

Hannibal left his winter quarters for Etruria with the intention of inducing that nation to join forces with him, either voluntarily or under compulsion.

During his passage of the Apennines he was overtaken by a storm of such severity as almost to surpass the horrors of the Alps. The rain was driven by the wind straight into the men's faces, and either they had to drop their weapons or if they tried to struggle against the hurricane it caught them and dashed them to the ground, so they came to a halt. Then they found that it was stopping their respiration so that they could not breathe, and they sat down for a short time with their backs to the wind. The heavens began to reverberate with terrific roar, and amidst the awful din lightning flashed and quivered. Sight and sound alike paralysed them with terror. At last, as the force of the gale increased owing to the rain having ceased, they saw that there was nothing for it but to pitch their camp on the ground where they had been caught by the storm. Now all their labour had to begin over again, for they could neither unroll anything nor fix anything, whatever was fixed did not stand, the wind tore everything into shreds and carried it off. Soon the moisture in the upper air above the cold mountain peaks froze and discharged such a shower of snow and hail that the men, giving up all further attempts, lay down as best they could, buried beneath their coverings rather than protected by them. This was followed by such intense cold that when any one attempted to rise out of that pitiable crowd of prostrate men and beasts it was a long time before he could get up, for his muscles being cramped and stiff with cold, he could hardly bend his limbs. At length, by exercising their arms and legs, they were able to move about, and began to recover their spirits; here and there fires were lighted, and those who were most helpless turned to their colleagues for help. They remained on that spot for two days like a force blockaded; many men and animals perished; of the elephants which survived the battle of the Trebia they lost seven.

LIX. After descending from the Apennines Hannibal advanced towards Placentia, and after a ten miles' march formed camp. The following day he marched against the enemy with 12,000 infantry and 5000 cavalry. Sempronius had by this time returned from Rome, and he did not decline battle. That day the two camps were three miles distant from each other; the following day they fought, and both sides exhibited the most determined courage, but the action was indecisive. At the first encounter the Romans were so far superior that they not only conquered in the field, but followed the routed enemy to his camp and soon made an attack upon it. Hannibal stationed a few men to defend the rampart and the gates, the rest he massed in the middle of the camp, and ordered them to be on the alert and wait for the signal to make a sortie. It was now about three o'clock; the Romans were worn out with their fruitless efforts as there was no hope of carrying the camp, and the consul gave the signal to retire. As soon as Hannibal heard it and saw that the fighting had slackened and that the enemy were retiring from the camp, he immediately launched his cavalry against them right and left, and sallied in person with the main strength of his infantry from the middle of the camp. Seldom has there been a more equal fight, and few would have been rendered more memorable by the mutual destruction of both armies had the daylight allowed it to be sufficiently prolonged; as it was, night put an end to a conflict which had been maintained with such determined courage. There was greater fury than bloodshed, and as the fighting had been almost equal on both sides, they separated with equal loss. Not more than 600 infantry and half that number of cavalry fell on either side, but the Roman loss was out of proportion to their numbers; several members of the equestrian order and five military tribunes as well as three prefects of the allies were killed.

Immediately after the battle Hannibal withdrew into Liguria, and Sempronius to Luca. Whilst Hannibal was entering Liguria, two Roman quaestors who had been ambushed and captured, C. Fulvius and L. Lucretius, together with three military tribunes and five members of the equestrian order, most of them sons of senators, were given up to him by the Gauls in order that he might feel more confidence in their maintenance of peaceful relations, and their determination to give him active support.

LX. *Cneius Scipio's Campaign in Spain.*—While these events were in progress in Italy, Cn. Cornelius Scipio, who had been sent with a fleet and an army to Spain, commenced operations in that country. Starting from the mouth of the Rhone, he sailed round the eastward end of the Pyrenees and brought up at Emporiae. Here he disembarked his army, and beginning with the Læetani, he brought the whole of the maritime populations as far as the Ebro within the sphere of Roman influence by renewing old alliances and forming new ones. He gained in this way a reputation for clemency which extended not only to the maritime populations but to the more warlike tribes in the interior and the mountain districts. He established peaceable relations with these, and more than that, he secured their support in arms and several strong cohorts were enrolled from amongst them.

The country on this side the Ebro was Hanno's province, Hannibal had left him to hold it for Carthage. Considering that he ought to oppose Scipio's further progress before the whole province was under Roman sway, he fixed his camp in full view of the enemy and offered battle. The Roman general, too, thought that battle ought not to be delayed; he knew he would have to fight both Hanno and Hasdrubal, and preferred dealing with each singly rather than meeting them both at once. The battle was not a hard-fought one. The enemy lost 6000; 2000, including those who were guarding the camp, were made prisoners; the camp itself was carried and the general with some of his chiefs was taken; Cissis, a town near the camp, was successfully attacked. The plunder, however, as it was a small place, was of little value, consisting mainly of the barbarians' household goods and some worthless slaves. The camp, however, enriched the soldiers with the property belonging not only to the army they had defeated but also to the one serving with Hannibal in Italy. They had left almost all their valuable possessions on the other side of the Pyrenees, that they might not have heavy loads to carry.

LXI. Before he had received definite tidings of this defeat, Hasdrubal had crossed the Ebro with 8000 infantry and 1000 cavalry, hoping to encounter the Romans as soon as they landed, but after hearing of the disaster at Cissis and the capture of the camp, he turned his route to the sea. Not far from Tarracona he found our marines and seamen wandering at will through the fields, success as usual producing carelessness. Sending his cavalry in all directions amongst them, he made a great slaughter and drove them pell-mell to their ships. Afraid to remain any longer in the neighbourhood lest he should be surprised by Scipio, he retreated across the Ebro. On hearing of this fresh enemy Scipio came down by forced marches, and after dealing summary punishment to some of the naval captains, returned by sea to Emporiae, leaving a small garrison in Tarracona. He had scarcely left when Hasdrubal appeared on the scene, and instigated the Ilergetes, who had given hostages to Scipio, to revolt, and in conjunction with the warriors of that tribe ravaged the territories of those tribes who remained loyal to Rome.

This roused Scipio from his winter quarters, on which Hasdrubal again disappeared beyond the Ebro, and Scipio invaded in force the territory of the Ilergetes, after the author of the revolt had left them to their fate. He drove them all into Antanagrum, their capital, which he proceeded to invest, and a few days later he received them into the protection and jurisdiction of Rome, after demanding an increase in the number of hostages and inflicting a heavy fine upon them. From there he advanced against the Ausetani, who lived near the Ebro and were also in alliance with the Carthaginians, and invested their city. The Læetani whilst bringing assistance to their neighbours by night were ambushed not far from the city which they intended to enter. As many as 12,000 were killed, almost all the survivors threw away their arms and fled to their homes in scattered groups all over the country. The only thing which saved the invested city from assault and storm was the severity of the weather. For the thirty days during which the siege lasted the snow was seldom less than four feet deep, and it covered up the mantlets and *vineae* so completely that it even served as a sufficient protection against the firebrands which the enemy discharged from time to time. At last, after their chief, Amusicus, had escaped to Hasdrubal's quarters, they surrendered and agreed to pay an indemnity of twenty talents.

The army returned to its winter quarters at Tarracona.

LXII. *Religious Excitement in Rome.*—During this winter many portents occurred in Rome and the neighbourhood, or at all events, many were reported and easily gained credence, for when once men's minds have been excited by superstitious fears they easily believe these things. A six-months-old child, of freeborn parents, is said to have shouted " Io Triumphe " in the vegetable market, whilst in the Forum Boarium an ox is reported to have climbed up of its own accord to the third story of a house, and then, frightened by the noisy crowd which gathered, it threw itself down. A phantom navy was seen shining in the sky; the temple of Hope in the vegetable market was struck by lightning; at Lanuvium Juno's spear had moved of itself, and a crow had flown down to her temple and settled upon her couch; in the territory of Amiternum beings in human shape and clothed in white were seen at a distance, but no one came close to them; in the neighbourhood of Picenum there was a shower of stones; at Caere the oracular tablets had shrunk in size; in Gaul a wolf had snatched a sentinel's sword from its scabbard and run off with it.[17]

With regard to the other portents, the decemvirs were ordered
to consult the Sacred Books, but in the case of the shower of
stones at Picenum a nine days' sacred feast was proclaimed, at
the close of which almost the whole community busied itself
with the expiation of the others. First of all the City was
purified, and full-grown victims were sacrificed to the deities
named in the Sacred Books; an offering of forty pounds' weight
of gold was conveyed to Juno at Lanuvium, and the matrons
dedicated a bronze statue of that goddess on the Aventine. At
Caere, where the tablets had shrunk, a *lectisternium* was enjoined, and a service of intercession was to be rendered to
Fortuna on Algidus. In Rome also a *lectisternium* was ordered
for Juventas and a special service of intercession at the temple
of Hercules, and afterwards one in which the whole population
were to take part at all the shrines. Five full-grown victims
were sacrificed to the Genius of Rome, and C. Atilius Serranus,
the praetor, received instructions to undertake certain vows
which were to be discharged should the commonwealth remain
in the same condition for ten years. These ceremonial observances and vows, ordered in obedience to the Sacred Books, did
much to allay the religious fears of the people.

LXIII. *C. Flaminius and the Senate.*—One of the consuls elect
was C. Flaminius, and to him was assigned by lot the command
of the legions at Placentia. He wrote to the consul giving orders
for the army to be in camp at Ariminum by the 15th of March.
The reason was that he might enter upon his office there, for he
had not forgotten his old quarrels with the senate, first as
tribune of the people, then afterwards about his consulship, the
election to which had been declared illegal, and finally about
his triumph.[18] He further embittered the senate against him
by his support of C. Claudius; he alone of all the members was
in favour of the measure which that tribune introduced. Under
its provisions no senator, no one whose father had been a
senator, was allowed to possess a vessel of more than 300
amphorae burden. This was considered quite large enough for
the conveyance of produce from their estates, all profit made by
trading was regarded as dishonourable for the patricians.[19] The
question excited the keenest opposition and brought Flaminius
into the worst possible odium with the nobility through his
support of it, but on the other hand made him a popular favourite
and procured for him his second consulship. Suspecting, therefore, that they would endeavour to detain him in the City by
various devices, such as falsifying the auspices or the delay

necessitated by the Latin Festival, or other hindrances to which as consul he was liable, he gave out that he had to take a journey, and then left the City secretly as a private individual and so reached his province. When this got abroad there was a fresh outburst of indignation on the part of the incensed senate; they declared that he was carrying on war not only with the senate but even with the immortal gods. " On the former occasion," they said, " when he was elected consul against the auspices and we recalled him from the very field of battle, he was disobedient to gods and men. Now he is conscious that he has despised them and has fled from the Capitol and the customary recital of solemn vows. He refuses to approach the temple of Jupiter Optimus Maximus on the day of his entrance upon office, to see and consult the senate, to whom he is so odious and whom he alone of all men detests, to proclaim the Latin Festival and offer sacrifice to Jupiter Latiaris on the Alban Mount, to proceed to the Capitol and after duly taking the auspices recite the prescribed vows, and from thence, vested in the paludamentum and escorted by lictors, go in state to his province. He has stolen away furtively without his insignia of office, without his lictors, just as though he were some menial employed in the camp and had quitted his native soil to go into exile. He thinks it, forsooth, more consonant with the greatness of his office to enter upon it at Ariminum rather than in Rome, and to put on his official dress in some wayside inn rather than at his own hearth and in the presence of his own household gods."

It was unanimously decided that he should be recalled, brought back if need be by force, and compelled to discharge, on the spot, all the duties he owed to God and man before he went to the army and to his province. Q. Terentius and M. Antistius were delegated for this task, but they had no more influence with him than the despatch of the senate in his former consulship.

A few days afterwards he entered upon office, and whilst offering his sacrifice, the calf, after it was struck, bounded away out of the hands of the sacrificing priests and bespattered many of the bystanders with its blood. Amongst those at a distance from the altar who did not know what the commotion was about there was great excitement ; most people regarded it as a most alarming omen.

Flaminius took over the two legions from Sempronius, the late consul, and the two from C. Atilius, the praetor, and commenced his march to Etruria through the passes of the Apennines.

BOOK XXII

THE DISASTER OF CANNAE

I. Spring was now coming on; Hannibal accordingly moved out of his winter quarters. His previous attempt to cross the Apennines had been frustrated by the insupportable cold; to remain where he was would have been to court danger. The Gauls had rallied to him through the prospect of booty and spoil, but when they found that instead of plundering other people's territory their own had become the seat of war and had to bear the burden of furnishing winter quarters for both sides, they diverted their hatred from the Romans to Hannibal. Plots against his life were frequently hatched by their chiefs, and he owed his safety to their mutual faithlessness, for they betrayed the plots to him in the same spirit of fickleness in which they had formed them. He guarded himself from their attempts by assuming different disguises, at one time wearing a different dress, at another putting on false hair. But these constant alarms were an additional motive for his early departure from his winter quarters.

About the same time Cn. Servilius entered upon his consulship at Rome, on the 15th of March. When he had laid before the senate the policy which he proposed to carry out, the indignation against C. Flaminius broke out afresh. "Two consuls had been elected, but as a matter of fact they only had one. What legitimate authority did this man possess? What religious sanctions? Magistrates only take these sanctions with them from home, from the altars of the State, and from their private altars at home after they have celebrated the Latin Festival, offered the sacrifice on the Alban Mount, and duly recited the vows in the Capitol. These sanctions do not follow a private citizen, nor if he has departed without them can he obtain them afresh in all their fulness on a foreign soil."

Various Portents.—To add to the general feeling of apprehension, information was received of portents having occurred simultaneously in several places. In Sicily several of the soldiers' darts were covered with flames; in Sardinia the same thing happened to the staff in the hand of an officer who was going his rounds to inspect the sentinels on the wall; the shores had been lit up by numerous fires; a couple of shields had sweated blood; some soldiers had been struck by lightning; an eclipse of the sun had been observed; at Praeneste there had been a shower of red-hot stones; at Arpi shields had been seen in the sky and the sun had appeared to be fighting with the moon; at Capena two moons were visible in the daytime; at Caere the waters ran mingled with blood, and even the spring of Hercules had bubbled up with drops of blood on the water; at Antium the ears of corn which fell into the reapers' basket were blood-stained; at Falerii the sky seemed to be cleft asunder as with an enormous rift and all over the opening there was a blazing light; the oracular tablets shrank and shrivelled without being touched and one had fallen out with this inscription, " MARS IS SHAKING HIS SPEAR "; and at the same time the statue of Mars on the Appian Way and the images of the Wolves sweated blood. Finally, at Capua the sight was seen of the sky on fire and the moon falling in the midst of a shower of rain. Then credence was given to comparatively trifling portents, such as that certain people's goats were suddenly clothed with wool, a hen turned into a cock, and a cock into a hen. After giving the details exactly as they were reported to him and bringing his informants before the senate, the consul consulted the House as to what religious observances ought to be proclaimed. A decree was passed that to avert the evils which these portents foreboded, sacrifices should be offered, the victims to be both full-grown animals and sucklings, and also that special intercessions should be made at all the shrines for three days. What other ceremonial was necessary was to be carried out in accordance with the instructions of the decemvirs after they had inspected the Sacred Books and ascertained the will of the gods. On their advice it was decreed that the first votive offering should be made to Jupiter in the shape of a golden thunderbolt weighing fifty pounds, gifts of silver to Juno and Minerva, and sacrifices of full-grown victims to Queen Juno on the Aventine and Juno Sospita at Lanuvium, whilst the matrons were to contribute according to their means and bear their gift to Queen Juno on the Aventine. A *lectisternium* was to be held, and even the freedwomen were to contribute what they could for a gift to the temple of Feronia. When these instructions had been carried out the decemvirs sacrificed full-grown victims in the forum at Ardea, and finally in the middle of December there was a sacrifice at the Temple of Saturn, a *lectisternium* was ordered (the senators prepared the couch), and a public banquet. For a day and a night the cry of the Saturnalia resounded through the City, and the people were ordered to make that day a festival and observe it as such for ever.

II. *Hannibal's Advance into Etruria.*—While the consul was occupied in these propitiatory ceremonies and also in the enrolment of troops, information reached Hannibal that Flaminius had arrived at Arretium, and he at once broke up his winter quarters. There were two routes into Etruria, both of which were pointed out to Hannibal; one was considerably longer than the other but a much better road, the shorter route, which he decided to take, passed through the marshes of the Arno, which was at the time in higher flood than usual. He ordered the Spaniards and Africans, the main strength of his veteran army, to lead, and they were to take their own baggage with them, so that, in case of a halt, they might have the necessary supplies; the Gauls were to follow so as to form the centre of the column; the cavalry were to march last, and Mago and his Numidian light horse were to close up the column, mainly to keep the Gauls up to the mark in case they fell out or came to a halt through the fatigue and exertion of so long a march, for as a nation they were unable to stand that kind of thing. Those in front followed wherever the guides led the way, through the deep and almost bottomless pools of water, and though almost sucked in by the mud through which they were half-wading, half-swimming, still kept their ranks. The Gauls could neither recover themselves when they slipped nor when once down had they the strength to struggle out of the pools; depressed and hopeless they had no spirits left to keep up their bodily powers. Some dragged their worn-out limbs painfully along, others gave up the struggle and lay dying amongst the baggage animals which were lying about in all directions. What distressed them most of all was want of sleep, from which they had been suffering for four days and three nights. As everything was covered with water and they had not a dry spot on which to lay their wearied bodies, they piled up the baggage in the water and lay on the top, whilst some snatched a few minutes' needful rest by making couches of the heaps of baggage animals which were everywhere standing out of the water. Hannibal himself, whose eyes were affected by the changeable and inclement spring weather, rode upon the only surviving elephant so that he might be a little higher above the water.

Owing, however, to want of sleep and the night mists and the malaria from the marshes, his head became affected, and as neither place nor time admitted of any proper treatment, he completely lost the sight of one eye.

III. After losing many men and beasts under these frightful circumstances, he at last got clear of the marshes, and as soon as he could find some dry ground he pitched his camp. The scouting parties he had sent out reported that the Roman army was lying in the neighbourhood of Arretium. His next step was to investigate as carefully as he possibly could all that it was material for him to know—what mood the consul was in, what designs he was forming, what the character of the country and the kind of roads it possessed, and what resources it offered for the obtaining of supplies.

The district was amongst the most fertile in Italy; the plains of Etruria, which extend from Faesulae to Arretium, are rich in corn and live stock and every kind of produce. The consul's overbearing temper, which had grown steadily worse since his last consulship, made him lose all proper respect and reverence even for the gods, to say nothing of the majesty of the senate and the laws, and this self-willed and obstinate side of his character had been aggravated by the successes he had achieved both at home and in the field. It was perfectly obvious that he would not seek counsel from either God or man, and whatever he did would be done in an impetuous and headstrong manner. By way of making him show these faults of character still more flagrantly, the Carthaginian prepared to irritate and annoy him. He left the Roman camp on his left, and marched in the direction of Faesulae to plunder the central districts of Etruria. Within actual view of the consul he created as widespread a devastation as he possibly could, and from the Roman camp they saw in the distance an extensive scene of fire and massacre.

Flaminius had no intention of keeping quiet even if the enemy had done so, but now that he saw the possessions of the allies of Rome plundered and pillaged almost before his very eyes, he felt it to be a personal disgrace that an enemy should be roaming at will through Italy and advancing to attack Rome with none to hinder him. All the other members of the council of war were in favour of a policy of safety rather than of display; they urged him to wait for his colleague, that they might unite their forces and act with one mind on a common plan, and pending his arrival they should check the wild excesses of the plundering enemy with cavalry and the light-armed auxiliaries. Enraged at these suggestions he dashed out of the council and ordered the trumpets to give the signal for march and battle; exclaiming at the same time: " We are to sit, I suppose, before the walls of Arretium, because our country and our household gods are here. Now that Hannibal has slipped through our hands, he is to ravage Italy, destroy and burn everything in his way till he reaches Rome, while we are not to stir from here until the senate summons C. Flaminius from Arretium as they once summoned Camillus from Veii." During this outburst, he ordered the standards to be pulled up with all speed and at the same time mounted his horse. No sooner had he done so than the animal stumbled and fell and threw him over its head. All those who were standing round were appalled by what they took to be an evil omen at the beginning of a campaign, and their alarm was considerably increased by a message brought to the consul that the standard could not be moved though the standard-bearer had exerted his utmost strength. He turned to the messenger and asked him: " Are you bringing a despatch from the senate, also, forbidding me to go on with the campaign? Go, let them dig out the standard if their hands are too benumbed with fear for them to pull it up." Then the column began its march. The superior officers, besides being absolutely opposed to his plans, were thoroughly alarmed by the double portent, but the great body of the soldiers were delighted at the spirit their general had shown; they shared his confidence without knowing on what slender grounds it rested.

IV. *Battle on the Lake Trasumennus.*—In order still further to exasperate his enemy and make him eager to avenge the injuries inflicted on the allies of Rome, Hannibal laid waste with all the horrors of war the land between Cortona and Lake Trasumennus. He had now reached a position eminently adapted for surprise tactics, where the lake comes up close under the hills of Cortona. There is only a very narrow road here between the hills and the lake, as though a space had been purposely left for it. Further on there is a small expanse of level ground flanked by hills, and it was here that Hannibal pitched camp, which was only occupied by his Africans and Spaniards, he himself being in command. The Balearics and the rest of the light infantry he sent behind the hills; the cavalry, conveniently screened by some low hills, he stationed at the mouth of the defile, so that when the Romans had entered it they would be completely shut in by the cavalry, the lake, and the hills.

Flaminius had reached the lake at sunset. The next morning, in a still uncertain light, he passed through the defile, without sending any scouts on to feel the way, and when the column began to deploy in the wider extent of level ground the only enemy they saw was the one in front, the rest were concealed in their rear and above their heads. When the Carthaginian saw his object achieved and had his enemy shut in between the lake and the hills with his forces surrounding them, he gave the signal for all to make a simultaneous attack, and they charged straight down upon the point nearest to them. The affair was all the more sudden and unexpected to the Romans because a fog which had risen from the lake was denser on the plain than on the heights ; the bodies of the enemy on the various hills could see each other well enough, and it was all the easier for them to charge all at the same time. The shout of battle rose round the Romans before they could see clearly from whence it came, or became aware that they were surrounded. Fighting began in front and flank before they could form line or get their weapons ready or draw their swords.

V. In the universal panic, the consul displayed all the coolness that could be expected under the circumstances. The ranks were broken by each man turning towards the discordant shouts; he re-formed them as well as time and place allowed, and wherever he could be seen or heard, he encouraged his men and bade them stand and fight. "It is not by prayers or entreaties to the gods that you must make your way out," he said, "but by your strength and your courage. It is the sword that cuts a path through the middle of the enemy, and where there is less fear there is generally less danger." But such was the uproar and confusion that neither counsel nor command could be heard, and so far was the soldier from recognising his standard or his company or his place in the rank, that he had hardly sufficient presence of mind to get hold of his weapons and make them available for use, and some who found them a burden rather than a protection were overtaken by the enemy. In such a thick fog ears were of more use than eyes; the men turned their gaze in every direction as they heard the groans of the wounded and the blows on shield or breastplate, and the mingled shouts of triumph and cries of panic. Some who tried to fly ran into a dense body of combatants and could get no further; others who were returning to the fray were swept away by a rush of fugitives. At last, when ineffective charges had been made in every direction and they found themselves completely hemmed in, by the lake and the hills on either side, and by the enemy in front and rear, it became clear to every man that his only hope of safety lay in his own right hand and his sword. Then each began to depend upon himself for guidance and encouragement, and the fighting began afresh, not the orderly battle with its three divisions of *principes*, *hastati*, and *triarii*, where the fighting line is in front of the standards and the rest of the army behind, and where each soldier is in his own legion and cohort and maniple. Chance massed them together, each man took his place in front or rear as his courage prompted him, and such was the ardour of the combatants, so intent were they on the battle, that not a single man on the field was aware of the earthquake which levelled large portions of many towns in Italy, altered the course of swift streams, brought the sea up into the rivers, and occasioned enormous landslips amongst the mountains.

VI. For almost three hours the fighting went on; everywhere a desperate struggle was kept up, but it raged with greater fierceness round the consul. He was followed by the pick of his army, and wherever he saw his men hard pressed and in difficulties he at once went to their help. Distinguished by his armour he was the object of the enemy's fiercest attacks, which his comrades did their utmost to repel, until an Insubrian horseman who knew the consul by sight—his name was Ducarius—cried out to his countrymen, " Here is the man who slew our legions and laid waste our city and our lands! I will offer him in sacrifice to the shades of my foully murdered countrymen." Digging spurs into his horse he charged into the dense masses of the enemy, and slew an armour-bearer who threw himself in the way as he galloped up lance in rest, and then plunged his lance into the consul; but the *triarii* protected the body with their shields and prevented him from despoiling it.

Then began a general flight, neither lake nor mountain stopped the panic-stricken fugitives, they rushed like blind men over cliff and defile, men and arms tumbled pell-mell on one another. A large number, finding no avenue of escape, went into the water up to their shoulders; some in their wild terror even attempted to escape by swimming, an endless and hopeless task in that lake. Either their spirits gave way and they were drowned, or else finding their efforts fruitless, they regained with great difficulty the shallow water at the edge of the lake and were butchered in all directions by the enemy's cavalry who had ridden into the water.

About 6000 men who had formed the head of the line of march cut their way through the enemy and cleared the defile, quite unconscious of all that had been going on behind them. They halted on some rising ground, and listened to the shouting below and the clash of arms, but were unable, owing to the fog, to see or find out what the fortunes of the fight were.

At last, when the battle was over and the sun's heat had dispelled the fog, mountain and plain revealed in the clear light the disastrous overthrow of the Roman army and showed only too plainly that all was lost. Fearing lest they should be seen in the distance and cavalry be sent against them, they hurriedly took up their standards and disappeared with all possible speed. Maharbal pursued them through the night with the whole of his mounted force, and on the morrow, as starvation, in addition to all their other miseries, was threatening them, they surrendered to Maharbal, on condition of being allowed to depart with one garment apiece. This promise was kept with Punic faith by Hannibal, and he threw them all into chains.[1]

VII. *Reception of the News in Rome.*—This was the famous battle at Trasumennus, and a disaster for Rome memorable as few others have been. Fifteen thousand Romans were killed in action; 1000 fugitives were scattered all over Etruria and reached the City by divers routes ; 2500 of the enemy perished on the field, many in both armies afterwards of their wounds. Other authors give the loss on each side as many times greater, but I refuse to indulge in the idle exaggerations to which writers are far too much given, and what is more, I am supported by the authority of Fabius, who was living during the war. Hannibal dismissed without ransom those prisoners who belonged to the allies and threw the Romans into chains. He then gave orders for the bodies of his own men to be picked out from the heaps of slain and buried; careful search was also made for the body of Flaminius that it might receive honourable interment, but it was not found.

As soon as the news of this disaster reached Rome the people flocked into the Forum in a great state of panic and confusion. Matrons were wandering about the streets and asking those they met what recent disaster had been reported or what news was there of the army. The throng in the Forum, as numerous as a crowded Assembly, flocked towards the Comitium and the Senate-house and called for the magistrates. At last, shortly before sunset, M. Pomponius, the praetor, announced, " We have been defeated in a great battle." Though nothing more definite was heard from him, the people, full of the reports which they had heard from one another, carried back to their homes the information that the consul had been killed with the greater part of his army; only a few survived, and these were either dispersed in flight throughout Etruria or had been made prisoners by the enemy.

The misfortunes which had befallen the defeated army were not more numerous than the anxieties of those whose relatives had served under C. Flaminius, ignorant as they were of the fate of each of their friends, and not in the least knowing what to hope for or what to fear. The next day and several days afterwards, a large crowd, containing more women than men, stood at the gates waiting for some one of their friends or for news about them, and they crowded round those they met with eager and anxious inquiries, nor was it possible to get them away, especially from those they knew, until they had got all the details from first to last. Then as they came away from their informants you might see the different expressions on their faces, according as each had received good or bad news, and friends congratulating or consoling them as they wended their way homewards. The women were especially demonstrative in their joy and in their grief. They say that one who suddenly met her son at the gate safe and sound expired in his arms, whilst another who had received false tidings of her son's death and was sitting as a sorrowful mourner in her house, no sooner saw him returning than she died from too great happiness.

For several days the praetors kept the senate in session from sunrise to sunset, deliberating under what general or with what forces they could offer effectual resistance to the victorious Carthaginian.

VIII. *Q. Fabius Maximus nominated Dictator.*—Before they had formed any definite plans, a fresh disaster was announced; 4000 cavalry under the command of C. Centenius, the propraetor, had been sent by the consul Servilius to the assistance of his colleague. When they heard of the battle at Trasumennus they marched into Umbria, and here they were surrounded and captured by Hannibal. The news of this occurrence affected men in very different ways. Some, whose thoughts were preoccupied with more serious troubles, looked upon this loss of cavalry as a light matter in comparison with the previous losses; others estimated the importance of the incident not by the

magnitude of the loss but by its moral effect.   Just as where
the constitution is impaired, any malady however slight is felt
more than it would be in a strong robust person, so any misfortune which befell the State in its present sick and disordered
condition must be measured not by its actual importance but
by its effect [on a State already exhausted and unable to bear
anything which would aggravate its condition.

Accordingly the citizens took refuge in a remedy which for a
long time had not been made use of or required, namely the
appointment of a Dictator.   As the consul by whom alone
one could be nominated was absent, and it was not easy for a
messenger or a despatch to be sent through Italy, overrun as it
was by the arms of Carthage, and as it would have been contrary
to all precedent for the people to appoint a Dictator, the
Assembly invested Q. Fabius Maximus with dictatorial powers [2]
and appointed M. Minucius Rufus to act as his Master of the
Horse.   They were commissioned by the senate to strengthen
the walls and towers of the City and place garrisons in whatever positions they thought best, and cut down the bridges over
the various rivers, for now it was a fight for their City and their
homes, since they were no longer able to defend Italy.

IX. *Hannibal's Advance to Apulia.*—Hannibal marched in a
straight course through Umbria as far as Spoletum, and after
laying the country round utterly waste, he commenced an attack
upon the city which was repulsed with heavy loss.   As a single
colony was strong enough to defeat his unfortunate attempt,
he was able to form some conjecture as to the difficulties attend-
ing the capture of Rome, and consequently diverted his march
into the territory of Picenum, a district which not only abounded
in every kind of produce but was richly stored with property
which the greedy and needy soldiers seized and plundered without restraint.   He remained in camp there for several days,
during which his soldiers recruited their strength after their
winter campaigns and their journey across the marshes, and
a battle which though ultimately successful was neither without
heavy loss nor easily won.

When sufficient time for rest had been allowed to men who
delighted much more in plundering and destroying than in ease
and idleness, Hannibal resumed his march and devastated the
districts of Praetutia and Hadria, then he treated in the same
way the country of the Marsi, the Marrucini, and the Peligni,
and the part of Apulia which was nearest to him, including the
cities of Arpi and Luceria.

Cn. Servilius had fought some insignificant actions with the Gauls and taken one small town, but when he heard of his colleague's death and the destruction of his army, he was alarmed for the walls of his native City, and marched straight for Rome that he might not be absent at this critical juncture.

The Appeal to Religion in Rome.—Q. Fabius Maximus was now Dictator for the second time. On the very day of his entrance upon office he summoned a meeting of the senate, and commenced by discussing matters of religion. He made it quite clear to the senators that C. Flaminius' fault lay much more in his neglect of the auspices and of his religious duties than in bad generalship and foolhardiness. The gods themselves, he maintained, must be consulted as to the necessary measures to avert their displeasure, and he succeeded in getting a decree passed that the decemvirs should be ordered to consult the Sibylline Books, a course which is only adopted when the most alarming portents have been reported. After inspecting the Books of Fate they informed the senate that the vow which had been made to Mars in view of that war had not been duly discharged, and that it must be discharged afresh and on a much greater scale. The Great Games must be vowed to Jupiter, a temple to Venus Erycina and one to Mens;[3] a *lectisternium* must be held and solemn intercessions made; a Sacred Spring must also be vowed. All these things must be done if the war was to be a successful one and the republic remain in the same position in which it was at the beginning of the war. As Fabius would be wholly occupied with the necessary arrangements for the war, the senate with the full approval of the pontifical college ordered the praetor, M. Æmilius, to take care that all these orders were carried out in good time.

X. After these resolutions had been passed in the senate the praetor consulted the pontifical college as to the proper means of giving effect to them, and L. Cornelius Lentulus, the Pontifex Maximus, decided that the very first step to take was to refer to the people the question of a " Sacred Spring," as this particular form of vow could not be undertaken without the order of the people. The form of procedure was as follows : " Is it," the praetor asked the Assembly, " your will and pleasure that all be done and performed in manner following? That is to say, if the commonwealth of the Romans and the Quirites be preserved, as I pray it may be, safe and sound through these present wars—to wit, the war between Rome and Carthage and the wars with the Gauls now dwelling on the hither side of the Alps—then shall the Romans and Quirites present as an offering whatever the spring shall produce from their flocks and herds, whether it be from swine or sheep or goats or cattle, and all that is not already devoted to any other deity shall be consecrated to Jupiter from such time as the senate and people shall order. Whosoever shall make an offering let him do it at whatsoever time and in whatsoever manner he will, and howsoever he offers it, it shall be accounted to be duly offered. If the animal which should have been sacrificed die, it shall be as though unconsecrated, there shall be no sin. If any man shall hurt or slay a consecrated thing unwittingly he shall not be held guilty. If a man shall have stolen any such animal, the people shall not bear the guilt, nor he from whom it was stolen. If a man offer his sacrifice unwittingly on a forbidden day, it shall be accounted to be duly offered. Whether he do so by night or day, whether he be slave or freeman, it shall be accounted to be duly offered. If any sacrifice be offered before the senate and people have ordered that it shall be done, the people shall be free and absolved from all guilt therefrom."

To the same end the Great Games were vowed at a cost of 333,333⅓ *ases*, and in addition 300 oxen to Jupiter, and white oxen and the other customary victims to a number of deities.

When the vows had been duly pronounced a litany of intercession was ordered, and not only the population of the City but the people from the country districts, whose private interests were being affected by the public distress, went in procession with their wives and children.

Then a *lectisternium* was held for three days under the supervision of the ten keepers of the Sacred Books. Six couches were publicly exhibited; one for Jupiter and Juno, another for Neptune and Minerva, a third for Mars and Venus, a fourth for Apollo and Diana, a fifth for Vulcan and Vesta, and the sixth for Mercury and Ceres.

This was followed by the vowing of temples. Q. Fabius Maximus, as Dictator, vowed the temple to Venus Erycina, because it was laid down in the Books of Fate that this vow should be made by the man who possessed the supreme authority in the State. T. Otacilius, the praetor, vowed the temple to Mens.

XI. *Military Measures.*—After the various obligations towards the gods had thus been discharged, the Dictator referred to the senate the question of the policy to be adopted with regard to the war, with what legions and how many the senators thought he ought to meet their victorious enemy. They decreed that he should take over the army from Cneius Servilius, and further that he should enrol from amongst the citizens and the allies as many cavalry and infantry as he considered requisite; all else was left to his discretion to take such steps as he thought desirable in the interests of the republic. Fabius said that he would add two legions to the army which Servilius commanded; these were raised by the Master of the Horse and he fixed a day for their assembling at Tibur. A proclamation was also issued that those who were living in towns and strongholds that were not sufficiently fortified should remove into places of safety, and that all the population settled in the districts through which Hannibal was likely to march should abandon their farms, after first burning their houses and destroying their produce, so that he might not have any supplies to fall back upon. He then marched along the Flaminian road to meet the consul.

As soon as he caught sight of the army in the neighbourhood of Ocriculum near the Tiber, and the consul riding forward with some cavalry to meet him, he sent an officer to tell him that he was to come to the Dictator without his lictors. He did so, and the way they met produced a profound sense of the majesty of the dictatorship amongst both citizens and allies, who had almost by this time forgotten that greatest of all offices.

Shortly afterwards a despatch was handed in from the City stating that some transports which were carrying supplies for the army in Spain had been captured by the Carthaginian fleet near the port of Cosa. The consul was thereupon ordered to man the ships which were lying off Rome or at Ostia with full complements of seamen and soldiers, and sail in pursuit of the hostile fleet and protect the coast of Italy. A large force was raised in Rome, even freedmen who had children and were of the military age had been sworn in. Out of these city troops, all under thirty-five years of age were placed on board the ships, the rest were left to garrison the City.

XII. *Fabius declines Hannibal's offer of Battle.*—The Dictator took over the consul's army from Fulvius Flaccus, the second in command, and marched through Sabine territory to Tibur, where he had ordered the newly raised force to assemble by the appointed day. From there he advanced to Praeneste, and taking a cross-country route, came out on the Latin road. From this point he proceeded towards the enemy, showing the

utmost care in reconnoitring all the various routes, and determined not to take any risks anywhere, except so far as necessity
should compel him. The first day he pitched his camp in view
of the enemy not far from Arpi; the Carthaginian lost no time
in marching out his men in battle order to give him the chance
of fighting. But when he saw that the enemy kept perfectly
quiet and that there were no signs of excitement in their camp,
he tauntingly remarked that the spirits of the Romans, those
sons of Mars, were broken at last, the war was at an end, and
they had openly foregone all claim to valour and renown. He
then returned into camp. But he was really in a very anxious
state of mind, for he saw that he would have to do with a very
different type of commander from Flaminius or Sempronius;
the Romans had been taught by their defeats and had at last
found a general who was a match for him. It was the wariness
not the impetuosity of the Dictator [4] that was the immediate
cause of his alarm; he had not yet tested his inflexible resolution. He began to harass and provoke him by frequently
shifting his camp and ravaging the fields of the allies of Rome
before his very eyes. Sometimes he would march rapidly out
of sight and then in some turn of the road take up a concealed
position in the hope of entrapping him, should he come down
to level ground. Fabius kept on high ground, at a moderate
distance from the enemy, so that he never lost sight of him and
never closed with him. Unless they were employed on necessary
duty, the soldiers were confined to camp. When they went in
quest of wood or forage they went in large bodies and only
within prescribed limits. A force of cavalry and light infantry
told off in readiness against sudden alarms, made everything
safe for his own soldiers and dangerous for the scattered foragers
of the enemy. He refused to stake everything on a general
engagement, whilst slight encounters, fought on safe ground
with a retreat close at hand, encouraged his men, who had been
demoralised by their previous defeats, and made them less
dissatisfied with their own courage and fortunes. But his
sound and commonsense tactics were not more distasteful to
Hannibal than they were to his own Master of the Horse.
Headstrong and impetuous in counsel and with an ungovernable
tongue, the only thing that prevented Minucius from making
shipwreck of the State was the fact that he was in a subordinate
command. At first to a few listeners, afterwards openly amongst
the rank and file, he abused Fabius, calling his deliberation
indolence and his caution cowardice, attributing to him faults

akin to his real virtues, and by disparaging his superior—a vile practice which, through its often proving successful, is steadily on the increase—he tried to exalt himself.

XIII. *Hannibal in Samnium and Campania.*—From the Hirpini Hannibal went across into Samnium; he ravaged the territory of Beneventum and captured the city of Telesia. He did his best to exasperate the Roman commander, hoping that he would be so incensed by the insults and sufferings inflicted on his allies that he would be able to draw him into an engagement on level ground.

Amongst the thousands of allies of Italian nationality who had been taken prisoners by Hannibal at Trasumennus and dismissed to their homes were three Campanian knights, who had been allured by bribes and promises to win over the affections of their countrymen. They sent a message to Hannibal to the effect that if he would bring his army up to Campania there would be a good chance of his obtaining possession of Capua. Hannibal was undecided whether to trust them or not, for the enterprise was greater than the authority of those who advised it; however, they at last persuaded him to leave Samnium for Campania. He warned them that they must make their repeated promises good by their acts, and after bidding them return to him with more of their countrymen, including some of their chief men, he dismissed them. Some who were familiar with the country told him that if he marched into the neighbourhood of Casinum and occupied the pass, he would prevent the Romans from rendering assistance to their allies. He accordingly ordered a guide to conduct him there. But the difficulty which the Carthaginians found in pronouncing Latin names led to the guide understanding Casilinum instead of Casinum. Quitting his intended route, he came down through the districts of Allifae, Callifae, and Cales on to the plains of Stella. When he looked round and saw the country shut in by mountains and rivers he called the guide and asked him where on earth he was. When he was told that he would that day have his quarters at Casilinum, he saw the mistake and knew that Casinum was far away in quite another country. The guide was scourged and crucified in order to strike terror into the others. After entrenching his camp he sent Maharbal with his cavalry to harry the Falernian land. The work of destruction extended to the Baths of Sinuessa;[5] the Numidians inflicted enormous losses, but the panic and terror which they created spread even further. And yet, though everything was wrapped in the flames of war, the allies did not allow their terrors to warp them from their loyalty, simply because they were under a just and equable rule, and rendered a willing obedience to their superiors—the only true bond of allegiance.

XIV. *Minucius attacks the Dictator's Authority.*—When Hannibal had encamped at the Vulturnus and the loveliest part of Italy was being reduced to ashes and the smoke was rising everywhere from the burning farms, Fabius continued his march along the Massic range of hills. For a few days the mutinous discontent amongst the troops had subsided, because they inferred from the unusually rapid marching that Fabius was hastening to save Campania from being ravaged and plundered. But when they reached the western extremity of the range and saw the enemy burning the farmsteads of the colonists of Sinuessa and those in the Falernian district, while nothing was said about giving battle, the feeling of exasperation was again roused, and studiously fanned by Minucius. "Are we come here," he would ask, "to enjoy the sight of our murdered allies and the smoking ruins of their homes? Surely, if nothing else appeals to us, ought we not to feel ashamed of ourselves as we see the sufferings of those whom our fathers sent as colonists to Sinuessa that this frontier might be protected from the Samnite foe, whose homes are being burnt not by our neighbours the Samnites but by a Carthaginian stranger from the ends of the earth who has been allowed to come thus far simply through our dilatoriness and supineness? Have we, alas! so far degenerated from our fathers that we calmly look on while the very country, past which they considered it an affront for a Carthaginian fleet to cruise, has now been filled with Numidian and Moorish invaders? We who only the other day in our indignation at the attack on Saguntum appealed not to men alone, but to treaties and to gods, now quietly watch Hannibal scaling the walls of a Roman colony! The smoke from the burning farms and fields is blown into our faces, our ears are assailed by the cries of our despairing allies who appeal to us for help more than they do to the gods, and here are we marching an army like a herd of cattle through summer pastures and mountain paths hidden from view by woods and clouds! If M. Furius Camillus had chosen this method of wandering over mountain heights and passes to rescue the City from the Gauls which has been adopted by this new Camillus, this peerless Dictator who has been found for us in our troubles, to recover

Italy from Hannibal, Rome would still be in the hands of the Gauls, and I very much fear that if we go on dawdling in this way the City which our ancestors have so often saved will only have been saved for Hannibal and the Carthaginians. But on the day that the message came to Veii that Camillus had been nominated Dictator by senate and people, though the Janiculum was quite high enough for him to sit there and watch the enemy, like the man and true Roman that he was, he came down into the plain, and in the very heart of the City where the Busta Gallica are now he cut to pieces the legions of the Gauls, and the next day he did the same beyond Gabii. Why, when years and years ago we were sent under the yoke by the Samnites at the Caudine Forks, was it, pray, by exploring the heights of Samnium or by assailing and besieging Luceria and challenging our victorious foe that L. Papirius Cursor took the yoke off Roman necks and placed it on the haughty Samnite? What else but rapidity of action gave C. Lutatius the victory? The day after he first saw the enemy he surprised their fleet laden with supplies and hampered by its cargo of stores and equipment. It is mere folly to fancy that the war can be brought to an end by sitting still or making vows to heaven. Your duty is to take your arms and go down and meet the enemy man to man. It is by doing and daring that Rome has increased her dominion not by these counsels of sloth which cowards call caution."

Minucius said all this before a host of Roman tribunes and knights, as if he were addressing the Assembly, and his daring words even reached the ears of the soldiery; if they could have voted on the question, there is no doubt that they would have superseded Fabius for Minucius.

XV. Fabius kept an equally careful watch upon both sides, upon his own men no less than upon the enemy, and he showed that his resolution was quite unshaken. He was quite aware that his inactivity was making him unpopular not only in his own camp, but even in Rome, nevertheless his determination remained unchanged and he persisted in the same tactics for the rest of the summer, and Hannibal abandoned all hopes of the battle which he had so anxiously sought for. It became necessary for him to look round for a suitable place to winter in, as the country in which he was, a land of orchards and vineyards, was entirely planted with the luxuries rather than the necessaries of life, and furnished supplies only for a few months not for the whole year. Hannibal's movements were reported to Fabius by his scouts. As he felt quite certain that he would return by the same pass through which he had entered the district of Falernum, he posted a fairly strong detachment on Mount Callicula and another to garrison Casilinum. The Vulturnus runs through the middle of this town and forms the boundary between the districts of Falernum and Campania. He led his army back over the same heights, having previously sent L. Hostilius Mancinus forward with 400 cavalry to reconnoitre. This man was amongst the throng of young officers who had frequently listened to the fierce harangues of the Master of the Horse. At first he advanced cautiously, as a scouting party should do, to get a good view of the enemy from a safe position. But when he saw the Numidians roaming in all directions through the villages, and had even surprised and killed some of them, he thought of nothing but fighting, and completely forgot the Dictator's instructions, which were to go forward as far as he could safely and to retire before the enemy observed him. The Numidians, attacking and retreating in small bodies, drew him gradually almost up to their camp, his men and horses by this time thoroughly tired. Thereupon Carthalo, the general in command of the cavalry, charged at full speed, and before they came within range of their javelins put the enemy to flight and pursued them without slackening rein for nearly five miles. When Mancinus saw that there was no chance of the enemy giving up the pursuit, or of his escaping them, he rallied his men and faced the Numidians, though completely outnumbered and outmatched. He himself with the best of his riders was cut off, the rest resumed their wild flight and reached Cales and ultimately by different by-paths returned to the Dictator.

It so happened that Minucius had rejoined Fabius on this day. He had been sent to strengthen the force holding the defile which contracts into a narrow pass just above Terracina close to the sea. This was to prevent the Carthaginian from utilising the Appian road for a descent upon the territory of Rome, when he left Sinuessa. The Dictator and the Master of the Horse with their joint armies moved their camp on to the route which Hannibal was expected to take. He was encamped two miles distant.

XVI. *Hannibal foils the Dictator.*—The next day the Carthaginian army began its march and filled the whole of the road between the two camps. The Romans had taken up a position immediately below their entrenchments, on unquestionably more advantageous ground, yet the Carthaginian came up with his cavalry and light infantry to challenge his enemy. They made repeated attacks and retirements, but the Roman line kept its ground; the fighting was slack and more satisfactory to the Dictator than to Hannibal; 200 Romans fell, and 800 of the enemy.

It now seemed as if Hannibal must be hemmed in. Capua and Samnium and all the rich land of Latium behind them were furnishing the Romans with supplies, while the Carthaginian would have to winter amongst the rocks of Formiae and the sands and marshes of Liternum and in gloomy forests. Hannibal did not fail to observe that his own tactics were being employed against him. As he could not get out through Casilinum, and would have to make for the mountains and cross the ridge of Callicula, he would be liable to be attacked by the Romans whilst he was shut up in the valleys. To guard against this he decided upon a stratagem which, deceiving the eyes of the enemy by its alarming appearance, would enable him to scale the mountains in a night march without fear of interruption. The following was the ruse which he adopted. Torchwood gathered from all the country round, and faggots of dry brushwood were tied on the horns of the oxen which he was driving in vast numbers, both broken and unbroken to the plough, amongst the rest of the plunder from the fields. About 2000 oxen were collected for the purpose. To Hasdrubal was assigned the task of setting fire to the bundles on the horns of this herd as soon as darkness set in, then driving them up the mountains and if possible mostly above the passes which were guarded by the Romans.

XVII. As soon as it was dark, the camp silently broke up; the oxen were driven some distance in front of the column. When they had reached the foot of the mountains where the roads began to narrow, the signal was given and the herds with their flaming horns were driven up the mountain side. The terrifying glare of the flames shooting from their heads and the heat which penetrated to the root of their horns made the oxen rush about as though they were mad. At this sudden scampering about, it seemed as though the woods and mountains were on fire, and all the brushwood round became alight and the incessant but useless shaking of their heads made the flames shoot out all the more, and gave the appearance of men running about in all directions. When the men who were guarding the pass saw fires moving above them high up on the mountains, they thought that their position was turned, and they hastily quitted it. Making their way up to the highest points, they took the direction where there appeared to be the fewest flames, thinking this to be the safest road. Even so, they came across stray oxen separated from the herd, and at first sight they stood still in astonishment at what seemed a preternatural sight of beings breathing fire. When it turned out to be simply a human device they were still more alarmed at what they suspected was an ambuscade, and they took to flight. Now they fell in with some of Hannibal's light infantry, but both sides shrank from a fight in the darkness and remained inactive till daylight. In the meantime Hannibal had marched the whole of his army through the pass, and after surprising and scattering some Roman troops in the pass itself, fixed his camp in the district of Allifae.

XVIII. *Hannibal's Continued March—Minucius in command.* —Fabius watched all this confusion and excitement, but as he took it to be an ambuscade, and in any case shrank from a battle in the night, he kept his men within their lines. As soon as it was light there was a battle just under the ridge of the mountain where the Carthaginian light infantry were cut off from their main body and would easily have been crushed by the Romans, who had considerably the advantage in numbers, had not a cohort of Spaniards come up, who had been sent back by Hannibal to their assistance. These men were more accustomed to the mountains and in better training for running amongst rocks and precipices, and being both more lightly made and more lightly armed they could easily by their method of fighting baffle an enemy drawn from the lowlands, heavily armed and accustomed to stationary tactics. At last they drew off from a contest which was anything but an equal one. The Spaniards being almost untouched, the Romans having sustained a heavy loss, each retired to their respective camps.

Fabius followed on Hannibal's track through the pass and encamped above Allifae in an elevated position and one of great natural strength. Hannibal retraced his steps as far as the Peligni, ravaging the country as he went, as though his intention was to march through Samnium upon Rome. Fabius continued to move along the heights, keeping between the enemy and the City, neither avoiding nor attacking him. The Carthaginian left the Peligni, and marching back into Apulia, reached Gereonium. This city had been abandoned by its inhabitants because a portion of the walls had fallen into ruin. The Dictator formed an entrenched camp near Larinum. From there he was recalled to Rome on business connected with religion. Before his departure he impressed upon the Master of the Horse, not only as commander-in-chief but as a friend giving good advice and even using entreaties, the necessity of trusting more to prudence than to luck, and following his own example rather than copying Sempronius and Flaminius. He was not to suppose that nothing had been gained now that the summer had been spent in baffling the enemy, even physicians often gained more by not disturbing their patients than by subjecting them to movement and exercises; it was no small advantage to have avoided defeat at the hands of a foe who had been so often victorious and to have obtained a breathing space after such a series of disasters. With these unheeded warnings to the Master of the Horse he started for Rome.

XIX. *Events in Spain.*—At the commencement of this summer war began in Spain both by land and sea. Hasdrubal added ten ships to those which he had received from his brother, equipped and ready for action, and gave Himilco a fleet of forty vessels. He then sailed from New Carthage, keeping near land, and with his army moving parallel along the coast, ready to engage the enemy whether by sea or land. When Cn. Scipio learnt that his enemy had left his winter quarters he at first adopted the same tactics, but on further consideration he would not venture on a contest by land, owing to the immense reputation of the new auxiliaries. After embarking the pick of his army he proceeded with a fleet of thirty-five ships to meet the enemy. The day after leaving Tarraco he came to anchor at a spot ten miles distant from the mouth of the Ebro. Two despatch boats belonging to Massilia had been sent to reconnoitre, and they brought back word that the Carthaginian fleet was riding at anchor in the mouth of the river and their camp was on the bank. Scipio at once weighed anchor and sailed towards the enemy, intending to strike a sudden panic amongst them by surprising them whilst off their guard and unsuspicious of danger.

There are in Spain many towers situated on high ground which are used both as look-outs and places of defence against pirates. It was from there that the hostile ships were first sighted, and the signal given to Hasdrubal; excitement and confusion prevailed in the camp on shore before it reached the ships at sea, as the splash of the oars and other sounds of advancing ships were not yet heard, and the projecting headlands hid the Roman fleet from view. Suddenly one mounted vidette after another

III   F

from Hasdrubal galloped up with orders to those who were
strolling about on the shore or resting in their tents, and expecting anything rather than the approach of an enemy or battle
that day, to embark with all speed and take their arms, for the
Roman fleet was now not far from the harbour. This order the
mounted men were giving in all directions, and before long
Hasdrubal himself appeared with the whole of his army. Everywhere there was noise and confusion, the rowers and the soldiers
scrambled on board more like men flying from the shore than
men going into action. Hardly were all on board, when some
unfastened the mooring ropes and drifted towards their anchors,
others cut their cables; everything was done in too much haste
and hurry, the work of the seamen was hampered by the preparations which the soldiers were making, and the soldiers were
prevented from putting themselves in fighting trim owing to
the confusion and panic which prevailed amongst the seamen.
By this time the Romans were not only near at hand, they had
actually lined up their ships for the attack. The Carthaginians
were paralysed quite as much by their own disorder as by the
approach of the enemy, and they brought their ships round for
flight, after abandoning a struggle which it would be more true
to say was attempted rather than begun. But it was impossible
for their widely extended line to enter the mouth of the river all
at once, and the ships were run ashore in all directions. Some
of those on board got out through the shallow water, others
jumped on to the beach, with arms or without, and made good
their escape to the army which was drawn up ready for action
along the shore. Two Carthaginian ships, however, were
captured to begin with and four sunk.

XX. Though the Romans saw that the enemy were in force
on land and that their army was extended along the shore, they
showed no hesitation in following up the enemy's panic-stricken
fleet. They secured all the ships which had not staved their
prows in on the beach, or grounded with their keels in the mud
by fastening hawsers to their sterns and dragging them into deep
water. Out of forty vessels twenty-five were captured in this
way.

This was not, however, the best part of the victory. Its main
importance lay in the fact that this one insignificant encounter
gave the mastery of the whole of the adjacent sea. The fleet
accordingly sailed to Onusa, and there the soldiers disembarked,
captured and plundered the place and then marched towards
New Carthage. They ravaged the entire country round, and

ended by setting fire to the houses which adjoined the walls and gates. Re-embarking laden with plunder, they sailed to Longuntica, where they found a great quantity of esparto grass which Hasdrubal had collected for the use of the navy, and after taking what they could use they burnt the rest. They did not confine themselves to cruising along the coast, but crossed over to the island of Ebusus, where they made a determined but unsuccessful attack upon the capital during the whole of two days. As they found that they were only wasting time on a hopeless enterprise, they took to plundering the country, and sacked and burnt several villages. Here they secured more booty than on the mainland, and after placing it on board, as they were on the point of sailing away, some envoys came to Scipio from the Balearic isles to sue for peace. From this point the fleet sailed back to the eastern side of the province where envoys were assembled from all the tribes in the district of the Ebro, and many even from the remotest parts of Spain. The tribes which actually acknowledged the supremacy of Rome and gave hostages amounted to more than a hundred and twenty. The Romans felt now as much confidence in their army as in their navy, and marched as far as the pass of Castulo. Hasdrubal retired to Lusitania where he was nearer to the Atlantic.

XXI. It now seemed as though the remainder of the summer would be undisturbed, and it would have been so as far as the Carthaginians were concerned. But the Spanish temperament is restless and fond of change, and after the Romans had left the pass and retired to the coast, Mandonius and Indibilis, who had previously been chief of the Ibergetes, roused their fellow-tribesmen and proceeded to harry the lands of those who were in peace and alliance with Rome. Scipio despatched a military tribune with some light-armed auxiliaries to disperse them, and after a trifling engagement, for they were undisciplined and without organisation, they were all put to rout, some being killed or taken prisoners, and a large proportion deprived of their arms. This disturbance, however, brought Hasdrubal, who was marching westwards, back to the defence of his allies on the south side of the Ebro. The Carthaginians were in camp amongst the Ilergavonians; the Roman camp was at Nova, when unexpected intelligence turned the tide of war in another direction. The Celtiberi, who had sent their chief men as envoys to Scipio and had given hostages, were induced by his representations to take up arms and invade the province of New Carthage with a powerful army. They took three fortified towns by storm, and fought two most successful actions with Hasdrubal himself, killing 15,000 of the enemy and taking 4000 prisoners with numerous standards.

XXII. *Publius Scipio despatched with Reinforcements to Spain.*—This was the position of affairs when P. Scipio, whose command had been extended after he ceased to be consul, came to the province which had been assigned to him by the senate. He brought a reinforcement of thirty ships of war and 8000 troops, also a large convoy of supplies. This fleet, with its enormous column of transports, excited the liveliest delight among the townsmen and their allies when it was seen in the distance and finally reached the port of Tarracona. There the soldiers were landed and Scipio marched up country to meet his brother; thenceforward they carried on the campaign with their united forces and with one heart and purpose.

As the Carthaginians were preoccupied with the Celtiberian war, the Scipios had no hesitation in crossing the Ebro and, as no enemy appeared, marching straight to Saguntum, where they had been informed that the hostages who had been surrendered to Hannibal from all parts of Spain were detained in the citadel under a somewhat weak guard. The fact that they had given these pledges was the only thing that prevented all the tribes of Spain from openly manifesting their leanings towards alliance with Rome; they dreaded lest the price of their defection from Carthage should be the blood of their own children. From this bond Spain was released by the clever but treacherous scheme of one individual.

Abelux was a Spaniard of high birth living at Saguntum, who had at one time been loyal to Carthage, but afterwards, with the usual fickleness of barbarians, as the fortunes of Carthage changed so he changed his allegiance. He considered that any one going over to the enemy without having something valuable to betray was simply a worthless and disreputable individual, and so he made it his one aim to be of the greatest service he could to his new allies. After making a survey of everything which Fortune could possibly put within his reach, he made up his mind to effect the delivery of the hostages; that one thing he thought would do more than anything else to win the friendship of the Spanish chieftains for the Romans. He was quite aware, however, that the guardians of the hostages would take no step without the orders of Bostar, their commanding officer, and so he employed his arts against Bostar himself. Bostar had fixed his camp outside the city quite on the shore that he might bar the approach of the Romans on that side. After obtaining a secret interview with him he warned him, as though he were unaware of it, as to the actual state of affairs. "Up to this time," he said, "fear alone has kept the Spaniards loyal because the Romans were far away; now the Roman camp is on our side the Ebro, a secure stronghold and refuge for all who want to change their allegiance. Those, therefore, who are no longer restrained by fear must be bound to us by kindness and feelings of gratitude." Bostar was greatly surprised, and asked him what boon could suddenly effect such great results. "Send the hostages," was the reply, "back to their homes. That will evoke gratitude from their parents, who are very influential people in their own country, and also from their fellow-countrymen generally. Every one likes to feel that he is trusted; the confidence you place in others generally strengthens their confidence in you. The service of restoring the hostages to their respective homes I claim for myself, that I may contribute to the success of my plan by my own personal efforts, and win for an act gracious in itself still more gratitude."

He succeeded in persuading Bostar, whose intelligence was not on a par with the acuteness which the other Carthaginians showed. After this interview he went secretly to the enemy's outposts, and meeting with some Spanish auxiliaries he was conducted by them into the presence of Scipio, to whom he explained what he proposed to do. Pledges of good faith were mutually exchanged and the place and time for handing over the hostages fixed, after which he returned to Saguntum. The following day he spent in receiving Bostar's instructions for the execution of the project. It was agreed between them that he should go at night in order, as he pretended, to escape the observation of the Roman outposts. He had already arranged with these as to the hour at which he would come, and after awakening those who were in guard of the boys he conducted the hostages, without appearing to be aware of the fact, into the trap which he had himself prepared. The outposts conducted them into the Roman camp; all the remaining details connected with their restoration to their homes were carried out as he had arranged with Bostar, precisely as if the business were being transacted in the name of Carthage. Yet though the service rendered was the same, the gratitude felt towards the Romans was considerably greater than would have been earned by the Carthaginians, who had shown themselves oppressive and tyrannical in the time of their prosperity, and now that they experienced a change of fortune their act might have appeared to be dictated by fear. The Romans, on the other hand, hitherto perfect strangers, had no sooner come into the country than they began with an act of clemency and generosity, and Abelux was considered to have shown his prudence in changing his allies to such good purpose. All now began with surprising unanimity to meditate revolt, and an armed movement would have begun at once had not the winter set in, which compelled the Romans as well as the Carthaginians to retire to their quarters.

XXIII. *Fabius' growing Unpopularity.*—These were the main incidents of the campaign in Spain during the second summer of the Punic war.

In Italy the masterly inaction of Fabius had for a short time stemmed the tide of Roman disasters. It was a cause of grave anxiety to Hannibal, for he fully realised that the Romans had chosen for their commander-in-chief a man who conducted war on rational principles and not by trusting to chance. But amongst his own people, soldiers and civilians alike, his tactics were viewed with contempt, especially after a battle had been brought about owing to the rashness of the Master of the Horse in the Dictator's absence which would be more correctly described as fortunate rather than as successful. Two incidents occurred which made the Dictator still more unpopular. One was due to the crafty policy of Hannibal. Some deserters had pointed out to him the Dictator's landed property, and after all the surrounding buildings had been levelled to the ground he gave orders for that property to be spared from fire and sword and all hostile treatment whatever in order that it might be thought that there was some secret bargain between them. The second cause of the Dictator's growing unpopularity was something which he himself did, and which at first bore an equivocal aspect because he had acted without the authority of the senate, but ultimately it was universally recognised as redounding very greatly to his credit. In carrying out the exchange of prisoners it had been agreed between the Roman and the Carthaginian commanders, following the precedent of the first Punic war, that whichever side received back more prisoners than they gave should strike a balance by paying two and a half pounds of silver for each soldier they received in excess of those they gave. The Roman prisoners restored were two hundred and forty-seven more than the Carthaginians. The question of this payment had been frequently discussed in the senate, but as Fabius had not consulted that body before making the agreement there was some delay in voting the money. The matter was settled by Fabius sending his son Quintus to Rome to sell the land which had been untouched by the enemy; he thus discharged the obligation of the State at his own private expense.

When Hannibal burnt Gereonium after its capture, he left a few houses standing to serve as granaries, and now he was occupying a standing camp before its walls. He was in the habit of sending out two divisions to collect corn, he remained in camp with the third ready to move in any direction where he saw that his foragers were being attacked.

XXIV. The Roman army was at the time in the neighbourhood of Larinum, with Minucius in command, owing, as stated above, to the Dictator having left for the City. The camp had been situated in a lofty and secure position; it was now transferred to the plain, and more energetic measures more in harmony with the general's temperament were being discussed; suggestions were made for an attack either on the dispersed parties of foragers or on the camp now that it was left with a weak guard. Hannibal soon found out that the tactics of his enemies had changed with the change of generals, and that they would act with more spirit than prudence, and, incredible as it may sound, though his enemy was in closer proximity to him, he sent out a whole division of his army to collect corn, keeping the other two in camp. The next thing he did was to move his camp still nearer the enemy, about two miles from Gereonium on rising ground within view of the Romans, so that they might know that he was determined to protect his foragers in case of attack. From this position he was able to see another elevated position still closer to the Roman camp, in fact looking down on it. There was no doubt that if he were to attempt to seize it in broad daylight the enemy, having less distance to go, would be there before him, so he sent a force of Numidians who occupied it during the night. The next day the Romans, seeing how small a number were holding the position, made short work of them and drove them off and then transferred their own camp there. By this time there was but a very small distance between rampart and rampart, and even that was almost entirely filled with Roman troops, who were demonstrating in force to conceal the movements of cavalry and light infantry who had been sent through the camp gate farthest from the enemy [6] to attack his foragers, upon whom they inflicted severe losses. Hannibal did not venture upon a regular battle because his

camp was so weakly guarded that it could not have repelled an
assault. Borrowing the tactics of Fabius he began to carry on
the campaign by remaining in almost complete inaction, and
withdrew his camp to its former position before the walls of
Gereonium. According to some authors a pitched battle was
fought with both armies in regular formation; the Carthaginians
were routed at the first onset and driven to their camp; from
there a sudden sortie was made and it was the Romans' turn
to flee, and the battle was once more restored by the sudden
appearance of Numerius Decimus, the Samnite general. Decimus was, as far as wealth and lineage go, the foremost man
not only in Bovianum, his native place, but in the whole of
Samnium. In obedience to the Dictator's orders he was bringing into camp a force of 8000 foot and 500 horse, and when he
appeared in Hannibal's rear both sides thought that it was a
reinforcement coming from Rome under Q. Fabius. Hannibal,
it is further stated, ordered his men to retire, the Romans
followed them up, and with the aid of the Samnites captured
two of their fortified positions the same day; 6000 of the enemy
were killed and about 5000 of the Romans, yet though the
losses were so evenly balanced an idle and foolish report of a
splendid victory reached Rome together with a despatch from
the Master of the Horse which was still more foolish.

XXV. *Proposal to divide the Dictator's Authority.*—This state
of affairs led to constant discussions in the senate and the
Assembly. Amidst the universal rejoicing the Dictator stood
alone; he declared that he did not place the slightest credence
in either the report or the despatch, and even if everything was
as it was represented, he dreaded success more than failure.
On this M. Metilius, tribune of the plebs, said it was really
becoming intolerable that the Dictator, not content with standing in the way of any success being achieved when he was on the
spot, should now be equally opposed to it after it had been
achieved in his absence. " He was deliberately wasting time
in his conduct of the war in order to remain longer in office as
sole magistrate and retain his supreme command. One consul
has fallen in battle, the other has been banished far from Italy
under pretext of chasing the Carthaginian fleet; two praetors
have their hands full with Sicily and Sardinia, neither of which
provinces needs a praetor at all at this time; M. Minucius, Master
of the Horse, has been almost kept under guard to prevent him
from seeing the enemy or doing anything which savoured of
war. And so, good heavens! not only Samnium, where we re-

treated before the Carthaginians as though it were some territory beyond the Ebro, but even the country of Falernum, have been utterly laid waste, while the Dictator was sitting idly at Casilinum, using the legions of Rome to protect his own property. The Master of the Horse and the army, who were burning to fight, were kept back and almost imprisoned within their lines; they were deprived of their arms as though they were prisoners of war. At length, no sooner had the Dictator departed than, like men delivered from a blockade, they left their entrenchments and routed the enemy and put him to flight. Under these circumstances I was prepared, if the Roman plebs still possessed the spirit they showed in old days, to take the bold step of bringing in a measure to relieve Q. Fabius of his command; as it is I shall propose a resolution couched in very moderate terms—' that the authority of the Master of the Horse be made equal to that of the Dictator.' But even if this resolution is carried Q. Fabius must not be allowed to rejoin the army before he has appointed a consul in place of C. Flaminius.''

As the line which the Dictator was taking was in the highest degree unpopular, he kept away from the Assembly. Even in the senate he produced an unfavourable impression when he spoke in laudatory terms of the enemy and put down the disasters of the past two years to rashness and lack of generalship on the part of the commanders. The Master of the Horse, he said, must be called to account for having fought against his orders. If, he went on to say, the supreme command and direction of the war remained in his hands, he would soon let men know that in the case of a good general Fortune plays a small part, intelligence and military skill are the main factors. To have preserved the army in circumstances of extreme danger without any humiliating defeat was in his opinion a more glorious thing than the slaughter of many thousands of the enemy.

But he failed to convince his audience, and after appointing M. Atilius Regulus as consul, he set off by night to rejoin his army. He was anxious to avoid a personal altercation on the question of his authority, and left Rome the day before the proposal was voted upon.

At daybreak a meeting of the plebs was held to consider the proposal. Though the general feeling was one of hostility to the Dictator and goodwill towards the Master of the Horse, few were found bold enough to give this feeling utterance and recommend a proposal which after all was acceptable to the plebs as a body, and so, notwithstanding the fact that the great

majority were in favour of it, it lacked the support of men of
weight and influence. One man was found who came forward
to advocate the proposal, C. Terentius Varro, who had been
praetor the year before, a man of humble and even mean origin.
The tradition is that his father was a butcher who hawked his
meat about and employed his son in the menial drudgery of his
trade.

XXVI. *Terentius Varro.*—The money made in this business
was left to his son, who hoped that his fortune might help him
to a more respectable position in society. He decided to become an advocate, and his appearances in the Forum, where
he defended men of the lowest class by noisy and scurrilous
attacks upon the property and character of respectable citizens,
brought him into notoriety and ultimately into office. After
discharging the various duties of the quaestorship, the two
ædileships, plebeian and curule, and lastly those of the praetor,
he now aspired to the consulship. With this view he cleverly
took advantage of the feeling against the Dictator to court the
gale of popular favour, and gained for himself the whole credit
of carrying the resolution.

Everybody, whether in Rome or in the army, whether friend
or foe, with the sole exception of the Dictator himself, looked
upon this proposal as intended to cast a slur on him. But he
met the injustice done to him by the people, embittered as they
were against him, with the same dignified composure with which
he had previously treated the charges which his opponents had
brought against him before the populace. While still on his
way he received a despatch containing the senatorial decree for
dividing his command, but as he knew perfectly well that an
equal share of military command by no means implied an equal
share of military skill, he returned to his army with a spirit
undismayed by either his fellow-citizens or the enemy.[7]

XXVII. *Minucius' Failure.* — Owing to his success and
popularity Minucius had been almost unbearable before, but
now that he had won as great a victory over Fabius as over
Hannibal, his boastful arrogance knew no bounds. "The
man," he exclaimed, "who was selected as the only general
who would be a match for Hannibal has now, by an order of
the people, been put on a level with his second in command;
the Dictator has to share his powers with the Master of the
Horse. There is no precedent for this in our annals, and it has
been done in that very State in which Masters of the Horse
have been wont to look with dread upon the rods and axes of

Dictators. So brilliant have been my good fortune and my merits. If the Dictator persists in that dilatoriness and inaction which have been condemned by the judgment of gods and men, I shall follow my good fortune wherever it may lead me."

Accordingly on his first meeting with Q. Fabius, he told him that the very first thing that had to be settled was the method in which they should exercise their divided authority. The best plan, he thought, would be for them each to take supreme command on alternate days, or, if he preferred it, at longer intervals. This would enable whichever general was in command to meet Hannibal with tactics and strength equal to his own should an opportunity arise of striking a blow. Q. Fabius met this proposal with a decided negative. Everything, he argued, which his colleague's rashness might prompt would be at the mercy of Fortune; though his command was shared with another, he was not wholly deprived of it; he would never therefore voluntarily give up what power he still possessed of conducting operations with common sense and prudence, and though he refused to agree to a division of days or periods of command, he was prepared to divide the army with him and use his best foresight and judgment to preserve what he could as he could not save all. So it was arranged that they should adopt the plan of the consuls and share the legions between them. The first and fourth went to Minucius, Fabius retained the second and third. The cavalry and the contingents supplied by the Latins and the allies were also divided equally between them. The Master of the Horse even insisted upon separate camps.

XXVIII. Nothing that was going on amongst his enemies escaped the observation of Hannibal, for ample information was supplied to him by deserters as well as by his scouts. He was doubly delighted, for he felt sure of entrapping by his own peculiar methods the wild rashness of Minucius, and he saw that Fabius' skilful tactics had lost half their strength.

Between Minucius' camp and Hannibal's there was some rising ground, and whichever side seized it would undoubtedly be able to render their adversaries' position less secure. Hannibal determined to secure it, and though it would have been worth while doing so without a fight, he preferred to bring on a battle with Minucius, who, he felt quite sure, would hurry up to stop him. The entire intervening country seemed, at a first glance, totally unsuited for surprise tactics, for there were no woods anywhere, no spots covered with brushwood and scrub, but in reality it naturally lent itself to such a purpose, and all the more so because in so bare a valley no stratagem of the kind could be suspected. In its windings there were caverns, some so large as to be capable of concealing two hundred men. Each of these hiding-places was filled with troops, and altogether 5000 horse and foot were placed in concealment. In case, however, the stratagem might be detected by some soldier's thoughtless movements, or the glint of arms in so open a valley, Hannibal sent a small detachment to seize the rising ground already described in order to divert the attention of the enemy. As soon as they were sighted, their small number excited ridicule, and every man begged that he might have the task of dislodging them. Conspicuous amongst his senseless and hot-headed soldiers the general sounded a general call to arms, and poured idle abuse and threats on the enemy.

He sent the light infantry first in open skirmishing order, these were followed by the cavalry in close formation, and at last, when he saw that reinforcements were being brought up to the enemy, he advanced with the legions in line. Hannibal on his side sent supports, both horse and foot, to his men wherever they were hard pressed, and the numbers engaged steadily grew until he had formed his entire army into order of battle and both sides were in full strength. The Roman light infantry moving up the hill from lower ground were the first to be repulsed and forced back to the cavalry who were coming up behind them. They sought refuge behind the front ranks of the legions, who alone amidst the general panic preserved their coolness and presence of mind. Had it been a straightforward fight, man to man, they would to all appearance have been quite a match for their foes, so much had their success, a few days previously, restored their courage. But the sudden appearance of the concealed troops and their combined attack on both flanks and on the rear of the Roman legions created such confusion and alarm that not a man had any spirit left to fight or any hope of escaping by flight.

XXIX. *Fabius comes to the Rescue.*—Fabius' attention was first drawn to the cries of alarm, then he observed in the distance the disordered and broken ranks. " Just so," he exclaimed, " Fortune has overtaken his rashness, but not more quickly than I feared. Fabius is his equal in command, but he has found out that Hannibal is his superior both in ability and in success. However, this is not the time for censure or rebuke, advance into the field! Let us wrest victory from the foe, and a confession of error from our fellow-citizens."

By this time the rout had spread over a large part of the field, some were killed, others looking round for the means of escape, when suddenly the army of Fabius appeared as though sent down from heaven to their rescue. Before they came within range of their missiles, before they could exchange blows, they checked their comrades in their wild flight and the enemy in their fierce attack. Those who had been scattered hither and thither after their ranks were broken, closed in from all sides and reformed their line; those who had kept together in their retreat wheeled round to face the enemy, and, forming square, at one moment slowly retired, and at another shoulder to shoulder stood their ground. The defeated troops and those who were fresh on the field had now practically become one line, and they were commencing an advance on the enemy when the Carthaginian sounded the retreat, showing clearly that whilst Minucius had been defeated by him he was himself vanquished by Fabius.

The greater part of the day had been spent in these varying fortunes of the field. On their return to camp Minucius called his men together and addressed them thus: " Soldiers, I have often heard it said that the best man is he who himself advises what is the right thing to do; next to him comes the man who follows good advice; but the man who neither himself knows what counsel to give nor obeys the wise counsels of another is of the very lowest order of intelligence. Since the first order of intelligence and capacity has been denied to us let us cling to the second and intermediate one, and whilst we are learning to command, let us make up our minds to obey him who is wise and far sighted. Let us join camp with Fabius. When we have carried the standards to his tent where I shall salute him as ' Father,' a title which the service he has done us and the greatness of his office alike deserve, you soldiers will salute as ' Patrons ' those whose arms and right hands protected you a little while ago. If this day has done nothing else for us, it has at all events conferred on us the glory of having grateful hearts."

XXX. *Fabius, a Popular Hero.*—The signal was given and the word passed to collect the baggage; they then proceeded in marching order to the Dictator's camp much to his surprise and to the surprise of all who were round him. When the standards had been stationed in front of his tribunal, the Master of the Horse stepped forward and addressed him as " Father," and the whole of his troops saluted those who were crowding round them as " Patrons." He then proceeded, " I have put you on a level, Dictator, with my parents as far as I can do so in words, but to them I only owe my life, to you I owe my preservation and the safety of all these men. The decree of the plebs, which I feel to be onerous rather than an honour, I am the first to repeal and annul, and with a prayer that it may turn out well for you, for me, and for these armies of yours, for preserved and preserver alike, I place myself again under your auspicious authority and restore to you these legions with their standards. I ask you, as an act of grace, to order me to retain my office and these, each man of them, his place in the ranks." Then each man grasped his neighbour's hand, and the soldiers were dismissed to quarters, where they were generously and hospitably entertained by acquaintances and strangers alike, and the day which had a short time ago been dark and gloomy and almost marked by disaster and ruin became a day of joy and gladness.

When the report of this action reached Rome and was confirmed by despatches from both commanders, and by letters from the rank and file of both armies, every man did his best to extol Maximus to the skies. His reputation was quite as great with Hannibal and the Carthaginians; now at last they felt that they were warring with Romans and on Italian soil. For the last two years they had felt such contempt for Roman generals and Roman troops that they could hardly believe that they were at war with that nation of whom they had heard such a terrible report from their fathers.

Hannibal on his return from the field is reported to have said, "The cloud which has so long settled on the mountain heights has at last burst upon us in rain and storm."

XXXI. While these events were occurring in Italy, the consul, Cn. Servilius Geminus, with a fleet of 120 vessels, visited Sardinia and Corsica and received hostages from both islands; from there he sailed to Africa. Before landing on the mainland he laid waste the island of Menix and allowed the inhabitants of Cercina to save their island from a similar visitation by paying an indemnity of ten talents of silver. After this he disembarked his forces on the African coast and sent them, both soldiers and seamen, to ravage the country. They dispersed far and wide just as though they were plundering uninhabited islands, and consequently their recklessness led them into an ambuscade. Straggling in small parties, they were surrounded by large numbers of the enemy who knew the country, whilst they were strangers to it, with the result that they were driven in wild flight and with heavy loss back to their ships. After losing as many as a thousand men—amongst them the quaestor Sempronius Blaesus—the fleet hastily put to sea from shores"lined with the enemy and held its course to Sicily. Here it was handed over to T. Otacilius, in order that his second in command, P. Sura, might take it back to Rome. Servilius himself proceeded overland through Sicily and crossed the Strait into Italy, in consequence of a despatch from Q. Fabius recalling him and his colleague, M. Atilius, to take over the armies, as his six months' tenure of office had almost expired.

All the annalists, with one or two exceptions, state that Fabius acted against Hannibal as Dictator; Caelius adds that he was the first Dictator who was appointed by the people. But Caelius and the rest have forgotten that the right of nominating a Dictator lay with the consul alone, and Servilius, who was the only consul at the time, was in Gaul. The citizens, appalled by three successive defeats, could not endure the thought of delay, and recourse was had to the appointment by the people of a man to act in place of a Dictator ("pro dictatore"). His subsequent achievements, his brilliant reputation as a commander, and the exaggerations which his descendants introduced into the inscription on his bust easily explain the belief which ultimately gained ground, that Fabius, who had only been pro-dictator, was actually Dictator.

XXXII. Fabius' army was transferred to Atilius, Servilius Geminus took over the one which Minucius had commanded. They lost no time in fortifying their winter quarters, and during the remainder of the autumn conducted their joint operations in the most perfect harmony on the line which Fabius had laid down. When Hannibal left his camp to collect supplies, they were conveniently posted at different spots to harass his main body and cut off stragglers; but they refused to risk a general engagement, though the enemy employed every artifice to bring one on. Hannibal was reduced to such extremities that he would have marched back into Gaul had not his departure looked like flight. No chance whatever would have been left to him of feeding his army in that part of Italy if the succeeding consuls had persevered in the same tactics.

Neapolis offers Pecuniary Assistance.—When the winter had brought the war to a standstill at Gereonium, envoys from Neapolis arrived in Rome. They brought with them into the Senate-house forty very heavy golden bowls, and addressed the assembled senators in the following terms : "We know that the Roman treasury is being drained by the war, and since this war is being carried on for the towns and fields of the allies quite as much as for the head and stronghold of Italy, the City of Rome and its empire, we Neapolitans have thought it but right to assist the Roman people with the gold which has been left by our ancestors for the enriching of our temples and for a reserve in time of need. If we thought that our personal services would have been of any use we would just as gladly have offered them. The senators and people of Rome will confer a great pleasure upon us if they look upon everything that belongs to the Neapolitans as their own, and deign to accept from us a gift, the value and importance of which lie rather in the cordial goodwill of those who gladly give it than in any intrinsic worth which it may itself possess." A vote of thanks was passed to the envoys for their munificence and their care for the interests of Rome, and one bowl, the smallest, was accepted.

XXXIII. About the same time a Carthaginian spy who for two years had escaped detection was caught in Rome, and after both his hands were cut off, he was sent away. Twenty-five slaves who had formed a conspiracy in the Campus Martius were crucified; the informer had his liberty given to him and 20,000 bronze *ases*. Ambassadors were sent to Philip, King of Macedon, to demand the surrender of Demetrius of Pharos, who had taken refuge with him after his defeat, and another embassy was despatched to the Ligurians to make a formal complaint as to the assistance they had given the Carthaginian in men and money, and at the same time to get a nearer view of what was going on amongst the Boii and the Insubres. Officials were also sent to Pineus, King of Illyria, to demand payment of the tribute which was now in arrears, or, if he wished for an extension of time, to accept personal securities for its payment. So, though they had an immense war on their shoulders, nothing escaped the attention of the Romans in any part of the world, however distant. A religious difficulty arose about an unfulfilled vow. On the occasion of the mutiny amongst the troops in Gaul two years before, the praetor, L. Manlius, had vowed a temple to Concord, but up to that time no contract had been made for its construction. Two commissioners were appointed for the purpose by M. Æmilius, the City praetor, namely, C. Pupius and Caeso Quinctius Flamininus, and they entered into a contract for the building of the temple within the precinct of the citadel.

The senate passed a resolution that Æmilius should also write to the consuls asking one of them, if they approved, to come to Rome to hold the consular elections, and he would give notice of the elections for whatever day they fixed upon. The consuls replied that they could not leave the army in the presence of the enemy without danger to the republic, it would be therefore better for the elections to be held by an interrex than that a consul should be recalled from the front. The senate thought it better for a Dictator to be nominated by the consul for the purpose of holding the elections. L. Veturius Philo was nominated; he appointed Manlius Pomponius Matho his Master of the Horse. Their election was found to be invalid, and they were ordered to resign office after holding it for four days; matters reverted to an interregnum.

XXXIV. *Stormy Election—C. Terentius Varro Consul* (B.C. 216.)—Servilius and Regulus had their commands extended for another year. The interreges appointed by the senate were C. Claudius Cento, son of Appius, and P. Cornelius Asina. The latter conducted the elections amidst a bitter struggle between the patricians and the plebs.

C. Terentius Varro, a member of their own order, had ingratiated himself with the plebs by his attacks upon the leading men in the State and by all the tricks known to the demagogue. His success in shaking the influence of Fabius and weakening the authority of the Dictator had invested him with a certain glory in the eyes of the mob, which was heightened by the other's unpopularity, and they did their utmost to raise him to the consulship. The patricians opposed him with their utmost strength, dreading lest it should become a common practice for men to attack them as a means of rising to an equality with them. Q. Baebius Herennius, a relation of Varro's, accused not only the senate, but even the augurs, because they had prevented the Dictator from carrying the elections through, and by thus embittering public opinion against them, he strengthened the feeling in favour of his own candidate. "It was by the nobility," he declared, "who had for many years been trying to get up a war, that Hannibal was brought into Italy, and when the war might have been brought to a close, it was they who were unscrupulously protracting it. The advantage which M. Minucius gained in the absence of Fabius made it abundantly clear that with four legions combined, a successful fight could be maintained, but afterwards two legions had been exposed to slaughter at the hands of the enemy, and then rescued at the very last moment in order that he might be called 'Father' and 'Patron' because he would not allow the Romans to conquer before they had been defeated. Then as to the consuls; though they had it in their power to finish the war they had adopted Fabius' policy and protracted it. This is the secret understanding that has been come to by all the nobles, and we shall never see the end of the war till we have elected as our consul a man who is really a plebeian, that is, one from the ranks. The plebeian nobility have all been initiated into the same mysteries;[8] when they are no longer looked down upon by the patricians, they at once begin to look down upon the plebs. Who does not see that their one aim and object was to bring about an interregnum in order that the elections might be controlled by the patricians? That was the object of the consuls in both staying with the army; then, afterwards, because they had to nominate a Dictator against their will to conduct the elections, they had carried their point by force, and the Dictator's appointment was declared invalid by the augurs. Well, they have got their interregnum; one consulship at all events belongs to the Roman plebs; the people will freely dispose of it and give it to the man who prefers an early victory to prolonged command."

XXXV. Harangues like these kindled intense excitement amongst the plebs. There were three patrician candidates in the field, P. Cornelius Merenda, L. Manlius Vulso, and M. Æmilius Lepidus; two plebeians who were now ennobled, C. Atilius Serranus and Q. Ælius Paetus, one of whom was a pontiff, the other an augur. But the only one elected was C. Terentius Varro, so that the elections for appointing his colleague were in his hands. The nobility saw that his rivals were not strong enough, and they compelled L. Æmilius Paulus to come forward. He had come off with a blasted reputation from the trial in which his colleague had been found guilty, and he narrowly escaped,[9] and for a long time stoutly resisted the proposal to become a candidate owing to his intense dislike of the plebs. On the next election day, after all Varro's opponents had retired, he was given to him not so much to be his colleague as to oppose him on equal terms. The elections of praetors followed; those elected were Manlius Pomponius Matho and P. Furius Philus. To Philus was assigned the jurisdiction over Roman citizens, to Pomponius the decision of suits between citizens and foreigners. Two additional praetors were appointed, M. Claudius Marcellus for Sicily, and L. Postumius Albinus to act in Gaul. These were all elected in their absence, and none of them, with the exception of Varro, were new to office. Several strong and capable men were passed over, for at such a time it seemed undesirable that a magistracy should be entrusted to new and untried men.

XXXVI. *Preparations for the Campaign.*—The armies were increased, but as to what additions were made to the infantry and cavalry, the authorities vary so much, both as to the numbers and nature of the forces, that I should hardly venture to assert anything as positively certain. Some say that 10,000 recruits were called out to make up the losses; others, that four new legions were enrolled so that they might carry on the war with eight legions. Some authorities record that both horse and foot in the legions were made stronger by the addition of 1000 infantry and 100 cavalry to each, so that they contained 5000 infantry and 300 cavalry, whilst the allies furnished double the number of cavalry and an equal number of infantry. Thus, according to these writers, there were 87,200 men in the Roman camp when the battle of Cannae was fought. One thing is quite certain; the struggle was resumed with greater vigour and energy than in former years, because the Dictator had given them reason to hope that the enemy might be conquered.

But before the newly raised legions left the City the decemvirs were ordered to consult the Sacred Books owing to the general alarm which had been created by fresh portents. It was reported that showers of stones had fallen simultaneously on the Aventine in Rome and at Aricia; that the statues of the gods amongst the Sabines had sweated blood, and cold water had flowed from the hot springs. This latter portent created more terror, because it had happened several times. In the colonnade near the Campus several men had been killed by lightning. The proper explation of these portents was ascertained from the Sacred Books.

Some envoys from Paestum brought golden bowls to Rome. Thanks were voted to them as in the case of the Neapolitans, but the gold was not accepted.

XXXVII. *Assistance from Hiero.*—About the same time a fleet which had been despatched by Hiero arrived at Ostia with a large quantity of supplies. When his officers were introduced into the senate they spoke in the following terms: " The news of the death of the consul C. Flaminius and the destruction of his army caused so much distress and grief to King Hiero that he could not have been more deeply moved by any disaster which could happen either to himself personally or to his kingdom. Although he well knows that the greatness of Rome is almost more to be admired in adversity than in prosperity, still, notwithstanding that, he has sent everything with which good and faithful allies can assist their friends in time of war, and he earnestly intreats the senate not to reject his offer. To begin with, we are bringing, as an omen of good fortune, a golden statue of Victory, weighing two hundred and twenty pounds. We ask you to accept it and keep it as your own for ever. We have also brought 300,000 pecks of wheat and 200,000 of barley that you may not want provisions, and we are prepared to transport as much more as you require to any place that you may decide upon. The king is quite aware that Rome does not employ any legionary soldiers or cavalry except Romans and those belonging to the Latin nation, but he has seen foreigners serving as light infantry in the Roman camp. He has, accordingly, sent 1000 archers and slingers, capable of acting against the Balearics and Moors and other tribes who fight with missile weapons." They supplemented these gifts by suggesting that the praetor to whom Sicily had been assigned should take the fleet over to Africa so that the country of the enemy, too, might be visited by war, and less facilities afforded him for sending reinforcements to Hannibal. The senate requested the officers to take back the following reply to the king: Hiero was a man of honour and an exemplary ally; he had been consistently loyal all through, and had on every occasion rendered most generous help to Rome, and for that Rome was duly grateful. The gold which had been offered by one or two cities had not been accepted, though the Roman people were very grateful for the offer. They would, however, accept the statue of Victory as an omen for the future, and would give and consecrate a place for her in the Capitol in the temple of Jupiter Optimus Maximus. Enshrined in that stronghold she will be gracious and propitious, constant and steadfast to Rome.

The archers and slingers and the corn were handed over to the consuls. The fleet which T. Otacilius had with him in Sicily was strengthened by the addition of twenty-five quinqueremes, and permission was given him to cross over to Africa if he thought it would be in the interest of the republic.

XXXVIII. *Troops enrolled—Preparations for Departure.*—After completing the enrolment the consuls waited a few days for the contingents furnished by the Latins and the allies to come in. Then a new departure was made; the soldiers were sworn in by the military tribunes. Up to that day there had only been the military oath binding the men to assemble at the bidding of the consuls and not to disband until they received orders to do so.

It had also been the custom among the soldiers, when the infantry were formed into companies of 100, and the cavalry into troops of 10, for all the men in each company or troop to take a voluntary oath to each other that they would not leave their comrades for fear or for flight, and that they would not quit the ranks save to fetch or pick up a weapon, to strike an enemy, or to save a comrade. This voluntary covenant was now changed into a formal oath taken before the tribunes.

Before they marched out of the City, Varro delivered several violent harangues, in which he declared that the war had been brought into Italy by the nobles, and would continue to feed on the vitals of the republic if there were more generals like Fabius; he, Varro, would finish off the war the very day he caught sight of the enemy. His colleague, Paulus, made only one speech, in which there was much more truth than the people cared to hear. He passed no strictures on Varro, but he did express surprise that any general, whilst still in the City before he had taken up his command, or become acquainted with either his own army or that of the enemy, or gained any information as to the lie of the country and the nature of the ground, should know in what way he should conduct the campaign and be able to foretell the day on which he would fight a decisive battle with the enemy. As for himself, Paulus said that he would not anticipate events by disclosing his measures, for, after all, circumstances determined measures for men much more than men made circumstances subservient to measures. He hoped and prayed that such measures as were taken with due caution and foresight might turn out successful; so far rashness, besides being foolish, had proved disastrous. He made it quite clear that he would prefer safe to hasty counsels, and in order to strengthen him in this resolve Fabius is said to have addressed him on his departure in the following terms:

XXXIX. *Fabius gives Advice.*—" L. Æmilius, if you were like your colleague or, if you had a colleague like yourself—and I would that it were so—my address would be simply a waste of words. For if you were both good consuls, you would, without any suggestions from me, do everything that the interests of the State or your own sense of honour demanded; if you were both alike bad, you would neither listen to anything I had to say, nor take any advice which I might offer. As it is, when I look at your colleague and consider what sort of a man you are, I shall address my remarks to you. I can see that your merits as a man and a citizen will effect nothing if one half of the commonwealth is crippled and evil counsels possess the same force and authority as good ones. You are mistaken, L. Paulus, if you imagine that you will have less difficulty with C. Terentius than with Hannibal; I rather think the former will prove a more dangerous enemy than the latter. With the one you will only have to contend in the field, the opposition of the other you will have to meet everywhere and always. Against Hannibal and his legions you will have your cavalry and infantry, when Varro is in command he will use your own men against you. I do not want to bring ill luck on you by mentioning the ill-starred Flaminius, but this I must say that it was only after he was consul and had entered upon his province and taken up his command that he began to play the madman, but this man was insane before he stood for the consulship and afterwards while canvassing for it, and now that he is consul, before he has seen the camp or the enemy he is madder than ever.[10] If he raises such storms amongst peaceful civilians as he did just now by bragging about battles and battlefields, what will he do, think you, when he is talking to armed men—and those young men— where words at once lead to action. And yet if he carries out his threat and brings on an action at once, either I am utterly ignorant of military science, of the nature of this war, of the enemy with whom we are dealing, or else some place or other will be rendered more notorious by our defeat than even Trasumennus. As we are alone, this is hardly a time for boasting, and I would rather be thought to have gone too far in despising glory than in seeking it, but as a matter of fact, the only rational method of carrying on war against Hannibal is the one which I have followed. This is not only taught us by experience— experience the teacher of fools—but by reasoning which has been and will continue to be unchanged as long as the conditions remain the same. We are carrying on war in Italy, in our own country on our own soil, everywhere round us are citizens and allies, they are helping us with men, horses, supplies, and they will continue to do so, for they have proved their loyalty thus far to us in our adversity; and time and circumstance are making us more efficient, more circumspect, more self-reliant. Hannibal, on the other hand, is in a foreign and hostile land, far from his home and country, confronted everywhere by opposition and danger; nowhere by land or sea can he find peace; no cities admit him within their gates, no fortified towns; nowhere does he see anything which he can call his own, he has to live on each day's pillage; he has hardly a third of the army with which he crossed the Ebro; he has lost more by famine than by the sword, and even the few he has cannot get enough to support life. Do you doubt then, that if we sit still we shall get the better of a man who is growing weaker day by day, who has neither supplies nor reinforcements nor money? How long has he been sitting before the walls of Gereonium, a poor fortress in Apulia, as though they were the walls of Carthage? But I will not sound my own praises even before you. See how the late consuls, Cn. Servilius and Atilius, fooled him. This, L. Paulus, is the only safe course to adopt, and it is one which your fellow citizens will do more to make difficult and dangerous for you than the enemy will. For your own soldiers will want the same thing as the enemy; Varro though he is a Roman consul will desire just what Hannibal the Carthaginian commander desires. You must hold your own single-handed against both generals. And you will hold your own if you stand your ground firmly against public gossip and private slander, if you remain unmoved by false misrepresentations and your colleague's idle boasting. It is said that truth is far too often eclipsed but never totally extinguished. The man who scorns false glory will possess the true. Let them call you a coward because you are cautious, a laggard because you are deliberate, unsoldierly because you are a skilful general. I would rather have you give a clever enemy cause for fear than earn the praise of foolish compatriots. Hannibal will only feel contempt for a man who runs all risks, he will be afraid of one who never takes a rash step. I do not advise you to do nothing, but I do advise you to be guided in what you do by common sense and reason and not by chance. Never lose control of your forces and yourself; be always prepared, always on the alert; never fail to seize an opportunity favourable to yourself, and never give a favourable opportunity to the enemy. The man who is not in a hurry will always see his way clearly; haste blunders on blindly."

XL. *The Consuls take the Field.*—The consul's reply was far from being a cheerful one, for he admitted that the advice given was true, but not easy to put into practice. If a Dictator had found his Master of the Horse unbearable, what power or authority would a consul have against a violent and headstrong colleague? "In my first consulship," he said, "I escaped, badly singed, from the fire of popular fury. I hope and pray that all may end successfully, but if any mischance befalls us I shall expose myself to the weapons of the enemy sooner than to the verdict of the enraged citizens."

With these words Paulus, it is said, set forward, escorted by the foremost men amongst the patricians; the plebeian consul was attended by his plebeian friends, more conspicuous for their numbers than for the quality of the men who composed the crowd. When they came into camp the recruits and the old soldiers were formed into one army, and two separate camps were formed, the new camp, which was the smaller one, being nearer to Hannibal, while in the old camp the larger part of the army and the best troops were stationed. M. Atilius, one of the consuls of the previous year, pleaded his age and was sent back to Rome; the other, Geminus Servilius, was placed in command of the smaller camp with one Roman legion and 2000 horse and foot of the allies.

Although Hannibal saw that the army opposed to him was half as large again as it had been he was hugely delighted at the advent of the consuls. For not only was there nothing left out of his daily plunder, but there was nothing left anywhere for him to seize, as all the corn, now that the country was unsafe, had been everywhere stored in the cities. Hardly ten days' rations of corn remained, as was afterwards discovered, and the Spaniards were prepared to desert, owing to the shortness of supplies, if only the Romans had waited till the time was ripe.

XLI. *A Brush with the Enemy—Hannibal's Stratagem foiled.*— An incident occurred which still further encouraged Varro's impetuous and headstrong temperament. Parties were sent to drive off the foragers; a confused fight ensued owing to the soldiers rushing forward without any preconcerted plan or orders from their commanders, and the contest went heavily against the Carthaginians. As many as 1700 of them were killed, the loss of the Romans and the allies did not amount to more than 100. The consuls commanded on alternate days, and that day happened to be Paulus' turn. He checked the victors who were pursuing the enemy in great disorder, for he feared an ambuscade. Varro was furious, and loudly exclaimed that the enemy had been allowed to slip out of their hands, and if the pursuit had not been stopped the war could have been brought to a close. Hannibal did not very much regret his losses, on the contrary he believed that they would serve as a bait to the impetuosity of the consul and his newly-raised troops, and that he would be more headstrong than ever. What was going on in the enemy's camp was quite as well known to him as what was going on in his own; he was fully aware that there were differences and quarrels between the commanders, and that two-thirds of the army consisted of recruits. The following night he selected what he considered a suitable position for an ambuscade, and marched his men out of camp with nothing but their arms, leaving all the property, both public and private, behind in the camp. He then concealed the force behind the hills which enclosed the valley, the infantry to the left and the cavalry to the right, and took the baggage train through the middle of the valley, in the hope of surprising the Romans whilst plundering the apparently deserted camp and hampered with their plunder. Numerous fires were left burning in the camp in order to create the impression that he wished to keep the consuls in their respective positions until he had traversed a considerable distance in his retreat. Fabius had been deceived by the same stratagem the previous year.

XLII. As it grew light the pickets were seen to have been withdrawn, then on approaching nearer the unusual silence created surprise. When it was definitely learnt that the camp was empty the men rushed in a body to the commanders' quarters with the news that the enemy had fled in such haste that they left the tents standing, and to secure greater secrecy for their flight had also left numerous fires burning. Then a loud shout arose demanding that the order should be given to advance, and that the men should be led in pursuit, and that the camp should be plundered forthwith. The one consul behaved as though he were one of the clamorous crowd; the other, Paulus, repeatedly asserted the need of caution and circumspection. At last, unable to deal with the mutinous crowd and its leader in any other way, he sent Marius Statilius with his troop of Lucanian horse to reconnoitre. When he had ridden up to the gates of the camp he ordered his men to halt outside the lines, he himself with two of his troopers entered the camp and after a careful and thorough examination he brought back word that there was certainly a trick somewhere, the fires were left on the side of the camp which fronted the Romans, the tents were standing open with all the valuables exposed to view, in some parts he had seen silver lying about on the paths as though it had been put there for plunder. So far from deterring the soldiers from satisfying their greed, as it was intended to do, this report only inflamed it, and a shout arose that if the signal was not given they would go on without their generals. There was no lack of a general, however, for Varro instantly gave the signal to advance. Paulus, who was hanging back, received a report from the keeper of the sacred chickens that they had not given a favourable omen, and he ordered the report to be at once carried to his colleague as he was just marching out of the camp gates. Varro was very much annoyed, but the recollection of the disaster which overtook Flaminius and the naval defeat which the consul Claudius sustained in the first Punic war made him afraid of acting in an irreligious spirit. It seemed as though the gods themselves on that day delayed, if they did actually do away, the fatal doom which was impending over the Romans. For it so happened that whilst the soldiers were ignoring the consul's order for the standards to be carried back into camp, two slaves, one belonging to a trooper from Formiae, the other to one from Sidicinum, who had been captured with the foraging parties when Servilius and Atilius were in command, had that day escaped to their former masters. They were taken before the consul and told him that the whole of Hannibal's army was lying behind the nearest hills. The opportune arrival of these men restored the authority of the consuls, though one of them in his desire to be popular had weakened his authority by his unscrupulous connivance at breaches of discipline.

XLIII. *Hannibal withdraws into Apulia.*—When Hannibal saw that the ill-considered movement which the Romans had commenced was not recklessly carried out to its final stage, and that his ruse had been detected, he returned to camp. Owing to the want of corn he was unable to remain there many days, and fresh plans were continually cropping up, not only amongst the soldiers, who were a medley of all nations, but even in the mind of the general himself. Murmurs gradually swelled into loud and angry protests as the men demanded their arrears of pay, and complained of the starvation which they were enduring, and in addition, a rumour was started that the mercenaries, chiefly those of Spanish nationality, had formed a plot to desert. Even Hannibal himself, it is said, sometimes thought of leaving his infantry behind and hurrying with his cavalry into Gaul. With these plans being discussed and this temper prevailing amongst the men, he decided to move into the warmer parts of Apulia, where the harvest was earlier and where, owing to the greater distance from the enemy, desertion would be rendered more difficult for the fickle-minded part of his force. As on the previous occasion, he ordered camp-fires to be lighted, and a few tents left where they could be easily seen, in order that the Romans, remembering a similar stratagem, might be afraid to move. However, Statilius was again sent to reconnoitre with his Lucanians, and he made a thorough examination of the country beyond the camp and over the mountains. He reported that he had caught a distant view of the enemy in line of march, and the question of pursuit was discussed. As usual, the views of the two consuls were opposed, but almost all present supported Varro, not a single voice was given in favour of Paulus, except that of Servilius, consul in the preceding year. The opinion of the majority of the council prevailed, and so, driven by destiny, they went forward to render Cannae famous in the annals of Roman defeats.

It was in the neighbourhood of this village that Hannibal had fixed his camp with his back to the Sirocco which blows from Mount Vultur and fills the arid plains with clouds of dust. This arrangement was a very convenient one for his camp, and it proved to be extremely advantageous afterwards, when he was forming his order of battle, for his own men, with the wind behind them, blowing only on their backs, would fight with an enemy who was blinded by volumes of dust.

XLIV. The consuls followed the Carthaginians, carefully examining the roads as they marched, and when they reached Cannae and had the enemy in view they formed two entrenched camps separated by the same interval as at Gereonium, and with the same distribution of troops in each camp. The river Aufidus, flowing past the two camps, furnished a supply of water which the soldiers got as they best could, and they generally had to fight for it. The men in the smaller camp, which was on the other side of the river, had less difficulty in obtaining it, as that bank was not held by the enemy. Hannibal now saw his hopes fulfilled, that the consuls would give him an opportunity of fighting on ground naturally adapted for the movements of cavalry, the arm in which he had so far been invincible, and accordingly he placed his army in order of battle, and tried to provoke his foe to action by repeated charges of his Numidians. The Roman camp was again disturbed by a mutinous soldiery and consuls at variance, Paulus bringing up against Varro the fatal rashness of Sempronius and Flaminius, Varro retorting by pointing to Fabius as the favourite model of cowardly and inert commanders, and calling gods and men to witness that it was through no fault of his that Hannibal had acquired, so to speak, a prescriptive right to Italy; [11] he had had his hands tied by his colleague; his soldiers, furious and eager for fight, had had their swords and arms taken away from them. Paulus, on the other hand, declared that if anything happened to the legions flung recklessly and betrayed into an ill-considered and imprudent action, he was free from all responsibility for it, though he would have to share in all the consequences. " See to it," he said to Varro, " that those who are so free and ready with their tongues are equally so with their hands in the day of battle."

XLV. *The Battle of Cannae.*—Whilst time was thus being wasted in disputes instead of deliberation, Hannibal withdrew the bulk of his army, who had been standing most of the day in order of battle, into camp. He sent his Numidians, however, across the river to attack the parties who were getting water for the smaller camp. They had hardly gained the opposite bank when with their shouting and uproar they sent the crowd flying in wild disorder, and galloping on as far as the outpost in front of the rampart, they nearly reached the gates of the camp. It was looked upon as such an insult for a Roman camp to be actually terrorised by irregular auxiliaries that one thing, and one thing alone, held back the Romans from instantly crossing the river and forming their battle line—the supreme command that day rested with Paulus.

The following day Varro, whose turn it now was, without any consultation with his colleague, exhibited the signal for battle and led his forces drawn up for action across the river. Paulus followed, for though he disapproved of the measure, he was bound to support it. After crossing, they strengthened their line with the force in the smaller camp and completed their formation. On the right, which was nearest to the river, the Roman cavalry were posted, then came the infantry; on the extreme left were the cavalry of the allies, their infantry were between them and the Roman legions. The javelin men with the rest of the light-armed auxiliaries formed the front line. The consuls took their stations on the wings, Terentius Varro on the left, Æmilius Paulus on the right.

XLVI. As soon as it grew light Hannibal sent forward the Balearics and the other light infantry. He then crossed the river in person and as each division was brought across he assigned it its place in the line. The Gaulish and Spanish horse he posted near the bank on the left wing in front of the Roman cavalry; the right wing was assigned to the Numidian troopers. The centre consisted of a strong force of infantry, the Gauls and Spaniards in the middle, the Africans at either end of them. You might fancy that the Africans were for the most part a body of Romans from the way they were armed, they were so completely equipped with the arms, some of which they had taken at the Trebia, but the most part at Trasumennus. The Gauls and Spaniards had shields almost of the same shape; their swords were totally different, those of the Gauls being very long and without a point, the Spaniard, accustomed to thrust more than to cut, had a short handy sword, pointed like a dagger. These nations, more than any other, inspired terror by the vastness of their stature and their frightful appearance: the Gauls were naked above the waist, the Spaniards had taken up their position wearing white tunics embroidered with purple, of dazzling brilliancy. The total number of infantry in the field was 40,000, and there were 10,000 cavalry. Hasdrubal was in command of the left wing, Maharbal of the right; Hannibal himself with his brother Mago commanded the centre. It was a great convenience to both armies that the sun shone obliquely on them, whether it was that they had purposely so placed themslves, or whether it happened by accident, since the Romans faced the north, the Carthaginans the South. The wind, called by the inhabitants the Vulturnus, was against the Romans, and blew great clouds of dust into their faces, making it impossible for them to see in front of them.

XLVII. When the battle shout was raised the auxiliaries ran forward, and the battle began with the light infantry. Then the Gauls and Spaniards on the left engaged the Roman cavalry on the right; the battle was not at all like a cavalry fight, for there was no room for manœuvring, the river on the one side and the infantry on the other hemming them in, compelled them to fight face to face. Each side tried to force their way straight forward, till at last the horses were standing in a closely pressed mass, and the riders seized their opponents and tried to drag them from their horses. It had become mainly a struggle of infantry, fierce but short, and the Roman cavalry was repulsed and fled. Just as this battle of the cavalry was finished, the infantry became engaged, and as long as the Gauls and Spaniards kept their ranks unbroken, both sides were equally matched in strength and courage. At length after long and repeated efforts the Romans closed up their ranks, echeloned their front, and by the sheer weight of their deep column bore down the division of the enemy which was stationed in front of Hannibal's line, and was too thin and weak to resist the pressure. Without a moment's pause they followed up their broken and hastily retreating foe till they took to headlong flight. Cutting their way through the mass of fugitives, who offered no resistance, they penetrated as far as the Africans who were stationed on both wings, somewhat further back than the Gauls and Spaniards who had formed the advanced centre. As the latter fell back the whole front became level, and as they continued to give ground it became concave and crescent-shaped, the Africans at either end forming the horns. As the Romans rushed on incautiously between them, they were enfiladed by the two wings, which extended and closed round them in the rear. On this, the Romans, who had fought one battle to no purpose, left the Gauls and Spaniards, whose rear they had been slaughtering, and commenced a fresh struggle with the Africans. The contest was a very one-sided one, for not only were they hemmed in on all sides, but wearied with the previous fighting they were meeting fresh and vigorous opponents.

XLVIII. By this time the Roman left wing, where the allied cavalry were fronting the Numidians, had become engaged, but the fighting was slack at first owing to a Carthaginian stratagem. About 500 Numidians, carrying, besides their usual arms and missiles, swords concealed under their coats of mail, rode out from their own line with their shields slung behind their backs as though they were deserters, and suddenly leaped from their horses and flung their shields and javelins at the feet of their enemy. They were received into their ranks, conducted to the rear, and ordered to remain quiet. While the battle was spreading to the various parts of the field they remained quiet, but when the eyes and minds of all were wholly taken up with the fighting they seized the large Roman shields which were lying everywhere amongst the heaps of slain and commenced a furious attack upon the rear of the Roman line. Slashing away at backs and hips, they made a great slaughter and a still greater panic and confusion. Amidst the rout and panic in one part of the field and the obstinate but hopeless struggle in the other, Hasdrubal, who was in command of that arm, withdrew some Numidians from the centre of the right wing, where the fighting was feebly kept up, and sent them in pursuit of the fugitives, and at the same time sent the Spanish and Gaulish horse to the aid of the Africans, who were by this time more wearied by slaughter than by fighting.

XLIX. Paulus was on the other side of the field. In spite of his having been seriously wounded at the commencement of the action by a bullet from a sling, he frequently encountered Hannibal with a compact body of troops, and in several places restored the battle. The Roman cavalry formed a bodyguard round him, but at last, as he became too weak to manage his horse, they all dismounted. It is stated that when some one reported to Hannibal that the consul had ordered his men to fight on foot, he remarked, " I would rather he handed them over to me bound hand and foot."[12] Now that the victory of the enemy was no longer doubtful this struggle of the dismounted cavalry was such as might be expected when men preferred to die where they stood rather than flee, and the victors, furious at them for delaying the victory, butchered without mercy those whom they could not dislodge. They did, however, repulse a few survivors exhausted with their exertions and their wounds. All were at last scattered, and those who could regained their horses for flight. Cn. Lentulus, a military tribune, saw, as he rode by, the consul covered with blood sitting on a boulder. " Lucius Æmilius," he said, " the one man whom the gods must hold guiltless of this day's disaster, take this horse while you have still some strength left, and I can lift you into the saddle and keep by your side to protect you. Do not make this day of battle still more fatal by a consul's death, there are enough tears and mourning without that." The consul replied: " Long may you live to do brave deeds, Cornelius, but do not waste in useless pity the few moments left in which to escape from the hands of the enemy. Go, announce publicly to the senate that they must fortify Rome and make its defence strong before the victorious enemy approaches, and tell Q. Fabius privately that I have ever remembered his precepts in life and in death. Suffer me to breathe my last among my slaughtered soldiers, let me not have to defend myself again when I am no longer consul, or appear as the accuser of my colleague and protect my own innocence by throwing the guilt on another." During this conversation a crowd of fugitives came suddenly upon them, followed by the enemy, who, not knowing who the consul was, overwhelmed him with a shower of missiles. Lentulus escaped on horseback in the rush.

Then there was flight in all directions ; 7000 men escaped to the smaller camp, 10,000 to the larger, and about 2000 to the village of Cannae. These latter were at once surrounded by Carthalo and his cavalry, as the village was quite unfortified. The other consul, who either by accident or design had not joined any of these bodies of fugitives, escaped with about fifty cavalry to Venusia; 45,500 infantry, 2700 cavalry—almost an equal proportion of Romans and allies—are said to have been killed. Amongst the number were both the quaestors attached to the consuls, L. Atilius and L. Furius Bibulcus, twenty-nine military tribunes, several ex-consuls, ex-praetors, and ex-ædiles (amongst them are included Cn. Servilius Geminus and M. Minucius, who was Master of the Horse the previous year and, some years before that, consul), and in addition to these, eighty men who had either been senators or filled offices qualifying them for election to the senate and who had volunteered for service with the legions. The prisoners taken in the battle are stated to have amounted to 3000 infantry and 1500 cavalry.[13]

L. Such was the battle of Cannae, a battle as famous as the disastrous one at the Allia; not so serious in its results, owing to the inaction of the enemy, but more serious and more horrible in view of the slaughter of the army. For the flight at the Allia saved the army though it lost the City, whereas at Cannae hardly fifty men shared the consul's flight, nearly the whole army met their death in company with the other consul. As those who had taken refuge in the two camps were only a defenceless crowd without any leaders, the men in the larger camp sent a message to the others asking them to cross over to them at night when the enemy, tired after the battle and the feasting in honour of their victory, would be buried in sleep. Then they would go in one body to Canusium. Some rejected the proposal with scorn. "Why," they asked, "cannot those who sent the message come themselves, since they are quite as able to join us as we to join them? Because, of course, all the country between us is scoured by the enemy and they prefer to expose other people to that deadly peril rather than themselves." Others did not disapprove of the proposal, but they lacked courage to carry it out.

P. Sempronius Tuditanus protested against this cowardice. "Would you," he asked, "rather be taken prisoners by a most avaricious and ruthless foe and a price put upon your heads and your value assessed after you have been asked whether you are a Roman citizen or a Latin ally, in order that another may win honour from your misery and disgrace? Certainly not, if you are really the fellow-countrymen of L. Æmilius, who chose a noble death rather than a life of degradation, and of all the brave men who are lying in heaps around him. But, before daylight overtakes us and the enemy gathers in larger force to bar our path, let us cut our way through the men who in disorder and confusion are clamouring at our gates. Good swords and brave hearts make a way through enemies, however densely they are massed. If you march shoulder to shoulder you will scatter this loose and disorganised force as easily as if nothing opposed you. Come then with me, all you who want to preserve yourselves and the State." With these words he drew his sword, and with his men in close formation marched through the very midst of the enemy. When the Numidians hurled their javelins on the right, the unprotected side, they transferred their shields to their right arms, and so got clear away to the larger camp. As many as 600 escaped on this occasion, and after another large body had joined them they at once left the camp and came through safely to Canusium. This action on the part of defeated men was due to the impulse of natural courage or of accident rather than to any concerted plan of their own or any one's generalship.

LI. *Events subsequent to the Battle.*—Hannibal's officers all surrounded him and congratulated him on his victory, and urged that after such a magnificent success he should allow himself and his exhausted men to rest for the remainder of the day and the following night. Maharbal, however, the commandant of the cavalry, thought that they ought not to lose a moment. "That you may know," he said to Hannibal, "what has been gained by this battle I prophesy that in five days you will be feasting as victor in the Capitol. Follow me; I will go in advance with the cavalry; they will know that you are come before they know that you are coming." To Hannibal the victory seemed too great and too joyous for him to realise all at once. He told Maharbal that he commended his zeal, but he needed time to think out his plans. Maharbal replied: "The gods have not given all their gifts to one man. You know how to win victory, Hannibal, you do not how to use it." That day's delay is believed to have saved the City and the empire.

The next day, as soon as it grew light, they set about gathering the spoils on the field and viewing the carnage, which was a ghastly sight even for an enemy. There all those thousands of Romans were lying, infantry and cavalry indiscriminately as chance had brought them together in the battle or the flight. Some covered with blood raised themselves from amongst the dead around them, tortured by their wounds which were nipped by the cold of the morning, and were promptly put an end to by the enemy. Some they found lying with their thighs and knees gashed but still alive; these bared their throats and necks and bade them drain what blood they still had left. Some were discovered with their heads buried in the earth, they had evidently suffocated themselves by making holes in the ground and heaping the soil over their faces. What attracted the attention of all was a Numidian who was dragged alive from under a dead Roman lying across him; his ears and nose were torn, for the Roman with hands too powerless to grasp his weapon had, in his mad rage, torn his enemy with his teeth, and while doing so expired.

LII. After most of the day had been spent in collecting the spoils, Hannibal led his men to the attack on the smaller camp and commenced operations by throwing up a breastwork to cut off their water supply from the river. As, however, all the defenders were exhausted by toil and want of sleep, as well as by wounds, the surrender was effected sooner than he had anticipated. They agreed to give up their arms and horses, and to pay for each Roman three hundred " chariot pieces," [14] for each ally two hundred, and for each officer's servant one hundred, on condition that after the money was paid they should be allowed to depart with one garment apiece. Then they admitted the enemy into the camp and were all placed under guard, the Romans and the allies separately.

Whilst time was being spent there, all those in the larger camp, who had sufficient strength and courage, to the number of 4000 infantry and 200 cavalry, made their escape to Canusium, some in a body, others straggling through the fields, which was quite as safe a thing to do. Those who were wounded and those who had been afraid to venture surrendered the camp on the same terms as had been agreed upon in the other camp. An immense amount of booty was secured, and the whole of it was made over to the troops with the exception of the horses and prisoners and whatever silver there might be. Most of this was on the trappings of the horses, for they used very little silver plate at table, at all events when on a campaign.

Hannibal then ordered the bodies of his own soldiers to be collected for burial; it is said that there were as many as 8000 of his best troops. Some authors state that he also had a search made for the body of the Roman consul, which he buried.

Those who had escaped to Canusium were simply allowed shelter within its walls and houses, but a high-born and wealthy Apulian lady, named Busa, assisted them with corn and clothes and even provisions for their journey. For this munificence the senate, at the close of the war, voted her public honours

LIII. *The Refugees at Canusium and Venusia.*—Although there were four military tribunes on the spot—Fabius Maximus of the first legion, whose father had been lately Dictator, L.

Publicius Bibulus and Publius Cornelius Scipio of the second legion, and Appius Claudius Pulcher of the third legion, who had just been ædile—the supreme command was by universal consent vested in P. Scipio, who was quite a youth, and Appius Claudius. They were holding a small council to discuss the state of affairs when P. Furius Philus, the son of an ex-consul, informed them that it was useless for them to cherish ruined hopes; the republic was despaired of and given over for lost; some young nobles with L. Caecilius Metellus at their head were turning their eyes seaward with the intention of abandoning Italy to its fate and transferring their services to some king or other. This evil news, terrible as it was and coming fresh on the top of all their other disasters, paralysed those who were present with wonder and amazement. They thought that a council ought to be summoned to deal with it, but young Scipio, the general destined to end this war, said that it was no business for a council. In such an emergency as that they must dare and act, not deliberate. "Let those," he cried, "who want to save the republic take their arms at once and follow me. No camp is more truly a hostile camp than one in which such treason is meditated." He started off with a few followers to the house where Metellus was lodging, and finding the young men about whom the report had been made gathered there in council, he held his naked sword over the heads of the conspirators and uttered these words: "I solemnly swear that I will not abandon the Republic of Rome, nor will I suffer any other Roman citizen to do so; if I knowingly break my oath, then do thou, O Jupiter Optimus Maximus, visit me, my home, my family, and my estate with utter destruction. I require you, L. Caecilius, and all who are here present, to take this oath. Whoever will not swear let him know that this sword is drawn against him." They were in as great a state of fear as though they saw the victorious Hannibal amongst them, and all took the oath and surrendered themselves into Scipio's custody.

LIV. Whilst these things were happening at Canusium, as many as 4500 infantry and cavalry, who had been dispersed in flight over the country, succeeded in reaching the consul at Venusia. The inhabitants received them with every mark of kindness and distributed them all amongst their households to be taken care of. They gave each of the troopers a toga and a tunic and twenty-five "chariot pieces," and to each legionary ten pieces, and whatever arms they required. All hospitality was shown them both by the government and by private citizens, for the people of Venusia were determined not to be outdone in kindness by a lady of Canusium. But the large number of men, which now amounted to something like 10,000, made the burden imposed upon Busa much heavier. For Appius and Scipio, on hearing that the consul was safe, at once sent to him to inquire what amount of foot and horse he had with him, and also whether he wanted the army to be taken to Venusia or to remain at Canusium. Varro transferred his forces to Canusium, and now there was something like a consular army; it seemed as though they would defend themselves successfully behind their walls if not in the open field.

The State of Things in Rome.—The reports which reached Rome left no room for hope that even these remnants of citizens and allies were still surviving; it was asserted that the army with its two consuls had been annihilated and the whole of the forces wiped out. Never before, while the City itself was still safe, had there been such excitement and panic within its walls. I shall not attempt to describe it, nor will I weaken the reality by going into details. After the loss of the consul and the army at Trasumennus the previous year, it was not wound upon wound but multiplied disaster that was now announced. For according to the reports two consular armies and two consuls were lost; there was no longer any Roman camp, any general, any single soldier in existence; Apulia, Samnium, almost the whole of Italy lay at Hannibal's feet. Certainly there is no other nation that would not have succumbed beneath such a weight of calamity. One might, of course, compare the naval defeat of the Carthaginians at the Ægates, which broke their power to such an extent that they gave up Sicily and Sardinia and submitted to the payment of tribute and a war indemnity; or, again, the battle which they lost in Africa, in which Hannibal himself was crushed. But there is no point of comparison between these and Cannae, unless it be that they were borne with less fortitude.

LV. P. Furius Philus and M. Pomponius, the praetors, called a meeting of the senate to take measures for the defence of the City, for no doubt was felt that after wiping out the armies the enemy would set about his one remaining task and advance to attack Rome. In the presence of evils the extent of which, great as they were, was still unknown, they were unable even to form any definite plans, and the cries of wailing women deafened their ears, for as the facts were not yet ascertained the living and the dead were being indiscriminately bewailed in almost every house. Under these circumstances Q. Fabius Maximus gave it as his opinion that swift horsemen should be sent along the Appian and Latin roads to make inquiries of those they met, for there would be sure to be fugitives scattered about the country, and bring back tidings as to what had befallen the consuls and the armies, and if the gods out of compassion for the empire had left any remnant of the Roman nation, to find out where those forces were. And also they might ascertain whither Hannibal had repaired after the battle, what plans he was forming, what he was doing or likely to do. They must get some young and active men to find out these things, and as there were hardly any magistrates in the City, the senators must themselves take steps to calm the agitation and alarm which prevailed. They must keep the matrons out of the public streets and compel them to remain indoors; they must suppress the loud laments for the dead and impose silence on the City; they must see that all who brought tidings were taken to the praetors, and that the citizens should, each in his own house, wait for any news which affected them personally. Moreover, they must station guards at the gates to prevent any one from leaving the City, and they must make it clear to every man that the only safety he can hope for lies in the City and its walls. When the tumult has once been hushed, then the senate must be again convened and measures discussed for the defence of the City.

LVI. This proposal was unanimously carried without any discussion. After the crowd was cleared out of the Forum by the magistrates and the senators had gone in various directions to allay the agitation, a despatch at last arrived from C. Terentius Varro. He wrote that L. Æmilius was killed and his army cut to pieces; he himself was at Canusium collecting the wreckage that remained from this awful disaster; there were as many as 10,000 soldiers, irregular, unorganised; the Carthaginian was still at Cannae, bargaining about the prisoners' ransom and the rest of the plunder in a spirit very unlike that of a great and victorious general. The next thing was the publication of the names of those killed, and the City was thrown into such universal mourning that the annual celebration of the festival of Ceres was suspended, because it is forbidden to those in mourning to take part in it, and there was not a single matron who was not a mourner during those days. In order that the same cause might not prevent other sacred observances from being duly honoured, the period of mourning was limited by a senatorial decree to thirty days.

When the agitation was quieted and the senate resumed its session, a fresh despatch was received, this time from Sicily. T. Otacilius, the propraetor, announced that Hiero's kingdom was being devastated by a Carthaginian fleet, and when he was preparing to render him the assistance he asked for, he received news that another fully equipped fleet was riding at anchor off the Ægates, and when they heard that he was occupied with the defence of the Syracusan shore they would at once attack Lilybaeum and the rest of the Roman province. If, therefore, the senate wished to retain the king as their ally and keep their hold on Sicily, they must fit out a fleet.

LVII. When the despatches from the consul and the praetor had been read it was decided that M. Claudius, who was commanding the fleet stationed at Ostia, should be sent to the army at Canusium and instructions forwarded to the consul requesting him to hand over his command to the praetor and come to Rome as soon as he possibly could consistently with his duty to the republic.

For, over and above these serious disasters, considerable alarm was created by portents which occurred. Two Vestal virgins, Opimia and Floronia, were found guilty of unchastity. One was buried alive, as is the custom, at the Colline Gate, the other committed suicide. L. Cantilius, one of the pontifical secretaries, now called " minor pontiffs," who had been guilty with Floronia, was scourged in the Comitium by the Pontifex Maximus so severely that he died under it. This act of wickedness, coming as it did amongst so many calamities, was, as often happens, regarded as a portent, and the decemvirs were ordered to consult the Sacred Books. Q. Fabius Pictor was sent to consult the oracle of Delphi as to what forms of prayer and supplication they were to use to propitiate the gods, and what was to be the end of all these terrible disasters. Meanwhile, in obedience to the Books of Destiny, some strange and unusual sacrifices were made, human sacrifices amongst them. A Gaulish man and a Gaulish woman and a Greek man and a Greek woman were buried alive under the Forum Boarium. They were lowered into a stone vault, which had on a previous occasion also been polluted by human victims, a practice most repulsive to Roman feelings.[15]

When the gods were believed to be duly propitiated, M. Claudius Marcellus sent from Ostia 1500 men who had been enrolled for service with the fleet to garrison Rome; the naval legion (the third) he sent on in advance with the military tribunes to Teanum Sidicinum, and then, handing the fleet over to his colleague, P. Furius Philus, hastened on by forced marches a few days later to Canusium.

On the authority of the senate M. Junius was nominated Dictator and Ti. Sempronius Master of the Horse. A levy was ordered, and all from seventeen years upwards were enrolled, some even younger; out of these recruits four legions were formed and 1000 cavalry. They also sent to the Latin confederacy and the other allied states to enlist soldiers according to the terms of their treaties. Armour, weapons, and other things of the kind were ordered to be in readiness, and the ancient spoils gathered from the enemy were taken down from the temples and colonnades. The dearth of freemen necessitated a new kind of enlistment; 8000 sturdy youths from amongst the slaves were armed at the public cost, after they had each been asked whether they were willing to serve or no. These soldiers were preferred, as there would be an opportunity of ransoming them when taken prisoners at a lower price.

LVIII. *Hannibal's Offer to allow the Prisoners to be ransomed refused by the Senate.*—After his great success at Cannae, Hannibal made his arrangements more as though his victory were a complete and decisive one than as if the war were still going on. The prisoners were brought before him and separated into two groups; the allies were treated as they had been at the Trebia and at Trasumennus, after some kind words they were dismissed without ransom; the Romans, too, were treated as they had never been before, for when they appeared before him he addressed them in quite a friendly way. He had no deadly feud, he told them, with Rome, all he was fighting for was his country's honour as a sovereign power. His fathers had yielded to Roman courage, his one object now was that the Romans should yield to his good fortune and courage. He now gave the prisoners permission to ransom themselves; each horseman at 500 " chariot pieces " and each foot-soldier at 300, and the slaves at 100 per head. This was somewhat more than the cavalry had agreed to when they surrendered, but they were only too glad to accept any terms. It was settled that they should elect ten of their number to go to the senate at Rome, and the only guarantee required was that they should take an oath to return. They were accompanied by Carthalo, a Carthaginian noble, who was to sound the feelings of the senators, and if they were inclined towards peace he was to propose terms. When the delegates had left the camp, one of them, a man of an utterly un-Roman temper, returned to the camp, as if he had forgotten something, and in this way hoped to free himself from his oath. He rejoined his comrades before nightfall. When it was announced that the party were on their way to Rome a lictor was despatched to meet Carthalo and order him in the name of the Dictator to quit the territory of Rome before night.

LIX. The Dictator admitted the prisoners' delegates to an audience of the senate. Their leader, M. Junius, spoke as follows: " Senators: we are every one of us aware that no State has held its prisoners of war of less account than our own, but, unless we think our case a better one than we have any right to do, we would urge that none have ever fallen into the hands of the enemy who were more deserving of consideration than we are. For we did not give up our arms during the battle from sheer cowardice; standing on the heaps of the slain we kept up the struggle till close on night, and only then did we retire into camp; for the remainder of the day and all through the night we defended our entrenchments; the following day we were surrounded by the victorious army and cut off from the water, and there was no hope whatever now of our forcing our way through the dense masses of the enemy. We did not think it a crime for some of Rome's soldiers to survive the battle of Cannae, seeing that 50,000 men had been butchered there, and therefore in the very last resort we consented to have a price fixed for our ransom and surrendered to the enemy those arms which were no longer of the slightest use to us. Besides, we had heard that our ancestors had ransomed themselves from the Gauls with gold, and that your fathers, sternly as they set themselves against all conditions of peace, did nevertheless send delegates to Tarentum to arrange the ransom of the prisoners. But neither the battle at the Alia against the Gauls nor that at Heraclea against Pyrrhus was disgraced by the actual losses sustained so much as by the panic and flight which marked them. The plains of Cannae are covered by heaps of Roman dead, and we should not be here now if the enemy had not lacked arms and strength to slay us. There are some amongst us who were never in the battle at all, but were left to guard the camp, and when it was surrendered they fell into the hands of the enemy. I do not envy the fortune or the circumstances of any man, whether he be a fellow-citizen or a fellow-soldier, nor would I wish it to be said that I had glorified myself by depreciating others, but this I will say, not even those who fled from the battle, mostly without arms, and did not stay their flight till they had reached Venusia or Canusium, can claim precedence over us or boast that they are more of a defence to the State than we are. But you will find both in them and in us good and gallant soldiers, only we shall be still more eager to serve our country because it will be through your kindness that we shall have been ransomed and restored to our fatherland. You have enlisted men of all ages and of every condition; I hear that eight thousand slaves are armed. Our number is no less, and it will not cost more to ransom us than it did to purchase them, but if I were to compare ourselves as soldiers with them, I should be offering an insult to the name of Roman. I should think, senators, that in deciding upon a matter like this, you should also take into consideration, if you are disposed to be too severe, to what sort of an enemy you are going to abandon us. Is it to a Pyrrhus, who treated his prisoners as though they were his guests? Is it not rather to a barbarian, and what is worse, a Carthaginian, of whom it is difficult to judge whether he is more rapacious or more cruel? Could you see the chains, the squalor, the disgusting appearance of your fellow-citizens, the sight would, I am sure, move you no less than if, on the other hand, you beheld your legions lying scattered over the plains of Cannae. You can behold the anxiety and the tears of our kinsmen as they stand in the vestibule of your House and await your reply. If they are in such anxiety and suspense about us and about those who are not here, what, think you, must be the feelings of the men themselves whose life and liberty are at stake? Why, good heavens! even if Hannibal, contrary to his nature, chose to be kind to us, we should still think life not worth living after you had decided that we did not deserve to be ransomed. Years ago the prisoners who were released by Pyrrhus without ransom returned to Rome, but they returned in company with the foremost men of the State who had been sent to effect their ransom. Am I to return to my native country as a citizen not thought worth three hundred coins? Each of us has his own feelings, senators. I know that my life and person are at stake, but I dread more the peril to my good name, in case we depart condemned and repulsed by you; for men will never believe that you grudged the cost."

LX. No sooner had he finished than a tearful cry arose from the crowd in the comitium; they stretched their hands towards the Senate-house and implored the senators to give them back their children, their brothers, and their relations. Fear and affection had brought even women amongst the crowd of men who thronged the Forum. After the strangers had withdrawn the debate commenced in the senate. There was great difference of opinion; some said that they ought to be ransomed at the expense of the State, others were of opinion that no public expense ought to be incurred, but they ought not to be prevented from defraying the cost from private sources, and in cases where ready money was not available it should be advanced from the treasury on personal security and mortgages. When it came to the turn of T. Manlius Torquatus, a man of old-fashioned and, some thought, excessive strictness, to give his opinion, he is said to have spoken in these terms: " If the delegates had confined themselves to asking that those who are in the hands of the enemy might be ransomed, I should have stated my opinion in few words without casting reflections on any of them, for all that would have been necessary would be to remind you that you should maintain the custom and usage handed down from our forefathers by setting an example necessary for military discipline. But as it is, since they have almost treated their surrender to the enemy as a thing to be proud of, and think it right that they should receive more consideration than the prisoners taken in the field or those who reached Venusia and Canusium, or even the consul himself, I will not allow you to remain in ignorance of what actually happened. I only wish that the facts which I am about to allege could be brought before the army at Canusium, which is best able to testify to each man's courage or cowardice, or at least that we had before us P. Sempronius Tuditanus, for if these men had followed him they would at this moment be in the Roman camp, not prisoners in the hands of the foe.

" The enemy had nearly all returned to their camp, tired out with fighting, to make merry over their victory, and these men had the night clear for a sortie. Seven thousand men could easily have made a sortie, even through dense masses of the enemy, but they did not make any attempt to do so on their own initiative, nor would they follow any one else. Nearly the whole night through P. Sempronius Tuditanus was continually warning them and urging them to follow him, whilst only a few of the enemy were watching their camp, whilst all was quiet and silent, whilst the night could still conceal their movements; before it was light they could reach safety and be protected by the cities of our allies. If he had spoken as that military tribune P. Decius spoke in the days of our fathers, or as Calpurnius Flamma, in the first Punic war, when we were young men, spoke to his three hundred volunteers whom he was leading to the capture of a height situated in the very centre of the enemy's position: ' Let us,' he exclaimed, ' die, my men, and by our death rescue our blockaded legions from their peril '—if, I say, P. Sempronius had spoken thus, I should not regard you as men, much less as Romans, if none had come forward as the comrade of so brave a man. But the way he pointed out to you led to safety quite as much as to glory, he would have brought you back to your country, your parents, your wives, and your children. You have not courage enough to save yourselves; what would you do if you had to die for your country? All round you on that day were lying fifty thousand dead, Romans and allies. If so many examples of courage did not inspire you, nothing ever will. If such an awful disaster did not make you hold your lives cheap, none will ever do so. It is whilst you are free men, with all your rights as citizens, that you must show your love for your country, or rather, while it is your country and you are its citizens. Now you are showing that love too late, your rights forfeited, your citizenship renounced, you have become the slaves of the Carthaginians. Is money going to restore you to the position which you have lost through cowardice and crime? You would not listen to your own countryman Sempronius when he bade you seize your arms and follow him, you did listen shortly afterwards to Hannibal when he bade you give up your arms and betray your camp. But why do I only charge these men with cowardice when I can prove them guilty of actual crime? For not only did they refuse to follow him when he gave them good advice, but they tried to stop him and keep him back, until a body of truly brave men drew their swords and drove back the cowards. P. Sempronius had actually to force his way through his own countrymen before he could do so through the enemy! Would our country care to have such as these for her citizens when, had all those who fought at Cannae been like them, she would not have had amongst them a single citizen worth the name! Out of seven thousand men in arms there were six hundred who had the courage to force their way, and returned to their country free men with arms in their hands. The enemy did not stop these six hundred, how safe the way would have been, do you not think? for a force of almost two legions. You would have to-day, senators, at Canusium 20,000 brave loyal soldiers; but as for these men, how can they possibly be good and loyal citizens? And as to their being 'brave,' they do not even themselves assert that—unless, indeed, some one chooses to imagine that whilst they were trying to stop the others from making the sortie, they were really encouraging them, or that, fully aware that their own timidity and cowardice was the cause of their becoming slaves, they feel no grudge towards the others for having won both safety and glory through their courage. Though they might have got away in the dead of the night, they preferred to skulk in their tents and wait for the daylight and with it the enemy. But you will say, if they lacked courage to leave the camp they had courage enough to defend it bravely; blockaded for several days and nights, they protected the rampart with their arms, and themselves with the rampart; at last, after going to the utmost lengths of endurance and daring, when every support of life failed, and they were so weakened by starvation that they had not strength to bear the weight of their arms, they were in the end conquered by the necessities of nature more than by the force of arms. What are the facts? At daybreak the enemy approached the rampart; within two hours, without trying their fortune in any conflict, they gave up their arms and themselves. This, you see, was their two days' soldiership. When duty called them to keep their line and fight they fled to their camp, when they ought to have fought at the rampart they surrendered their camp; they are useless alike in the field and in the camp. Am I to ransom you? When you ought to have made your way out of the camp you hesitated and remained there, when it was obligatory for you to remain there and defend the camp with your arms you gave up camp, arms, and yourselves to the enemy. No, senators, I do not think that those men ought to be ransomed any more than I should think it right to surrender to Hannibal the men who forced their way out of the camp through the midst of the enemy and by that supreme act of courage restored themselves to their fatherland."

LXI. Although most of the senators had relations among the prisoners, there were two considerations which weighed with them at the close of Manlius' speech. One was the practice of the State which from early times had shown very little indulgence to prisoners of war. The other was the amount of money that would be required, for they were anxious that the treasury should not be exhausted, a large sum having been already paid out in purchasing and arming the slaves, and they did not wish to enrich Hannibal who, according to rumour, was in particular need of money. When the melancholy reply was given that the prisoners were not ransomed, the prevailing grief was intensified by the loss of so many citizens, and the delegates were accompanied to the gates by a weeping and protesting crowd. One of them went to his home because he considered himself released from his vow by his pretended return to the camp. When this became known it was reported to the senate, and they unanimously decided that he should be arrested and conveyed to Hannibal under a guard furnished by the State. There is another account extant as to the fate of the prisoners. According to this tradition ten came at first, and there was a debate in the senate as to whether they should be allowed within the City or not; they were admitted on the understanding that the senate would not grant them an audience. As they stayed longer than was generally expected, three other delegates arrived—L. Scribonius, C. Calpurnius, and L. Manlius —and a relative of Scribonius who was a tribune of the plebs made a motion in the senate to ransom the prisoners. The senate decided that they should not be ransomed, and the three who came last returned to Hannibal, but the ten remained in Rome. They alleged that they had absolved themselves from their oath because after starting on their journey they had returned to Hannibal under the pretext of reviewing the list of the prisoners' names. The question of surrendering them was hotly debated in the senate, and those in favour of this course were beaten by only a few votes. Under the next censors, however, they were so crushed beneath every mark of disgrace and infamy that some of them immediately committed suicide; the others not only avoided the Forum for all their after life, but almost shunned the light of day and the faces of men. It is easier to feel astonishment at such discrepancies amongst our authorities than to determine what is the truth.

How far that disaster surpassed previous ones is shown by one simple fact. Up to that day the loyalty of our allies had remained unshaken, now it began to waver, for no other reason, we may be certain, than that they despaired of the maintenance of our empire. The tribes who revolted to the Carthaginians were the Atellani, the Calatini, the Hirpini, a section of the Apulians, all the Samnite cantons with the exception of the Pentri, all the Bruttii and the Lucanians. In addition to these, the Uzentini and almost the whole of the coast of Magna Graecia, the people of Tarentum Crotona and Locri, as well as all Cisalpine Gaul.[16] Yet, in spite of all their disasters and the revolt of their allies, no one anywhere in Rome mentioned the word " Peace," either before the consul's return or after his arrival, when all the memories of their losses were renewed. Such a lofty spirit did the citizens exhibit in those days that though the consul was coming back from a terrible defeat for which they knew he was mainly responsible, he was met by a vast concourse drawn from every class of society, and thanks were formally voted to him because he " had not despaired of the republic." Had he been commander-in-chief of the Carthaginians there was no torture to which he would not have been subjected.

BOOK XXIII

HANNIBAL AT CAPUA

I. *Hannibal at Capua.*—Immediately after the battle of Cannae and the capture and plunder of the Roman camp, Hannibal moved out of Apulia into Samnium, in consequence of an invitation he had received from a man named Statius Trebius, who promised to hand over Compsa to him if he would visit the territory of the Hirpini. Trebius was a native of Compsa, a man of note amongst his people, but his influence was less than that of the faction of the Mopsii, a family which owed its predominance to the favour and support of Rome. After the report of the battle of Cannae had reached the town, and Trebius was telling everybody that Hannibal was coming, the Mopsian party left the city. It was then peacefully handed over to the Carthaginian and a garrison placed in it.

There Hannibal left all his booty and his baggage, and then forming his army into two divisions, gave Mago the command of one and retained the other himself. He gave Mago instructions to receive the submission of the cities in the district which were revolting from Rome and to compel those which were hanging back to revolt, whilst he himself marched through the Campanian district towards the Lower Sea with the view of attacking Neapolis so that he might have a city accessible from the sea. When he entered the confines of Neapolis he placed some of his Numidians wherever he conveniently could in ambuscade, for the roads are mostly deep, with many unseen windings. The others he ordered to ride up to the gates driving ostentatiously before them the plunder they had collected from the fields. As they appeared to be a small and disorganised force, a troop of cavalry came out against them, they were drawn on by the retreating Numidians into the ambuscade and surrounded. Not a man would have escaped had not the proximity of the sea, and some ships, mostly fishing vessels, which they saw not far from the shore, afforded a means of escape to those who were good swimmers. Several young nobles, however, were either taken or killed in the skirmish, amongst them Hegeas, the commandant of the cavalry, who fell whilst following the retreating foe too incautiously. The aspect of the walls deterred the Carthaginian from attacking the city; they by no means offered facilities for an assault.

II. From there he directed his march towards Capua. This city had become demoralised by a long course of prosperity and the indulgence of Fortune, but most of all by the universal corruption produced by the wild excesses of a populace who exercised their liberty without any restraint.

Pacuvius Calavius had got the senate of Capua entirely in his own power and that of the populace. He was a noble, and at the same time a favourite with the people, but he had gained his influence and power by resorting to base practices. He happened to be chief magistrate in the year in which the defeat at Trasumennus occurred, and knowing the hatred which the populace had long felt towards the senate, he thought it highly probable that they would seize their opportunity, create a violent revolution, and, if Hannibal with his victorious army should visit their neighbourhood, murder the senators and hand over Capua to him. Bad as the man was, he was not utterly abandoned, since he preferred to play the autocrat in a commonwealth which was constitutionally sound rather than in one that was ruined, and he knew that no political constitution could be sound where there was no council of state. He embarked on a plan by which he could save the senate and at the same time render it completely subservient to himself and to the populace.

He summoned a meeting of the senate and commenced his speech by saying that any idea of a revolt from Rome would have been quite repugnant to him had it not been a necessity, seeing that he had children by the daughter of Appius Claudius and had given his own daughter in marriage to M. Livius in Rome. " But," he went on, " there is a much more serious and formidable danger impending, for the populace are not simply contemplating beginning their revolt from Rome by banishing the senate from the city, they mean to murder the senators and then hand over the city to Hannibal and the Carthaginians. It is in my power to save you from this peril if you will put yourselves in my hands, and, forgetting all our past quarrels, trust me." Overcome by their fears they all placed themselves in his hands. " I will," he then said, " shut you in your House, and whilst appearing myself to participate in their act by approving of designs which I should in vain attempt to oppose, I will discover a way of safety for you.

Take any guarantee in this matter which you please." When he had given the guarantee he went out and ordered the doors to be fastened, and left a guard in the vestibule to prevent any one from entering or leaving without his orders.

Next, he called an assembly of the people and addressed them thus: "You have often wished, citizens of Capua, that you had the power to execute summary justice on the unscrupulous and infamous senate. You can do so now safely, and none can call you to account. You need not risk your lives in desperate attempts to force the houses of individual senators, guarded as they are by their clients and slaves; take them as they now are, locked up in the Senate-house, all by themselves, unarmed. Do not be in a hurry, do nothing rashly. I will put you in a position to pass sentence of life and death so that each of them in turn may pay the penalty he deserves. But whatever you do see that you do not go too far in satisfying your feelings of resentment, make the security and welfare of the State your first consideration. For, as I understand it, it is these particular senators that you hate, you do not want to go without a senate altogether; for you must either have a king, which is an abomination, or a senate, which is the only consultative body that can exist in a free commonwealth. So you have to do two things at once, remove the old senate and choose a fresh one. I shall order the senators to be summoned one by one and I shall take your opinion as to their fate, and whatever decision you arrive at shall be carried out. But before punishment is inflicted on any one found guilty you must choose a strong and energetic man to take his place as senator."

He then sat down, and after the names of the senators had been cast into the urn he ordered the man whose name was drawn first to be brought out of the Senate-house. As soon as they heard the name they all shouted that he was a worthless scoundrel and richly deserved to be punished. Then Pacuvius said: "I see clearly what you think of this man; in place of a worthless scoundrel you must choose a worthy and honest man as senator." For a few minutes there was silence as they were unable to suggest a better man. Then one of them, laying aside his diffidence, ventured to suggest a name, and a greater clamour than ever arose. Some said they had never heard of him, others imputed to him shameful vices and humble birth, sordid poverty, and a low class of occupation or trade. A still more violent demonstration awaited the second and third senators who were summoned, and it was obvious that while they intensely disliked the man, they had no one to put in his place. It was no use mentioning the same names again and again, for it only led to everything that was bad being said about them, and the succeeding names were those of people much more low born and unknown than those which were first suggested. So the crowd dispersed saying to one another that the evils they were best acquainted with were the easiest to bear.

IV. The senate had to thank Pacuvius for its life, and it was much more under his control than under that of the populace. By common consent he now wielded supreme power and needed no armed support. Henceforth the senators, forgetting their rank and independence, flattered the populace, saluted them courteously, invited them as guests, received them at sumptuous banquets, undertook their cases, always appeared on their side, and when they were trying suits they always decided the actions in a way to secure the favour of the mob. In fact, the proceedings in the senate were exactly as though it had been a popular assembly. The city had always been disposed to luxury and extravagance, not only through the weakness of the character of its citizens, but also through the superabundance of the means of enjoyment and the incitements to every kind of pleasure which land or sea could furnish, and now, owing to the obsequiousness of the nobility and the licence of the populace, it was becoming so demoralised that the sensuality and extravagance which prevailed exceeded all bounds. They treated the laws, the magistrates, the senate with equal contempt, and now after the defeat of Cannae they began to feel contempt for the one thing which they had hitherto held in some respect—the power of Rome. The only circumstances which prevented them from immediately revolting were the old established right of intermarriage which had led to many of their illustrious and powerful families becoming connected with Rome and the fact that several citizens were serving with the Romans. The strongest tie of this nature was the presence of three hundred cavalry, from the noblest families in Capua, in Sicily, whither they had been specially sent by the Roman authorities to garrison the island. The parents and relatives of these troopers succeeded after much difficulty in getting envoys sent to the Roman consul.

V. The consul had not yet started for Canusium; they found him and his scanty, insufficiently armed force still at Venusia, an object calculated to arouse the deepest compassion in trusty allies, and nothing but contempt amongst arrogant and treacher-

ous ones like the Campanians. The consul made matters worse
and increased the contempt felt for himself and his fortunes
by revealing too plainly and openly the extent of the disaster.
When the envoys assured him that the senate and people of
Capua were much grieved that any mischance had happened to
the Romans and expressed their readiness to supply all that was
needed for the war, he replied: " In bidding us requisition from
you what we need for the war you have preserved the tone in
which we speak to allies instead of suiting your language to the
actual state of our circumstances. For what was left us at
Cannae that we should wish what is lacking—as though we still
possessed something—to be made up by our allies? Are we to ask
you to furnish infantry as though we still possessed any cavalry?
Are we to say that we want money, as though that were the only
thing we want? Fortune has not even left us anything which
we can supplement. Legions, cavalry, arms, standards, men and
horses, money, supplies—all have gone either on the battle-
field or when the two camps were lost the following day. So
then, men of Capua, you have not to help us in the war but
almost to undertake the war for us. Call to mind how once
when your forefathers were driven in hurried flight within their
walls in dread of the Sidicine as well as the Samnite we took
them under our protection at Saticula, and how the war which
then commenced with the Samnites on your behalf was
kept up by us with all its changeful fortunes for nearly a century. Besides all this you must remember that after you had
surrendered we gave you a treaty on equal terms, we allowed
you to retain your own laws, and—what was, before our defeat
at Cannae at all events, the greatest privilege—we granted our
citizenship to most of you and made you members of our commonwealth. Under these circumstances, men of Capua, you ought
to realise that you have suffered this defeat as much as we
have, and to feel that we have a common country to defend. It
is not with the Samnites or the Etruscans that we have to do;
if they deprived us of our power it would still be Italians who
would hold it. But the Carthaginian is dragging after him an
army that is not even made up of natives of Africa, he has
collected a force from the furthest corners of the earth, from the
ocean straits, and the Pillars of Hercules, men devoid of any
sense of right, destitute of the condition, and almost of the
speech of men. Savage and barbarous by nature and habit, their
general has made them still more brutal by building up bridges
and barriers with human bodies and—I shudder to say it—

teaching them to feed on human flesh. What man, if he were merely a native of Italy, would not be horrified at the thought of looking upon men who feast upon what it is impious even to touch as his lords and masters, looking to Africa and above all to Carthage for his laws, and having to submit to Italy becoming a dependency of the Numidians and the Moors? It will be a splendid thing, men of Capua, if the dominion of Rome, which has collapsed in defeat, should be saved and restored by your loyalty, your strength. I think that in Campania you can raise 30,000 infantry and 4000 cavalry; you have already sufficient money and corn. If you show a loyalty corresponding to your means Hannibal will not feel that he has conquered or that the Romans are vanquished."

VI. After this speech of the consul's, the envoys were dismissed. As they were on their way home, one of their number, Vibius Virrius, told them that the time had come when the Campanians could not only recover the territory wrongfully taken from them by the Romans, but even achieve the dominion over Italy. They could make a treaty with Hannibal on any terms they chose, and there was no disputing the fact that when the war was over and Hannibal after his conquest returned with his army to Africa, the sovereignty over Italy would fall to the Campanians. They all agreed with what Virrius said, and they gave such an account of their interview with the consul as to make everybody think that the very name of Rome was blotted out. The populace and a majority of the senate began at once to prepare for a revolt; it was owing to the exertions of the senior members that the crisis was staved off for a few days. At last the majority carried their point, and the same envoys who had been to the Roman consul were now sent to Hannibal. I find it stated in some annalists that before they started or it was definitely decided to revolt, envoys were sent from Capua to Rome to demand as the condition of their rendering assistance that one consul should be a Campanian, and amidst the indignation which this demand aroused the envoys were ordered to be summarily ejected from the Senate-house, and a lictor told off to conduct them out of the City with orders not to remain a single day on Roman territory. As, however, this demand is too much like one made by the Latins in earlier times, and Caelius amongst others would not have omitted to mention it without good reason, I will not venture to vouch for the truth of the statement.

VII. The envoys came to Hannibal and negotiated a peace

with him on the following terms: No Carthaginian commander
or magistrate was to have any jurisdiction over the citizens of
Capua nor was any Campanian citizen to be obliged to serve
in any military or other capacity against his will; Capua was
to retain its own magistrates and its own laws; and the Carthaginian was to allow them to choose three hundred Romans out
of his prisoners of war whom they were to exchange for the
Campanian troopers who were serving in Sicily.

These were the terms agreed upon, but the Campanians went
far beyond the stipulations in their criminal excesses. The
populace seized officers in command of our allies and other
Roman citizens, some whilst occupied with their military duties,
others whilst engaged in their private business, and ordered
them to be shut up in the baths on the pretence of keeping them
in safe custody; unable to breathe owing to the heat and fumes
they died in great agony.

Decius Magius was a man who, if his fellow-citizens had been
rational, would have gained very great authority with them.
He did his best to prevent these crimes and to stop the envoys
from going to Hannibal. When he heard that troops were
being sent by Hannibal to garrison the city, he protested most
earnestly against their being admitted and referred, as warning
examples, to the tyranny of Pyrrhus and the wretched servitude
into which the Tarentines fell. After they were admitted he
urged that they should be expelled, or what was better, if the
Capuans wished to clear themselves by a deed which would be
remembered from their guilt in revolting from ancient allies
and blood-relations, let them put the Carthaginian garrison to
death and be once more friends with Rome.

When this was reported to Hannibal — for there was no
secrecy about Magius' action—he sent to summon him to his
camp. Magius sent a spirited refusal; Hannibal, he said, had
no legal authority over a citizen of Capua. The Carthaginian,
furious at the rebuff, ordered the man to be thrown into chains
and brought to him. Fearing, however, on second thoughts,
that the use of force might create a tumult and feelings once
aroused might lead to a sudden outbreak, he sent a message
to Marius Blossius, the chief magistrate of Capua, that he would
be there on the morrow, and started with a small escort for the
city. Marius called the people together and gave public notice
that they should assemble in a body with their wives and children
and go to meet Hannibal. The whole population turned out,
not because they were ordered, but because the mob were

enthusiastic in favour of Hannibal, and were eager to see a commander famous for so many victories. Decius Magius did not go to meet him, nor did he shut himself up at home, as this might have implied a consciousness of guilt; he strolled leisurely about the Forum with his son and a few of his clients, whilst the whole city was in a state of wild excitement at seeing and welcoming Hannibal.

When he had entered the city Hannibal asked that the senate should be convened at once. The leading Campanians, however, implored him not to transact any serious business then, but to give himself up to the joyous celebration of a day which had been made such a happy one by his arrival. Though he was naturally impulsive in his anger, he would not begin with a refusal, and spent most of the day in viewing the city.

VIII. He stayed with two brothers, Sthenius and Pacuvius, men distinguished for their high birth and wealth. Pacuvius Calavius, whom we have already mentioned, the leader of the party which brought the city over to the Carthaginians, brought his young son to the house. The youth was closely attached to Decius Magius, and had stood up most resolutely with him for the alliance with Rome and against any terms with the Carthaginians, and neither the changing over of the city to the other side nor the authority of his father had been able to shake his resolution. Pacuvius dragged him away from Magius' side and now sought to obtain Hannibal's pardon for the youth by intercessions rather than by any attempts at exculpation. He was overcome by the father's prayers and tears and went so far as to order him to be invited to a banquet to which none were to be admitted but his hosts and Vibellius Taureas, a distinguished soldier. The banquet began early in the day, and was not at all in accordance with Carthaginian customs or military discipline, but as was natural in a city, still more in a house full of wealth and luxury, the table was furnished with every kind of dainty and delicacy. Young Calavius was the only one who could not be persuaded to drink, though his hosts and occasionally Hannibal invited him; he excused himself on the ground of health, and his father alleged as a further reason his not unnatural excitement under the circumstances. It was nearly sunset when the guests rose. Young Calavius accompanied his father out of the banquet chamber and when they had come to a retired spot in the garden behind the house, he stopped and said: " I have a plan to propose to you, father, by which we shall not only obtain pardon for the Romans for our offence in revolting to Hannibal, but also possess much more influence and prestige in Capua than we have ever done before." When his father asked him in great surprise what his plan was, he threw his toga back from his shoulder and showed him a sword belted on to his side. "Now," he said, "this very moment will I ratify our treaty with Rome in Hannibal's blood. I wanted you to know first, in case you would rather be away when the deed is done." The old man, beside himself with terror at what he saw and heard, as though he were actually witnessing the act his son had spoken of, exclaimed: "I pray and beseech you, my son, by all the sacred bonds which unite parents and children, not to insist upon doing and suffering everything that is horrible before your father's eyes. It is only a few hours ago that we pledged our faith, swearing by all the gods and joining hand to hand, and do you want us, when we have just separated after friendly talk, to arm those hands, consecrated by such a pledge, against him? Have you risen from the hospitable board to which you were invited by Hannibal with only two others out of all Capua that you may stain that board with your host's blood? I, your father, was able to make Hannibal friendly towards my son, am I powerless to make my son friendly towards Hannibal? But let nothing sacred hold you back, neither the plighted word, nor religious obligation, nor filial affection; dare infamous deeds, if they do not bring ruin as well as guilt upon us. But what then? Are you going to attack Hannibal single-handed? What of that throng of free men and slaves, with all their eyes intent on him alone? What of all those right hands? Will they hang down listlessly during that act of madness? Armed hosts cannot bear even to gaze on the face of Hannibal, the Roman people dread it, and will *you* endure it? Though other help be lacking, will you have the courage to strike me, me your father, when I interpose myself to protect Hannibal? And yet it is through my breast that you must pierce his. Suffer yourself to be deterred here rather than vanquished there. Let my prayers prevail with you as they have already to-day prevailed for you."

By this time the youth was in tears, and seeing this, the father flung his arms round him, clung to him with kisses, and persisted in his entreaties until he made his son lay aside his sword and give his word that he would do nothing of the kind. Then the son spoke: "I must pay to my father the dutiful obedience which I owe to my country. I am indeed grieved on your account for you have to bear the guilt of a threefold betraya of your country; first when you instigated the revolt from Rome; secondly when you urged peace with Hannibal, and now once more when you are the one let and hindrance in the way of restoring Capua to the Romans. Do you, my country, receive this sword with which I armed myself in your defence when I entered the stronghold of the enemy." With these words he flung the sword over the garden wall into the public road, and to allay all suspicions returned to the banqueting room.

X. The following day there was a full meeting of the senate to hear Hannibal. At first his tone was very gracious and winning; he thanked the Capuans for preferring his friendship to alliance with Rome, and amongst other magnificent promises he assured them that Capua would soon be the head of all Italy and that Rome, in common with all the other nationalities, would have to look to her for their laws. Then his tone changed. There was one man, he thundered, who was outside the friendship of Carthage and the treaty they had made with him, a man that was not, and ought not to be called a Campanian—Decius Magius. He demanded his surrender and asked that this matter should be discussed and a decision arrived at before he left the House. They all voted for surrendering the man, though a great many thought that he did not deserve such a cruel fate and felt that a long step had been taken in the abridgment of their rights and liberties.

On leaving the Senate-house Hannibal took his seat on the magistrates' tribunal and ordered Decius Magius to be arrested, brought before him, and put on his defence, alone and unbefriended. The high spirit of the man was still unquelled, he said that by the terms of the treaty this could not be insisted on, but he was at once placed in irons and ordered to be conducted to the camp, followed by a lictor. As long as his head was uncovered he was incessantly haranguing and shouting to the crowds round him: " You have got the liberty, you Campanians, that you asked for. In the middle of the Forum, in the broad daylight, with you looking on, I a man second to none in Capua am being hurried off in chains to death. Could any greater outrage have been committed if the city had been taken? Go and meet Hannibal, decorate your city, make the day of his arrival a public holiday that you may enjoy the spectacle of this triumph over a fellow-citizen! As the mob appeared to be moved by these outbursts, his head was muffled up and orders were given to hurry him more quickly outside the city gate. In this way he was brought into the camp and then at once put on board a ship and sent to Carthage. Hannibal's fear was that if any disturbance broke out in Capua in consequence of such scandalous treatment the senate might repent of having surrendered their foremost citizen, and if they sent to ask for his restoration he would either offend his new allies by refusing the first request they made, or, if he granted it, would have in Capua a fomenter of disorder and sedition. The vessel was driven by a storm to Cyrenae which was then under a monarchy. Here Magius fled for sanctuary to the statue of King Ptolemy, and his guards conveyed him to the King of Alexandria. After he had told him how he had been thrown into chains by Hannibal in defiance of all treaty rights, he was liberated from his fetters and permission accorded to him to go to Rome or Capua, whichever he preferred. Magius said that he would not be safe at Capua, and as there was at that time war between Rome and Capua, he would be living in Rome more like a deserter than a guest. There was no place where he would sooner live than under the rule of the man whom he had known as the champion and asserter of his freedom.

XI. During these occurrences Q. Fabius Pictor returned home from his mission to Delphi. He read the response of the oracle from a manuscript, in which were contained the names of the gods and goddesses to whom supplications were to be made, and the forms to be observed in making them. This was the closing paragraph: " If ye act thus, Romans, your estate will be better and less troubled, your republic will go forward as ye would have it, and the victory in the war will belong to the people of Rome. When your commonwealth is prosperous and safe send to Pythian Apollo a gift from the gains you have earned and honour him with your substance out of the plunder, the booty, and the spoils. Put away from you all wanton and godless living."

He translated this from the Greek as he read it, and when he had finished reading he said that as soon as he left the oracle he offered sacrifice with wine and incense to all the deities who were named, and further that he was instructed by the priest to go on board wearing the same laurel garland in which he had visited the oracle and not to lay it aside till he got to Rome. He stated that he had carried out all his instructions most carefully and conscientiously, and had laid the garland on the altar of Apollo. The senate passed a decree that the sacrifices and intercessions which were enjoined should be carefully performed at the earliest opportunity.

Reception of the News at Carthage.—During these occurrences in Rome and Italy, Mago, Hamilcar's son, had arrived at Carthage with the news of the victory of Cannae. He had not been sent by his brother immediately after the battle, but had been detained for some days in receiving into alliance Bruttian communities as they successively revolted. When he appeared before the senate he unfolded the story of his brother's successes in Italy, how he had fought pitched battles with six commanders-in-chief, four of whom were consuls and two a Dictator and his Master of Horse, and how he had killed about 200,000 of the enemy and taken more than 50,000 prisoners. Out of four consuls two had fallen, of the two survivors one was wounded and the other, after losing the whole of his army, had escaped with fifty men. The Master of the Horse, whose powers were those of a consul, had been routed and put to flight, and the Dictator, because he had never fought an action, was looked upon as a matchless general. The Bruttians and Apulians, with some of the Samnite and Lucanian communities, had gone over to the Carthaginians. Capua, which was not only the chief city of Campania, but now that the power of Rome had been shattered at Cannae was the head of Italy, had surrendered to Hannibal. For all these great victories he felt that they ought to be truly grateful and public thanksgivings ought to be offered to the immortal gods.

XII. As evidence that the joyful tidings he brought were true, he ordered a quantity of gold rings to be piled up in the vestibule of the Senate-house, and they formed such a great heap that, according to some authorities, they measured more than three *modii*;[1] the more probable account, however, is that they did not amount to more than one *modius*. He added by way of explanation, to show how great the Roman losses had been, that none but knights, and amongst them only the highest in rank, wore that ornament. The main purport of his speech was that the nearer Hannibal's chances were of bringing the war to a speedy close the more need there was to render him every possible assistance; he was campaigning far from home, in the midst of a hostile country; vast quantities of corn were being consumed and much money expended, and all those battles, whilst they destroyed the armies of the enemy, at the same time wasted very appreciably the forces of the victor. Reinforcements, therefore, must be sent, money must be sent to pay the troops, and supplies of corn to the soldiers who had done such splendid service for Carthage.

Amidst the general delight with which Mago's speech was received, Himilco, a member of the Barcine party, thought it a favourable moment for attacking Hanno. "Well, Hanno," he began, "do you still disapprove of our commencing a war against Rome? Give orders for Hannibal to be surrendered, put your veto upon all thanksgivings to the gods after we have received such blessings, let us hear the voice of a Roman senator in the Senate-house of Carthage?"

Then Hanno spoke to the following effect: "Senators, I would have kept silence on the present occasion, for I did not wish on a day of universal rejoicing to say anything which might damp your happiness. But as a senator has asked me whether I still disapprove of the war we have commenced against Rome, silence on my part would show either insolence or cowardice; the one implies forgetfulness of the respect due to others, the other of one's own self-respect. My reply to Himilco is this: I have never ceased to disapprove of the war, nor shall I ever cease to censure your invincible general until I see the war ended upon conditions that are tolerable. Nothing will banish my regret for the old peace that we have broken except the establishment of a new one. Those details which Mago has proudly enumerated make Himilco and the rest of Hannibal's caucus very happy; they might make me happy too, for a successful war, if we choose to make a wise use of our good fortune, will bring us a more favourable peace. If we let this opportunity slip, when we are in a position to offer rather than submit to terms of peace, I fear that our rejoicing will become extravagant and finally turn out to be groundless. But even now, what is it that you are rejoicing at? 'I have slain the armies of the enemy; send me troops.' What more could you ask for, if you had been defeated? 'I have captured two of the enemy's camps, filled, of course, with plunder and supplies; send me corn and money.' What more could you want if you had been despoiled, stripped of your own camp? And that I may not be the only one to be surprised at your delight—for as I have answered Himilco, I have a perfect right to ask questions in my turn—I should be glad if either Himilco or Mago would tell me, since, you say, the battle of Cannae has all but destroyed the power of Rome and the whole of Italy is admittedly in revolt, whether, in the first place, any single community of the Latin nation has come over to us, and, secondly, whether a single man out of the thirty-five Roman tribes has deserted to Hannibal." Mago answered both questions in the negative.

" Then there are still," Hanno continued, " far too many of the enemy left. But I should like to know how much courage and confidence that vast multitude possess."

XIII. Mago said he did not know. " Nothing," replied Hanno, " is easier to find out. Have the Romans sent any envoys to Hannibal to sue for peace? Has any rumour reached your ears of any one even mentioning the word ' peace ' in Rome? " Again Mago replied in the negative. " Well, then," said Hanno, " we have as much work before us in this war as we had on the day when Hannibal first set foot in Italy. Many of us are still alive who can remember with what changeful fortunes the first Punic war was fought. Never did our cause appear to be prospering more by sea and land than immediately before the consulship of C. Lutatius and A. Postumius. But in their year of office we were utterly defeated off the Ægates. But if (which heaven forfend!) fortune should now turn to any extent, do you hope to obtain when you are defeated a peace which no one offers to give you now that you are victorious? If any one should ask my opinion about offering or accepting terms of peace I would say what I thought. But if the question before us is simply whether Mago's demands should be granted, I do not think that we are concerned with sending supplies to a victorious army, much less do I consider that they ought to be sent if we are being deluded with false and empty hopes."

Very few were influenced by Hanno's speech. His well-known dislike of the Barcas deprived his words of weight and they were too much pre-occupied with the delightful news they had just heard to listen to anything which would make them feel less cause for joy. They fancied that if they were willing to make a slight effort the war would soon be over. A resolution was accordingly passed with great enthusiasm to reinforce Hannibal with 4000 Numidians, 40 elephants, and 500 talents of silver. Bostar [2] also was sent with Mago into Spain to raise 20,000 infantry and 4000 cavalry to make good the losses of the armies in Italy and Spain.

XIV. *Hannibal fails to secure Nola.*—As usual, however, in seasons of prosperity, these measures were executed with great remissness and dilatoriness. The Romans, on the other hand, were kept from being dilatory by their native energy and still more by the necessities of their position. The consul did not fail in any single duty which he had to perform, nor did the Dictator show less energy. The force now available comprised the two legions which had been enrolled by the consuls at the beginning of the year, a levy of slaves and the cohorts which had been raised in the country of Picenum and Cisalpine Gaul. The Dictator decided to still further increase his strength by adopting a measure to which only a country in an almost hopeless state could stoop, when honour must yield to necessity. After duly discharging his religious duties and obtaining the necessary permission to mount his horse,[3] he published an edict that all who had been guilty of capital offences or who were in prison for debt and were willing to serve under him would by his orders be released from punishment and have their debts cancelled. 6000 men were raised in this way, and he armed them with the spoils taken from the Gauls and which had been carried in the triumphal procession of C. Flaminius. He then started from the City with 25,000 men.

After taking over Capua, and making another fruitless appeal to the hopes and fears of Neapolis, Hannibal marched into the territory of Nola. He did not at once treat it in a hostile manner as he was not without hope that the citizens would make a voluntary surrender, but if they delayed, he intended to leave nothing undone which could cause them suffering or terror. The senate, especially its leading members, were faithful supporters of the Roman alliance, the populace as usual were all in favour of revolting to Hannibal; they conjured up the prospect of ravaged fields and a siege with all its hardships and indignities; nor were there wanting men who were actively instigating a revolt. The senate were afraid that if they openly opposed the agitation they would not be able to withstand the popular excitement, and they found a means of putting off the evil day by pretending to go with the mob. They represented that they were in favour of revolting to Hannibal, but nothing was settled as to the conditions on which they were to enter into a new treaty and alliance. Having thus gained time, they sent delegates in great haste to Marcellus Claudius the praetor, who was with his army at Casilinum, to inform him of the critical position of Nola, how their territory was in Hannibal's hand, and the city would be in the possession of the Carthaginians unless it received succour, and how the senate, by telling the populace that they might revolt when they pleased, had made them less in a hurry to do so. Marcellus thanked the delegates and told them to adhere to the same policy and postpone matters till he arrived. He then left Casilinum for Caiatia and from there he marched across the Vulturnus, through the

districts of Saticula and Trebia, over the hills above Suessula,
and so arrived at Nola.

XV. On the approach of the Roman praetor the Carthaginian
evacuated the territory of Nola and marched down to the coast
close to Neapolis, as he was anxious to secure a seaport town
to which there might be a safe passage for ships coming from
Africa. When, however, he learnt that Neapolis was held by
a Roman officer, M. Junius Silanus, who had been invited by
the Neapolitans, he left Naples, as he had left Nola, and went to
Nuceria. He spent some time in investing the place, often
attacking it, and often making tempting proposals to the chief
men of the place and to the leaders of the populace, but all to
no purpose. At last famine did its work, and he received the
submission of the town, the inhabitants being allowed to depart
without arms and with one garment apiece. Then, to keep
up his character of being friendly to all the Italian nationalities
except the Romans, he held out honours and rewards to those
who consented to remain in his service. Not a single man was
tempted by the prospect; they all dispersed, wherever they
had friends, or wherever each man's fancy led him, amongst the
cities of Campania, mainly Nola and Neapolis. About thirty
of their senators, and, as it happened, their principal ones,
endeavoured to enter Capua, but were refused admission because
they had closed their gates against Hannibal. They accordingly went on to Cumae. The plunder of Nuceria was given
to the soldiers, the city itself was burnt.

Marcellus retained his hold on Nola quite as much by the
support of its leading men as by the confidence he felt in his
troops. Fears were entertained as to the populace and especially L. Bantius. This enterprising young man was at that
time almost the most distinguished among the allied cavalry,
but the knowledge that he had attempted revolt and his fear
of the Roman praetor were driving him on to betray his country
or, if he found no means of doing that, to become a deserter.
He had been discovered lying half-dead on a heap of bodies on
the field of Cannae, and after being taken the utmost care of,
Hannibal sent him home loaded with presents. His feelings
of gratitude for such kindness made him wish to place the
government of Nola in the hands of the Carthaginian, and his
anxiety and eagerness for a revolution attracted the observation of the praetor. As it was necessary either to restrain the
youth by punishment or to win him by kindness, the praetor
chose the latter course, preferring to secure such a brave and

enterprising youth as a friend rather than to lose him to the enemy. He invited him to come and see him and spoke to him most kindly. " You can easily understand," he told him, " that many of your countrymen are jealous of you, from the fact that not a single citizen of Nola has pointed out to me your many distinguished military services. But the bravery of a man who has served in a Roman camp cannot be hidden. Many of your fellow-soldiers tell me what a young hero you are, and how many perils and dangers you have undergone in defence of the safety and honour of Rome. I am told that you did not give up the struggle on the field of Cannae until you were buried, almost lifeless, beneath a falling mass of men and horses and arms. May you long live to do still more gallant deeds! With me you will gain every honour and reward, and you will find that the more you are in my company the more will it lead to your profit and promotion." The young man was delighted with these promises. The praetor made him a present of a splendid charger and authorised the quaestor to pay him 500 silver coins;[4] he also instructed his lictors to allow him to pass whenever he wished to see him.

XVI. The high-spirited youth was so completely captivated by the attention Marcellus paid him that for the future none among the allies of Rome gave her more efficient or more loyal help.

Hannibal once more moved his camp from Nuceria to Nola, and when he appeared before its gates the populace again began to look forward to revolting. As the enemy approached Marcellus retired within the walls, not because he feared for his camp, but because he would not give any opportunity to the large number of citizens who were bent on betraying their city.

Both armies now began to prepare for battle; the Romans before the walls of Nola and the Carthaginians in front of their camp. Slight skirmishes took place between the city and the camp with varying success, as the generals would not prohibit their men from going forward in small parties to offer defiance to the enemy nor would they give the signal for a general action.

Day after day the two armies took up their respective stations in this way, and during this time the leading citizens of Nola informed Marcellus that nocturnal interviews were taking place between the populace and the Carthaginians, and that it had been arranged that when the Roman army had passed out of the gates they should plunder their baggage and kits, then close the gates and man the walls so that having become masters of their city and government they might forthwith admit the Carthaginians instead of the Romans.

On receiving this information Marcellus warmly thanked the Nolan senators and made up his mind to try the fortune of a battle before any disturbances arose in the city. He formed his army into three divisions and stationed them at the three gates which faced the enemy, he ordered the baggage to follow close behind, and the camp-servants, sutlers, and disabled soldiers were to carry stakes. At the centre gate he posted the strongest part of the legions and the Roman cavalry, at the two on either side he stationed the recruits, the light infantry, and the cavalry of the allies. The Nolans were forbidden to approach the walls or gates and a special reserve was placed in charge of the baggage to prevent any attack upon it whilst the legions were engaged in the battle. In this formation they remained standing inside the gates. Hannibal had his troops drawn up for battle, as he had had for several days, and remained in this position till late in the day. At first it struck him with surprise that the Roman army did not move outside the gates and that not a single soldier appeared on the walls. Then, supposing that the secret interviews had been betrayed and that his friends were afraid to move, he sent back a portion of his troops to their camp with orders to bring all the appliances for attacking the town as soon as possible to the front of the line. He felt fairly confident that if he attacked them whilst thus hesitating .the populace would raise some disturbance in the town. Whilst his men were hurrying up to the front ranks, each to his allotted task, and the whole line was approaching the walls, Marcellus ordered the gates to be suddenly flung open, the attack sounded, and the battle shout raised; the infantry, followed by the cavalry, were to attack with all the fury possible. They had already carried enough confusion and alarm into the enemies' centre when P. Valerius Flaccus and C. Aurelius, divisional commanders, burst out from the other two gates and charged. The sutlers and camp-servants and the rest of the troops who were guarding the baggage joined in the shouting, and this made the Carthaginians, who had been despising the fewness of their numbers, think that it was a large army. I would hardly venture to assert, as some authorities do, that 2800 of the enemy were killed, and that the Romans did not lose more than 500. But whether the victory was as great as that or not, I do not think that an action more important in its consequences was fought during the whole war, for it was more difficult for those who conquered to escape being defeated by Hannibal than it was afterwards to conquer him.

XVII. *Siege and Capture of Casilinum.*—As there was no hope of his getting possession of Nola, Hannibal withdrew to Acerrae. No sooner had he departed than Marcellus shut the gates and posted guards to prevent any one from leaving the city. He then opened a public inquiry in the forum into the conduct of those who had been holding secret interviews with the enemy. Above seventy were found guilty of treason and beheaded and their property confiscated. Then, after handing the government over to the senate, he left with his entire force and took up a position above Suessula, where he encamped.

At first the Carthaginian tried to persuade the men of Acerrae to make a voluntary surrender, but when he found that their loyalty remained unshaken he made preparations for a siege and an assault. The Acerrans possessed more courage than strength, and when they saw that the blockade was being carried round their walls and that it was hopeless to attempt any further defence, they decided to escape before the enemies' line of circumvallation was closed, and stealing away in the dead of night through any unguarded gaps in the earthworks they fled, regardless of roads or paths, as chance or design led them. They escaped to those cities of Campania which they had every reason to believe had not changed their allegiance.

After plundering and burning Acerrae Hannibal marched to Casilinum in consequence of information he received of the Dictator's march on Capua with his legions.[5] He was apprehensive that the proximity of the Roman army might create a counter-revolution in Capua. At that time Casilinum was held by 500 Praenestines with a few Roman and Latin troops, who had gone there when they heard of the disaster at Cannae. The levy at Praeneste had not been completed by the appointed day, and these men started from home too late to be of use at Cannae. They reached Casilinum before news of the disaster arrived, and, joined by Romans and allies, they advanced in great force. Whilst on the march they heard of the battle and its result and returned to Casilinum. Here, suspected by the Campanians and fearing for their own safety, they passed some days in forming and evading plots. When they were satisfied that Capua was in revolt and that Hannibal would be admitted, they massacred the townsmen of Casilinum at night and took possession of the part of the city on this side of the Vulturnus—the river divides the city in two—and held it as a

Roman garrison. They were joined also by a cohort of Perusians numbering 460 men who were driven to Casilinum by the same intelligence that sent the Praenestines there a few days previously. The force was quite adequate for the small circuit of walls, protected, too, as they were on one side by the river, but the scarcity of corn made even that number appear too large.

XVIII. When Hannibal was now not far from the place he sent on in advance a troop of Gaetulians under an officer named Isalca, to try and get a parley with the inhabitants and persuade them by fair words to open their gates and admit a Carthaginian detachment to hold the town. If they refused, they were to use force and make an attack, wherever it seemed feasible, on the place. When they approached the walls the town was so silent that they thought it was deserted, and taking it for granted that the inhabitants had fled through fear they began to force the gates and break down the bars. Suddenly the gates were thrown open and two cohorts which had been standing inside ready for action dashed out and made a furious charge, utterly discomfiting the enemy. Maharbal was sent with a stronger force to their assistance, but even he was unable to withstand the impetuosity of the cohorts. At last Hannibal pitched his camp before the walls, and made preparations for assaulting the little town and its small garrison with the combined strength of his entire army. After completing the circle of his investing lines he began to harass and annoy the garrison, and in this way lost some of his most daring soldiers who were hit with missiles from the wall and turrets. On one occasion when the defenders were taking the aggressive in a sortie he nearly cut them off with his elephants and drove them in hasty flight into the city; the loss, considering their numbers, was quite severe enough, and more would have fallen had not night intervened.

The next day there was a general desire to begin the assault. The enthusiasm of the men had been kindled by the offer of a " mural crown " of gold and also by the way in which the general himself remonstrated with the men who had taken Saguntum for their slackness in attacking a little fortress situated in open country, and also reminded them one and all of Cannae, Trasumennus, and the Trebia. The *vineae* were brought up and mines commenced, but the various attempts of the enemy were opposed with equal strength and skill by the defenders, the allies of Rome; they created defences against the *vineae*, intercepted their mines with counter-mines, and met all their attacks above ground or below with steady resistance until at last Hannibal for very shame gave up his project. He contented himself with fortifying his camp and leaving a small force to defend it, so that it might not be supposed that the siege was entirely abandoned; after which he settled in Capua as his winter quarters.

There he kept his army under shelter for the greater part of the winter. A long and varied experience had inured that army to every form of human suffering, but it had not been habituated to or had any experience of ease and comfort. So it came about that the men whom no pressure of calamity had been able to subdue fell victims to a prosperity too great and pleasures too attractive for them to withstand, and fell all the more utterly the more greedily they plunged into new and untried delights. Sloth, wine, feasting, women, baths, and idle lounging, which became every day more seductive as they became more habituated to them, so enervated their minds and bodies that they were saved more by the memory of past victories than by any fighting strength they possessed now. Authorities in military matters have regarded the wintering at Capua as a greater mistake on the part of Hannibal than his not marching straight to Rome after his victory at Cannae. For his delay at that time might be looked upon as only postponing his final victory, but this may be considered as having deprived him of the strength to win victory. And it certainly did look as if he left Capua with another army altogether; it did not retain a shred of its former discipline. A large number who had become entangled with women went back there, and as soon as they took to tents again and the fatigue of marching and other military toils had to be endured their strength and spirits alike gave way just as though they were raw recruits. From that time all through the summer campaign a large number left the standards without leave, and Capua was the only place where the deserters sought to hide themselves.

XIX. *Casilinum Surrenders.*—However, when the mild weather came, Hannibal led his army out of their winter quarters and marched back to Casilinum. Although the assault had been suspended, the uninterrupted investment had reduced the townsfolk and the garrison to the extremity of want. Tiberius Sempronius Gracchus was in command of the Roman camp, as the Dictator had to leave for Rome to take the auspices afresh. Marcellus was equally anxious to assist the besieged garrison, but he was detained by the Vulturnus being in flood, and also by the entreaties of the people of Nola and Acerrae who feared the Campanians in case the Romans withdrew their protection. Gracchus simply watched Casilinum, for the Dictator had given strict orders that no active operations should be undertaken in his absence. He therefore kept quiet, though the reports from Casilinum might easily have been too much for any man's patience. It was stated as a fact that some, unable to endure starvation any longer, had flung themselves from the walls, others had stood there unarmed and exposed their defenceless bodies to the missiles of the enemy. These tidings sorely tried his patience, for he durst not fight against the Dictator's orders, and he saw that he would have to fight if he were seen getting corn into the place, and there was no chance of getting it in without being seen. He gathered in a supply of corn from all the fields round and filled a number of casks with it, and then sent a messenger to the chief magistrate at Casilinum asking him to pick up the casks which the river carried down. The next night, while all were intently watching the river, after their hopes had been raised by the Roman messenger, the casks floated down in the middle of the stream; and the corn was divided in equal shares amongst them all. The same thing happened on the two following days; they were sent off by night and reached their destination; so far they had escaped the notice of the enemy. Then, owing to the perpetual rain, the river became more rapid than usual and the cross currents carried the casks to the bank which the enemy were guarding. They caught sight of them as they stuck amongst the osier beds which grew on the bank and a report was made to Hannibal, in consequence of which greater caution was observed and a closer watch was kept, so that nothing could be sent by the Vulturnus to the city without being detected. Nuts, however, were scattered on the river from the Roman camp; these floated down the mid-stream and were caught in baskets. At last things came to such a pitch that the inhabitants tried to chew the leather straps and hides which they tore from their shields, after softening them in boiling water, nor did they refuse mice and other animals; they even dug up from the bottom of their walls grass and roots of all sorts. When the enemy had ploughed up all the grass outside the walls they sowed it with rape, which made Hannibal exclaim: " Am I to sit here before Casilinum until these seeds have grown? " and whereas he had never allowed any terms of surrender to be mentioned in his hearing, he now consented to proposals for the ransom of all the free-born citizens. The price agreed upon was seven ounces of gold for each person. When their liberty was guaranteed they surrendered, but were kept in custody till all the gold was paid, then in strict observance of the terms they were released.[6] This is much more likely to be true than that after they had left cavalry were sent after them and put them all to death. The great majority were Praenestines. Out of the 570 who formed the garrison not less than half had perished by sword and famine, the rest returned in safety to Praeneste with their commanding officer, M. Anicius, who had formerly been a notary. To commemorate the event his statue was set up in the forum of Praeneste, wearing a coat of mail with a toga over it and having the head veiled. A bronze plate was affixed with this inscription: " Marcus Anicius has discharged the vow he made for the safety of the garrison of Casilinum." The same inscription was affixed to the three images standing in the temple of Fortune.[7]

XX. The town of Casilinum was given back to the Campanians, and a garrison of 700 men from Hannibal's army was placed in it in case the Romans should attack it after Hannibal's departure. The senate decreed that double pay and an exemption for five years from further service should be granted to the Praenestine troops. They were also offered the full Roman citizenship, but they preferred not to change their status as citizens of Praeneste. There is more obscurity as to what happened to the Perusians, as there is no light thrown upon it by any monument of their own or any decree of the senate.

The people of Petelia, who alone of all the Bruttii had remained friendly to Rome, were now attacked not only by the Carthaginians, who were overrunning that district, but also by the rest of the Bruttii who had adopted the opposite policy. Finding themselves helpless in the presence of all these dangers, they sent envoys to Rome to ask for support. The senate told them that they must look after themselves, and on hearing this they broke into tears and entreaties and flung themselves on the floor of the vestibule. Their distress excited the deep sympathy of both senate and people, and the praetor, M. Æmilius, asked the senators to reconsider their decision. After making a careful survey of the resources of the empire, they were compelled to admit that they were powerless to protect their distant allies. They advised the envoys to return home and now that they had proved their loyalty to the utmost they must adopt such measures as their present circumstances demanded. When the result of their mission was reported to the Petelians, their

senate was so overcome by grief and fear that some were in favour
of deserting the city and seeking refuge wherever they could,
others thought that as they had been abandoned by their old
allies they had better join the rest of the Bruttii and surrender
to Hannibal. The majority, however, decided that no rash
action should be taken, and that the question should be further
debated. When the matter came up the next day a calmer
tone prevailed and their leading statesmen persuaded them to
collect all their produce and possessions from the fields and put
the city and the walls into a state of defence.

XXI. *Events in Sicily and Sardinia.*—About this time despatches arrived from Sicily and Sardinia. The one sent from
T. Otacilius, the propraetor commanding in Sicily, was read in
the senate. It stated in effect that P. Furius had reached
Lilybaeum with his fleet; that he himself was seriously wounded
and his life in great danger; that the soldiers and sailors had
no pay or corn given them from day to day, nor was there any
means of procuring any, and he strongly urged that both should
be sent as soon as possible, and that, if the senate agreed, one of
the new praetors should be sent to succeed him.

The despatch from A. Cornelius Mammula dealt with the
same difficulty as to pay and corn. The same reply was sent
to both; there was no possibility of sending either, and they
were instructed to make the best arrangements they could for
their fleets and armies. T. Otacilius sent envoys to Hiero, the
one man whom Rome could fall back upon, and received in
reply as much money as he needed and a six months' supply of
corn. In Sicily the allied cities sent generous contributions.
Even in Rome, too, the scarcity of money was felt and a measure
was carried by M. Minucius, one of the tribunes of the plebs, for
the appointment of three finance commissioners. The men
appointed were: L. Æmilius Papus, who had been consul and
censor; M. Atilius Regulus, who had been twice consul; and
L. Scribonius Libo, one of the tribunes of the plebs. Marcus
and Caius Atilius, two brothers, were appointed to dedicate the
temple of Concord which L. Manlius had vowed during his
praetorship. Three new pontiffs were also chosen—Q. Caecilius
Metellus, Q. Fabius Maximus, and Q. Fulvius Flaccus—in the
place of P. Scantinius who had died, and of L. Æmilius
Paulus, the consul, and Q. Ælius Paetus, both of whom fell
at Cannae.

XXII. *Additions made to the Senate.*—When the senate had
done their best—so far as human wisdom could do so—to make

good the losses which Fortune had inflicted in such an uninterrupted series of disasters, they at last turned their attention to the emptiness of the Senate-house and the small number of those who attended the national council. There had been no revision of the roll of the senate since L. Æmilius and C. Flaminius were censors, though there had been such heavy losses amongst the senators during the last five years on the field of battle, as well as from the fatalities and accidents to which all are liable. In compliance with the unanimous wish, the subject was brought forward by the praetor, M. Æmilius, in the absence of the Dictator, who after the loss of Casilinum had rejoined the army. Sp. Carvilius spoke at considerable length about the dearth of senators, and also the very small number of citizens from whom senators could be chosen. He went on to say that for the purpose of filling up the vacancies, and also of strengthening the union between the Latins and Rome, he should strongly urge that the full citizenship be granted to two senators out of each Latin city, to be approved by the senate, and that these men should be chosen into the senate in the place of those who had died.

The senate listened to these proposals with quite as much impatience as they had previously felt at the demand of the Latins.[8] A murmur of indignation went through the House. T. Manlius in particular was heard asserting that there was even still one man of the stock to which that consul belonged who once in the Capitol threatened that he would kill with his own hand any Latin whom he saw sitting in the senate. Q. Fabius Maximus declared that no proposal had ever been mooted in the senate at a more inopportune time than this; it had been thrown out at a moment when the sympathies of their allies were wavering and their loyalty doubtful, and it would make them more restless than ever; those rash inconsiderate words uttered by one man ought to be stifled by the silence of all men. Whatever secret or sacred matter had at any time imposed silence on that House, this most of all must be concealed, buried, forgotten, considered as never having been uttered. All further allusion to the subject was accordingly suppressed.

It was ultimately decided to nominate as Dictator a man who had been censor before, and was the oldest man living who had held that office, in order that the roll of senators might be revised. C. Terentius was recalled to nominate the Dictator. Leaving a garrison in Apulia he returned to Rome by forced marches, and the night after his arrival nominated in accordance with ancient custom M. Fabius Buteo to act as Dictator for six months without any Master of the Horse.

XXIII. Accompanied by his lictors, Fabius mounted the rostra and made the following speech: " I do not approve of there being two Dictators at the same time, a thing wholly unprecedented, nor of there being a Dictator without a Master of the Horse, nor of the censorial powers being entrusted to one individual and that for the second time, nor of the supreme authority being placed in the hands of a Dictator for six months unless he has been created to wield executive powers. These irregularities may perhaps be necessary at this juncture, but I shall fix a limit to them. I shall not remove from the roll any of those whom C. Flaminius and L. Æmilius, the last censors, placed on it, I shall simply order their names to be transcribed and read out, as I do not choose to allow the power of judging and deciding upon the reputation or character of a senator to rest with any single indvidual. I shall fill up the places of those who are dead in such a way as to make it clear that preference is given to rank and not to persons."

After the names of the old senate had been read out, Fabius began his selection. The first chosen were men who, subsequent to the censorship of L. Æmilius and C. Flaminius, had filled a curule office, but were not yet in the senate, and they were taken according to the order of their previous appointments. They were followed by those who had been ædiles, tribunes of the plebs, or quaestors. Last of all came those who had not held office, but had the spoils of an enemy set up in their houses or had received a " civic crown." In this way 177 names were added to the senatorial roll, amidst general approbation. Having completed his task he at once laid down his Dictatorship and descended from the rostra as a private citizen. He ordered the lictors to cease their attendance and mingled with the throng of citizens who were transacting their private business, deliberately idling his time away in order that he might not take the people out of the Forum to escort him home. The public interest in him, however, did not slacken through their having to wait, and a large crowd escorted him to his house.

The following night the consul made his way back to the army, without letting the senate know, as he did not want to be detained in the City for the elections.

XXIV. The next day the senate, on being consulted by M. Pomponius, the praetor, passed a decree to write to the

Dictator[9] asking him, if the interests of the State permitted, to come to Rome to conduct the election of fresh consuls. He was to bring with him his Master of the Horse and M. Marcellus, the praetor, so that the senate might learn from them on the spot in what condition the affairs of the Republic were, and form their plans accordingly. On receiving the summons they all came, after leaving officers in command of the legions.

The Dictator spoke briefly and modestly about himself; he gave most of the credit to Tiberius Sempronius Gracchus, his Master of the Horse, and then gave notice of the elections. The consuls elected were L. Postumius for the third time—he was elected in his absence, as he was then administering the province of Gaul—and Ti. Sempronius Gracchus, Master of the Horse, and at that time curule ædile also. Then the praetors were elected. They were M. Valerius Laevinus, for the second time, Appius Claudius Pulcher, Q. Fulvius Flaccus, and Q. Mucius Scaevola. After the various magistrates had been elected the Dictator returned to his army in winter quarters at Teanum. The Master of the Horse was left in Rome; as he would be entering upon office in a few days, it was desirable for him to consult the senate about the enrolment and equipment of the armies for the year.

L. Postumius and his Army lost in Gaul.—While these matters were engrossing attention a fresh disaster was announced, for Fortune was heaping one disaster upon another this year. It was reported that L. Postumius, the consul elect, and his army had been annihilated in Gaul. There was a wild forest called by the Gauls Litana, and through this the consul was to conduct his army. The Gauls cut through the trees on both sides of the road in such a way that they remained standing as long as they were undisturbed, but a slight pressure would make them fall. Postumius had two Roman legions, and he had also levied a force from the country bordering on the Upper Sea, sufficiently large to bring the force with which he entered the hostile territory up to 25,000 men. The Gauls had posted themselves round the outskirts of the forest, and as soon as the Roman army entered they pushed the sawn trees on the outside, these fell upon those next to them, which were tottering and hardly able to stand upright, until the whole mass fell in on both sides and buried in one common ruin arms and men and horses. Hardly ten men escaped, for when most of them had been crushed to death by the trunks or broken branches of the trees, the remainder, panic-struck at the unexpected disaster, were killed by the

Gauls who surrounded the forest. Out of the whole number only very few were made prisoners, and these, whilst trying to reach a bridge over the river, were intercepted by the Gauls who had already seized it. It was there that Postumius fell whilst fighting most desperately to avoid capture. The Boii stripped the body of its spoils and cut off the head, and bore them in triumph to the most sacred of their temples. According to their custom they cleaned out the skull and covered the scalp with beaten gold; it was then used as a vessel for libations and also as a drinking cup for the priest and ministers of the temple. The plunder, too, which the Gauls secured was as great as their victory, for although most of the animals had been buried beneath the fallen trees, the rest of the booty, not having been scattered in flight, was found strewn along the whole line where the army lay.

XXV. *Preparations for continuing the War.*—When the news of this disaster arrived the whole community was in such a state of alarm that the shops were shut up and a solitude like that of night pervaded the City. Under these circumstances the senate instructed the ædiles to make a round of the City and order the citizens to re-open their shops and lay aside the aspect of public mourning. Ti. Sempronius then convened the senate, and addressed them in a consolatory and encouraging tone. "We," he said, "who were not crushed by the overthrow at Cannae must not lose heart at smaller calamities. If we are successful, as I trust we shall be, in our operations against Hannibal and the Carthaginians, we can safely leave the war with the Gauls out of account for the present; the gods and the Roman people will have it in their power to avenge that act of treachery. It is with regard to the Carthaginians and the armies with which the war is to be carried on that we have now to deliberate and decide." He first gave details as to the strength of infantry and cavalry, and the proportion in each of Roman and allied troops, which made up the Dictator's army; Marcellus followed with similar details as to his own force. Then inquiry was made of those who were acquainted with the facts as to the strength of the force with C. Terentius Varro in Apulia. No practical method suggested itself for bringing up the two consular armies to sufficient strength for such an important war. So in spite of the justifiable resentment which was generally felt they decided to discontinue the campaign in Gaul for that year.

The Dictator's army was assigned to the consul. It was decided that those of Marcellus' troops who were involved in

the flight from Cannae should be transported to Sicily to serve
there as long as the war continued in Italy. All the least efficient in the Dictator's army were also to be removed there, no
period of service being fixed in their case, except that they
must each serve out their time. The two legions raised in the
City were allocated to the other consul who should succeed
L. Postumius; and it was arranged that he should be elected as
soon as favourable auspices could be obtained. The two legions
in Sicily were to be recalled at the earliest possible moment, and
the consul to whom the legions from the City had been assigned
was to take out of those what men he required. C. Terentius
had his command extended for another year, and no reduction
was to be made in the army with which he was protecting Apulia.

XXVI. *The War in Spain.*—Whilst these preparations were
going on in Italy, the war in Spain was being carried on with as
much energy as ever and, so far, in favour of the Romans. The
two Scipios, Publius and Cnaeus, had divided their forces between
them, Cnaeus was to operate on land and Publius by sea. Hasdrubal, the Carthaginian commander, did not feel himself
strong enough in either arm, and kept himself safe by taking up
strong positions at a distance from the enemy; until, in response
to his many earnest appeals for reinforcements, 4000 infantry
and 1000 cavalry were sent to him from Africa. Then, recovering his confidence, he moved nearer the enemy, and gave orders
for the fleet to be put into readiness to protect the islands and the
coast. In the very middle of his preparations for a fresh campaign he was dismayed by news of the desertion of the naval
captains. After they had been heavily censured for their
cowardice in abandoning the fleet at the Ebro they had never
been very loyal either to their general or to the cause of Carthage.
These deserters had started an agitation amongst the tribe of the
Tartesii and had induced several cities to revolt, and one they
had actually taken by storm. The war was now diverted from
the Romans to this tribe, and Hasdrubal entered their territories
with an invading army. Chalbus, a distinguished general
amongst them, was encamped with a strong force before the
walls of a city which he had captured a few days before, and
Hasdrubal determined to attack him. He sent forward skirmishers to draw the enemy into an engagement and told off a
part of his cavalry to lay waste the surrounding country and
pick up stragglers. There was confusion in the camp and panic
and bloodshed in the fields, but when they had regained the
camp from all directions their fears so suddenly left them that

they became emboldened, not only to defend their camp, but even to take the aggressive against the enemy. They burst in a body out of their camp, executing war dances after their manner, and this unexpected daring on their part carried terror into the hearts of the enemy, who had shortly before been challenging them. Hasdrubal thereupon withdrew his force to a fairly lofty hill, which was also protected by a river which served as a barrier. He retired his skirmishers and his scattered cavalry also to this same position. Not, however, feeling sufficiently protected by either hill or river he strongly entrenched himself. Several skirmishes took place between the two sides who were alternately frightening and fearing each other, and the Numidian trooper proved to be no match for the Spaniard, nor were the darts of the Moor very effective against the ox-hide shields of the natives, who were quite as rapid in their movements and possessed more strength and courage.

XXVII. When they found that though they rode up to the Carthaginian lines they could not entice the enemy into action, whilst an attack upon the camp was a far from easy matter, they successfully assaulted the town of Ascua, where Hasdrubal had stored his corn and other supplies on entering their territories, and became masters of all the country round.

Now there was no longer any discipline amongst them, whether on the march or in camp. Hasdrubal soon became aware of this, and seeing that success had made them careless, he urged his men to attack them whilst they were scattered away from their standards; he himself meanwhile descended from the hill and marched with his men in attack formation straight to their camp. News of his approach was brought by men rushing in from the look-out stations and outposts and there was a general call to arms. As each man seized his weapons he hurried with the others into battle, without order or formation, or word of command or standards. The foremost of them were already engaged, whilst others were still running up in small groups and some had not yet left the camp. Their reckless daring, however, at first checked the enemy, but soon, finding that whilst loose and scattered themselves, they were charging an enemy in close formation, and that their scanty numbers imperilled their safety, they looked round at one another, and as they were being repulsed in every direction they formed a square. Standing close together with their shields touching they were gradually driven into such a close mass that they had hardly room to use their weapons, and for a great part of the day were simply cut down by the enemy who completely surrounded them. A very few cut their way out and made for the woods and hills. The camp was abandoned in the same panic and the whole tribe made their surrender the following day.

But they did not remain quiet long, for just after this battle an order was received from Carthage for Hasdrubal to lead his army as soon as he could into Italy. This became generally known throughout Spain and the result was that there was a universal feeling in favour of Rome. Hasdrubal at once sent a despatch to Carthage pointing out what mischief the mere rumour of his departure had caused, and also that if he did really leave Spain it would pass into the hands of the Romans before he crossed the Ebro. He went on to say that not only had he neither a force nor a general to leave in his place, but the Roman generals were men whom he found it difficult to oppose even when his strength was equal to theirs. If, therefore, they were at all anxious to retain Spain they should send a man with a powerful army to succeed him, and even though all went well with his successor he would not find it an easy province to govern.

XXVIII. Although this despatch made a great impression on the senate, they decided that as Italy demanded their first and closest attention, the arrangements about Hannibal and his forces must not be altered. Himilco was sent with a large and well-appointed army and an augmented fleet to hold and defend Spain by sea and land. As soon as he had brought his military and naval forces across he formed an entrenched camp, hauled his ships up on the beach and surrounded them with a rampart. After providing for the safety of his force he started with a picked body of cavalry, and marching as rapidly as possible, and being equally on the alert whether passing through doubtful or through hostile tribes, succeeded in reaching Hasdrubal. After laying before him the resolutions and instructions of the senate and being in his turn shown in what way the war was to be managed in Spain, he returned to his camp. He owed his safety most of all to the speed at which he travelled, for he had got clear of each tribe before they had time for any united action.

Before Hasdrubal commenced his march, he levied contributions on all the tribes under his rule, for he was quite aware that Hannibal had secured a passage through some tribes by paying for it, and had obtained his Gaulish auxiliaries simply by hiring them. To commence such a march without money would hardly bring him to the Alps. The contributions were therefore hurriedly called in and after receiving them he marched down to the Ebro.

When the resolutions of the Carthaginians and Hasdrubal's march were reported to the Roman generals, the two Scipios at once put aside all other matters and made preparations to meet him at the outset with their joint forces and stop his further progress. They believed that if Hannibal, who single-handed was almost too much for Italy, were joined by such a general as Hasdrubal and his Spanish army it would mean the end of the Roman empire. With so much to make them anxious they concentrated their forces at the Ebro and crossed the river. They deliberated for some considerable time as to whether they should meet him, army against army, or whether it would be enough for them to hinder his proposed march by attacking the tribes in alliance with the Carthaginians. The latter plan seemed the best, and they made preparations for attacking a city which from its proximity to the river was called Hibera, the wealthiest city in that country. As soon as Hasdrubal became aware of this, instead of going to the assistance of his allies he proceeded to attack a city which had recently put itself under the protection of Rome. On this the Romans abandoned the siege which they had begun and turned their arms against Hasdrubal himself.

XXIX. *Hasdrubal completely Defeated*.—For some days they remained encamped at a distance of about five miles from each other, and though frequent skirmishes took place there was no general action. At last on the same day, as though by previous agreement, the signal was given on both sides and they descended with their entire forces on to the plain. The Roman line was in three divisions. Some of the light infantry were posted between the leading ranks of the legions, the rest amongst those behind; the cavalry closed the wings. Hasdrubal strengthened his centre with his Spaniards, on the right wing he posted the Carthaginians, on the left the Africans and the mercenaries, the Numidian horse he stationed in front of the Carthaginian infantry, and the rest of the cavalry in front of the Africans. Not all the Numidian horse, however, were on the right wing, but only those who were trained to manage two horses at the same time like circus-riders and, when the battle was at the hottest, were in the habit of jumping off the wearied horse on to the fresh one, such were the agility of the riders and the docility of the horses.

These were the dispositions on each side, and whilst the two armies were standing ready to engage, their commanders felt almost equally confident of victory, for neither side was much superior to the other either in the numbers or the quality of the troops. With the men themselves it was far otherwise. Though the Romans were fighting far away from their homes their generals had no difficulty in making them realise that they were fighting for Italy and for Rome. They knew that it hung upon the issue of that fight whether they were to see their homes again or not, and they resolutely determined either to conquer or to die. The other army possessed nothing like the same determination, for they were most of them natives of Spain and would rather be defeated in Spain than win the victory and be dragged to Italy. At the first onset, almost before they had hurled their javelins, the centre gave ground, and when the Romans came on in a tremendous charge they turned and fled. The brunt of the fighting now fell upon the wings; the Carthaginians pressed forward on the right, the Africans on the left, and slowly wheeling round attacked the advancing Roman infantry on both flanks. But the whole force had now concentrated on the centre, and forming front in both directions beat back the attack on their flanks. So two separate actions were going on. The Romans, having already repulsed Hasdrubal's centre, and having the advantage as regarded both the numbers and the strength of their men, proved themselves undoubtedly superior on both fronts. A very large number of the enemy fell in these two attacks, and had not their centre taken to hasty flight almost before the battle began, very few would have survived out of their whole army. The cavalry took no part whatever in the fighting, for no sooner did the Moors and Numidians see the centre of the line giving way than they fled precipitately, leaving the wings exposed, and even driving the elephants before them. Hasdrubal waited to see the final issue of the battle and then escaped out of the slaughter with a few followers. The camp was seized and plundered by the Romans. This battle secured for Rome all the tribes who were wavering and deprived Hasdrubal of all hopes of taking his army to Italy or even of remaining with anything like safety in Spain. When the contents of the despatch from the Scipios was made known in Rome, the gratification felt was not so much on account of the victory as that Hasdrubal's march into Italy was at an end.

XXX. *Events in Italy.*—During these incidents in Spain, Petelia in Bruttium was taken by Himilco, one of Hannibal's lieutenants, after a siege which lasted several months. That

victory cost the Carthaginians heavy losses in both killed and
wounded, for the defenders only yielded after they had been
starved out. They had consumed all their corn and eaten every
kind of animal whether ordinarily used as food or not, and at
last kept themselves alive by eating leather and grass and roots
and the soft bark of trees and leaves picked from shrubs. It
was not until they had no longer strength to stand on the walls
or to bear the weight of their armour that they were subdued.

After the capture of Petelia the Carthaginian marched his
army to Consentia. The defence here was less obstinate and
the place surrendered in a few days.

About the same time an army of Bruttians invested the Greek
city of Croton. At one time this city had been a military power,
but it had been overtaken by so many and such serious reverses
that its whole population was now reduced to less than 2000 souls.
The enemy found no difficulty in gaining possession of a city so
denuded of defenders; the citadel alone was held, after some
had sought refuge there from the massacre and confusion which
followed the capture of the city. Locri also went over to the
Bruttians and Carthaginians after the aristocracy of the city
had betrayed the populace. The people of Rhegium alone in
all that country remained loyal to the Romans and kept their
independence to the end.

The same change of feeling extended to Sicily and even the
house of Hiero did not altogether shrink from deserting Rome.
Gelo, the eldest son of the family, treating with equal contempt
his aged father and the alliance with Rome, after the defeat of
Cannae, went over to the Carthaginians. He was arming the
natives and making friendly overtures to the cities in alliance
with Rome and would have brought about a revolution in Sicily
had he not been removed by the hand of death, a death so opportune that it cast suspicion even on his father.

Such were the serious occurrences in Italy, Africa, Sicily, and
Spain during the year (216 B.C.).

Towards the close of the year Q. Fabius Maximus asked the
senate to allow him to dedicate the temple of Venus Erycina
which he had vowed when Dictator. The senate passed a
decree that Tiberius Sempronius the consul - elect should immediately upon his entering office propose a resolution to the
people [10] that Q. Fabius be one of the two commissioners appointed to dedicate the temple. After the death of M. Æmilius
Lepidus, who had been augur and twice consul, his three sons,
Lucius, Marcus, and Quintus, celebrated funeral games in his

honour for three days and exhibited twenty-two pairs of gladiators in the Forum.

The curule ædiles, C. Laetorius and Ti. Sempronius Gracchus, consul elect, who during his ædileship had been Master of the Horse, celebrated the Roman Games; the celebration lasted three days. The Plebeian Games given by the ædiles Marcus Aurelius Cotta and Marcus Claudius Marcellus were solemnised three times.

The third year of the Punic war had run its course when Ti. Sempronius entered on his consulship on March 15. The praetors were Q. Fulvius Flaccus, who had been previously censor and twice consul, and M. Valerius Laevinus; the former exercised jurisdiction over citizens, the latter over foreigners. App. Claudius Pulcher had the province of Sicily allotted to him, Q. Mucius Scaevola that of Sardinia. The people made an order investing M. Marcellus with the powers of a proconsul, because he was the only one out of the Roman commanders who had gained any successes in Italy since the disaster at Cannae.

XXXI. *Preparations for War.* — The first day the senate met for business at the Capitol they passed a decree that the war-tax for that year should be doubled, and that half the whole amount should be collected at once to furnish pay for all the soldiers, except those who had been present at Cannae. As regarded the armies they decreed that Ti. Sempronius should fix a day on which the two City legions were to muster at Cales, and that they should march from there to Claudius' camp above Suessula. The legions there, mostly made up from the army which fought at Cannae, were to be transferred by App. Claudius Pulcher to Sicily and the legions in Sicily were to be brought to Rome. M. Claudius Marcellus was sent to take command of the army which had been ordered to assemble at Cales and he received orders to conduct it to Claudius' camp. Ti. Maecilius Croto was sent by App. Claudius to take over the lod army and conduct it to Sicily.

At first people waited in silent expectation for the consul to hold an Assembly for the election of a colleague, but when they saw that M. Marcellus, whom they particularly wished to have as consul this year after his brilliant success as praetor, was kept out of the way, murmurs began to be heard in the Senate-house. When the consul became aware of this he said, " It is to the interest of the State, senators, that M. Claudius has gone into Campania to effect the exchange of armies, and it is equally to

the interest of the State that notice of election should not be
given until he has discharged the commission entrusted to him
and returned home, so that you may have for your consul the
man whom the circumstances of the republic call for and whom
you most of all wish for.'' After this nothing more was said
about the election till Marcellus returned.

Meanwhile the two commissioners were appointed for the
dedication of temples: T. Otacilius Crassus dedicated the temple
to Mens, Q. Fabius Maximus the one to Venus Erycina.   Both
are on the Capitol, separated only by a water channel.   In the
case of the three hundred Campanian knights, who after loyally
serving their time in Sicily had now come to Rome, a proposal
was made to the people that they should receive the full rights
of Roman citizenship and should be entered on the roll of the
burghers of Cumae, reckoning from the day previous to the
revolt of the Campanians from Rome.   The main reason for
this proposal was their declaration that they did not know to
what people they belonged, as they had abandoned their old
country and had not yet been admitted as citizens into that to
which they had returned.

On Marcellus' return from the army notice was given of the
election of a consul in the place of L. Postumius.   Marcellus
was elected by a quite unanimous vote in order that he might
take up his magistracy at once.   Whilst he was assuming the
duties of the consulship thunder was heard; the augurs were
summoned and gave it as their opinion that there was some
informality in his election.   The patricians spread a report that
as that was the first time that two plebeian consuls were
elected together, the gods were showing their displeasure.
Marcellus resigned his office and Q. Fabius Maximus was
appointed in his place; this was his third consulship.

This year the sea appeared to be on fire; at Sinuessa a cow
brought forth a colt; the statues in the temple of Juno Sospita
at Lanuvium sweated blood and a shower of stones fell round
the temple.   For this portent there were the usual nine
days' religious observances; the other portents were duly
expiated.

XXXII. The consuls divided the armies between them; the
army at Teanum which M. Junius the Dictator had been commanding passed to Fabius, Sempronius took command of the
volunteer slaves there and 25,000 troops furnished by the
allies; the legions which had returned from Sicily were assigned
to M. Valerius the praetor; M. Claudius was sent to the army

which was in camp above Suessa to protect Nola; the praetors went to their respective provinces in Sicily and Sardinia.

The consuls issued a notice that whenever the senate was summoned the senators and all who had the right of speaking in the senate should meet at the Capena gate. The praetors whose duty it was to hear cases set up their tribunals near the public bathing place [11] and ordered all litigants to answer to their recognisances at that place, and there they administered justice during the year.

In the meanwhile the news was brought to Carthage that things had gone badly in Spain and that almost all the communities in that country had gone over to Rome. Mago, Hannibal's brother, was preparing to transport to Italy a force of 12,000 infantry, 1500 cavalry, and 20 elephants, escorted by a fleet of 60 war-ships. On the receipt of this news, however, some were in favour of Mago, with such a fleet and army as he had, going to Spain instead of Italy, but whilst they were deliberating there was a sudden gleam of hope that Sardinia might be recovered. They were told that " there was only a small Roman army there, the old praetor, A. Cornelius, who knew the province well, was leaving and a fresh one was expected; the Sardinians, too, were tired of their long subjection, and during the last twelve months the government had been harsh and rapacious and had crushed them with a heavy tax and an unfair exaction of corn. Nothing was wanting but a leader to head their revolt." This report was brought by some secret agents from their leaders, the prime mover in the matter being Hampsicora, the most influential and wealthy man amongst them at that time. Perturbed by the news from Spain, and at the same time elated by the Sardinian report, they sent Mago with his fleet and army to Spain and selected Hasdrubal to conduct the operations in Sardinia, assigning to him a force about as large as the one they had furnished to Mago.[12]

After they had transacted all the necessary business in Rome the consuls began to prepare for war. Ti. Sempronius gave his soldiers notice of the date when they were to assemble at Sinuessa, and Q. Fabius, after previously consulting the senate, issued a proclamation warning every one to convey the corn from their fields into the fortified cities by the first day of the following June, all those who failed to do so would have their land laid waste, their farms burnt, and they themselves would be sold into slavery. Even the praetors who had been appointed to administer the law were not exempted from military duties. It was decided that

Valerius should be sent to Apulia to take over the army from
Terentius: when the legions came from Sicily he was to employ
them mainly for the defence of that district and send the army
of Terentius under one of his lieutenants to Tarentum. A fleet
of twenty-five vessels was also supplied him for the protection of
the coast between Brundisium and Tarentum. A fleet of equal
strength was assigned to Q. Fulvius, the praetor in charge of the
City, for the defence of the coast near Rome. C. Terentius, as
proconsul, was commissioned to raise a force in the territory of
Picenum to defend that part of the country. Lastly, T. Otacilius Crassus was despatched to Sicily, after he had dedicated
the temple of Mens, with full powers as propraetor to take
command of the fleet.

XXXIII. *Alliance between Hannibal and Philip, King of
Macedon.*—This struggle between the most powerful nations in
the world was attracting the attention of all men, kings and
peoples alike, and especially of Philip, the King of Macedon, as
he was comparatively near to Italy, separated from it only
by the Ionian Sea. When he first heard the rumour of Hannibal's passage of the Alps, delighted as he was at the outbreak
of war between Rome and Carthage, he was still undecided,
till their relative strength had been tested, which of the two
he would prefer to have the victory. But after the third battle
had been fought and the victory rested with the Carthaginians
for the third time, he inclined to the side which Fortune favoured
and sent ambassadors to Hannibal. Avoiding the ports of
Brundisium and Tarentum which were guarded by Roman
ships, they landed near the temple of Juno Lacinia. Whilst
traversing Apulia on their way to Capua they fell into the
midst of the Roman troops who were defending the district,
and were conducted to Valerius Laevinus, the praetor, who was
encamped near Luceria. Xenophanes, the head of the legation,
explained, without the slightest fear or hesitation, that he had
been sent by the king to form a league of friendship with Rome,
and that he was conveying his instructions to the consuls and
senate and people. Amidst the defection of so many old allies,
the praetor was delighted beyond measure at the prospect of a
new alliance with so illustrious a monarch, and gave his enemies
a most hospitable reception. He assigned them an escort, and
pointed out carefully what route they should take, what places
and passes were held by the Romans and what by the enemy.
Xenophanes passed through the Roman troops into Campania
and thence by the nearest route reached Hannibal's camp.

He made a treaty of friendship with him on these terms: King Philip was to sail to Italy with as large a fleet as possible—he was, it appears, intending to fit out two hundred ships—and ravage the coast, and carry on war by land and sea to the utmost of his power; when the war was over the whole of Italy, including Rome itself, was to be the possession of the Carthaginians and Hannibal, and all the plunder was to go to Hannibal; when the Carthaginians had thoroughly subdued Italy they were to sail to Greece and make war upon such nations as the king wished; the cities on the mainland and the islands lying off Macedonia were to form part of Philip's kingdom.

XXXIV. These were, in effect, the terms on which the treaty was concluded between the Carthaginian general and the King of Macedon. On their return the envoys were accompanied by commissioners sent by Hannibal to obtain the king's ratification of the treaty: they were Gisgo, Bostar, and Mago. They reached the spot near the temple of Juno Lacinia, where they had left their ship moored in a hidden creek, and set sail for Greece. When they were out to sea they were descried by the Roman fleet which was guarding the Calabrian coast. Valerius Flaccus sent some light boats to chase and bring back the strange vessel. At first the king's men attempted flight, but finding that they were being overhauled they surrendered to the Romans. When they were brought before the admiral of the fleet he questioned them as to who they were, where they had come from, and whither they were sailing. Xenophanes, who had so far been very lucky, began to make up a tale; he said that he had been sent by Philip to Rome and had succeeded in reaching M. Valerius, as he was the only person he could get to safely; he had not been able to go through Campania as it was beset by the enemy's troops. Then the Carthaginian dress and manner of Hannibal's agents aroused suspicion, and on being questioned their speech betrayed them. Their comrades were at once taken aside and terrified by threats, a letter from Hannibal to Philip was discovered, and also the articles of agreement between the King of Macedon and the Carthaginian general. When the investigation was completed, it seemed best to carry the prisoners and their companions as soon as possible to the senate at Rome or to the consuls, wherever they were. Five of the swiftest ships were selected for the purpose and L. Valerius Antias was placed in charge of the expedition with instructions to distribute the envoys amongst the ships under guard and to be careful that no conversation was allowed amongst them or any communication of plans.

During this time A. Cornelius Mammula on leaving his province made a report on the condition of Sardinia. All, he said, were contemplating war and revolt; Q. Mucius, who had succeeded him, had been affected by the unhealthy climate and impure water and had fallen into an illness which was tedious rather than dangerous, and would make him for some considerable time unfit to bear the responsibilities of war. The army, too, which was quartered there, though strong enough for the occupation of a peaceable province, was quite inadequate for the war which seemed likely to break out. The senate made a decree that Q. Fulvius Flaccus should raise a force of 5000 infantry and 400 cavalry and arrange for its immediate transport to Sardinia, and further that he should send whom he considered the most suitable man, invested with full powers, to conduct operations until Mucius recovered his health. He selected T. Manlius Torquatus, who had been twice consul as well as censor, and during his consulship had subdued the Sardinians.

About the same time a Carthaginian fleet which had been despatched to Sardinia under the command of Hasdrubul, surnamed " the Bald," was caught in a storm and driven on the Balearic Isles. So much damage was caused, not only to the rigging but also to the hulls, that the vessels were hauled ashore and a considerable time was spent in repairing them.

XXXV. *The Campanians unsuccessfully attempt Cumae.*—In Italy the war had been less vigorously conducted since the battle of Cannae; for the strength of the one side was broken and the temper of the other enervated. Under these circumstances the Campanians made an attempt by themselves to become masters of Cumae. They first tried persuasion, but as they could not succeed in inducing them to revolt from Rome, they decided to employ stratagem. All the Campanians held a sacrificial service at stated intervals at Hamae. They informed the Cumans that the Campanian senate was going there, and they asked the Cuman senate also to be present in order to come to a common understanding, so that both peoples might have the same allies and the same enemies. They also promised that they would have an armed force there, to guard against any danger from either Romans or Carthaginians. Although the Cumans suspected a plot, they made no difficulty

about going, for they thought that by thus consenting they
would be able to conceal a manœuvre of their own.

The consul Tiberius Sempronius had in the meanwhile purified
his army at Sinuessa,[13] the appointed rendezvous, and after
crossing the Vulturnus pitched his camp near Liternum. As
there was nothing for them to do in camp, he put his men
through frequent war manœuvres to accustom the recruits, most
of whom were volunteer slaves, to follow the standards and
know their places in the ranks when in action. In carrying
out these exercises, the general's main object—and he had given
similar instructions to the officers—was that there should be
no class-feeling in the ranks, through the slaves being twitted
with their former condition; the old soldiers were to regard
themselves as on a perfect equality with the recruits, the free
men with the slaves; all to whom Rome had entrusted her
standards and her arms were to be regarded as equally honourable, equally well-born; Fortune had compelled them to adopt
this state of things, and now that it was adopted she compelled
them to acquiesce to it. The soldiers were quite as anxious to
obey these instructions as the officers were to enforce them, and
in a short time the men had become so fused together that it
was almost forgotten what condition of life each man had been
in before he became a soldier.

While Gracchus was thus occupied messengers from Cumae
informed him of the proposals made by the Campanians a few
days previously and of their reply, and that the festival was to
be held in three days' time, when not only the whole senate
would be there but also the Campanian army in camp. Gracchus gave the Cumans orders to remove everything from their
fields into the city and to remain within their walls, whilst he
himself moved his camp to Cumae the day before the Campanians
were to perform their sacrifice. Hamae was about three miles
distant. The Campanians had already, as arranged, assembled
there in large numbers and not far away Marius Alfius, the
" Medixtuticus " (the chief magistrate of the Campanians),
was secretly encamped with 14,000 troops, but he was more
intent on making preparations for the sacrifice and the stratagem he was to execute during its performance than on fortifying
his camp or any other military duty. The ceremonial took place
at night and was over by midnight. Gracchus thought this
the best time for his purpose, and after stationing guards at
the camp gate to prevent any one from conveying information
of his design, he ordered his men to refresh themselves and get

what sleep they could at four o'clock in the afternoon so that they might be ready to assemble round the standards as soon as it was dark. About the first watch he ordered the advance to be made and the army marched in silence to Hamae, which they reached at midnight. The Campanian camp, as might be expected during a nocturnal festival, was negligently guarded, and he made a simultaneous attack on all sides of it. Some were slain whilst stretched in slumber, others whilst returning unarmed after the ceremony. In the confusion and terror of the night more than 2000 men were killed, including their general, Marius Alfius, and 34 standards seized.

XXXVI. After getting possession of the enemies' camp with a loss of less than 100 men, Gracchus speedily retired, fearing an attack from Hannibal, who had his camp at Tifata, overlooking Capua. Nor were his anticipations groundless. No sooner had the news of the disaster reached Capua than Hannibal, expecting to find at Hamae an army, composed mostly of raw recruits and slaves, wildly delighted at their victory, despoiling their vanquished foes and carrying off the plunder, hurried on with all speed past Capua, and ordered all the Campanian fugitives he met to be escorted to Capua and the wounded to be carried there in wagons. But when he got to Hamae he found the camp abandoned, nothing was to be seen but the traces of the recent slaughter and the bodies of his allies lying about everywhere. Some advised him to march straight to Cumae and attack the place. Nothing would have suited his wishes better for, after his failure to secure Neapolis, he was very anxious to get possession of Cumae that he might have one maritime city at all events. As, however, his soldiers in their hurried march had brought nothing with them beyond their arms he returned to his camp on Tifata. The next day, yielding to the importunities of the Campanians, he marched back to Cumae with all the necessary appliances for attacking the city, and after effectually devastating the neighbourhood, fixed his camp at the distance of one mile from the place. Gracchus still remained in occupation of Cumae, more because he was ashamed to desert the allies who were imploring his protection and that of the Roman people than because he felt sufficiently assured as to his army. The other consul, Fabius, who was encamped at Cales, did not venture to cross the Vulturnus; his attention was occupied first with taking fresh auspices and then with the portents which were being announced one after another, and which the soothsayers assured him would be very difficult to avert.

XXXVII. Whilst these causes kept Fabius from moving, Sempronius was invested, and the siege works were now actually in operation. A huge wooden tower on wheels had been brought up against the walls and the Roman consul constructed another still higher upon the wall itself, which was fairly high and which served as a platform, after he had placed stout beams across. The besieged garrison protected the walls of the city by hurling stones and sharpened stakes and other missiles from their tower; at last when they saw the other tower brought up to the walls they flung blazing brands over it and caused a large fire. Terrified by the conflagration the crowd of soldiers in it flung themselves down and at the same moment a sortie was made from two of the gates, the outposts of the enemy were overpowered and driven in flight to their camp, so that for that day the Carthaginians were more like a besieged than a besieging force. As many as 1300 Carthaginians were killed and 59 taken prisoners who had been surprised while standing careless and unconcerned round the walls or at the outposts, and least of all fearing a sortie. Before the enemy had time to recover from their panic Gracchus gave the signal to retire and withdrew with his men inside the walls. The following day, Hannibal, expecting that the consul, elated with his success, would be prepared to fight a regular battle, formed his line on the ground between his camp and the city; when, however, he saw that not a single man moved from his usual post of defence and that no risks were being taken through rash confidence, he returned to Tifata without accomplishing anything.

Just at the time when the siege of Cumae was raised Ti. Sempronius, surnamed "Longus," fought a successful action with the Carthaginian Hanno at Grumentum in Lucania. Over 2000 were killed, 280 men and 41 military standards were captured. Driven out of Lucania, Hanno retreated to Bruttium. Amongst the Hirpini, also, three towns which had revolted from Rome, Vercellium, Vescellium, and Sicilinum, were retaken by the praetor M. Valerius, and the authors of the revolt beheaded. Over 5000 prisoners were sold, the rest of the booty was presented to the soldiers, and the army marched back to Luceria.

XXXVIII. During these incidents amongst the Lucanians and Hirpini, the five ships which were carrying the Macedonian and Carthaginian agents to Rome, after sailing almost round the whole of Italy in their passage from the upper to the lower sea were off Cumae, when Gracchus, uncertain whether they belonged to friends or foes, sent vessels from his own fleet to intercept them. After mutual questionings those on board learnt that the consul was at Cumae. The vessels accordingly were brought into the harbour and the prisoners were brought before the consul and the letters placed in his hands. He read the letters of Philip and Hannibal through and sent everything under seal by land to the senate, the agents he ordered to be taken by sea. The letters and the agents both reached Rome the same day, and when it was ascertained that what the agents said in their examination agreed with the letters, the senate were filled with very gloomy apprehensions. They recognised what a heavy burden a war with Macedon would impose upon them at a time when it was all they could do to bear the weight of the Punic war. They did not, however, so far give way to despondency as not to enter at once upon a discussion as to how they could divert the enemy from Italy by themselves commencing hostilities against him. Orders were given for the agents to be kept in chains and their companions to be sold as slaves; they also decided to equip twenty vessels in addition to the twenty-five which P. Valerius Flaccus already had under his command. After these had been fitted out and launched, the five ships which had carried the agents were added and thirty vessels left Ostia for Tarentum. Publius Valerius was instructed to place on board the soldiers which had belonged to Varro's army and which were now at Tarentum under the command of L. Apustius, and with his combined fleet of fifty-five vessels he was not only to protect the coast of Italy but try to obtain information about the hostile attitude of Macedon. If Philip's designs should prove to correspond to the captured despatches and the statements of the agents, he was to write to Marcus Valerius, the praetor, to that effect and then, after placing his army under the command of L. Apustius, go to the fleet at Tarentum and sail across to Macedonia at the first opportunity and do his utmost to confine Philip within his own dominions. A decree was made that the money which had been sent to Appius Claudius in Sicily to be returned to King Hiero should now be devoted to the maintenance of the fleet and the expenses of the Macedonian war, and it was conveyed to Tarentum through L. Antistius. Two hundred thousand *modii* of wheat and barley were sent at the same time by King Hiero.

XXXIX. While these various steps were being taken, one of the captured ships which were on their way to Rome escaped during the voyage to Philip, and he then learnt that his agents had been captured together with his despatches. As he did not know what understanding they had come to with Hannibal, or what proposals Hannibal's agents were bringing to him, he despatched a second embassy with the same instructions. Their names were Heraclitus, surnamed Scotinus, Crito of Boeotia, and Sositheus the Magnesian. They accomplished their mission successfully, but the summer passed away before the king could attempt any active measures. So important was the seizure of that one ship with the king's agents on board in delaying the outbreak of the war which now threatened Rome!

Fabius at last succeeded in expiating the portents and crossed the Vulturnus; both consuls now resumed the campaign round Capua. Combulteria, Trebula, and Austicula, all of which had revolted to Hannibal, were successfully attacked by Fabius, and the garrisons which Hannibal had placed in them as well as a large number of Campanians were made prisoners. At Nola, the senate were on the side of the Romans, as they had been the year before, and the populace, who were on the side of Hannibal, were hatching secret plots for the murder of the aristocrats and the betrayal of the city. To prevent them from carrying out their intentions Fabius marched between Capua and Hannibal's camp on Tifata and established himself in Claudius' camp overlooking Suessula. From there he sent M. Marcellus, who was propraetor, with the force under his command to occupy Nola.

XL. *The Campaign in Sardinia.*—The active operations in Sardinia which had been dropped owing to the serious illness of Q. Mucius were resumed under the direction of T. Manlius. He hauled ashore his war-ships and furnished the seamen and rowers with arms, so that they might be available for service on land; with these and the army he had taken over from the praetor he made up a force of 22,000 infantry and 1200 cavalry. With this combined force he invaded the hostile territory and fixed his camp at no great distance from Hampsicora's lines. Hampsicora himself happened to be absent; he had paid a visit to the Pelliti-Sardinians [14] in order to arm the younger men amongst them so as to increase his own strength. His son Hostus was in command and in the impetuosity of youth he rashly offered battle, with the result that he was defeated and put to flight. 3000 Sardinians were killed in that battle and 800 taken alive; the rest of the army after wandering in their flight through fields and woods heard that their general had fled to a place called

Cornus, the chief town of the district, and thither they directed their flight.

That battle would have finished the war had not the Carthaginian fleet under Hasdrubal, which had been driven by a storm down to the Balearic Isles, arrived in time to revive their hopes of renewing the war. When Manlius heard of its arrival he retired upon Carales, and this gave Hampsicora an opportunity of forming a junction with the Carthaginian. Hasdrubal disembarked his force and sent the ships back to Carthage, and then, under Hampsicora's guidance, proceeded to harry and waste the land belonging to the allies of Rome. He would have gone as far as Carales if Manlius had not met him with his army and checked his widespread ravages. At first the two camps faced each other, with only a small space between; then small sorties and skirmishes took place with varying results; at last it came to a battle, a regular action, which lasted for four hours. For a long time the Carthaginians made the issue doubtful, the Sardinians, who were accustomed to defeat, being easily beaten, but at last when they saw the whole field covered with dead and flying Sardinians they too gave way, but when they turned to flee the Roman wing which had routed the Sardinians wheeled round and hemmed them in. Then it was more of a massacre than a battle. 12,000 of the enemy, Sardinians and Carthaginians, were slain, about 3700 were made prisoners, and 27 military standards were captured.

XLI. What more than anything else made the battle glorious and memorable was the capture of the commander-in-chief, Hasdrubal, and also of Hanno and Mago, two Carthaginian nobles. Mago was a member of the house of Barca, a near relative of Hannibal; Hanno had taken the lead in the Sardinian revolt and was unquestionably the chief instigator of the war. The battle was no less famous for the fate which overtook the Sardinian generals; Hampsicora's son, Hostus, fell on the field, and when Hampsicora, who was fleeing from the carnage with a few horsemen, heard of his son's death, he was so crushed by the tidings, coming as it did on the top of all the other disasters, that in the dead of night, when none could hinder his purpose, he slew himself with his own hand. The rest of the fugitives found shelter as they had done before in Cornus, but Manlius leading his victorious troops against it effected its capture in a few days. On this the other cities which had espoused the cause of Hampsicora and the Carthaginians gave hostages and surrendered to him. He imposed upon each of them a tribute of money and corn; the amount was proportioned to their resources and also to the share they had taken in the revolt. After this he returned to Carales. There the ships which had been hauled ashore were launched, the troops he had brought with him were re-embarked, and he sailed for Rome. On his arrival he reported to the senate the complete subjugation of Sardinia, and made over the money to the quaestors, the corn to the ædiles, and the prisoners to Q. Fulvius, the praetor.

During this time T. Otacilius had crossed with his fleet from Lilybaeum to the coast of Africa and was ravaging the territory of Carthage, when rumours came to him that Hasdrubal had recently sailed from the Balearic Isles to Sardinia. He set sail for that island and fell in with the Carthaginian fleet returning to Africa. A brief action followed on the high seas in which Otacilius took seven ships with their crews. The rest dispersed in a panic far and wide, as though they had been scattered by a storm.

It so happened at this time that Bomilcar arrived at Locri with reinforcements of men and elephants and also with supplies. Appius Claudius intended to surprise him, and with this view he led his army hurriedly to Messana as though he were going to make a circuit of the province, and finding the wind and tide favourable, crossed over to Locri. Bomilcar had already left to join Hanno in Bruttium and the Locrians shut their gates against the Romans; Appius after all his efforts achieved no results and returned to Messana.

The Hirpini and the Samnites appeal to Hannibal for Protection.—This same summer Marcellus made frequent excursions from Nola, which he was holding with a garrison, into the territory of the Hirpini and in the neighbourhood of Samnite Caudium. Such utter devastation did he spread everywhere with fire and sword that he revived throughout Samnium the memory of her ancient disasters.

XLII. Both nations sent envoys simultaneously to Hannibal, who addressed him thus: " We have been the enemies of Rome, Hannibal, from very early times. At first we fought her in our own might as long as our arms, our strength, sufficed to protect us. When we could trust them no more we took our place by the side of King Pyrrhus; when we were abandoned by him we were compelled to accept terms of peace and by those terms we stood for almost fifty years, down to the time of your arrival in Italy. It was your conspicuous courtesy and kindness towards our fellow-countrymen who were your prisoners and whom you sent back to us, quite as much as your courage and success, which have so won our hearts that as long as you, our friend, are safe and prosperous we should not fear—I do not say the Romans, but—even the wrath of heaven, if I may say so without irreverence. But, good heavens! while you are not only safe and victorious but actually here amongst us, when you could almost hear the shrieks of our wives and children and see our blazing houses, we have suffered such repeated devastations this summer that it would seem as if M. Marcellus and not Hannibal had been the victor at Cannae, and as if the Romans had good cause to boast that you have only strength enough for one blow, and that like a bee that has left its sting you are now inert and powerless. For a hundred years we have been at war with Rome and no general, no army from without, has come to our aid save for the two years when Pyrrhus used our soldiers to increase his strength rather than use his strength to defend us. I will not boast of our successes—the two consuls with their armies whom we sent under the yoke, and all the other fortunate or glorious events which we can recall. The trials and sufferings we then went through can be recounted with less bitter feelings than those which are happening to-day. *Then* great Dictators with their Masters of the Horse would invade our borders, two consuls and two consular armies found it necessary to act together against us, and they took every precaution, careful scouting, reserves duly posted, their army in order of battle, when they ravaged our country; *now* we are the prey of a solitary propraetor and a small garrison at Nola! They do not even march in military detachments, but they scour the whole of our country like brigands and more carelessly than if they were roaming about on Roman ground. The reason is simply this: you do not defend us, and our soldiery who could protect us if they were at home are all serving under your standards. I should be utterly ignorant of you and your army if I did not think it an easy task for the man, by whom to my knowledge so many Roman armies have been routed and laid low, to crush these plunderers of our country while they are roving about in disorder and wandering wherever any one is led by hopes of plunder, however futile such hopes may be. They will be the prey of a few Numidians, and you will relieve both us and Nola of its garrison [15] if only you count the men whom you thought worthy of your alliance still worthy of your protection."

XLIII. To all this Hannibal replied: "You Samnites and

Hirpini are doing everything at once; you point out your sufferings and ask for protection and complain of being unprotected and neglected. But you ought to have first made your representations, then asked for protection, and if you did not obtain it then only should you have complained that you had sought help in vain. I shall not lead my army into the country of the Hirpini and Samnites because I do not want to be a burden to you, but I shall march into those districts belonging to the allies of Rome which are nearest to me. By plundering these I shall satisfy and enrich my soldiers and shall frighten the enemy sufficiently to make him leave you alone. As to the war with Rome, if Trasumennus was a more famous battle than the Trebia, if Cannae was more famous than Trasumennus, I shall make even the memory of Cannae fade in the light of a greater and more brilliant victory."

With this reply and with munificent presents he dismissed the envoys, and then leaving a somewhat small detachment on Tifata marched with the rest of his army to Nola, whither Hanno also came with the reinforcements he had brought from Carthage and the elephants. Encamping at no great distance, he found out, on inquiry, that everything was very different from the impression he had received from the envoys. No one who watched Marcellus' proceedings could ever say that he trusted to Fortune or gave the enemy a chance through his rashness. Hitherto his plundering expeditions had been made after careful reconnoitring, with strong supports for the marauding parties and a secure retreat. Now when he became aware of the enemy's approach, he kept his force within the fortifications and ordered the senators of Nola to patrol the ramparts and keep a sharp lookout all round and find out what the enemy were doing.

Hanno had come close up to the walls, and, seeing amongst the senators Herennius Bassus and Herius Pettius, asked for an interview with them. Having obtained permission from Marcellus they went out to him. He addressed them through an interpreter. After magnifying the merits and good fortune of Hannibal and dwelling upon the decaying strength and greatness of Rome, he went on to urge that even if Rome were what she once had been, still men who knew by experience how burdensome the Roman government was to their allies and with what indulgence Hannibal had treated all those of his prisoners who belonged to any Italian nation must surely prefer the alliance and friendship of Carthage to those of Rome. If both the con-

suls and their two armies had been at Nola, they would still be
no more a match for Hannibal than they were at Cannae, how
then could one praetor with a few raw soldiers defend the place?
It was of more importance to them whether the town were taken
or surrendered than it was to Hannibal; he would get possession
of it in any case as he had got possession of Capua and Nuceria.
But what a difference there was between the fate of Capua and
that of Nola, they knew best, situated as they were midway
between the two places. He did not want to prophesy what
would happen to the city if it were captured; he preferred to
pledge his word that if they would give up Marcellus and his
garrison and the city of Nola no one but themselves should
dictate the terms on which they would become allies and friends
of Hannibal.

XLIV. Herennius Bassus briefly replied that the friendship
between Rome and Nola had now lasted many years, and up
to that day neither party had had any reason to regret it. If
they had wished to change their allegiance when the change
came in their fortunes, it was too late to do so now. If they
had thought of surrendering to Hannibal would they have
asked for a Roman garrison? They were in perfect accord with
those who had come to protect them, and they would continue
to be so to the last.

This interview destroyed any expectations Hannibal might
have formed of securing Nola by treachery. He therefore drew
his lines completely round the town so that a simultaneous
attack might be made on all sides. When Marcellus saw that
he was close up to the ramparts, he drew up his men inside
one of the gates and then burst out in a fierce tumultuous
charge. A few were overthrown and killed in the first shock,
but as men ran up into the fighting line and the two sides became more equalised, the contest was beginning to be a severe
one, and few battles would have been more memorable had not
a very heavy storm of rain and wind separated the combatants.
They retired for that day after only a brief encounter but in a
state of great exasperation, the Romans to the city, the Carthaginians to their camp. Of the latter not more than thirty
fell in the first attack; the Romans lost fifty. The rain fell
without any intermission all through the night and continued till
the third hour of the following day, so, though both sides were
eager for battle, they remained that day within their lines. The
following day Hannibal sent part of his force on a plundering
expedition in the Nolan territory. No sooner was Marcellus

aware of it than he formed his line of battle, nor did Hannibal decline the challenge. There was about a mile between his camp and the city, and within that space—it is all level ground round Nola—the armies met. The battle shout raised on both sides brought back the nearest amongst the cohorts who had been sent off to plunder; the Nolans, too, on the other side, took their place in the Roman line. Marcellus addressed a few words of encouragement and thanks to them, and told them to take their station amongst the reserve and help to carry the wounded from the field, they were to keep out of the fighting unless they received the signal from him.

XLV. The battle was obstinately contested; the generals encouraged the men, and the men fought to the utmost of their strength. Marcellus urged his men to press vigorously on those whom they had vanquished only three days ago, who had been driven in flight from Cumae, and whom he had himself, with another army, defeated the year before. " All his forces," he said, " are not in the field, some are roving through the land bent on plunder, whilst those who are fighting are enervated by the luxury of Capua and have worn themselves out through a whole winter's indulgence in wine and women and every kind of debauchery. They have lost their force and vigour, they have dissipated that strength of mind and body in which they surmounted the Alpine peaks. The men who did that are mere wrecks now; they can hardly bear the weight of their armour on their limbs while they fight. Capua has proved to be Hannibal's Cannae. All soldierly courage, all military discipline, all glory won in the past, all hopes for the future have been extinguished there."

By showing his contempt for the enemy, Marcellus raised the spirits of his men. Hannibal, on the other hand, reproached his own men in much more severe terms. "I recognise," he said, " the same arms and standards here which I saw and used at the Trebia, at Trasumennus, and finally at Cannae, but not the same soldiers. It is quite certain that I led one army into winter quarters at Capua and marched out with quite a different one. Are you, whom two consular armies never withstood, hardly able now to hold your own against a subordinate officer, with his one legion and its contingent of allies? Is Marcellus to challenge us with impunity a second time with his raw recruits and Nolan supports? Where is that soldier of mine who dragged the consul, C. Flaminius, from his horse and struck off his head? Where is the one who slew L. Paulus at Cannae? Has the sword lost its edge; have your right hands lost their power? Or has any other miracle happened? Though but few your- selves, you have been wont to vanquish an enemy that far out- numbered you; now you can hardly stand up against a force far smaller than your own. You used to boast, tongue-valiant as you are, that you would take Rome by storm if any one would lead you. Well, I want you to try your courage and your strength in a smaller task. Carry Nola; it is a city in a plain, with no protection from river or from sea. When ye have loaded yourselves with the plunder of such a wealthy city as this, I will lead you or follow you wherever you wish."

XLVI. Neither his censures nor his promises had any effect in strengthening the morale of his men. When they began to fall back in all directions the spirits of the Romans rose, not only because of their general's cheering words, but also because the Nolans raised encouraging shouts and fired them with the glow of battle, until the Carthaginians fairly turned to flee and were driven to their camp. The Romans were anxious to storm the camp, but Marcellus marched them back to Nola amid the joyous congratulations even of the populace who had before been more inclined to the Carthaginians. More than 5000 of the enemy were killed that day and 600 made prisoners, 18 mili- tary standards were taken and two elephants; four had been killed in the battle. The Romans had less than a thousand killed. The next day was spent by both sides in burying those killed in battle, under an informal truce. Marcellus burnt the spoils taken from the enemy in fulfilment of a vow to Vulcan. Three days later, owing, I fancy, to some disagreement or in hope of more liberal pay, 272 troopers, Numidians and Spaniards, deserted to Marcellus. The Romans often availed themselves of their brave and loyal help in the war. At its close a gift of land was made in Spain to the Spaniards and in Africa to the Numidians as a reward for their valour.

Hanno was sent back into Bruttium with the force he had brought, and Hannibal went into winter quarters in Apulia and encamped in the neighbourhood of Arpi. As soon as Q. Fabius heard that Hannibal had left for Apulia, he had a quantity of corn from Nola and Neapolis conveyed into the camp above Suessula, and after strengthening its defences and leaving a force sufficient to hold the position through the winter months, he moved his own camp nearer to Capua and laid waste its terri- tory with fire and sword. The Campanians had no confidence whatever in their strength, but they were at last compelled to come out of their gates into the open and form an entrenched camp in front of the city. They had 6000 men under arms, the infantry were absolutely useless, but the mounted men were more efficient, so they kept harassing the enemy by cavalry skirmishes. There were several Campanian nobles serving as troopers, amongst them Cerrinus Vibellius, surnamed Taurea. He was a citizen of Capua and by far the finest soldier in the Campanian horse, so much so indeed that when he was serving with the Romans there was only one Roman horseman that enjoyed an equal reputation, and that was Claudius Asellus. Taurea had for a long time been riding up to the enemy's squadrons to see if he could find this man, and at last when there was a moment's silence he asked where Claudius Asellus was. "He has often," he said, "argued with me about our respective merits, let him settle the matter with the sword, and if he is vanquished yield me the *spolia opima*,[16] or if he is the victor take them from me."

XLVII. When this was reported to Asellus in the camp, he only waited till he could ask the consul whether he would be allowed, against the regulations, to fight his challenger. Permission being granted he at once armed himself and, riding in front of the outposts, called Taurea by name and told him to meet him wherever he pleased. The Romans had already gone out in crowds to watch the duel, and the Campanians had not only lined the rampart of their camp, but had gathered in large numbers on the fortifications of the city. After a great flourish of words and expressions of mutual defiance they levelled their spears and spurred their horses. As there was plenty of space they kept evading each other's thrusts and the fight went on without either being wounded. Then the Campanian said to the Roman: "This will be a trial of skill between the horses and not their riders unless we leave the open and go down into this hollow lane. There will be no room for swerving aside there, we shall fight at close quarters."

Almost before the words were out of his mouth, Claudius leaped his horse into the lane, and Taurea, bolder in words than deeds, shouted, "Never be an ass in a ditch," and this expression became a rustic proverb.[17] After riding some distance along the lane and finding no opponent, Claudius got into the open and returned to camp, saying strong things about the cowardice of his adversary. He was welcomed as victor with cheers and congratulations by his comrades. In the accounts of this duel on horseback some annalists record an additional circumstance

—how far there is any truth in it each must judge for himself, but it is at least remarkable. They say that Claudius went in pursuit of Taurea who fled to the city, and galloped in through one open gate and out through another unhurt, the enemy standing dumbfounded at the extraordinary sight.

XLVIII. After this incident the Roman camp was undisturbed; the consul even shifted his camp further away that the Campanians might complete their sowing, and he did not inflict any injury on their land until the corn was high enough in the blade to yield fodder. Then he carried it off to Claudius' camp above Suessula and built huts for his men to winter in there. M. Claudius, the proconsul, received orders to keep a force at Nola sufficient to protect the place and send the rest of his troops to Rome to prevent their being a burden to the allies and an expense to the republic. And Ti. Gracchus, having marched his legions from Cumae to Luceria in Apulia, sent the praetor, M. Valerius, to Brundisium with the army he had had at Luceria, and gave him orders to protect the coast of the Sallentine territory and to make such provision as might be necessary with regard to Philip and the Macedonian war.

Towards the end of the summer in which the events we have been describing occurred, despatches from P. and Cn. Scipio arrived, giving an account of the great successes they had achieved, but also stating that money to pay the troops was needed, as also clothing and corn for the army, whilst the seamen were destitute of everything. As regarded the pay, if the treasury were low they (the Scipios) would devise some means by which they could obtain it from the Spaniards, but all the other things must in any case be sent from Rome, otherwise they could neither keep their army nor the province. When the despatches had been read there was no one present who did not admit that the statements were true and the demands fair and just. But other considerations were present to their minds—the enormous land and sea forces they had to keep up; the large fleet that would have to be fitted out if the war with Macedon went forward; the condition of Sicily and Sardinia, which before the war had helped to fill the treasury and were now hardly able to support the armies which were protecting those islands; and, above all, the shrinkage in the revenue. For the war-tax from which the national expenditure was met had diminished with the number of those who paid it after the destruction of the armies at Trasumennus and at Cannae, and if the few survivors had to pay at a very much higher rate, they too, would perish, though not in battle. If, therefore, the State could not be upheld by credit it could not stand by its own resources. After thus reviewing the position of affairs the senate decided that Fulvius, one of the praetors, should appear before the Assembly and point out to the people the pressing needs of the State and ask those who had augmented their patrimonies by making contracts with the government to extend the date of payment [18] for the State, out of which they had made their money, and contract to supply what was needed for the army in Spain on condition that as soon as there was money in the treasury they should be the first to be paid.

After making this proposal, the praetor fixed a date for making the contracts for the supply of clothing and corn to the army in Spain, and for furnishing all that was required for the seamen.

XLIX. On the appointed day three syndicates appeared, consisting each of nineteen members, prepared to tender for the contracts. They insisted on two conditions — one was that they should be exempt from military service whilst they were employed on this public business, and the other that the cargoes they shipped should be insured by the government against storm or capture. Both demands were conceded, and the administration of the State was carried on with private money. Such were the moral tone and lofty patriotism which pervaded all ranks of society! As the contracts had been entered into from a generous and noble spirit, so they were executed with the utmost conscientiousness; the soldiers received as ample supplies as though they had been furnished, as they once were, from a rich treasury.

When these supplies reached Spain, the town of Iliturgi, which had gone over to the Romans, was being attacked by three Carthaginian armies under Hasdrubal, Mago, and Hannibal, the son of Bomilcar. Between these three camps the Scipios forced their way into the town after hard fighting and heavy losses. They brought with them a quantity of corn, of which there was a great scarcity, and encouraged the townsfolk to defend their walls with the same courage that they saw the Roman army display when fighting on their behalf. Then they advanced to attack the largest of the three camps, of which Hasdrubal was in command. The other two commanders and their armies saw that the decisive struggle would be fought there and they hastened to its support. As soon as they had emerged from their camps the fighting began. There were 60,000 of the enemy engaged that day and about 16,000 Romans. And yet the victory was such a crushing one that the Romans slew more than their own number of the enemy, made prisoners of more than 3000, captured somewhat less than 1000 horses, 59 military standards, 7 elephants, 5 having been killed in the battle, and got possession of the three camps—all in that one day.

After the siege of Iliturgi was thus raised, the Carthaginian armies marched to attack Intibili. They had repaired their losses out of that province which, above all others, was eager for fighting, if only plunder and money were to be got out of it, and which, too, abounded in young men. A pitched battle was again fought with the same result for both sides. Over 13,000 of the enemy were killed, more than 2000 made prisoners, 42 standards and 9 elephants were also taken.

And now nearly all the tribes of Spain went over to Rome, and the successes gained in Spain that summer were far greater than those in Italy.[19]

BOOK XXIV

THE REVOLUTION IN SYRACUSE

I. *The Carthaginians in Bruttium.*—After his return to Bruttium, Hanno, with the assistance and guidance of the Bruttians, made an attempt on the Greek cities. They were steadfast in their adherence to Rome, and all the more so because they saw that the Bruttians, whom they feared and hated, were taking sides with the Carthaginians. Rhegium was the first place he attempted, and several days were spent there without any result. Meanwhile the Locrians were hastily carrying their corn and wood and everything else they might want out of the fields into the city, not only for safety, but also that no plunder whatever might be left for the enemy. Every day larger numbers of people poured out of all the gates, till at last only those remained in the city whose duty it was to repair the walls and gates and provide a store of weapons on the ramparts. Against this miscellaneous crowd of all ranks and ages wandering through the fields mostly unarmed, Hamilcar sent his cavalry with orders not to injure any one but simply to scatter them in flight and then cut them off from returning to the city. He had taken up his position upon some high ground where he had a view of the country and the city, and he sent orders to one of the Bruttian cohorts to go up to the walls and invite the principal men of the place to a conference, and if they consented they were to endeavour to persuade them to betray the city, promising them, if they did so, Hannibal's friendship. The conference took place, but no credence was placed in what the Bruttians said, until the Carthaginians showed themselves on the hills and a few who escaped to the city brought the news that the whole population was in the hands of the enemy. Unnerved by terror they replied that they would consult the people, and a meeting was at once convened. All who were restless and discontented preferred a fresh policy and a fresh alliance, whilst those whose kinsfolk had been shut out of the city by the enemy felt as much pledged as though they had given hostages. A few were in favour of maintaining their loyalty to Rome, but

they kept silence rather than venture to defend their opinion.
A resolution was passed with apparent unanimity in favour of
surrendering to the Carthaginians. L. Atilius, the commandant
of the garrison, and his men were conducted down to the harbour and placed on board ship for conveyance to Regium;
Hamilcar and his Carthaginians were received into the city on
the understanding that a treaty with equal rights should be at
once concluded. This condition was within a very little of
being broken, for the Carthaginians charged the Locrians with
treachery in sending away the Romans, whilst the Locrians
pleaded that they had escaped. Some cavalry went in pursuit
in case the tide in the straits should either delay the departure
of the ships or drift them ashore. They did not overtake those
whom they were in pursuit of, but they saw some other ships
crossing the straits from Messana to Regium. These were
Roman soldiers who had been sent by Claudius to hold the
city. So the Carthaginians at once retired from Regium. By
Hannibal's orders peace was granted to the Locrians; they
were to be independent and live under their own laws; the
city was to be open to the Carthaginians, the Locrians were to
have sole control of the harbour, and the alliance was to be
based on the principle of mutual support: the Carthaginians
were to help the Locrians and the Locrians the Carthaginians
in peace and in war.

II. Thus the Carthaginians marched back from the straits
amidst the protests of the Bruttians, who complained that the
cities which they had marked for themselves for plunder had
been left unmolested. They determined to act on their own
account, and after enrolling and arming 15,000 of their own
fighting men they proceeded to attack Croto, a Greek city
situated on the coast. They imagined that they would gain an
immense accession of strength if they possessed a seaport with
a strongly fortified harbour. What troubled them was that
they could not quite venture to summon the Carthaginians to
their aid lest they should be thought not to have acted as allies
ought to act, and again, if the Carthaginian should for the second
time be the advocate of peace rather than of war, they were
afraid that they would fight in vain against the freedom of
Croto as they had against that of Locri. It seemed the best
course to send to Hannibal and obtain from him an assurance
that on its capture Croto should pass to the Bruttians. Hannibal told them that it was a matter for those on the spot to
arrange and referred them to Hanno, for neither he nor Hanno

wanted that famous and wealthy city to be plundered, and they hoped that when the Bruttians attacked it and it was seen that the Carthaginians neither assisted nor approved of the attack, the defenders would come over to Hannibal all the sooner.

In Croto there was neither unity of purpose nor of feeling; it seemed as though a disease had attacked all the cities of Italy alike, everywhere the populace were hostile to the aristocracy. The senate of Croto were in favour of the Romans, the populace wanted to place their state in the hands of the Carthaginians. This division of opinion in the city was reported by a deserter to the Bruttians. According to his statements, Aristomachus was the leader of the populace and was urging the surrender of the city, which was extensive and thickly populated, with fortifications covering a large area. The positions where the senators kept watch and ward were few and scattered, wherever the populace kept guard the way lay open into the city. At the suggestion of the deserter and under his guidance the Bruttians completely invested the town, and at the very first assault were admitted by the populace and took possession of the whole place with the exception of the citadel. This was held by the aristocrats, who had prepared it beforehand as a place of refuge in case anything of this sort should happen. Aristomachus, too, fled there, and gave out that he had advised the surrender of the city to the Carthaginians, not to the Bruttians.[1]

III. Before Pyrrhus' arrival in Italy, the city of Croto had walls which formed a circuit of twelve miles. After the devastation caused by that war hardly half the place was inhabited; the river which used to flow through the middle of the city now ran outside the part where the houses were, and the citadel was at a considerable distance from them. Sixteen miles from this famous city there was a still more famous temple to Juno Lacinia, an object of veneration to all the surrounding communities. There was a grove here enclosed by a dense wood and lofty fir-trees, in the middle of which there was a glade affording delightful pasture. In this glade cattle of every kind, sacred to the goddess, used to feed without any one to look after them, and at nightfall the different herds separated each to their own stalls without any beasts of prey lying in wait for them or any human hands to steal them. These cattle were a source of great profit, and a column of solid gold was made from the money thus gained and dedicated to the goddess.[2] Thus the temple became celebrated for its wealth as well as for its sanctity, and as generally happens in these famous spots, some miracles also were attributed to it. It was commonly reported that an altar stood in the porch of the temple, the ashes on which were never stirred by any wind.

The citadel of Croto, which overhung the sea on one side and on the other faced the land, was formerly protected by its natural position; afterwards it was further protected by a wall, on the side where Dionysius, the Sicilian tyrant, had captured it by stratagem, scaling it on the side away from the sea. It was this citadel that the aristocrats of Croto now occupied, regarding it as a fairly safe stronghold, while the populace in conjunction with the Bruttians besieged them. At last the Bruttians saw that they could never take the place in their own strength, and found themselves compelled to appeal to Hanno for help. He tried to bring the Crotonians to a surrender on condition that they would admit a Bruttian colony and allow their city, wasted and desolate as it was by war, to recover its ancient populousness. Not a single man amongst them, except Aristomachus, would listen to him. They said that they would sooner die than be mingled with Bruttians and change to alien ceremonies, customs, and laws, and soon even to a foreign speech. Aristomachus, finding himself powerless to persuade them to surrender and not getting any opportunity of betraying the citadel as he had betrayed the city, went off by himself to Hanno. Shortly after some envoys from Locri, who had, with Hanno's permission, obtained access to the citadel, persuaded them to suffer themselves to be transferred to Locri instead of facing the last extremity. They had already sent to Hannibal and obtained his consent to this course. So they left Croto and were conducted to the sea and put on board ship and sailed in a body for Locri.

In Apulia even the winter did not pass quietly so far as the Romans and Hannibal were concerned. Sempronius was wintering at Luceria and Hannibal not far from Arpi; skirmishes took place between them as occasion offered or either side saw its opportunity, and these brushes with the enemy made the Romans more efficient every day and more familiar with the cunning methods of their opponents.

IV. *Fall and Death of Hieronymus in Syracuse.*—In Sicily the position of the Romans was totally altered by the death of Hiero and the demise of the crown to his grandson, Hieronymus, who was but a boy and hardly likely to use his own liberty much

less his sovereign power with moderation. At such an age and
with such a temperament guardians and friends alike sought to
plunge him into every kind of excess. Hiero, it is said, seeing
what was going to happen, was anxious at the close of his long
life to leave Syracuse as a free State, lest the kingdom which had
been acquired and built up by wise and honourable statesman-
ship should go to ruin by being made the sport of a boy tyrant.
His project met with the most determined opposition from his
daughters. They imagined that whilst the boy retained the
name of king, the supreme power would really rest with them
and their husbands, Andranodorus and Zoippus, whom the
king purposed to leave as the boy's principal guardians. It
was no easy matter for a man in his ninetieth year, subject
night and day to the coaxing and blandishments of two women,
to keep an open mind and make public interests predominant
over private ones in his thoughts. So all he could do was to
leave fifteen guardians for his son, and he implored them on his
deathbed to maintain unimpaired the loyal relations with Rome
which he had cultivated for fifty years, and to see to it that the
young man, above all things, followed in his footsteps and
adhered to the principles in which he had been brought up.

Such were his instructions. When the king had breathed his
last the guardians produced the will and brought the boy, who
was then about fifteen, before the assembled people. Some
who had taken their places in different parts to raise acclama-
tions shouted their approval of the will, the majority, feeling
that they had lost a father, feared the worst now that the State
was orphaned. Then followed the king's funeral, which was
honoured more by the love and affection of his subjects than by
any grief amongst his own kindred. Shortly afterwards Andranodorus got rid of the other guardians by giving out that
Hieronymus was now a young man and capable of assuming the
government; by himself resigning the guardianship which he
shared with several others, he concentrated all their powers in
his own person.

V. Even a good and sensible prince would have found it
difficult to win popularity with the Syracusans as successor to
their beloved Hiero. But Hieronymus, as though he were
anxious by his own vices to make the loss of his grandfather
more keenly felt, showed on his very first appearance in public
how everything was changed. Those who had for so many
years seen Hiero and his son, Gelo, going about with nothing in
their dress or other marks of royalty to distinguish them from

the rest of their countrymen, now saw Hieronymus clad in purple, wearing a diadem, surrounded by an armed escort, and sometimes even proceeding from his palace in a chariot drawn by four white horses, after the style of Dionysius the tyrant. Quite in harmony with this extravagant assumption of state and pomp was the contempt he showed for everybody; the insolent tone in which he addressed those who sought audiences of him; the way he made himself difficult of access not only to strangers but even to his guardians; his monstrous lusts; his inhuman cruelty. Such terror seized everybody that some of his guardians anticipated a death of torture by suicide or flight. Three of them, the only ones who had familiar access to the palace, Andranodorus and Zoippus, Hiero's sons-in-law, and a certain Thraso, did not rouse much interest in him when talking of other matters, but as two of them took the side of the Carthaginians and Thraso that of the Romans, their heated arguments and quarrels attracted the young king's attention. A conspiracy formed against the despot's life was disclosed by a certain Callo, a lad of about the same age as Hieronymus and accustomed from his boyhood to associate with him on terms of perfect familiarity. The informer was able to give the name of one of the conspirators, Theodotus, by whom he had himself been invited to join in the plot. This man was at once arrested and handed over to Andranodorus for torture. He confessed his own complicity without any hesitation, but was silent about the others. At last, when he was racked with tortures too terrible for human endurance, he pretended to be overcome by his sufferings, and instead of disclosing the names of the guilty informed against an innocent man, and falsely accused Thraso of being the ringleader of the plot. Unless, he said, they had had such an influential man to lead them they would never have ventured upon so serious an undertaking. He went on inventing his story amidst groans of anguish and mentioning names just as they occurred to him, taking care to select the most worthless amongst the king's courtiers. It was the mention of Thraso that weighed most in persuading the king of the truth of the story; he accordingly was at once given up for punishment, and the others, as innocent as he was, shared his fate. Though their accomplice was under torture for a long time, not one of the actual conspirators either concealed himself or sought safety in flight, so great was their confidence in the courage and honour of Theodotus, and so great the firmness with which he kept their secret.

VI. The one link with Rome had now gone with Thraso, and there was no doubt about the movement towards revolt. Envoys were sent to Hannibal, and he sent back, together with a young noble, also named Hannibal, two other agents, Hippocrates and Epicydes, natives of Carthage and Carthaginians on the mother's side, but their grandfather was a refugee from Syracuse. Through their agency an alliance was formed between Hannibal and the Syracusan tyrant, and with Hannibal's consent they stayed on with Hieronymus.

As soon as Appius Claudius, who was commanding in Sicily, heard of this, he sent envoys to the king. When they announced that they had come to renew the alliance which had existed with his grandfather, they were laughed at, and as they were leaving the king asked them in jest what fortune they had met with in the battle of Cannae, for he could hardly believe what Hannibal's envoys told him; he wanted to know the truth so that he might make up his mind which course to follow as offering the best prospects. The Romans said that they would come back to him when he had learnt to receive embassies seriously, and, after warning him, rather than asking him, not to abandon their alliance lightly, they departed.

Hieronymus sent envoys to Carthage to conclude a treaty in the terms of their alliance with Hannibal. It was agreed in this compact that after they had expelled the Romans from Sicily—and that would soon be done if they sent a fleet and an army—the river Himera, which almost equally divides the island, was to be the boundary between the dominions of Syracuse and that of Carthage. Puffed up by the flattery of people who told him to remember not only Hiero but his maternal grandfather, King Pyrrhus, Hieronymus sent a second legation to Hannibal to tell him that he thought it only fair that the whole of Sicily should be ceded to him and that Carthage should claim the empire of Italy as their own. They expressed neither surprise nor displeasure at this fickleness and levity in the hot-headed youth provided only they could keep him from declaring for Rome.

VII. But everything was hurrying him headlong into ruin. He had sent Hippocrates and Epicydes in advance, each with 2000 troops, to attempt some cities which were held by Roman garrisons, whilst he himself advanced to Leontini with 15,000 foot and horse, which comprised the rest of his army. The conspirators, all of whom happened to be in the army, took an empty house overlooking the narrow road by which the king usually went down to the forum. Whilst they were all standing in front of the house, fully armed, waiting for the king to pass, one of them, Dinomenes by name, in the royal body-guard, had the task assigned to him of keeping back the crowd in the rear, by some means or other, when the king approached the gate of the house. All was done as had been arranged. Pretending to loosen a knot which was too tight on his foot, Dinomenes stopped the crowd and made so wide a gap in it that when the king was attacked in the absence of his guards he was stabbed in several places before help could reach him. As soon as the shouting and tumult were heard the guard hurled their missiles on Dinomenes who was now unmistakably stopping the way, but he escaped with only two wounds. When they saw the king lying on the ground the attendants fled. Some of the assassins went to the people who had assembled in the forum, rejoicing in their recovered liberty, others hastened to Syracuse to forestall the designs of Andranodorus and the rest of the king's men.

In this critical state of affairs Appius Claudius saw that a war was beginning close at hand, and he sent a despatch to the senate informing them that Sicily was being won over to Carthage and Hannibal. To frustrate the plans being formed at Syracuse, he moved all the garrisons to the frontier between the Roman province and the late king's dominion.

The Consular Elections.—At the close of the year Q. Fabius was authorised by the senate to fortify Puteoli, where there had grown up a considerable trade during the war, and also to place a garrison in it. On his way to Rome, where he was to conduct the elections, he gave notice that they would be held on the first election day that he could fix, and then to save time he marched past the City straight to the Campus Martius. That day the first voting fell by lot to the junior century of the tribe of the Anio, and they were giving their vote for T. Otacilius and M. Æmilius Regillus, when Q. Fabius, having obtained silence, made the following address:

" If Italy were at peace, or if we had on our hands such a war and such an enemy as to allow room for less care on our part, I should consider any one who sought to check the eagerness with which you have come here to confer honour on the men of your choice as very forgetful of your liberties. But in this war, in dealing with this enemy, none of our generals has ever made a single mistake which has not involved us in the gravest disasters, and therefore it is only right that you should exercise your franchise in the election of consuls with as much circumspection as you show when going armed into battle. Every man must say to himself, ' I am nominating a consul who is to be a match for Hannibal.' It was during this year that Vibellius Taurea, the foremost of the Campanian knights, challenged and was met by Asellus Claudius, the finest Roman horseman, at Capua. Against a Gaul, who once offered his defiance on the bridge over the Anio, our ancestors sent T. Manlius, a man of undaunted courage and prowess. Not many years later it was in the same spirit of fearless confidence, I will make bold to say, that M. Valerius armed himself against the Gaul who challenged him in the same way to single combat. Just as we desire to have our infantry and cavalry stronger, or if that is impossible at least equal to the enemy, so we should look for a commander equal to his. Even if we choose as our commander the finest general in the republic, still he is only chosen for a year, and immediately after his election he will be pitted against a veteran and permanent strategist who is not shackled by any limitations of time or authority, or prevented from forming and executing any plans which the necessities of war may require. In our case, on the other hand, the year is gone simply in making preparations and commencing a campaign.

" I have said enough as to the sort of men you ought to elect as your consuls; let me say a word about the men in whose favour the first vote has already been given. M. Æmilius Regillus is a Flamen or Quirinus; we cannot discharge him from his sacred duties without neglecting our duty to the gods, nor can we keep him at home without neglecting proper attention to the war. Otacilius married my sister's daughter and has children by her, but the obligations you have conferred on me and my ancestors are not such that I can place private relationship before the welfare of the State. In a calm sea any sailor, any passenger, can steer the ship, but when a violent storm arises and the vessel is driven by the wind over the raging waters then you want a man who is really a pilot. We are not sailing now in smooth water, already we have almost foundered in the many storms that have overtaken us, and therefore you must use the utmost foresight and caution in choosing the man who is to take the helm.

" As for you, T. Otacilius, we have had some experience of your conduct of comparatively unimportant operations, and you have certainly not shown any grounds for our entrusting you with more important ones. There were three objects for which we equipped the fleet this year which you commanded: it was to ravage the African coast, to render the coast of Italy safe for us, and, what was most important of all, to prevent any reinforcements, money, or supplies from being sent from Carthage to Hannibal. If T. Otacilius has carried out—I will not say all, but—any one of these objects for the State, then by all means elect him consul. But if, whilst you were in command of the fleet, everything required reached Hannibal safe and sound from home, if the coast of Italy has this year been in greater danger than the coast of Africa, what possible reason can you give why they should put you up, most of all, to oppose Hannibal? If you were consul we should have to follow the example of our forefathers and nominate a Dictator, and you could not take it as an insult that somebody amongst all the citizens of Rome was looked upon as a better strategist than yourself. It is of more importance to you, T. Otacilius, than it can be to any one else that you should not have a burden placed upon your shoulders whose weight would crush you.

" And to you, my fellow-citizens, I appeal most solemnly to remember what you are about to do. Imagine yourselves standing in your armed ranks on the field of battle; suddenly you are called upon to choose two commanders under whose auspicious generalship you are to fight. In the same spirit choose the consuls to-day to whom your children must take the oath, at whose edict they must assemble, under whose tutelage and protection they must serve. Trasumennus and Cannae are melancholy precedents to recall, but they are solemn warnings to guard against similar disasters. Usher! call back the century of juniors in the tribe of the Anio to give their votes again."

IX. T. Otacilius was in a state of great excitement, loudly exclaiming that Fabius wanted to have his consulship prolonged, and as he persisted in creating a disturbance the consul ordered the lictors to approach him and warned him that as he had marched straight to the Campus without entering the City, the axes were still bound up in the *fasces*.[3] The voting had in the meantime recommenced, and the first was given in favour of Q. Fabius Maximus as consul for the fourth time and M. Marcellus for the third. All the other centuries voted without exception for the same men. One praetor was re-elected, Q. Fulvius Flaccus, the others were fresh appointments; T. Otacilius Crassus, now praetor for the second time; Q. Fabius, a son of the consul and curule aedile at the time of his election; and P. Cornelius Lentulus. When the election of the praetors was finished the senate passed a resolution that Quintus Fulvius should have the City as his special province, and when the consuls had gone to the war he should command at home.

There were two great floods this year; the Tiber inundated the fields, causing widespread destruction of farm-buildings and stock and much loss of life.

It was in the fifth year of the second Punic war that Q. Fabius Maximus assumed the consulship for the fourth time and M. Claudius Marcellus for the third time. Their election excited an unusual amount of interest amongst the citizens, for it was many years since there had been such a pair of consuls. Old men remembered that Maximus Rullus had been similarly elected with P. Decius in view of the Gaulish war, and in the same way afterwards Papirius and Carvilius had been chosen consuls to act against the Samnites and Bruttians and also against the Lucanians and Tarentines.

Marcellus was elected in his absence whilst he was with the army. Fabius was re-elected when he was on the spot and actually conducting the election. Irregular as this was, the circumstances at the time, the exigencies of the war, the critical position of the State prevented any one from inquiring into precedents or suspecting the consul of love of power. On the contrary, they praised his greatness of soul, because when he knew that the republic needed its greatest general, and that he was unquestionably himself the one, he thought less of any personal odium which he might incur than of the interest of the republic.

X. On the day when the consuls entered upon office, a meeting of the senate was held in the Capitol. The very first decree passed was that the consuls should either draw lots or arrange between themselves which of them should conduct the election of censors before he left for the army. A second decree extended the command of the former consuls who were with their armies, and they were ordered to remain in their respective provinces; Ti. Gracchus at Luceria, where he was stationed with his army of volunteer slaves; C. Terentius Varro in the district of Picenum; Manius Pomponius in the land of the Gauls. The praetors of the former year were to act as propraetors; Q. Mucius was to hold Sardinia, and M. Valerius was to continue in command of the coast with his headquarters at Brundisium, where he was to be on the watch against any movement on the part of Philip of Macedon. The province of Sicily was assigned to P. Cornelius Lentulus, one of the praetors, and

T. Otacilius was to command the same fleet which he had had the previous year, to act against the Carthaginians.

Many portents were announced that year, and the more readily men of simple and pious minds believed in them the more numerously were they reported. Right in the inside of the temple of Juno Sospita at Lanuvium some crows had built a nest; in Apulia a green palm-tree had caught fire; at Mantua a pool formed by the overflow of the Mincius presented the appearance of blood; at Cales there was a rain of chalk stones, and at Rome, in the Forum Boarium, one of blood; in the Insteian quarter a subterranean spring flowed with such violence that it carried off some casks and jars in the cellars there as though they had been swept away by a torrent; various objects were struck by lightning, a public hall in the Capitol, the temple of Vulcan in the Campus Martius, some farm buildings in the Sabine territory; [4] and the public road, the walls, and one of the gates of Gabii. Then other marvels were reported; the spear of Mars at Praeneste had moved of its own accord; in Sicily an ox had spoken; amongst the Marrucini an infant had cried "Io triumphe" in its mother's womb; at Spoletum a woman had been turned into a man; at Hadria an altar had been seen in the sky with men clothed in white standing round it; and lastly at Rome, in the very City itself, a swarm of bees was seen in the Forum and immediately afterwards some people raised the cry "To arms!" declaring that they saw armed legions on the Janiculum, though the people who were on the hill at the time said that they saw no one except those who were usually at work in the gardens there.

These portents were expiated by victims of the larger kind in accordance with the directions of the diviners, and solemn intercessions were ordered to be made to all the deities who possessed shrines in Rome.

XI. *Preparations for War.*—When all had been done to secure "the peace of the gods," the consuls brought before the senate the questions relating to the policy of the State, the conduct of the war, and the amount and disposition of the military and naval forces of the republic. It was decided to place eighteen legions in the field. Each of the consuls was to have two, Gaul, Sicily, and Sardinia were each to be held by two, Q. Fabius, the praetor, was to take command of two in Apulia, and Ti. Gracchus was to keep his two legions of volunteer slaves at Luceria. One legion was left with C. Terentius at Picenum, and one also with M. Valerius at Brundisium for the fleet, and two were to defend the City. To make up this number of legions six new ones had to be raised. The consuls were directed to raise these as quickly as possible, and to fit out a fleet so that with the vessels stationed off the Calabrian coast the navy might that year be increased to 150 vessels of war. After the troops were levied and 100 new vessels launched, Q. Fabius held the election for the appointment of censors; those elected were M. Atilius Regulus and P. Furius Philus.

As the rumours of war in Sicily became more frequent, T. Otacilius was directed to sail thither with his fleet. As there was a deficiency of sailors, the consuls, acting upon the instructions of the senate, published an order to meet the case. Every one who had been assessed or whose father had been assessed in the censorship of L. Æmilius and C. Flaminius at from 50,000 to 100,000 *ases* or whose property had since reached that amount, was to furnish one sailor with six months' pay; those whose assessment was from 100,000 to 300,000 were to supply three sailors with twelve months' pay; from 300,000 to 1,000,000 the contribution was to be five sailors, and above that amount seven. The senators were to furnish eight sailors and a year's pay.[5] The sailors forthcoming under this order, after being armed and equipped by their masters, went on board with thirty days' rations. This was the first occasion on which a Roman fleet was manned by seamen provided at private cost.

XII. *Progress of the Campaign.*—The extraordinary scale on which these preparations were made threw the Campanians into a state of consternation; they were in dread lest the Romans should begin their campaigns for the year by besieging Capua. So they sent to Hannibal imploring him to move his army to Capua; fresh armies, they informed him, had been raised in Rome with a view to attacking them, and there was no city whose defection the Romans more bitterly resented than theirs. Owing to the urgency of the message, Hannibal felt he ought to lose no time in case the Romans anticipated him, and leaving Arpi he took up his position in his old camp at Tifata, overlooking Capua. Leaving his Numidians and Spaniards to protect the camp and Capua at the same time, he descended with the rest of his army to Lake Avernus, ostensibly for the purpose of offering sacrifice,[6] but really to make an attempt on Puteoli and the garrison there. As soon as the news of Hannibal's departure from Arpi and his return to Campania reached Maximus, he returned to his army, travelling night and day, and sent orders to Ti. Gracchus to move his forces from Luceria to

Beneventum, whilst Q. Fabius, the praetor, the consul's son, was instructed to take Gracchus' place at Luceria. Two praetors started at the same time for Sicily, P. Cornelius to the army and T. Otacilius to take charge of the coast and direct the naval affairs. The others all left for their respective provinces, and those whose command had been extended kept the districts they had held the year before.

XIII. While Hannibal was at Lake Avernus he was visited by five young nobles from Tarentum who had been made prisoners, some at Trasumennus and the others at Cannae, and afterwards sent to their homes with the same courteous treatment that the Carthaginian had shown to all the allies of Rome. They told him that they had not forgotten his kindness, and out of gratitude had persuaded most of the younger men in Tarentum to choose the friendship and alliance of Hannibal in preference to that of the Romans; they had been sent by their compatriots to ask him to march his army nearer to Tarentum. "If only," they declared, "your standards and camp are visible at Tarentum, there will be no hesitation in making the city over to you. The populace is in the hands of the younger men, and the government of Tarentum is in the hands of the populace." Hannibal expressed his warm approval of their sentiments, loaded them with splendid promises, and bade them return home to mature their plans. He would himself be with them at the right time. With this hope the Tarentines were dismissed. Hannibal himself was extremely anxious to gain possession of Tarentum; he saw that it was a wealthy and famous city, and, what was more, it was a maritime city on the coast opposite Macedonia, and as the Romans were holding Brundisium, this would be the port that King Philip would make for if he sailed to Italy.

After performing the sacred rites which were the object of his coming, and having during his stay laid waste the territory of Cumae as far as the promontory of Misenum, he suddenly marched to Puteoli, hoping to surprise the Roman garrison. There were 6000 troops there, and the place was not only one of great strength, but had also been strongly fortified. The Carthaginian spent three days there in attempting the fortress on every side, and as he met with no success he proceeded to ravage the district round Naples, more out of disappointed rage than in hopes of gaining possession of the city. The populace of Nola, who had long been disaffected towards Rome and at variance with their own senate, were greatly excited by his presence in a territory so close to their own. Their envoys accordingly came to invite Hannibal and brought him a positive assurance that the city would be delivered up to him. Their design was forestalled by the consul Marcellus, who had been summoned by the leading citizens. In one day he marched from Cales to Suessula in spite of the delay involved in crossing the Vulturnus, and the following night he threw into Nola 6000 infantry and 500 cavalry as a protection to the senate. While the consul was acting with the utmost energy in making Nola safe against attack, Hannibal was losing time, and after two unsuccessful attempts was less inclined to put faith in the populace of Nola.

XIV. *Carthaginian Defeat at Beneventum.*—During this time the consul, Q. Fabius, made an attempt on Casilinum, which was held by a Carthaginian garrison, while, as though they were acting in concert, Hanno, marching from Bruttium with a strong body of horse and foot, reached Beneventum on the one side and Ti. Gracchus, from Luceria, approached it in the opposite direction. He got into the town first, and hearing that Hanno had encamped by the river Caloris about three miles from the city and was ravaging the country, he moved out of the place and fixed his camp about a mile from the enemy. Here he harangued his troops. His legions were composed mostly of volunteer slaves who had made up their minds to earn their liberty, without murmuring, by another year's service rather than demand it openly. He had, however, on leaving his winter quarters noticed that there were discontented grumblings going on in the army, men were asking whether they would ever serve as free men. In consequence of this he had sent a despatch to the senate in which he stated that the question was not so much what they wanted as what they deserved; they had rendered him good and gallant service up to that day, and they only fell short of the standard of regular soldiers in the matter of personal freedom. On that point permission had been granted to him to do what he thought best in the interests of the State. So before closing with the enemy he announced that the hour which they had so long hoped for, when they would gain their freedom, had now come. The next day he was going to fight a pitched battle in a free and open plain where there would be full scope for true courage without any fear of ambuscade. Whoever brought back the head of an enemy would be at once by his orders declared to be a free man; whoever quitted his place in the ranks he would punish with a slave's death. Every man's fortune was in his own hands. It was not he alone that guaranteed their liberty, but the consul Marcellus also and the whole of the senate whom he had consulted and who had left the question of their liberty to him. He then read the despatch from Marcellus and the resolution passed in the senate.

These were greeted with a loud and ringing cheer. They demanded to be led at once to battle and pressed him forthwith to give the signal. Gracchus announced that the battle would take place the next day and then dismissed the men to quarters. The soldiers were in high spirits, those especially who had the prospect of earning their freedom by one day's strenuous work, and they spent the rest of the day in getting their arms and armour ready.

XV. When the bugles began to sound the next morning the volunteer slaves were the first to muster in front of the head-quarters' tent, armed and ready. As soon as the sun was risen Gracchus led his forces into the field, and the enemy showed no slackness in meeting him. He had 17,000 infantry, mostly Bruttians and Lucanians, and 1200 cavalry, amongst whom were very few Italians, the rest were almost all Numidians and Moors. The battle was a severe and protracted one; for four hours neither side gained any advantage. Nothing hampered the Romans more than the setting a price upon the heads of their foes, the price of liberty, for no sooner had any one made a furious attack upon an enemy and killed him than he lost time in cutting off his head—a difficult matter in the tumult and turmoil of the battle—and then, as their right hands were occupied in holding the heads all the best soldiers were no longer able to fight, and the battle was left to the slow and the timid. The military tribunes reported to their general that not a man of the enemy was being wounded as he stood, whilst those who had fallen were being butchered and the soldiers were carrying human heads in their right hands instead of swords. Gracchus made them at once give the order to throw down the heads and attack the enemy, and to tell them that their courage was sufficiently clear and conspicuous, and that there would be no question about liberty for brave men. On this the fighting was renewed and even the cavalry were sent against the enemy. The Numidians made a countercharge with great impetuosity, and the fighting became as fierce between the cavalry as it was amongst the infantry, making the issue of the contest again uncertain.

The generals on both sides now appealed to their men; the Roman pointed to the Bruttians and Lucanians who had been so often defeated and crushed by their ancestors; the Carthaginian showered contempt upon Roman slaves and soldiers taken out of the workshops. At last Gracchus gave out that there would be no hope whatever of liberty if the enemy were not routed and put to flight that day.

XVI. These words so kindled their courage that they seemed like different men; they raised the battle shout again and flung themselves on the enemy with such force that their attack could no longer be withstood. The Carthaginian ranks in front of the standards were broken, then the soldiers round the standards were thrown into disorder, and at last their entire army became a scene of confusion. Soon they were unmistakably routed, and they rushed to their camp in such haste and panic that not even in the gates or on the rampart was there any attempt at resistance. The Romans followed almost on their heels and commenced a fresh battle inside the enemies' rampart. Here the combatants had less space to move and the battle was all the more bloody. The prisoners in the camp also helped the Romans, for they snatched up swords amid the confusion and, forming a solid phalanx, they fell upon the Carthaginians in the rear and stopped their flight.

Out of that large army not 2000 men escaped, and amongst these were the greater part of the cavalry who got clear away with their general, all the rest were either killed or made prisoners, and thirty-eight standards were captured. Of the victors hardly 2000 fell. The whole of the plunder, with the exception of the prisoners, was given to the soldiers; whatever cattle the owners claimed within thirty days were also excepted.

On their return to camp, laden with booty, some 4000 of the volunteer slaves who had shown remissness in the fighting and had not joined in the rush into the camp took possession of a hill not far from their own camp as they were afraid of punishment. The next day Gracchus ordered a parade of his army, and these men were brought down by their officers and entered the camp after the rest of the army was mustered. The proconsul first bestowed military rewards on the veterans, according to the courage and activity they had shown in the battle. Then turning to the volunteer slaves he said that he would much rather have praised all alike, whether deserving or undeserving, than that any man should be punished that day. "And," he continued, " I pray that what I am now doing may

prove to be for the benefit, happiness, and felicity of yourselves
and of the commonwealth—I bid you all be free." At these
words they broke out into a storm of cheering; at one moment
they embraced and congratulated each other, at another they
lifted up their hands to heaven and prayed that every blessing
might descend upon the people of Rome and upon Gracchus
himself. Gracchus continued: " Before making you all equal
as free men I did not want to affix any mark by which the brave
soldier could be distinguished from the coward, but now that
the State has fulfilled its promise to you I shall not let all distinction between courage and cowardice be lost. I shall require
the names to be brought to me of those who, conscious of their
skulking in battle, lately seceded from us, and when they have
been summoned before me I shall make each of them take an
oath that he will never as long as he is with the colours, unless
prevented by illness, take his meals other than standing. You
will be quite reconciled to this small penalty when you reflect
that it would have been impossible to mark you with any lighter
stigma for your cowardice."

He then gave orders for the tents and other things to be
packed up, and the soldiers carrying their plunder or driving it
in front of them with mirth and jest returned to Beneventum
in such happy laughing spirits that they seemed to be coming
back after a day of revelry rather than after a day of battle.
The whole population of Beneventum poured out in crowds to
meet them at the gates; they embraced and congratulated the
soldiers and invited them to partake of their hospitality. Tables
had been spread for them all in the forecourts of the houses;
the citizens invited the men and begged Gracchus to allow his
troops to enjoy a feast. Gracchus consented on condition that
they all banqueted in public view, and each citizen brought out
his provision and placed his tables in front of his door. The
volunteers, now no longer slaves, wore white caps or fillets of
white wool round their heads [7] at the feast; some were reclining,
others remained standing, waiting on the others and taking
their food at the same time. Gracchus thought the scene worth
commemorating, and on his return to Rome he ordered a re-
presentation of that celebrated day to be painted in the temple
of Liberty; the temple which his father had built and dedicated
on the Aventine out of the proceeds of the fines.

XVII. During these proceedings at Beneventum, Hannibal,
after ravaging the Neapolitan territory, shifted his camp to
Nola. As soon as the consul became aware of his approach

he sent for Pomponius, the propraetor, to join him with the army which was in camp above Suessula, and prepared to meet the enemy without delay. He sent C. Claudius Nero with the best of the cavalry out through the camp gate which was furthest from the enemy, in the dead of night, with instructions to ride round to the rear of the enemy without being observed and follow him slowly, and when he saw the battle begin, throw himself across his rear. Nero was unable to follow out his instructions, whether because he lost his way or because he had not sufficient time is uncertain.

The battle commenced in his absence and the Romans undoubtedly had the advantage, but owing to the cavalry not making their appearance in time the general's plans were all upset. Marcellus did not venture to pursue the retreating Carthaginians, and gave the signal for retreat though his soldiers were actually conquering. It is asserted that more than 2000 of the enemy were killed that day, whilst the Romans lost less than 400. About sunset Nero returned with his horses and men tired out to no purpose and without having even seen the enemy. He was severely censured by the consul who even went so far as to say that it was entirely his fault that they had not inflicted on the enemy in his turn a defeat as crushing as the one at Cannae. The next day the Romans marched into the field, but the Carthaginian remained in camp, thereby tacitly admitting that he was vanquished.⁸ The following day he gave up all hope of gaining possession of Nola, his attempts having been always foiled, and proceeded to Tarentum, where he had better hopes of securing the place through treachery.

XVIII. *Activity of the Censors.*—The government showed quite as much energy at home as in the field. Owing to the emptiness of the treasury the censors were released from the task of letting out public works to contract, and they devoted their attention to the regulation of public morals and the castigation of the vices which sprang up during the war, just as constitutions enfeebled by long illness naturally develop other evils.

They began by summoning before them those who were reported to have formed plans for abandoning Italy after the defeat of Cannae; the principal person concerned, M. Caecilius Metellus, happened to be praetor at the time. He and the rest who were involved in the charge were put upon their trial, and as they were unable to clear themselves the censors pronounced them guilty of having uttered treasonable language both

privately and publicly in order that a conspiracy might be
formed for abandoning Italy. Next to these were summoned
those who had been too clever in explaining how they were
absolved from their oath, the prisoners who imagined that when
they had furtively gone back, after once starting, to Hannibal's
camp they were released from the oath which they had taken
to return. In their case and in that of those above mentioned,
all who possessed horses at the cost of the State were deprived
of them, and they were all removed from their tribes and disfranchised. Nor were the attentions of the censors confined to
the senate or the equestrian order, they took out from the
registers of the junior centuries the names of all those who had
not served for four years, unless formally exempted or incapacitated by sickness, and the names of above 2000 men
were removed from the tribes and the men disfranchised. This
drastic procedure of the censors was followed by severe action
on the part of the senate. They passed a resolution that all
those whom the censors had degraded were to serve as foot
soldiers and be sent to the remains of the army of Cannae in
Sicily. This class of soldiers was only to terminate its service
when the enemy had been driven out of Italy.

As the censors were now abstaining, owing to the emptiness of
the treasury, from making any contracts for repairs to the
sacred edifices or for supplying chariot horses or similar objects,
they were frequently approached by those who had been in the
habit of tendering for these contracts, and urged to conduct
all their business and let out the contracts just as if there was
money in the treasury. No one, they said, would ask for
money from the exchequer till the war was over. Then came
the owners of the slaves whom Tiberius Sempronius had manu-
mitted at Beneventum. They stated that they had had notice
from the financial commissioners that they were to receive the
value of their slaves, but they would not accept it till the war
was at an end. While the plebeians were thus showing their
readiness to meet the difficulties of an empty exchequer, the
moneys of minors and wards and then of widows began to be
deposited, those who brought the money believing that their
deposits would not be safer or more scrupulously protected anywhere than when they were under the guarantee of the State.
Whatever was bought or provided for the minors and widows
was paid for by a bill of exchange on the quaestor. This generous spirit on the part of individual citizens spread from the
City to the camp, so that not a single horse soldier, not a single

centurion would accept pay; whoever did accept it received the opprobrious epithet of " mercenary."

XIX. *The Campaign in Italy*.—It has been stated above that the consul, Q. Fabius, was encamped near Casilinum, which was held by a garrison of 2000 Campanians and 700 of Hannibal's troops. Statius Metius had been sent by Gnaevius Magius of Atella, who was the " medixtuticus " for that year, to take command, and he had armed the populace and the slaves indiscriminately in order to attack the Roman camp while the consul was engaged in the assault on the town. Fabius was perfectly aware of all that was going on, and he sent word to his colleague at Nola that a second army would be needed to hold the Campanians while he was delivering the assault, and either he should come himself and leave a sufficient force at Nola, or, if there was still danger to be apprehended from Hannibal and Nola required his presence, he should recall Tiberius Gracchus from Beneventum. On receipt of this message Marcellus left 2000 men to protect Nola and came with the rest of his army to Casilinum.

His arrival put an end to any movement on the part of the Campanians, and Casilinum was now besieged by both consuls. Many of the Roman soldiers were wounded by rashly venturing too near the walls, and the operations were by no means successful. Fabius thought that the enterprise, which was of small importance though quite as difficult as more important ones, ought to be abandoned, and that they ought to go where more serious business awaited them. Marcellus urged that while there were many things which a great general ought not to undertake, still, when he had undertaken them, he ought not to let them drop, as in either case it had great influence on public opinion. He succeeded in preventing the siege from being abandoned.

Now the assault commenced in earnest, and when the *vineae* and siege works and artillery of every kind were brought against the walls, the Campanians begged Fabius to be allowed to depart under safe conduct to Capua. After a few had got outside the town Marcellus occupied the gate through which they were leaving, and an indiscriminate slaughter began, first amongst those near the gate and then, after the troops burst in, in the city itself. About fifty of the Campanians had already passed out and they fled to Fabius, under whose protection they reached Capua. During these parleys, and the delay occasioned by those who appealed for protection, the besiegers found their opportunity and Casilinum was taken. The Campanians and

those of Hannibal's troops who were made prisoners were sent
to Rome and shut up in prison; the mass of the townsfolk were
distributed amongst the neighbouring communities to be kept
in custody.

XX. Just at the time when the consuls were withdrawing from
Casilinum after their success, Gracchus sent some cohorts, which
he had raised in Lucania under an officer of the allies, on a
plundering expedition in the enemy's territory. Whilst they
were scattered in all directions Hanno attacked them and inflicted on them as great a loss as he had suffered at Beneventum,
after which he hurriedly retreated into Bruttium lest Gracchus
should be on his track.

Marcellus went back to Nola, Fabius marched into Samnium
to lay waste the country and to recover by force of arms the
cities which had revolted. His hand fell most heavily on
Caudium; the crops were burnt far and wide, cattle and men
were driven away as plunder, their towns were taken by assault;
Compulteria, Telesia, Compsa, and after these Fugifulae and
Orbitanium, amongst the Lucanians Blandae and the Apulian
town of Æcae, were all captured. In these places 25,000 of
the enemy were either killed or made prisoners and 370 deserters
were taken, whom the consul sent on to Rome; they were all
scourged in the Comitium and then flung from the rock. All
these successes were gained by Q. Fabius within a few days.
Marcellus was compelled to remain quiet at Nola owing to
illness. The praetor, Q. Fabius, was also meeting with success;
he was operating in the country round Luceria and captured the
town of Acuca, after which he established a standing camp at
Ardaneae.

While the Roman generals were thus engaged elsewhere
Hannibal had reached Tarentum, utterly ruining and destroying
everything as he advanced. It was not till he was in the
territory of Tarentum that his army began to advance peace-
ably; no injury was inflicted, no foragers or plunderers left the
line of march, and it was quite apparent that this self-restraint
on the part of the general and his men was solely with a view
to winning the sympathies of the Tarentines. When, however,
he went up to the walls and there was no such movement as he
expected at the sight of his army, he went into camp about a
mile from the city.

Three days before his arrival M. Valerius, the propraetor,
who was in command of the fleet at Brundisium, had sent M.
Livius to Tarentum. He speedily embodied a force out of the

young nobility, and posted detachments at the gates and on the walls wherever it seemed necessary, and by being ever on the alert day and night gave no chance to either the enemy or the untrustworthy allies of making any attempt themselves or hoping for anything from Hannibal. After spending some days there fruitlessly and finding that none of those who had paid him a visit at Lake Avernus either came in person or sent any messenger or letter, he recognised that he had been misled by empty promises and withdrew his army. He still abstained from doing any injury to the Tarentine territory, although this affectation of mildness had done him no good so far. He still clung to the hope of undermining their loyalty to Rome.

When he came to Salapia the summer was now over, and as the place seemed suitable for winter quarters he provisioned it with corn collected from the country round Metapontum and Heraclea. From this centre the Numidians and Moors were sent on marauding expeditions through the Sallentine district and the pasture lands bordering on Apulia; they brought away mostly quantities of horses, not much plunder of other kinds, and as many as 4000 of these were distributed amongst the troopers to be trained.

XXI. *Revolution in Sicily.*—A war was threatening in Sicily which could by no means be treated lightly, for the death of the tyrant had rather furnished the Syracusans with able and energetic leaders than produced any change in their political sentiments. The senate accordingly placed the other consul, M. Marcellus, in charge of that province.

Immediately after the death of Hieronymus a disturbance broke out among the soldiery at Leontini; they loudly demanded that the murder of the king should be atoned for by the blood of the conspirators. When, however, the words, so delightful to hear, " the restoration of liberty," were constantly uttered, and they were led to hope that they would receive a largesse out of the royal treasure and would henceforth serve under more able generals, when, too, the foul crimes and still fouler lusts of the late tyrant were recounted to them, their feelings were so completely changed that they allowed the body of the king, whose loss they had regretted, to lie unburied. The rest of the conspirators remained behind to secure the army, whilst Theodotus and Sosis, mounting the king's horses, rode at full speed to Syracuse to crush the royalists while still ignorant of all that had happened. Rumour, however, which on such occasions travels more quickly than anything else, reached the city before them, and also one of the royal servants had brought the news. Thus forewarned, Andranodorus had occupied with strong garrisons the Island, the citadel, and all the other suitable positions.[9] Theodotus and Sosis rode in through the Hexapylon [10] after sunset when it was growing dark and displayed the blood-stained robe of the king and the diadem that had adorned his head. Then they rode on through the Tycha, and summoning the people to liberty and to arms bade them assemble in the Achradina. Some of the population ran out into the streets, others stood in the doorways, others looked out from the windows and the roofs inquiring what was the matter. Lights were visible everywhere and the whole city was in an uproar. Those who had arms mustered in the open spaces of the city; those who had none tore down the spoils of the Gauls and Illyrians which the Roman people had given to Hiero and which he had hung up in the temple of Olympian Jupiter, and as they did so prayed to the deity that he would of his grace and mercy lend them those consecrated arms to use in defence of the shrines of the gods and in defence of their liberty. The citizens were joined by the troops who had been posted in the different parts of the city. Amongst the other places in the Island Andranodorus had strongly occupied the public granary. This place, enclosed by a wall of large stone blocks and fortified like a citadel, was held by a body of young men told off for its defence, and they sent messengers to the Achradina to say that the granaries and the corn stored there were in the possession of the senate.

XXII. As soon as it was light the whole population, armed and unarmed, assembled at the Senate-house in the Achradina. There, in front of the temple of Concord, which was situated there, Polyaenus, one of the prominent citizens, made a speech which breathed of freedom but at the same time counselled moderation. " Men," he said, " who have experienced the fear and the humiliation of slavery are stung to rage against an evil which they know well. What disasters civil discord brings in its train, you, Syracusans, have heard from your fathers rather than witnessed yourselves. I praise your action in so promptly taking up arms, I shall praise you more if you do not use them unless compelled to do so as a last resort. I should advise you to send envoys at once to Andranodorus and warn him to submit to the authority of the senate and people, to open the gates of the Island, and surrender the fort. If he chooses to usurp the sovereignty of which he has been appointed guardian, then I tell you you must show much more determination in recovering your liberties from him than you did from Hieronymus."

Envoys were accordingly sent. A meeting of the senate was then held. During the reign of Hiero this body had continued to act as the great council of the nation, but after his death it had never up to that day been summoned or consulted about any matter whatever. Andranodorus, on the arrival of the envoys, was much impressed by the unanimity of the people and also by the seizure of various points in the city, especially in the Island, the most strongly fortified position in which had been betrayed to his opponents. But his wife, Demarata, a daughter of Hiero, with all the spirit of a princess and the ambition of a woman, called him aside from the envoys and reminded him of an oft-quoted saying of Dionysius the tyrant that one ought to relinquish sovereign power when dragged by the heels not when mounted on a horse. It was easy for any one who wished to resign in a moment a great position, but to create and secure it was a difficult and arduous task. She advised him to ask the envoys for time for consultation, and to employ that time in summoning the troops from Leontini; if he promised to give them the royal treasure, he would have everything in his own power. These feminine suggestions Andranodorus did not wholly reject, nor did he at once adopt them. He thought the safest way of gaining power was to yield for the time being, so he told the envoys to take back word that he should submit to the authority of the senate and people. The next day as soon as it was light he opened the gates of the Island and entered the forum in the Achradina. He went up to the altar of Concord, from which the day before Polyaenus had addressed the people, and began his speech by apologising for his delay. " I have," he went on, " it is true, closed the gates, but not because I regard my interests as separate from those of the State, but because I felt misgivings, when once the sword was drawn, as to how far the thirst for blood might carry you, whether you would be content with the death of the tyrant, which amply secures your liberty, or whether every one who had been connected with the palace by relationship or by official position was to be put to death as being involved in another's guilt. As soon as I saw that those who freed their country meant to keep it free and that all were consulting the public good, I had no hesitation in giving back to my country my person and all that had been entrusted to my protection now that he who committed them to me has

perished through his own madness." Then turning to the
king's assassins and addressing Theodotus and Sosis by name,
he said, " You have wrought a deed that will be remembered,
but, believe me, your reputation has yet to be made, and unless
you strive for peace and concord there is a most serious danger
ahead; the State will perish in its freedom."

XXIII. With these words he laid the keys of the gates and of
the royal treasury at their feet. The assembly was then dismissed for the day and the joyful citizens accompanied by their
wives and children offered thanksgivings at all the temples.
The next day the election was held for the appointment of
praetors. Amongst the first to be elected was Andranodorus,
the rest were mostly men who had taken part in the tyrant's
death; two were elected in their absence, Sopater and Dinomenes. These two, on hearing what had happened at Syracuse,
brought that part of the royal treasure which was at Leontini
and delivered it into the charge of specially appointed quaestors,
that portion which was in the Island was also handed over to them
in Achradina. That part of the wall which shut off the Island
from the city by a needlessly strong barrier was with the unanimous approval of the citizens thrown down,[11] and all the other
measures taken were in harmony with the general desire for
liberty.

As soon as Hippocrates and Epicydes heard of the tyrant's
death, which Hippocrates had tried to conceal by putting the
messenger to death, finding themselves deserted by their soldiers they returned to Syracuse, as this seemed the safest course
under the circumstances. To avoid attracting observation or
being suspected of plotting a counter-revolution, they approached the praetors, and through them were admitted to an
audience of the senate. They declared publicly that they had
been sent by Hannibal to Hieronymus as to a friend and ally;
they had obeyed the commands of the men whom their general
Hannibal had wished them to obey, and now they were anxious
to return to Hannibal. The journey, however, was not a safe
one, for the Romans were to be found in every part of Sicily;
they requested therefore that they might have an escort to conduct them to Socri in Italy, in this way the Syracusans would
confer a great obligation on Hannibal with very little trouble to
themselves. The request was very readily granted, for they
were anxious to see the last of the king's generals who were not
only able commanders but also needy and daring adventurers.
But Hippocrates and Epicydes did not execute their purpose

with the promptness which seemed necessary. These young men, thorough soldiers themselves and living in familiar intercourse with soldiers, went about amongst the troops, amongst the deserters, consisting to a large extent of Roman seamen, and even amongst the dregs of the populace, spreading libellous charges against the senate and the aristocracy, whom they accused of secretly plotting and contriving to bring Syracuse under the suzerainty of Rome under the pretence of renewing the alliance. Then, they hinted, the small faction which had been the prime agents in renewing the treaty would be the masters of the city.

XXIV. These slanders were listened to and believed in by the crowds which flocked to Syracuse in greater numbers every day, and not only Epicydes but even Andranodorus began to entertain hopes of a successful revolution. The latter was constantly being warned by his wife that now was the time to seize the reins of power whilst a new and unorganised liberty had thrown everything into confusion, while a soldiery, battening on the royal donative, was ready to his hand, and while Hannibal's emissaries, generals who could handle troops, were able to aid his enterprise. Wearied out at last by her importunity he communicated his design to Themistus, the husband of Gelo's daughter, and a few days later he incautiously disclosed it to a certain Aristo, a tragic actor to whom he had been in the habit of confiding other secrets. Aristo was a man of respectable family and position, nor did his profession in any way disgrace him, for among the Greeks nothing of that kind is a thing to be ashamed of. This being his character, he thought that his country had the first and strongest claim on his loyalty, and he laid an information before the praetors. As soon as they ascertained by decisive evidence that it was no merely trumped up affair they consulted the elder senators and on their authority placed a guard at the door and slew Themistus and Andranodorus as they entered the Senate-house. A disturbance was raised at what appeared an atrocious crime by those who were ignorant of the reason, and the praetors, having at last obtained silence, introduced the informer into the senate.

The man gave all the details of the story in regular order. The conspiracy was first started at the time of the marriage of Gelo's daughter Harmonia to Themistus; some of the African and Spanish auxiliary troops had been told off to murder the praetor and the rest of the principal citizens and had been promised their property by way of reward; further, a band of mercenaries, in the pay of Andranodorus, were in readiness to seize the Island a second time. Then he put before their eyes the several parts which each were to play and the whole organisation of the conspiracy with the men and the arms that were to be employed.

The senate were quite convinced that the death of these men was as justly deserved as that of Hieronymus, but clamours arose from the crowd in front of the Senate-house, who were divided in their sympathies and doubtful as to what was going on. As they pressed forward with threatening shouts into the vestibule, the sight of the conspirators' bodies so appalled them that they became silent and followed the rest of the population who were proceeding calmly to hold an assembly. Sopater was commissioned by the senate and by his colleages to explain the position of affairs.

He began by reviewing the past life of the dead conspirators, as though he were putting them on their trial, and showed how all the scandalous and impious crimes that had been committed since Hiero's death were the work of Andranodorus and Themistus. "For what," he asked, "could a boy like Hieronymus, who was hardly in his teens, have done on his own initiative? His guardians and masters reigned unmolested because the odium fell on another; they ought to have perished before Hieronymus or at all events when he did. Yet these men, deservedly marked out for death, committed fresh crimes after the tyrant's decease; at first openly, when Andranodorus closed the gates of the Island and, by declaring himself heir to the crown, seized, as though he were the rightful owner, what he had held simply as trustee. Then, when he was abandoned by all in the Island and kept at bay by the whole body of the citizens who held the Achradina, he tried by secret craft to attain the sovereignty which he had failed to secure by open violence. He could not be turned from his purpose even by the favour shown him and the honour conferred, when he who was plotting against liberty was elected praetor with those who had won their country's freedom. But it was really the wives who were responsible and who, being of royal blood, had filled their husbands with a passion for royalty, for one of the men had married Hiero's daughter, the other a daughter of Gelo."

At these words shouts rose from the whole assembly declaring that neither of these women ought to live, and that no single member of the royal family ought to survive. Such is the character of the mob; either they are cringing slaves or ruthless tyrants. As for the liberty which lies between these extremes, they are incapable of losing it without losing their self-respect, or possessing it without falling into licentious excesses. Nor are there, as a rule, wanting men, willing tools, to pander to their passions and excite their bitter and vindictive feelings to bloodshed and murder. It was just in this spirit that the praetors at once brought forward a motion which was adopted almost before it was proposed, that all the blood royal should be exterminated. Emissaries from the praetors put to death Demarata and Harmonia, the daughters of Hiero and Gelo and the wives of Andranodorus and Themistus.

XXVI. There was another daughter of Hiero's, Heraclia, the wife of Zoippus, a man whom Hieronymus had sent on an embassy to Ptolemy, and who had chosen to remain in voluntary exile. As soon as she learned that the executioners were coming to her she fled for sanctuary into the private chapel where the household gods were, accompanied by her unmarried daughters with their hair dishevelled and everything in their appearance which could appeal to pity. This silent appeal she strengthened by remonstrances and prayers. She implored the executioners by the memory of her father Hiero and her brother Gelo not to allow an innocent woman like her to fall a victim to the hatred felt for Hieronymus. "All that I have gained by his reign is my husband's exile; in his lifetime my sisters' fortunes were very different from mine, and now that he has been killed our interests are not the same. Why! had Andranodorus' designs succeeded, her sister would have shared her husband's throne, and the rest would have been her slaves. Is there one of you who doubts that if any one were to announce to Zoippus the assassination of Hieronymus and the recovery of liberty for Syracuse, he would not at once take ship and return to his native land? How are all human hopes falsified! Now his country is free and his wife and children are battling for their lives, and in what are they opposing freedom and law? What danger is there for any man in a lonely, all but widowed woman and daughters who are living in orphanhood? Ah, but even if there is no danger to be feared from us, we are of the hated royal birth. Then banish us far from Syracuse and Sicily, order us to be transported to Alexandria, send the wife to her husband, the daughters to their father."

She saw that ears and hearts were deaf to her appeals and that some were getting their swords ready without further loss of time. Then, no longer praying for herself, she implored them to spare her daughters; their tender age even an exasperated enemy would respect. "Do not," she cried, "in wreaking vengeance on tyrants, imitate the crimes which have made them so hated." In the midst of her cries they dragged her out of the chapel and killed her. Then they attacked the daughters who were bespattered with their mother's blood. Distracted by grief and terror they dashed like mad things out of the chapel, and, could they have escaped into the street, they would have created a tumult all through the city. Even as it was, in the confined space of the house they for some time eluded all those armed men without being hurt, and freed themselves from those who got hold of them, though they had to struggle out of so many strong hands. At last, exhausted by wounds, while the whole place was covered by their blood, they fell lifeless to the ground. Their fate, pitiable in any case, was made still more so by an evil chance, for very soon after all was over a messenger came to forbid their being killed. The popular sentiment had changed to the side of mercy, and mercy soon passed into self-accusing anger for they had been so hasty to punish that they had left no time for repentance or for their passions to cool down. Angry remonstrances were heard everywhere against the praetors, and the people insisted upon an election to fill the places of Andranodorus and Themistus, a proceeding by no means to the liking of the other praetors.

XXVII. When the day fixed for the election arrived, to the surprise of all, a man from the back of the crowd proposed Epicydes, then another nominated Hippocrates. The voices of their supporters become more and more numerous and evidently carried with them the assent of the people. As a matter of fact the gathering was a very mixed one; there were not only citizens, but a crowd of soldiers present, and a large proportion of deserters, ripe for a complete revolution, were mingled with them. The praetors pretended at first not to hear and tried hard to delay the proceedings; at last, powerless before a unanimous assembly, and dreading a seditious outbreak, they declared them to be duly elected praetors.

Relations of the new Government with Rome.—They did not reveal their designs immediately they were appointed, though they were extremely annoyed at envoys having gone to Appius Claudius to arrange a ten days' truce, and at others having been sent, after it was arranged, to discuss the renewal of the ancient treaty. The Romans had at the time a fleet of a hundred vessels at Murgantia awaiting the issue of the disturbances which the massacre of the royal family had created in Syracuse and the effect upon the people of their new and untried freedom. During that time the Syracusan envoys had been sent by Appius to Marcellus on his arrival in Sicily, and Marcellus, after hearing the proposed terms of peace, thought that the matter could be arranged and accordingly sent envoys to Syracuse to discuss publicly with the praetors the question of renewing the treaty. But now there was nothing like the same state of quiet and tranquillity in the city. As soon as news came that a Carthaginian fleet was off Pachynum, Hippocrates and Epicydes, throwing off all fear, went about amongst the mercenaries and then amongst the deserters declaring that Syracuse was being betrayed to the Romans. When Appius brought his ships to anchor at the mouth of the harbour in the hope of increasing the confidence of those who belonged to the other party, these groundless insinuations received to all appearance strong confirmation, and at the first sight of the fleet the people ran down to the harbour in a state of great excitement to prevent them from making any attempt to land.

XXVIII. As affairs were in such a disturbed condition it was decided to hold an assembly. Here the most divergent views were expressed and things seemed to be approaching an outbreak of civil war when one of their foremost citizens, Apollonides, rose and made what was under the circumstances a wise and patriotic speech. " No city," he said, " has ever had a brighter prospect of permanent security or a stronger chance of being utterly ruined than we have at the present moment. If we are all agreed in our policy, whether it take the side of Rome or the side of Carthage, no state will be in a more prosperous and happy condition; if we all pull different ways, the war between the Carthaginians and the Romans will not be a more bitter one than between the Syracusans themselves, shut up as they are within the same walls, each side with its own army, its own munitions of war, its own general. We must then do our very utmost to secure unanimity. Which alliance will be the more advantageous to us is a much less important question, and much less depends upon it, but still I think that we ought to be guided by the authority of Hiero in choosing our allies rather than by that of Hieronymus; in any case we ought to prefer a tried friendship of fifty years' standing to one of which we now know nothing and once found untrustworthy. There is also another serious consideration—we can decline to come to terms with the Carthaginians without having to fear immediate hostilities with them, but with the Romans it is a question of either peace or an immediate declaration of war."

The absence of personal ambition and party spirit from this speech gave it all the greater weight, and a council of war was at once summoned, in which the praetors and a select number of senators were joined by the officers and commanders of the auxiliaries. There were frequent heated discussions, but finally, as there appeared to be no possible means of carrying on a war with Rome, it was decided to conclude a peace and to send an embassy along with the envoys who had come from Marcellus to obtain its ratification.

XXIX. *The Syracusans break with Rome.*—Not many days elapsed before a deputation came from Leontini begging for a force to protect their territory. This request seemed to afford a most favourable opportunity for relieving the city of a number of insubordinate and disorderly characters and getting rid of their leaders. Hippocrates received orders to march the deserters to Leontini, with these and a large body of mercenaries he made up a force of 4000 men. The expedition was welcomed both by those who were despatched and those who were despatching them: the former saw the opportunity, long hoped for, of effecting a revolution; the latter were thankful that the dregs of the city were being cleared out. It was, however, only a temporary alleviation of the disease, which afterwards became all the more aggravated. For Hippocrates began to devastate the country adjacent to the Roman province; at first making stealthy raids, then, when Appius had sent a detachment to protect the fields of the allies of Rome, he made an attack with his entire force upon one of the outposts and inflicted heavy loss.

When Marcellus was informed of this he promptly sent envoys to Syracuse to say that the peace they had guaranteed was broken, and that an occasion of war would never be wanting until Hippocrates and Epicydes had been banished far away, not only from Syracuse, but from Sicily. Epicydes feared that if he remained he should be held responsible for the misdeeds of his absent brother, and also should be unable to do his share in stirring up war, so he left for Leontini, and finding the people there sufficiently exasperated against Rome, he tried to detach them from Syracuse as well. "The Syracusans," he said, "have concluded a peace with Rome on condition that all the communities which were under their kings should remain under their rule; they are no longer content to be free themselves unless they can rule and tyrannise over others. You must make them understand that the Leontines also think it right that they should be free, and that for two reasons; it was on Leontine soil that the tyrant fell, and it was at Leontini that the cry of liberty was first raised, and from Leontini the people flocked to Syracuse, after deserting the royal leaders. Either that provision of the treaty must be struck out, or if it is insisted upon, the treaty must not be accepted."

They had no difficulty in persuading the people, and when the Syracusan envoys made their protest against the massacre of the Roman outpost and demanded that Hippocrates and Epicydes should go to Locri or any other place which they preferred so long as they left Sicily, they received the defiant reply that the Leontines had given no mandate to the Syracusans to conclude a treaty with Rome, nor were they bound by any compacts which other people made. The Syracusans reported this to the Romans, and said that the Leontines were not under their control, " in which case," they added, " the Romans may carry on war with them without any infringement of their treaty with us, nor shall we stand aloof in such a war, if it is clearly understood that when they have been subjugated they will again form part of our dominions in accordance with the terms of the treaty."

XXX. Marcellus advanced with his whole force against Leontini and summoned Appius to attack it on the opposite side. The men were so furious at the butchery of the outpost while negotiations were actually going on that they carried the place at the first assault. When Hippocrates and Epicydes saw that the enemy were getting possession of the walls and bursting in the gates, they retreated with a small following to the citadel, and during the night made their escape secretly to Herbesus. The Syracusans had already started with an army of 8000 men, and were met at the river Myla with the news that the city was captured. The rest of the message was mostly false: their informant told them that there had been an indiscriminate massacre of soldiers and civilians, and he thought that not a single adult was left alive; the city had been looted and the property of the wealthy citizens given to the troops.

On receiving this shocking intelligence the army halted; there was great excitement in all ranks, and the generals, Sosis and Dinomenes, consulted as to what was to be done. What lent a certain plausibility to the story and afforded apparent grounds for alarm was the scourging and beheading of as many as two thousand deserters, but otherwise not one of the Leontines or the regular troops had been injured after the city was taken and every man's property was restored to him beyond what had been destroyed in the first confusion of the assault. The men could not be induced to continue their march to Leontini, though they loudly protested that their comrades had been given up to massacre, nor would they consent to remain where they were and wait for more definite intelligence. The praetors saw that they were inclined to mutiny, but they did not believe that the excitement would last long if those who were leading them in their folly were put out of the way. They conducted the army to Megara and rode on with a small body of cavalry to Herbesus, hoping in the general panic to secure the betrayal of the place. As this attempt failed, they resolved to resort to force, and the following day marched from Megara with the intention of attacking Herbesus with their full strength. Now that all hope was cut off, Hippocrates and Epicydes thought that their only course, and that not at first sight a very safe one, was to give themselves up to the soldiers, who knew them well, and were highly incensed at the story of the massacre. So they went to meet the army. It so happened that the front ranks consisted of a body of 600 Cretans who had served under these very men in Hieronymus's army and had had experience of Hannibal's kindness, having been taken prisoners with other auxiliary troops at Trasumennus and afterwards released. When Hippocrates and Epicydes recognised them by their standards and the fashion of their arms they held out olive branches and other suppliant emblems and begged them to receive and protect them and not give them up to the Syracusans, who would surrender them to the Romans to be butchered.

XXXI. "Be of good heart," came back the answering shout, "we will share all your fortunes." During this colloquy the standards had halted and the whole army was stopped, but the generals had not yet learnt the cause of the delay. As soon as the rumour spread that Hippocrates and Epicydes were there, and cries of joy from the whole army showed unmistakably how glad they were that they had come, the praetors rode up to the front and sternly demanded: "What is the meaning of this conduct? What audacity is this on the part of the Cretans, that they should dare to hold interviews with an enemy and admit him against orders into their ranks?" They ordered Hippocrates to be arrested and thrown into chains. At this order such angry protests were made by the Cretans, and then by others, that the praetors saw that if they went any further their lives would be in danger. Perplexed and anxious they

issued orders to return to Megara, and sent messengers to
Syracuse to report as to the situation they were in. Upon men
who were ready to suspect everybody Hippocrates practised a
fresh deceit. He sent some of the Cretans to lurk near the
roads, and read a despatch which he had put together himself,
giving out that it had been intercepted. It bore the address,
" The praetors of Syracuse to the consul Marcellus," and after the
usual salutation went on to say, " You have acted rightly and
properly in not sparing a single Leontine, but all the mercenaries
are making common cause and Syracuse will never be at peace
as long as there are any foreign auxiliaries either in the city or in
our army. Do your best, therefore, to get into your power those
who are with our praetors in camp at Megara and by their
punishment secure liberty at last for Syracuse."

After the reading of this letter there was a general rush to
arms and such angry shouts were raised that the praetors,
appalled by the tumult, rode off to Syracuse. Not even their
flight quieted the disturbance, and the Syracusan soldiers were
being attacked by the mercenaries, nor would a single man have
escaped their violence had not Epicydes and Hippocrates withstood their rage, not from any feeling of pity or humanity, but
the fear of cutting off all hopes of their return. Besides, by
thus protecting the soldiers they would have them as faithful
adherents as well as hostages, and they would at the same time
win over their friends and relations in the first place by doing so
great a service and afterwards by keeping them as guarantees of
loyalty. Having learnt by experience how easy it is to excite
the senseless mob, they got hold of one of the men who had been
in Leontini when it was captured, and bribed him to carry intelligence to Syracuse similar to what they had been told at Myla,
and to rouse the passions of the populace by personally vouching
for the truth of his story and silencing all doubts by declaring
that he had been an eyewitness of what he narrated.

XXXII. This man not only obtained credence with the mob,
but after being introduced into the senate actually produced an
impression on that body. Some of those present who were by no
means lacking in sense openly averred that it was a very good
thing that the Romans had displayed their rapacity and cruelty
at Leontini for, had they entered Syracuse, they would have
behaved in the same way or even worse, since there was more
to feed their rapacity. It was the unanimous opinion that the
gates should be shut and the city put in a state of defence, but
they were not unanimous in their fears and hates. To the whole

of the soldiery and to a large proportion of the population the
Romans were the objects of detestation; the praetor and a few
of the aristocracy were anxious to guard against a nearer and
more pressing danger, though they too were excited by the false
intelligence. For as a matter of fact, Hippocrates and Epicydes
were already at the Hexapylon, and conversations were going
on amongst the relations of the Syracusan soldiers about opening
the gates and letting their common country be defended from
any attack by the Romans.

One of the gates of the Hexapylon had already been thrown
open and the troops were beginning to be admitted when the
praetors appeared on the scene. At first they used commands
and threats, then they brought their personal authority to
bear, and at last, finding all their efforts useless, they resorted
to entreaties, regardless of their dignity, and implored the
citizens not to betray their country to men who had once danced
attendance on a tyrant and were now corrupting the army.
But the ears of the maddened people were deaf to their appeals
and the gates were battered as much from within as from without.
After they had all been burst open the army was admitted
through the whole length of the Hexapylon.

The praetors and the younger citizens took refuge in the
Achradina. The enemies' numbers were swelled by the mercenaries, the deserters, and all the late king's guards who had been
left in Syracuse, with the result that the Achradina was captured
at the first attempt, and all the praetors who had failed to make
their escape in the confusion were put to death. Night put an
end to the massacre. The following day the slaves were called
up to receive the cap of freedom and all who were in gaol were
released. This motley crowd elected Hippocrates and Epicydes
praetors, and Syracuse, after its short-lived gleam of liberty, fell
back into its old bondage.

XXXIII. *The Siege of Syracuse.*—When the Romans received
information of what was going on they at once broke their camp
at Leontini and marched to Syracuse. Some envoys had been
sent by Appius to pass through the harbour on board a quin-
quereme, and a quadrireme which had sailed in advance of
them was captured, the envoys themselves making their escape
with great difficulty.

It soon became apparent that not only the laws of peace but
even the laws of war were no longer respected. The Roman
army had encamped at the Olympium—a temple of Jupiter—
about a mile and a half from the city. It was decided to send

envoys again from there; and Hippocrates and Epicydes met them with their attendants outside the gate, to prevent them from entering the city. The spokesman of the Romans said they were not bringing war to the Syracusans but help and succour, both for those who had been cowed by terror and for those who were enduring a servitude worse than exile, worse even than death itself. " The Romans," he said, " will not allow the infamous massacre of their allies to go unavenged. If, therefore, those who have taken refuge with us are at liberty to return home unmolested, if the ringleaders of the massacre are given up and if Syracuse is allowed once more to enjoy her liberty and her laws, there is no need of arms; but if these things are not done we shall visit with all the horrors of war those, whoever they are, who stand in the way of our demands being fulfilled." To this Epicydes replied: " If we had been the persons to whom your demands are addressed we should have replied to them; when the government of Syracuse is in the hands of those to whom you were sent, then you can return again. If you provoke us to war you will learn by experience that to attack Syracuse is not quite the same thing as attacking Leontini." With these words he left the envoys and closed the gates.

Then a simultaneous attack by sea and land was commenced on Syracuse. The land attack was directed against the Hexapylon; that by sea against Achradina, the walls of which are washed by the waves. As they had carried Leontini at the first assault owing to the panic they created, so the Romans felt confident that they would find some point where they could penetrate into the wide and scattered city, and they brought up the whole of their siege artillery against the walls.

XXXIV. An assault begun so vigorously would have undoubtedly succeeded had it not been for one man living at the time in Syracuse. That man was ARCHIMEDES. Unrivalled as he was as an observer of the heavens and the stars, he was still more wonderful as the inventor and creator of military works and engines by which with very little trouble he was able to baffle the most laborious efforts of the enemy. The city wall ran over hills of varying altitude, for the most part lofty and difficult of access, but in some places low and admitting of approach from the level of the valleys. This wall he furnished with artillery of every kind, according to the requirements of the different positions. Marcellus with sixty quinqueremes attacked the wall of Achradina, which as above stated is washed by the sea. In the other ships were archers, slingers, and even light

infantry, whose missile is an awkward one to return for those
who are not expert at it, so they hardly allowed any one to
remain on the walls without being wounded. As they needed
space to hurl their missiles, they kept their ships some distance
from the walls. The other quinqueremes were fastened together
in pairs, the oars on the inside being shipped so as to allow of
the sides being brought together; they were propelled like one
ship by the outside set of oars, and when thus fastened together
they carried towers built up in stories and other machinery for
battering the wall.

To meet this naval attack Archimedes placed on the ramparts
engines of various sizes. The ships at a distance he bombarded
with immense stones, the nearer ones he raked with lighter
and therefore more numerous missiles; lastly he pierced the
entire height of the walls with loopholes about eighteen inches
wide so that his men might discharge their missiles without
exposing themselves. Through these openings they aimed
arrows and small so-called "scorpions" at the enemy. Some
of the ships which came in still more closely in order to be
beneath the range of the artillery were attacked in the following
way. A huge beam swinging on a pivot projected from the
wall and a strong chain hanging from the end had an iron
grappling hook fastened to it. This was lowered on to the
prow of a ship and a heavy lead weight brought the other end
of the beam to the ground, raising the prow into the air and
making the vessel rest on its stern. Then the weight being
removed, the prow was suddenly dashed on to the water as
though it had fallen from the wall, to the great consternation of
the sailors; the shock was so great that if it fell straight it
shipped a considerable amount of water.

In this way the naval assault was foiled, and all the hopes of
the besiegers now rested upon an attack from the side of the
land, delivered with their entire strength.

But here too Hiero had for many years devoted money and
pains to fitting up military engines of every kind, guided and
directed by the unapproachable skill of Archimedes. The
nature of the ground also helped the defence. The rock on
which the foundations of the wall mostly rested was for the
greater part of its length so steep that not only when stones
were hurled from the engines but even when rolled down with
their own weight they fell with terrible effect on the enemy.
The same cause made any approach to the foot of the walls
difficult and the foothold precarious.

A council of war was accordingly held and it was decided, since all their attempts were frustrated, to desist from active operations and confine themselves simply to a blockade, and cut off all supplies from the enemy both by land and sea.

XXXV. Marcellus in the meanwhile proceeded with about one-third of his army to recover the cities which in the general disturbance had seceded to the Carthaginians. Helorum and Herbesus at once made their submission, Megara was taken by assault and sacked and then completely destroyed in order to strike terror into the rest, especially Syracuse. Himilco, who had been for a considerable time cruising with his fleet off the promontory of Pachynus, returned to Carthage as soon as he heard that Syracuse had been seized by Hippocrates. Supported by the envoys from Hippocrates and by a despatch from Hannibal in which he said that the time had arrived for winning back Sicily in the most glorious way, and by the weight of his own personal presence, he had no difficulty in persuading the government to send to Sicily as large a force as they could of both infantry and cavalry. Sailing back to the island he landed at Heraclea an army of 20,000 infantry, 3000 cavalry, and twelve elephants, a very much stronger force than he had with him at Pachynus. Immediately on his arrival he took Heraclea and a few days later Agrigentum. Other cities which had taken the side of Carthage were now so hopeful of expelling the Romans from Sicily that even the spirits of the blockaded Syracusans began to rise. Their generals considered that a portion of their army would be adequate for the defence of the city, and accordingly divided their force; Epicydes was to superintend the defence of the city, whilst Hippocrates was to conduct the campaign against the Roman consul in conjunction with Himilco. Hippocrates marched out of the city in the night through an unguarded part of the Roman lines and selected a site for his camp near the city of Acrillae. Marcellus came upon them while they were entrenching themselves. He had marched hastily to Agrigentum in the hope of reaching it before the enemy, but, finding it already occupied, was returning to his position before Syracuse and expected least of all to find a Syracusan force at that time and in that place. Knowing that he was no match with the troops he had for Himilco and his Carthaginians, he had advanced with the utmost caution, keeping a sharp look-out and guarding against any possible surprise.

XXXVI. Whilst thus on the alert he fell in with Hippocrates, and the preparations he had made to meet the Carthaginians served him in good stead against the Syracusans. He caught them whilst forming their camp, dispersed and in disorder, and for the most part unarmed. The whole of their infantry were cut off, the cavalry offered but slight resistance and escaped with Hippocrates to Acrae.

That battle checked the Sicilians in their revolt from Rome and Marcellus returned to Syracuse. A few days later Himilco, who had been joined by Hippocrates, fixed his camp by the river Anapus, about eight miles from Syracuse. A Carthaginian fleet of fifty-five vessels of war sailed about the same time into the great harbour of Syracuse from the high seas; and a Roman fleet, also, of thirty quinqueremes, landed the first legion at Panormus. It looked as if the war had been wholly diverted from Italy, so completely were both peoples devoting their attention to Sicily. Himilco fully expected that the legion which had been landed at Panormus would fall into his hands on its march to Syracuse, but he was disappointed as it did not take the route he expected. Whilst he marched inland, the legion proceeded along the coast, accompanied by the fleet, and joined Appius Claudius who had come to meet it with a portion of his force.

Now the Carthaginians despaired of relieving Syracuse and left it to its fate. Bomilcar did not feel sufficient confidence in his fleet as the Romans had one of double the number, and he saw that by remaining there inactive he was only aggravating the scarcity which prevailed amongst his allies, so he put out to sea and sailed across to Africa. Himilco had followed upon Marcellus' track to Syracuse, hoping for a chance of fighting before he was joined by superior forces; and as no opportunity of doing so occurred and he saw that the enemy were in great strength and safe within their lines round Syracuse he marched away, not caring to waste time by looking on in idleness at the investment of his allies. He also wished to be free to march wherever any hope of defection from Rome summoned him, that he might by his presence encourage those whose sympathies were with Carthage. He began with the capture of Murgantia, where the populace betrayed the Roman garrison, and where a large quantity of corn and provisions of all kinds had been stored for the use of the Romans.

XXXVII. *Roman Treatment of Henna.*—Other cities took courage from this example of defection, and the Roman garrisons were either expelled from their strongholds or treacherously overpowered.

Henna, situated on a lofty position precipitous on all sides, was naturally impregnable, and it had also a strong Roman garrison and a commandant who was not at all a suitable man for traitors to approach. L. Pinarius was a keen soldier and trusted more to his own vigilance and alertness than to the fidelity of the Sicilians. The numerous betrayals and defections which reached his ears and the massacre of Roman garrisons made him more than ever careful to take every possible precaution. So by day and night alike, everything was in readiness, every position occupied by guards and sentinels, and the soldiers never laid aside their arms or left their posts. The chief citizens of Henna had already come to an understanding with Himilco about betraying the garrison, and when they observed all this vigilance and recognised that the Romans were not open to any treacherous surprise, they saw that they would have to use forcible measures. "The city and its stronghold," they said, "are under our authority; if as free men we accepted the Roman alliance we did not hand ourselves over to be kept in custody as slaves. We think it right, therefore, that the keys of the gates should be given up to us; the strongest bond between good allies is to trust one another's loyalty; it is only if we remain friends with Rome voluntarily and not by constraint that your people can feel grateful to us."

To this the Roman commandant replied: "I have been placed in charge here by my commanding officer, it is from him that I have received the keys of the gates and the custody of the citadel; I do not hold these things at my own disposal or at the disposal of the citizens of Henna, but at the disposal of the man who committed them to my charge. To quit one's post is with the Romans a capital offence, and fathers have even punished it as such in the case of their own children. The consul Marcellus is not far away, send to him, he has the right and authority to act in the matter." They said that they should not send, and if argument failed they would seek some other method of vindicating their liberty. To this Pinarius answered: "Well, if you think it too much trouble to send to the consul, you can, at all events, give me an opportunity of consulting the people, that it may be made clear whether this demand proceeds from a few or from the whole body of the citizens." They agreed to convene a meeting of the assembly the following day.

XXXVIII. After he had returned from the interview to the citadel, he called his men together and addressed them as follows: "I think, soldiers, you have heard what has happened lately and how the Roman garrisons have been surprised and overwhelmed by the Sicilians. That treachery you have escaped, in the first place by the good providence of the gods and next by your own steady courage and by your persistent watchfulness and remaining under arms night and day. I only hope the rest of our time may be spent without suffering or inflicting things too horrible to speak about. The precautions we have so far taken have been against secret treachery; as that has proved unsuccessful they are now openly demanding the keys of the gates; and no sooner will they be delivered than Henna will be in the power of the Carthaginians, and we here shall be butchered with greater cruelty than the garrison of Murgantia. I have succeeded with difficulty in getting one night allowed for deliberation so that I could inform you of the impending peril. At daybreak they are going to hold an assembly of the people at which they will fling charges against me and stir up the populace against you. So to-morrow Henna will run with blood, either yours or that of its own citizens. If you are not beforehand with them, there is no hope for you; if you are, there is no danger. Victory will fall to him who first draws the sword. So all be on the alert and wait attentively for the signal. I shall be in the assembly and will spin out the time by speaking and arguing till everything is perfectly ready, and when I give the signal with my toga, raise a loud shout and make an attack on the crowd from all sides and cut everything down with the sword, and take care that nothing survives from which either open violence or treachery is to be feared." Then he continued, " You, Mother Ceres and Proserpina, and all ye deities, celestial and infernal, who have your dwelling in this city and these sacred lakes and groves—I pray and beseech you to be gracious and merciful to us if we are indeed purposing to do this deed not that we may inflict but that we may escape treachery and murder. I should say more to you, soldiers, if you were going to fight with an armed foe; it is those who are unarmed and unsuspecting whom you will slay till you are weary of slaughter. The consul's camp, too, is in the neighbourhood, so nothing need be feared from Himilco and the Carthaginians."

XXXIX. After this speech he dismissed them to seek refreshment and rest. The next morning some of them were posted in various places to block the streets and close the exits from the theatre, the majority took their stand round the theatre and on the ground above it; they had frequently watched the proceedings of the assembly from there, and so their appearance aroused no suspicion. The Roman commandant was introduced to the assembly by the magistrates. He said that it was the consul and not he who had the right and the power to decide the matter, and went pretty much over the same ground as on the day before. At first one or two voices were heard and then several, demanding the surrender of the keys, till the whole assembly broke out into loud and threatening shouts, and seemed on the point of making a murderous attack upon him as he still hesitated and delayed. Then, at last, he gave the agreed signal with his toga, and the soldiers, who had long been ready and waiting, raised a shout and rushed down upon the crowd, while others blocked the exits from the densely packed theatre. Hemmed in and caged, the men of Henna were ruthlessly cut down and lay about in heaps; not only where the dead were piled up, but where in trying to escape they scrambled over each other's heads and fell one upon another, the wounded stumbling over the unwounded, the living over the dead. Then the soldiers dispersed in all directions and the city was filled with dead bodies and people fleeing for their lives, for the soldiers slew the defenceless crowd with as much fury as though they were fighting against an equal foe, and glowing with all the ardour of battle.

So Henna was saved for Rome by a deed which was criminal if it was not unavoidable. Marcellus not only passed no censure on the transaction, but even bestowed the plundered property of the citizens upon his troops, thinking that by the terror thus inspired the Sicilians would be deterred from any longer betraying their garrisons. The news of this occurrence spread through Sicily almost in a day, for the city, lying in the middle of the island, was no less famous for the natural strength of its position than it was for the sacred associations which connected every part of it with the old story of the Rape of Proserpine. It was universally felt that a foul and murderous outrage had been offered to the abode of gods as well as to the dwellings of men, and many who had before been wavering now went over to the Carthaginians. Hippocrates and Himilco, who had brought up their forces to Henna on the invitation of the would-be betrayers, finding themselves unable to effect anything retired, the former to Murgantia, the latter to Agrigentum. Marcellus marched back to Leontini, and after collecting supplies of corn and other provisions for the camp he left a small detachment to hold the city and returned to the blockade of Syracuse. He gave Appius Claudius leave to go to Rome to carry on his candidature for the consulship, and placed T. Quinctius Crispinus in his stead in command of the fleet and the old camp, whilst he himself constructed and fortified winter quarters in a place called Leon about five miles from Hexapylon.

These were the main incidents in the Sicilian campaign up to the beginning of the winter.

XL. *Events in Greece.*—The war with Philip which had been for some time apprehended actually broke out this summer. The praetor, M. Valerius, who had his base at Brundisium and was cruising off the Calabrian coast, received information from Oricum that Philip had made an attempt on Apollonia by sending a fleet of 120 light vessels up the river Aous, and then finding that matters were moving too slowly, he had brought up his army by night to Oricum, and as the place lay in a plain and was not strong enough to defend itself either by its fortifications or its garrison, it was taken at the first assault. His informants begged him to send help and to keep off one who was unmistakably an enemy to Rome from injuring the cities on the coast which were in danger solely because they lay opposite to Italy. M. Valerius complied with their request, and leaving a small garrison of 2000 men under P. Valerius, set sail with his fleet ready for action, and such soldiers as the warships had not room for he placed on the cargo boats. On the second day he reached Oricum, and as the king on his departure had only left a weak force to hold it, it was taken with very little fighting. Whilst he was there envoys came to him from Apollonia with the announcement that they were undergoing a siege because they refused to break with Rome, and unless the Romans protected them, they should be unable to withstand the Macedonians any longer. Valerius promised to do what they wanted and he sent a picked force of 2000 men on warships to the mouth of the river under the command of Q. Naevius Crista, an active and experienced soldier. He disembarked his men and sent the ships back to rejoin the fleet at Oricum, whilst he marched at some distance from the river, where he would be least likely to meet any of the king's troops, and entered the city by night, without being observed by any of the enemy. The following day they rested to give him an opportunity of making a thorough inspection of the armed force of Apollonia and the strength of the city. He was much encouraged by the result of his inspection and also by the account which his scouts gave of the indolence and negligence which prevailed amongst the enemy.

Marching out of the city in the dead of the night, without the slightest noise or confusion, he got within the enemy's camp, which was so unguarded and open that it is credibly stated that more than a thousand men were inside the lines before they were detected, and if they had only refrained from using their swords they could actually have reached the king's tent. The slaughter of those nearest the camp gates aroused the enemy, and such universal panic and terror ensued that no one seized his weapons or made any attempt to drive out the invaders. Even the king himself, suddenly wakened from sleep, fled half-dressed, in a state not decent for a common soldier, to say nothing of a king, and escaped to his ships in the river. The rest fled wildly in the same direction. The losses in killed and prisoners were under three thousand, the prisoners being much the most numerous. After the camp had been plundered the Apollonians removed the catapults, the ballistae, and the other siege artillery, which had been put in readiness for the assault, into the city for the defence of their own walls if such an emergency should ever occur again; all the other booty was given to the Romans.

As soon as the news of this action reached Oricum, Valerius sent the fleet to the mouth of the river to prevent any attempt on the part of Philip to escape by sea. The king did not feel sufficient confidence in risking a contest either by sea or land, and hauled his ships ashore or burnt them and made his way to Macedonia by land, the greater part of his army having lost their arms and all their belongings. M. Valerius wintered with his fleet at Oricum.

XLI. *The Campaign in Spain.* — The fighting went on in Spain this year with varying success. Before the Romans crossed the Ebro Mago and Hasdrubal defeated enormous forces of Spaniards. All Spain west of the Ebro would have abandoned the side of Rome had not P. Cornelius Scipio hurriedly crossed the Ebro and by his timely appearance confirmed the wavering allies. The Romans first fixed their camp at Castrum Album,[12] a place made famous by the death of the great Hamilcar, and had accumulated supplies of corn there. The country round, however, was infested by the enemy, and his cavalry had attacked the Romans while on the march with impunity; they lost as many as 2000 men who had fallen behind or were straying from the line of march. They decided to withdraw to a less hostile part and entrenched themselves at the Mount of Victory. Cn. Scipio joined them here with his entire force, and Hasdrubal, the son of Gisgo, came up also with a complete army. There were now three Carthaginian generals and they all encamped on the other side of the river opposite the Roman camp.

Publius Scipio went out with some light cavalry to reconnoitre, but in spite of all his precautions he did not remain unobserved, and would have been overpowered in the open plain had he not seized some rising ground that was near. Here he was surrounded and it was only his brother's timely arrival that rescued him.

Castulo, a powerful and famous city of Spain, and in such close alliance with Carthage that Hannibal took a wife from there, seceded to Rome.

The Carthaginians commenced an attack upon Illiturgis, owing to the presence of a Roman garrison there, and it looked as if they would certainly reduce it by famine. Cn. Scipio went to the assistance of the besieged with a legion in light marching order, and fighting his way between the two Carthaginian camps, entered the town after inflicting heavy losses upon the besiegers. The following day he made a sortie and was equally successful. Above 12,000 men were killed in the two battles and more than a thousand were made prisoners; thirty-six standards were also captured. In this way the siege of Illiturgis was raised.

Their next move was to Bigerra—also in alliance with Rome— which they proceeded to attack, but on Cn. Scipio's appearance they retired without striking a blow.

XLII. The Carthaginian camp was next shifted to Munda, and the Romans instantly followed them. Here a pitched battle was fought for four hours and the Romans were winning a splendid victory when the signal was given to retire. Cn. Scipio was wounded in the thigh with a javelin and the soldiers round him were in great fear lest the wound should prove fatal. There was not the smallest doubt that if that delay had not occurred the Carthaginian camp could have been captured that same day, for the men and the elephants, too, had been driven back to their lines, and thirty-nine of the latter had been transfixed by the heavy Roman javelins. It is stated that 12,000 men were killed in this battle and about 3000 made prisoners, whilst fifty-seven standards were taken.

From there the Carthaginians retreated to Auringis, the Romans following them up slowly and allowing them no time to recover from their defeats. There another battle was fought, and Scipio was carried into the field on a litter. The victory was decisive, though not half as many of the enemy were killed as on the previous occasion, for there were fewer left to fight. But the Spaniards have a natural instinct for repairing the losses in war, and when Mago was sent by his brother to raise troops, they very soon filled up the gaps in the army and encouraged their generals to try another battle.   Though they were mostly fresh soldiers, yet as they had to defend a cause which had been repeatedly worsted in so short a time, they fought with the same spirit and the same result as those before them had done. More than 8000 men were killed, not less than 1000 made prisoners, and fifty-eight standards were captured.   Most of the spoil had belonged to Gauls, there were a large number of golden armlets and chains, and two distinguished Gaulish chieftains, Moenia-coepto and Vismaro, fell in the battle.   Eight elephants were captured and three killed.[13]

As things were going so prosperously in Spain, the Romans at last began to feel ashamed of having left Saguntum, the primary cause of the war, in the possession of the enemy for almost eight years.   So after expelling the Carthaginian garrison they recovered the town and restored it to all the former inhabitants whom the ravages of war had spared.   The Turdetani, who had brought about the war between Saguntum and Carthage, were reduced to subjection and sold as slaves; their city was utterly destroyed.

XLIII. *Affairs in Rome.*—Such was the course of events in Spain in the year when Q. Fabius and M. Claudius were consuls.

Immediately the new tribunes of the plebs entered office, M. Metellus, one of their number, indicted the censors, P. Furius and M. Atilius, and demanded that they should be put on their trial before the people.   His reason for taking this course was that the year before they had deprived him of his horse, degraded him from his tribe, and disfranchised him on the ground that he was involved in the plot which had been formed after the battle of Cannae for abandoning Italy.   The other nine tribunes, however, interposed their veto against their being tried whilst holding office, and the matter fell through.   The death of P. Furius prevented them from completing the *lustrum* and M. Atilius resigned office.

The consular elections were held under the presidency of Q. Fabius Maximus, the consul.   Both consuls were elected in their absence—Q. Fabius Maximus, the son of the consul, and Tiberius Sempronius Gracchus, for the second time.   The praetors elected were M. Atilius and three who were at the time

curule ædiles, namely, P. Sempronius Tuditanus, Cnaeus
Fulvius Centimalus, and M. Æmilius Lepidus. It is recorded
that the scenic games were celebrated for the first time this year
by the curule ædiles and that the celebration lasted four days.
The ædile Tuditanus was the officer who led his men through the
midst of the enemy after the defeat at Cannae when all the others
were paralysed with terror.[14]

As soon as the elections were over, the consuls elect were, on
the advice of Q. Fabius, recalled to Rome to enter upon their
duties. After they had returned they consulted the senate on
the conduct of the war, the allocation of provinces to themselves
and the praetors, the armies to be raised, and the men who were
to command them.

XLIV. The following was the distribution of the provinces
and the armies. The operations against Hannibal were entrusted to the two consuls, and Sempronius was to retain the
army he had been commanding. Fabius was to take over his
father's army. Each consisted of two legions. M. Æmilius,
the praetor, who had the jurisdiction over aliens, was to have
Luceria for his province and the two legions which Q. Fabius,
the newly elected consul, had been commanding as praetor;
P. Sempronius Tuditanus received Ariminum as his province
and Cn. Fulvius, Suessula, each likewise with two legions,
Fulvius being in command of the City legions and Tuditanus
taking over those from Manius Pomponius. The commands
were extended in the following cases: M. Claudius was to retain
that part of Sicily which had constituted Hiero's kingdom,
Lentulus as propraetor was to administer the old province;
Titus Otacilius was to continue in command of the fleet, no fresh
troops being supplied him, and M. Valerius was to operate in
Greece and Macedonia with the legion and ships which he had;
Q. Mucius was to continue in command of his old army of two
legions in Sardinia, and C. Terentius was to keep his one legion
at Picenum. Orders were given for two legions to be raised in
the City and 20,000 men to be furnished by the allies.[15]

These were the generals and the troops that were to be the
bulwark of Rome against the many wars, some actually going on,
some anticipated, that were threatening the existence of her
dominion.

After raising the City contingent, and recruiting fresh drafts
for other legions, the two consuls before they left the City set
about the expiation of certain portents which had been announced.
Part of the City wall and some of the gates had been struck by

lightning, as had also the temple of Jupiter at Aricia. Other things which people imagined they had seen or heard were believed to be true; warships were supposed to have been seen in the river at Tarracina, whilst there were none there; a clashing of arms was heard in the temple of Jupiter Vicilinus in the neighbourhood of Compsa, and the river at Amiternum was said to have run with blood.

When these portents had been expiated in accordance with the directions of the pontiffs, the consuls left for the front; Sempronius for Lucania, Fabius for Apulia. Old Fabius came into his son's camp at Suessula as his lieutenant. The son went out to meet him with the twelve lictors preceding him in single file. The old man rode past eleven of them, all of whom out of respect for him remained silent, whereupon the consul ordered the remaining lictor who was immediately in front of him to do his duty. The man thereupon called to Fabius to dismount, and he springing from his horse said to his son, " I wanted to find out, my son, whether you sufficiently realised that you are consul."

XLV. *Capture of Arpi.*—One night, Dasius Altinius of Arpi paid a stealthy visit to this camp, accompanied by three slaves, and offered for a fitting reward to betray Arpi. Fabius referred the matter to the council of war, and some thought he ought to be treated as a deserter, scourged and beheaded. They said he was a trimmer, an enemy to both sides, for, after the defeat of Cannae, as though loyalty depended on success, he had gone over to Hannibal and had drawn Arpi over with him, and now that the cause of Rome was, in the teeth of all his hopes and wishes, springing up, as it were, again from its roots, he was promising a fresh treason by way of indemnifying those whom he betrayed before. He openly espoused one side while all his sympathies were with the other, faithless as an ally, contemptible as an enemy; like the man who would have betrayed Falerii, or the man who offered to poison Pyrrhus, let him be made a third warning to all renegades.

The consul's father took a different view. " Some men," he said, " oblivious of times and seasons, pass judgment upon everything as calmly and impartially in the excitement of war as though they were at peace. The more important matter for us to discuss and decide is how we can possibly prevent our allies from deserting us, but this is the last thing we are thinking about; we are talking about the duty of making an example of any one who sees his error and looks back with regret to the old alliance. But if a man is at liberty to forsake Rome, but not at liberty to return to her, who can fail to see that in a short time the Roman empire, bereft of its allies, will find every part of Italy bound by treaty to Carthage? Still I am not going to advise that any confidence be placed in Altinius; I shall suggest a middle course in dealing with him. I should recommend that he be treated neither as an enemy nor as a friend, but be interned in some city we can trust not far from our camp and kept there during the war. When that is over, then we should discuss whether he deserves punishment for his former disloyalty more than he merits pardon for his coming back to us now."

Fabius' suggestions met with general approval, and Altinius was handed over to some officials from Cales together with those who accompanied him. He had brought with him a considerable amount of gold, and this was ordered to be taken care of for him. At Cales he was free to move about in the daytime, but was always followed by a guard, who kept him in confinement at night. At Arpi he was missed from home and a search was commenced, rumours soon ran through the city and naturally caused intense excitement, seeing they had lost their leader. Fears were entertained of a revolution, and messengers were at once despatched to Hannibal. The Carthaginian was not at all concerned at what had happened; he had long suspected the man and doubted his loyalty, and he had now a plausible reason for seizing and selling the property of a very rich man. But, in order to create a belief that he was swayed more by anger than by avarice, he aggravated his rapacity by an act of atrocious cruelty. He sent for the wife and children, and after questioning them first about the circumstances under which Altinius had disappeared, and then about the amount of gold and silver which he had left at home, and so finding out all he wanted to know, he had them burnt alive.

XLVI. Fabius broke up his camp at Suessula and decided to begin by an attack on Arpi. He encamped about half a mile from it, and on examining from a near position the situation of the city and its fortifications, he saw one part where it was most strongly fortified and, therefore, less carefully guarded, and at this point he determined to deliver his assault. After seeing that everything required for the storm was in readiness, he selected out of the whole army the pick of the centurions and placed them under the command of tribunes who were distinguished for courage. He then furnished them with six hundred of the rank and file, a number which he deemed quite sufficient for his purpose, and gave them orders to carry scaling ladders to that point when they heard the bugles sound the fourth watch. There was a low narrow gate which led into an unfrequented street running through a lonely part of the city. His orders were that they were first to scale the wall with their ladders, and then open the gate or break the bolts and bars from the inside, and when they were in possession of that quarter of the city they were to give a signal on the bugle, so that the rest of the troops might be brought up, and he would have everything in order and ready. His instructions were carried out to the letter, and what seemed likely to prove a hindrance turned out to be of the greatest help in concealing their movements. A rain storm which began at midnight drove all the sentries and outposts to seek shelter in the houses, and the roar of the rain which at first came down like a deluge prevented the noise of those who were at work on the gate from being heard. Then when the sound of the rain fell upon the ear more gently and regularly, it soothed most of the defenders to sleep. As soon as they were in possession of the gate, they placed the buglers at equal distances along the street and ordered them to sound the signal to give notice to the consul. This having been done as previously arranged, the consul ordered a general advance, and shortly before daylight he entered the city through the broken down gate.

XLVII. Now at last the enemy was roused; there was a lull in the storm and daylight was approaching. Hannibal's garrison in the city amounted to about 5000 men, and the citizens themselves had raised a force of 3000. These the Carthaginians put in front to meet the enemy, that there might be no attempt at treachery in their rear. The fighting began in the dark in the narrow streets, the Romans having occupied not only the streets near the gate but the houses also, that they might not be assailed from the roofs. Gradually as it grew light some of the citizen troops and some of the Romans recognised one another, and entered into conversation. The Roman soldiers asked what it was that the Arpinians wanted, what wrong had Rome done them, what good service had Carthage rendered them that they, Italians bred and born, should fight against their old friends the Romans on behalf of foreigners and barbarians, and wish to make Italy a tributary province of Africa. The people of Arpi urged in their excuse that they knew nothing of what was going on, they had in fact been sold by their leaders to the Carthaginians, they had been victimised and enslaved by a small oligarchy. When a beginning had been once made the conversations became more and more general; at last the praetor of Arpi was conducted by his friends to the consul, and after they had given each other mutual assurances, surrounded by the troops under their standards, the citizens suddenly turned against the Carthaginians and fought for the Romans. A body of Spaniards also, numbering something less than a thousand, transferred their services to the consul upon the sole condition that the Carthaginian garrison should be allowed to depart uninjured. The gates were opened for them and they were dismissed, according to the stipulation, in perfect safety, and went to Hannibal at Salapia. Thus Arpi was restored to the Romans without the loss of a single life, except in the case of one man who had long ago been a traitor and had recently deserted. The Spaniards were ordered to receive double rations, and the republic availed itself on very many occasions of their courage and fidelity.

While one of the consuls was in Apulia and the other in Lucania some hundred and twelve Campanian nobles left Capua by permission of the magistrates for the purpose, as they alleged, of carrying away plunder from the enemy's territory. They really, however, rode off to the Roman camp above Suessula, and when they came up to the outposts they told them that they wished for an interview with the commander, Cn. Fulvius. On being informed of their request he gave orders for ten of their number to be conducted to him, after they had laid aside their arms. When he heard what they wanted, which was simply that, after the recapture of Capua, their property might be restored to them, he received them all under his protection.

The other praetor took the town of Atrinum by storm. More than 7000 were taken prisoners and a considerable quantity of bronze and silver coinage seized.

At Rome there was a dreadful fire which lasted for two nights and a day. All the buildings between the Salinae and the Porta Carmentalis, including the Æquimaelium, the Vicus Jugarius, and the temples of Fortune and Mater Matuta were burnt to the ground. The fire travelled for a considerable distance outside the gate and destroyed much property and many sacred objects.

XLVIII. *Roman Support in Africa.* — The two Scipios, Publius and Cnaeus, after their successful operations in Spain, in the course of which they won back many old allies and gained new ones, during the year began to hope for similar results in Africa. Syphax, king of the Numidians, had suddenly taken up a hostile attitude towards Carthage. The Scipios sent three centurions on a mission to him, with instructions to conclude a friendly alliance with him and to assure him that if he would go on persistently harassing the Carthaginians he would confer an obligation on the senate and people of Rome, and it would be their endeavour to repay the debt of gratitude at a fitting time and with large interest. The barbarian was delighted at the mission and held frequent conversations with the centurions upon the methods of warfare. As he listened to the seasoned soldiers he found out how many things he was ignorant of, and how great the contrast was between his own practice and their discipline and organisation. He asked that whilst two of them carried back the report of their mission to their commanders, the third might remain with him as a military instructor. He explained that the Numidians made very poor infantry soldiers, they were only useful as mounted troops; he explained that this was the style of warfare which his ancestors had adopted from the very earliest times, it was the style to which he had been trained from his boyhood. They had an enemy who depended mainly upon his infantry, and if he wished to meet him with equal strength he must provide himself also with infantry. His kingdom contained an abundant population fit for the purpose, but he did not know the proper method of arming and equipping and drilling them. All was disorderly and haphazard, just like a crowd collected together by chance.

The envoys replied that for the time being they would do what he wished, on the distinct understanding that if their commanders did not approve of the arrangement he would at once send back the one who remained. This man's name was Statorius. The king sent some Numidians to accompany the two Romans to Spain and obtain sanction for the arrangement from the commanders. He also charged them to take immediate steps to persuade the Numidians who were acting as auxiliaries with the Carthaginian troops to come over to the Romans.

Out of the large number of young men which the country contained Statorius enrolled a force of infantry for the king. These he formed into companies pretty much on the Roman model, and by drilling and exercising them he taught them to follow their standards and keep their ranks. He also made them so familiar with the work of entrenchment and other regular military tasks that the king placed quite as much confidence in his infantry as in his cavalry, and in a pitched battle fought on a level plain he proved superior to the Carthaginians.

The presence of the king's envoys in Spain proved very serviceable to the Romans, for on the news of their arrival numerous desertions took place amongst the Numidians. So between Syphax and the Romans friendly relations were established.

As soon as the Carthaginians heard what was going on, they sent envoys to Gala, who reigned in the other part of Numidia over a tribe called Maesuli.

XLIX. Gala had a son called Masinissa, seventeen years old, but a youth of such a strong character that even then it was evident that he would make the kingdom greater and wealthier than he received it. The envoys pointed out to Gala that since Syphax had joined the Romans in order to strengthen his hands, by their alliance, against the kings and peoples of Africa, the best thing for him to do would be to unite with the Carthaginians as soon as possible, before Syphax crossed into Spain or the Romans into Africa. Syphax, they said, could easily be crushed, for he had got nothing out of the Roman alliance except the name.

Gala's son asked to be entrusted with the management of the war and easily persuaded his father to send an army, which in conjunction with the Carthaginians conquered Syphax in a great battle, in which it is stated that 30,000 men were killed. Syphax with a few of his horse fled from the field to the Maurusii, a tribe of Numidians who dwell at almost the furthest point of Africa near the ocean, opposite Gades. At the news of his arrival the barbarians flocked to him from all sides and in a short time he armed an immense force.

Whilst he was preparing to cross over with them into Spain, which was only separated by a narrow strait, Masinissa arrived with his victorious army, and won a great reputation by the way in which he concluded the war against Syphax without any help from the Carthaginians.

In Spain nothing of any importance took place except that the Romans secured for themselves the services of the Celtiberians by offering them the same pay which the Carthaginians had agreed to pay. They also sent to Italy three hundred of the leading Spanish nobility to win over their countrymen who were serving with Hannibal. That is the solitary incident in Spain worth recording for the year, and its interest lies in the fact that the Romans had never had a mercenary soldier in their camp until they employed the Celtiberians.

BOOK XXV

FALL OF SYRACUSE

1. *Foreign Superstitions in Rome.*—While these operations in Spain and Africa were going on, Hannibal spent the whole summer in the Sallentine territory in the hope of securing the city of Tarentum by treachery, and whilst he was there some unimportant towns seceded to him. Out of the twelve communities in Bruttium who had gone over to the Carthaginians the year before, two, namely Consentia and Thurii, returned to their old allegiance to Rome, and more would have done so had it not been for T. Pomponius Veientanus, an officer of allies. He had made several successful raids in Bruttium and had in consequence began to be regarded as a regularly commissioned general. With the raw and undisciplined army which he had got together he engaged Hanno. In that battle a great number of men, who were simply a confused crowd of peasants and slaves, were killed or made prisoners; the least important loss was that of the officer himself, who was made prisoner. For not only was he responsible for such a reckless and ill-advised battle, but in his capacity as a public contractor he had previously been guilty of all sorts of dishonest practices and robbed both the State and the City guilds.

The consul Sempronius fought several trifling actions in Lucania, none of which are worth recording, and took some unimportant towns belonging to the Lucanians.

The longer the war continued, and the more men's minds as well as their fortunes were affected by the alternations of success and failure, so much the more did the citizens become the victims of superstitions, and those for the most part foreign ones. It seemed as though either the characters of men or the nature of the gods had undergone a sudden change. The Roman ritual was growing into disuse not only in secret and in private houses; even in public places, in the Forum and the Capitol, crowds of women were to be seen who were offering neither sacrifices nor prayers in accordance with ancient usage. Unauthorised sacrificers and diviners had got possession of men's minds and the numbers of their dupes were swelled by the crowds of country people whom poverty or fear had driven into the City, and whose fields had lain untilled owing to the length of the war or had been desolated by the enemy. These impostors found their profit in trading upon the ignorance of others, and they practiced their calling with as much effrontery as if they had been duly authorised by the State. Respectable citizens protested in private against the state of things, and ultimately the matter became a public scandal and formal complaint was made to the senate. The ædiles and commissioners of police were severely reprimanded by the senate for not preventing these abuses, but when they attempted to remove the crowds from the Forum and destroy the altars and other preparations for their rites they narrowly escaped being roughly handled. As the mischief appeared to be too much for the inferior magistrates to deal with, M. Æmilius, the City praetor, was entrusted with the task of delivering the people from these superstitions. He read the resolution of the senate before the Assembly and gave notice that all those who had in their possession any manuals of divination or forms of prayers or sacrificial ritual in writing were to bring all their books and writings to him before the first of April, and no one was to use any strange or foreign form of sacrifice in any public or consecrated place.

II. Several officials connected with the State religion died this year: L. Cornelius Lentulus the chief pontiff, C. Papirius, son of C. Masso, one of the pontiffs, P. Furius Philus the augur, and C. Papirius, son of L. Maso, one of the Keepers of the Sacred Books. M. Cornelius Cethegus was appointed chief pontiff in place of Lentulus, and Cn. Servilius Caepio in place of Papirius. L. Quintius Flamininus was appointed augur and L. Cornelius Lentulus Keeper of the Sacred Books.

Arrangements for the Year.—The time for the consular elections was now drawing near, and as it was decided not to recall the consuls who were engaged in the war, Tiberius Sempronius nominated C. Claudius Cento Dictator for the purpose of conducting the elections. He appointed Q. Fulvius Flaccus as his Master of the Horse. The elections were completed on the first day; the Dictator returned as duly elected consuls Q. Fulvius Flaccus, Master of the Horse, and Appius Claudius Pulcher, who was at the time praetor in Sicily. Then the praetors were elected; Cn. Fulvius Flaccus, C. Claudius Nero, M. Junius Silanus, and P. Cornelius Sulla. When the elections were over the Dictator resigned. The curule ædiles for the year were

M. Cornelius Cethegus and P. Cornelius Scipio, who was subsequently known as Africanus. When the latter offered himself as a candidate, the tribunes of the plebs objected to him, and said that he could not be allowed to stand because he had not yet reached the legal age.[1]   His reply was: " If the Quirites are unanimous in their desire to appoint me ædile, I am quite old enough." On this the people hurried to give their tribal votes for him with such eagerness that the tribunes abandoned their opposition. The new ædiles discharged their functions with great munificence; the Roman Games were celebrated on a grand scale considering their resources at the time; they were repeated a second day and a *congius*[2] of oil was distributed in each street.

L. Villius Tappulus and M. Fundanius Fundulus, the plebeian ædiles, summoned several matrons before the people on a charge of misconduct; some of them were convicted and sent into exile. The celebration of the Plebeian Games lasted two days and there was a solemn banquet in the Capitol on the occasion of the Games.

III. Q. Fulvius Flaccus and Appius Claudius entered on their consulship, the former for the third time. The praetors drew lots for their provinces; P. Cornelius Sulla had assigned to him both the home and foreign jurisdiction, which had previously been held separately; Apulia fell to Cn. Fulvius Flaccus; Suessula to C. Claudius Nero; Etruria to M. Junius Silanus. Two legions were decreed for each of the consuls in the operations against Hannibal; one consul took over the army from Q. Fabius, the consul of the previous year, the other that of Fulvius Centumalus. With regard to the praetors, Fulvius Flaccus was to have the legions which were at Luceria under Æmilius, Claudius Nero those which were serving in Picenum under C. Terentius, and they were each to raise their force to its full complement. The City legions raised the previous year were assigned to M. Junius to meet any movement from Etruria. Ti. Sempronius Gracchus and P. Sempronius Tuditanus had their commands extended in their respective provinces of Lucania and Cis-Alpine Gaul, as also had P. Lentulus in the Roman province of Sicily and M. Marcellus in Syracuse and that part of the island over which Hiero had reigned. The command of the fleet was left in the hands of T. Otacilius, the operations in Greece in those of M. Valerius, the campaign in Sardinia was still to be under the conduct of Q. Mucius Scaevola, whilst the two Scipios were to continue their work in Spain.

In addition to the existing armies two fresh legions were raised in the City by the consuls, thus bringing up the total number to twenty-three legions for the year.

Dishonest Conduct of the Public Contractors.—The enrolment was interrupted by the conduct of M. Postumius Pyrgensis which might have endangered the stability of the republic. This man was a public contractor and for many years had had only one man to match him in dishonesty and greed, and that was T. Pomponius Veientanus, whom the Carthaginians under Hanno got hold of while he was recklessly raiding Lucania. The State had made itself responsible where supplies intended for the armies were lost through storms at sea, and these men invented stories of shipwrecks, and when they did not invent, the shipwrecks which they reported were due to their dishonesty, not to accident. They placed small and worthless cargoes on old shattered ships, which they sank when out at sea, the sailors being taken into boats which were kept in readiness, and then they made a false declaration as to the cargo, putting it at many times its real value. This fraud had been disclosed to M. Æmilius, the praetor, and he laid the matter before the senate, but they had taken no action because they were anxious not to offend the body of public contractors at such a time as that. The people, however, took a much severer view of the case, and at length two tribunes of the plebs, Spurius Carvilius and L. Carvilius, seeing the public indignation and disgust aroused, demanded that a fine of 200,000 *ases* should be imposed on them. When the day came for the question to be decided, the plebs were present in such great numbers that the space on the Capitol hardly held them, and after the case had been gone through, the only hope left to the defence was the chance of C. Servilius Casca, a tribune of the plebs and a near relative of Postumius, interposing his veto before the tribes proceeded to vote. When the evidence had been given, the tribunes ordered the people to withdraw and the voting urn was brought in, in order that it might be determined in what tribe the Latins were to vote.[3] While this was being done the contractors urged Casca to stop the proceedings for the day, and the people loudly opposed that step. Casca happened to be sitting in front at the end of the tribunal seats, and he was labouring under the conflicting emotions of fear and shame. Seeing that no dependence was to be placed upon him, the contractors determined to create a disturbance and rushed in a compact body into the space left vacant by the withdrawal of the Assembly, loudly abusing both the people and the tribunes. As there was every prospect of a hand-to-hand fight the consul Fulvius said to the tribunes: "Do you not see that your authority has gone, and that there will certainly be a riot if you do not dismiss the meeting?"

After the Assembly of the plebs was dismissed a meeting of the senate was called, and the consuls brought forward the question of "the disturbance of a meeting of the plebs through the violence and audacity of the public contractors."

"M. Furius Camillus," they said, "whose exile was followed by the downfall of Rome, submitted to condemnation at the hands of the irate citizens; before his time the decemvirs—whose laws are in force to-day—and after him many of our foremost citizens have bowed to the sentence of the people. Whereas Postumius Pyrgensis has deprived the people of their right to vote, broken up a meeting of the plebs, destroyed the authority of the tribunes, levied war upon the people of Rome, made forcible seizure of a position in the City to cut off the plebs from its tribunes, and prevented the tribes from being called to vote. There was nothing to restrain men from fighting and bloodshed except the forbearance of the magistrates, who for the time being yielded to the furious audacity of a few men and allowed themselves and the Roman people to be successfully defied, and, rather than give any occasion for a conflict to those who were seeking one, they voluntarily closed the elections which the accused was going to stop by armed force."

This indictment was listened to by all good citizens with feelings of indignation proportioned to the atrocity of the outrage, and the senate passed a decree affirming that "that violent conduct was an offence against the republic and set a most vicious precedent."

Immediately on this the two Carvilii dropped the proposal for a fine and indicted Postumius for high treason, and ordered him to find sureties for his appearance on the day of trial, or failing that to be at once arrested and taken to prison. He found sureties, but did not appear. The resolution proposed by the tribunes and adopted by the plebs was in the following terms: "If M. Postumius does not enter an appearance before the first day of May and when cited into court does not answer his name on that day, and has not been lawfully excused from so appearing, he shall be deemed to be an exile, his goods shall be sold, and he himself placed under outlawry." Then all those who had taken the lead in the riotous disturbance were one by one indicted on the same charge and ordered to find sureties.

Those who did not find them and afterwards even those who could find them were alike cast into prison. Most of them, to escape the danger, went into exile.[4]

V. Such was the issue of the dishonesty of the State contractors, and their daring attempt to screen themselves. The next thing was the election of the chief pontiff. The new pontiff, M. Cornelius Cethegus, conducted the election, which was very keenly contested. There were three candidates: Q. Fulvius Flaccus, the consul, who had previously been twice consul as well as censor; T. Manlius Torquatus, who could also point to two consulships and the censorship; and P. Licinius Crassus, who was about to stand for the curule ædileship. This young man defeated his old and distinguished competitors; before him there had been no one for a hundred and twenty years, with the sole exception of P. Cornelius Calussa, who had been elected chief pontiff without having first sat in a curule chair.

The consuls found the levying of troops a difficult task, for there were not sufficient men of the required age to answer both purposes, that of raising the new City legions and also bringing the existing armies up to their full strength. The senate, however, would not allow them to give up the attempt, and ordered two commissions, each consisting of three members, to be appointed, one to work within a radius of fifty miles from the City, the other outside that radius. They were to inspect all the villages, market towns, and boroughs, and ascertain the total number of free-born men in each, and were to make soldiers of all who appeared strong enough to bear arms, even though they were below the military age. The tribunes of the plebs might, if they thought good, make a proposal to the people that those who had taken the military oath when under seventeen years of age should have their pay reckoned to them on the same scale as if they had been enlisted at seventeen, or older. The commissions so appointed recruited all the free-born men in the country districts.

The Survivors of Cannae.—About this time a despatch was read in the senate from M. Marcellus in Sicily, in which he put forward the request made to him by the soldiers who were serving with P. Lentulus. These were the remains of the army of Cannae, they had been sent away to Sicily, as has been stated above, and were not to be brought back to Italy before the Punic war had come to an end.

VI. The principal officers of the cavalry, with the centurions of highest rank and the pick of the legionaries, had been allowed by Lentulus to send a deputation to M. Marcellus in Italy. One was allowed to speak on behalf of the rest, and this is what he said: " We should have approached you, Marcellus, when you were consul, in Italy, as soon as that severe if not unjust resolution of the senate was passed concerning us, had we not hoped that after being sent into a province thrown into confusion by the death of its kings, to take part in a serious war against Sicilians and Carthaginians combined, we should have made reparation to the senate by our blood and our wounds in the same way that those who were taken by Pyrrhus at Heraclea, within the memory of our fathers, made reparation by fighting against Pyrrhus afterwards. And yet, what have we done, senators, that you should be wrath with us then or that we should deserve your anger now? I seem to myself to be gazing on the faces of both the consuls and of the whole senate when I look at you, Marcellus; if we had had you as our consul at Cannae, both we and the republic would have met with better fortune.

" Allow me, I pray you, before I complain of our treatment, to clear ourselves of the guilt which is laid to our charge. If it was not through the anger of the gods or through the ordering of that destiny by whose laws the chain of human affairs is immutably linked together, but by the fault of man that we perished at Cannae, whose fault, pray, was it? The fault of the soldiers or of their commanders? As a soldier I will never say a word about my commander, though I know that he was specially thanked by the senate because he did not despair of the republic, and has had his command extended every year since his flight from Cannae. Those of the survivors from that disaster, who were our military tribunes at the time, solicited and obtained office, as we have heard, and are in command of provinces. Do you lightly forgive yourselves and your children, senators, whilst you reserve your anger for poor wretches like us? While it was no disgrace for the consul and the foremost men in the State to flee when all hope was lost, did you send us, the common soldiers, to meet certain death in the battle field? At the Alia almost the entire army fled, at the Caudine Forks they delivered up their arms to the enemy without even attempting to fight, not to mention other shameful defeats that our armies have suffered. But so far were those armies from having any humiliation inflicted upon them, that the City of Rome was recovered by the very army which had fled from the Alia to Veii, and the Caudine legions who had returned to Rome without their arms were sent back armed to Samniun, and made that same enemy pass under the yoke who had enjoyed seeing them undergo that humiliation. Can any man charge the army at Cannae with flight or cowardice when more than 50,000 men fell there, when the consul fled with only seventy horsemen, when not one survives who fought there except those whom the enemy, wearied with slaughter, left alone. When the ransom of the prisoners was vetoed we were universally praised because we had saved ourselves for our country, because we returned to the consul at Venusia and presented the appearance of a regular army. But as it is, we are in a worse case than those prisoners in our fathers' days; for all that they had to endure was a change in their arms, in their military status, in their quarters in camp, and these they recovered by the one service they rendered to the State in fighting a successful battle. Not one of them was sent into exile, not one was deprived of the prospect of obtaining his discharge, and above all they had the chance of putting an end either to their life or their disgrace by fighting the enemy. But we, against whom no charge can be brought except that it is through our fault that a single Roman soldier is left alive after the battle of Cannae—we, I say, have not only been sent far away from our native soil and from Italy, but we have been placed out of reach of the enemy, we are to grow old in exile, with no hope, no chance, of wiping out our shame, or of appeasing our fellow-citizens, or even of dying an honourable death. We are not asking for an end to our ignominy or for the rewards of valour, we only ask to be allowed to prove our mettle and to show our courage. We ask for labours and dangers, for a chance of doing our duty as men and as soldiers. This is the second year of the war in Sicily with all its hard-fought battles. The Carthaginians are capturing some cities, the Romans are taking others, infantry and cavalry meet in the shock of battle, at Syracuse a great struggle is going on by land and sea, we hear the shouts of the combatants and the clash of their arms, and we are sitting idly by, as though we had neither weapons nor hands to use them. The legions of slaves have fought many pitched battles under Tiberius Sempronius; they have as their reward freedom and citizenship; we implore you to treat us at least as slaves who have been purchased for this war, and to allow us to meet and fight the enemy and so win our freedom. Are you willing to make proof of our courage by sea or by land, in the open field or against city walls? We ask for whatever brings the hardest toil and the greatest danger, if only what ought to have been done at Cannae may be done as soon as we can do it, now. For all our life since has been but one long agony of shame."

VII. When he had finished speaking they prostrated themselves at the knees of Marcellus. He told them that he had not the authority or the power to grant their request, but said that he would write to the senate and would be guided entirely by their decision.

The despatch was delivered into the hands of the new consuls and read by them to the senate. After discussing its contents, the senate decided that they saw no reason why the safety of the republic should be entrusted to soldiers who had deserted their comrades at Cannae. If M. Claudius, the propraetor, thought otherwise, he was to act as he thought best in the interests of the State, but only on this condition, that none of them should get their discharge or receive any reward for valour or be conveyed back to Italy as long as the enemy remained on Italian soil.

After this an election was held by the City praetor, in accordance with a decision of the senate and a resolution of the plebs, for the appointment of special commissioners of works. Five commissioners were chosen to undertake the repair of the walls and towers of the City, and two boards, each consisting of three members, were selected; one to inspect the contents of the temples and to make an inventory of the offerings; the other to rebuild the temples of Fortune and Mater Matuta inside the Porta Carmentalis and the temple of Spes outside, all of which had been destroyed by fire the previous year.

Frightful storms occurred: on the Alban Mount it rained stones incessantly for two days. Many places were struck by lightning, two buildings in the Capitol, the rampart of the camp above Suessula in many places, two sentinels being killed. The wall and some of the towers at Cumae were not only struck, but even thrown down by the lightning. At Reate a huge rock was seen to fly about, and the sun was unusually red, in fact the colour of blood. By reason of these portents a day was set apart for special intercessions, and for several days the consuls devoted their attention to religious matters, and special services were held for nine days.

Hannibal Captures Tarentum.—The betrayal of Tarentum had long been an object of hope with Hannibal and of suspicion with the Romans, and now an incident which occurred outside its walls hastened its capture.

Phileas had been a long time in Rome, ostensibly as the Tarentine envoy. He was a restless character and chafed under the inaction in which he seemed likely to spend the greater part of his life. The hostages from Tarentum and Thurii were kept in the Hall of Liberty, but not under strict surveillance, because it was neither for their own interest nor for that of their city to play the Romans false. Phileas found means of access to them and had frequent interviews, in which he won them over to his design, and by bribing two of the watchmen he brought them out of confinement as soon as it was dark, and they made their secret escape from Rome. As soon as it was light their flight became known throughout the City, and a party was sent in pursuit. They were caught at Tarracina and brought back; then they were marched into the Comitium and, with the approval of the people, scourged with rods and thrown from the Rock.

VIII. The cruelty of this punishment produced a feeling of bitter resentment in the two most important Greek cities in Italy, not only amongst the population at large, but especially amongst those who were connected by ties of relationship or friendship with the men who had met with such a horrible fate. Amongst these there were thirteen young nobles of Tarentum who entered into a conspiracy; the ringleaders were Nico and Philemenus. Before taking any action they thought that they ought to have an interview with Hannibal. They left the city by night on the pretence that they were going on a hunting expedition and took the direction of his camp. When they were not far from it, the others concealed themselves in a wood near the road while Nico and Philemenus went on to the outposts. They were seized, as they intended to be, and were conducted to Hannibal. After explaining to him the motives which had prompted them and the nature of the step they were contemplating they were warmly thanked and loaded with promises, and Hannibal advised them to drive to the city some cattle belonging to the Carthaginians which had been turned out to pasture, so that they might make their fellow-townsmen believe that they had really gone out, as they said, to get plunder. He promised that they should be safe and unmolested while so engaged. Every one saw the plunder which the young men had brought, and as they did the same thing over and over again people wondered less at their daring. At their next interview with Hannibal they obtained from him a solemn promise that the Tarentines should preserve their freedom and retain their own laws and all that belonged to them, they were to pay no taxes or tribute to Carthage, nor be required to admit a Carthaginian garrison against their will. The Roman garrison was to be at the mercy of the Carthaginians.[5]

When this understanding had been arrived at, Philemenus made a regular habit of leaving the city and returning to it by night. He was noted for his passion for hunting and he had his dogs and other requisites for the sport with him. Generally he brought back something which had purposely been placed in his way and gave it either to the commanders or the men on guard. They imagined that he chose night time for his expeditions through fear of the enemy. When they had become so accustomed to his movements that the gate was opened at whatever hour of the night he gave the signal by whistling, Hannibal thought the time had come for action. He was three days' march distant, and in order to lessen any surprise that might be felt at his remaining encamped on one and the same spot so long he feigned illness. The Romans who were garrisoning Tarentum had ceased to view his remaining there with suspicion.

IX. When he had made up his mind to march to Tarentum, he picked out a force of 10,000 infantry and cavalry, who, from their agility and the lightness of their armour, would be most suitable for a dash upon the city. At the fourth watch of the night he made his advance and sent forward about eighty Numidian troopers with orders to patrol the roads in the neighbourhood and keep a sharp look out so that none of the rustics might espy his movements from a distance. Those in front of them they were to bring back, any whom they met they were to kill in order that the inhabitants of the district might take them for a marauding force rather than an army. Marching his men rapidly forward he encamped about fifteen miles from Tarentum, and without saying a word as to where they were going he called his men together and warned them all to keep in the line of march and not to allow any one to fall out or leave the ranks. They were above all things to listen to orders with attention and not to do anything that they were not told to do. He would tell them, when the time came, what he wanted them to do.

Almost at the same hour a rumour reached Tarentum that a small body of Numidian horse were ravaging their fields and creating a panic far and wide amongst the peasantry. This news did not disturb the Roman commandant farther than that he ordered a portion of his cavalry to ride out the next morning early to drive off the enemy. As to guarding against any other contingency, so little care was shown that this movement on the part of the Numidians was actually taken as a proof that Hannibal and his army had not stirred from their camp.

Hannibal resumed his advance soon after dark; Philemenus leading the way with the usual load of game on his shoulders, the rest of the conspirators waiting inside the town to carry out their part in the plot. The arrangement was that Philemenus should carry his prey through the wicket gate which he always used and at the same time admit some armed men; Hannibal was to approach the Temenide gate from another direction. This gate was on the landward part of the city and looked eastwards near the public cemetery inside the walls. As he approached the gate Hannibal gave the signal by showing a light, the signal was answered in the same way by Nico; then both lights were extinguished. Hannibal marched up to the gate in silence; Nico made a sudden attack upon the sentinels who were sleeping soundly in their beds and killed them, then he opened the gate. Hannibal entered with his infantry, but the cavalry were ordered to remain outside, ready to meet any attack in the open plain. In the other direction Philemenus also reached the wicket gate which he had been in the habit of using, and whilst he was calling out that they could hardly stand the weight of the huge beast they were carrying, his voice and well-known signal roused the sentry and the gate was opened. Two young men carrying a wild boar entered, Philemenus and a lightly equipped huntsman followed close after, and whilst the sentinel, astonished at its size, turned unsuspectingly towards those who were carrying it, Philemenus ran him through with a hunting spear. Then about thirty armed men ran in and massacred the rest of the sentinels and broke open the large gate adjoining and the army at once entered in fighting order and marched in perfect silence to the forum where they joined Hannibal. The Carthaginian general formed 2000 of his Gauls into three divisions, furnishing each with Tarentines to guide them, and sent them into different parts of the city with orders to occupy the main streets, and if a tumult arose they were to cut down the Romans and spare the townsfolk. To secure this latter object he gave instructions to the conspirators to tell any of their people whom they saw at a distance to keep quiet and silent and fear nothing.

X. By this time there was as much shouting and uproar as

usually happens when a city is taken, but nobody knew for certain what had happened. The Tarentines thought that the Roman garrison had started to pillage the town; the Romans were under the impression that the townsfolk had got up a disturbance with some treacherous design. The commandant, awakened by the tumult, hurried away to the harbour, and getting into a boat was rowed round to the citadel. To add to the confusion the sound of a trumpet was heard from the theatre. It was a Roman trumpet which the conspirators had procured for the purpose, and being blown by a Greek who did not know how to use it, no one could make out who gave the signal or for whom it was intended.

When it began to grow light, the Romans recognised the arms of the Carthaginians and Gauls, and all doubt was removed; the Greeks, too, seeing the bodies of the Romans lying about everywhere, became aware that the city had been taken by Hannibal. When the light grew clearer and the Romans who survived the massacre had taken refuge in the citadel, the tumult having somewhat subsided, Hannibal ordered the Tarentines to assemble without their arms. After they had all assembled, with the exception of those who had accompanied the Romans into the citadel to share their fate whatever it might be, Hannibal addressed some kind words to them, and reminded them of the way he had treated their compatriots whom he had taken in the battle of Cannae. He went on to inveigh bitterly against the tyranny of Roman domination, and ended by ordering them each to return to their homes and write their names over their doors; if any houses were not so inscribed he should at once give the signal for them to be plundered, and if any one placed an inscription on a house occupied by a Roman—they were in a separate quarter—he should treat him as an enemy. The people were dismissed, and after the inscriptions had been placed on the doors, so that the houses could be distinguished from those of the enemy, the signal was given and the troops dispersed in all directions to plunder the Roman houses. There was a considerable amount of plunder seized.

XI. The next day he advanced to attack the citadel. It was protected by lofty cliffs on the side of the sea which surrounded the greater part of it like a peninsula, and on the side of the city it was enclosed by a wall and a very deep moat; Hannibal saw at once that it could successfully defy any attack either by storm or by siege works. As he did not wish to be delayed from undertaking more important operations by having to protect the

Tarentines nor to leave them without adequate defence against any attacks which the Romans might make at their pleasure from the citadel, he decided to cut off communication between the city and the citadel by earthworks. He rather hoped, too, that the Romans might attempt to interfere whilst these were being constructed and give him a chance of fighting, and in case they made a sortie in force he might inflict such heavy loss upon them and so weaken them that the Tarentines could easily hold their own against them unaided.

No sooner was the work commenced than the Romans suddenly flung open the citadel gates and attacked the working party. The detachment who were on guard along the front allowed themselves to be driven in, and the Romans, emboldened by success, followed them up in greater numbers and to a greater distance. Then a signal was given and the Carthaginians whom Hannibal had drawn up in readiness rushed upon them from all sides. The Romans could not withstand their attack, but their flight was checked by the narrow space and the obstructions caused by the work which had been begun and the preparations made for continuing it. A great many flung themselves headlong into the fosse, and more were killed in the flight than in the fighting. After this the work proceeded without molestation. An enormous fosse was dug and on its inner side a breastwork and parapet thrown up, and a little further off in the same direction he made preparations for adding a wall, so that the town could protect itself against the Romans without his aid. He left, however, a small detachment to garrison the place and also help to complete the wall, while he himself with the rest of his force fixed his camp by the river Galaesus about five miles from Tarentum.

Returning from this position to inspect the work, and finding it much more advanced than he expected, he became hopeful of successfully attacking the citadel. It was not, like other similar places, protected by its lofty position, as it stood on level ground and was separated from the city by a moat and a wall.[6] While the attack was being pressed with siege works, machines, and artillery of every kind, reinforcements arrived from Metapontum, and thus strengthened, the Romans were encouraged to make a night attack upon the enemies' works. Some they broke up, others they burnt, and that was the end of Hannibal's attempts to storm the walls. His only hope now was to invest the citadel, but that seemed useless, for standing as it did on a promontory and overlooking the mouth of the harbour, those who held it could make free use of the sea. The city, on the other hand, was cut off from all sea-borne supplies, and the besiegers were more likely to starve than the besieged.

Hannibal called the principal men of the place together and explained all the difficulties of the situation. He told them that he saw no way of carrying a citadel so strongly fortified by storm, and there was nothing to hope for from a blockade as long as the enemy were masters of the sea. If he had ships, so that all supplies could be stopped from reaching them, they would then have to evacuate the citadel or surrender. The Tarentines quite agreed with him, but they thought that the man who gave the advice ought to help in carrying it out. If he sent for Carthaginian vessels from Sicily the thing could be done, but their own ships were locked up in a narrow bay; so how could they escape into the open sea as long as the enemy held the mouth of the harbour? " They shall escape," Hannibal replied. " Many things which nature makes difficult become easy to the man who uses his brains. You have a city situated in a flat country; broad and level roads lead in all directions. I will transport your ships without much trouble on wagons and along the road which leads from the harbour through the heart of the city to the sea. Then the sea which the enemy are now masters of will be ours, we shall invest the citadel by sea on the one side, by land on the other, or rather I would say we shall very soon capture it, either after the enemy have evacuated it or with the enemy inside as well."

These words excited not only hopes of success but also an intense feeling of admiration for the general. Wagons were speedily collected from all sides and fastened together; machines were employed for hauling the ships ashore, and the surface of the road was made good so that the wagons could be drawn more easily and the transport effected with less difficulty. Then draught animals and men were got together, and the work promptly began. After a few days a completely equipped fleet sailed round the citadel and cast anchor off the very mouth of the harbour.

Such was the condition of affairs which Hannibal left behind him at Tarentum when he returned to his winter quarters. Authorities, however, are divided on the question whether the defection of Tarentum occurred this year or last, but the majority, including those who lived nearest to the time of the events, assert that it happened this year.

XII. *The Prophecies of Marcius.*—The consuls and praetors

were detained in Rome by the Latin Festival until the 27th of April. That day the sacred rites were completed on the Alban Mount, and they all set out for their various provinces. Subsequently the need of fresh religious observances was brought to their notice in consequence of the prophetic utterances of Marcius. This Marcius was a famous seer and his prophecies had come to light the previous year when by order of the senate an inspection was made of all books of a similar character. They first came into the hands of M. Æmilius who, as City praetor, was in charge of the business, and he at once handed them to the new praetor, Sulla. One of the two referred to events which had already happened before it saw the light, and the authority thus acquired by its fulfilment gained more credence for the other, which had yet to be fulfilled. In the first the disaster of Cannae was foretold in words to this effect:

> " Thou who art sprung from Trojan blood, beware
> The stream by Canna. Let not aliens born
> Force thee to battle on the fatal plain
> Of Diomed. But thou wilt give no heed
> To this my rede until that all the plain
> Be watered by thy blood, and mighty hosts
> The stream shall bear into the boundless deep
> From off the fruitful earth, and they who till
> Its soil shall be for food to birds and beasts
> And fishes. Such is Great Jove's word to me."

Those who had fought there recognised the truth of the description—the plains of Argive Diomed and the river Canna and the very picture of the disaster.

Then the second prophecy was read. It was not only more obscure than the first because the future is more uncertain than the past, but it was also more unintelligible owing to its phraseology. It ran as follows:

> " If, Romans, ye would drive the foemen forth,
> Who come from far to mar your land, then see
> That Games be held as each fourth year comes round
> In honour of Apollo and your State
> Shall bear its part and all your folk shall share
> The holy work, each for himself and his.
> Your praetor, who shall justice do for each
> And all, shall have the charge. Then let there be
> Ten chosen who shall offer sacrifice
> In Grecian fashion. This if ye will do,
> Then shall ye evermore rejoice and all
> Your State shall prosper; yea, the god shall bring
> Your foes to nought, who now eat up your land."

They spent one day interpreting this prophecy. The day following, the senate passed a resolution that the Ten should inspect the sacred books with reference to the institution of Games to Apollo and the proper form of sacrifice. After they had made their investigations and reported to the senate, a resolution was passed " that Games be vowed and celebrated in honour of Apollo, and that when they were finished, 12,000 *ases* were to be given to the praetor for the expenses of the sacrifice and two victims of large size." A second resolution was passed that " the Ten should sacrifice according to Greek ritual the following victims: to Apolla, on ox with gilded horns and two white she-goats with gilded horns, and to Latona a heifer with gilded horns." When the praetor was about to celebrate the Games in the Circus Maximus he gave notice that during the Games the people should contribute a gift to Apollo, according to each man's convenience.

Such is the origin of the Apollinarian Games, which were instituted for the cause of victory and not, as is generally thought, in the interests of the public health. The people wore garlands whilst witnessing them, the matrons offered up intercessions; feasting went on in the forecourts of the houses with open doors, and the day was observed with every kind of ceremonious rite.[7]

XIII. *Fighting round Capua.*—Hannibal was still in the neighbourhood of Tarentum and both the consuls were in Samnium apparently making preparations for besieging Capua. Famine, generally the result of a long siege, was already beginning to press upon the Campanians, as they had been prevented by the Roman armies from sowing their crops. They sent a message to Hannibal asking him to give orders for corn to be conveyed to Capua from places in the neighbourhood before the consuls sent their legions into their fields and all the roads were rendered impassable by the enemy. Hannibal ordered Hanno who was in Bruttium to march his army into Campania and see to it that the people of Capua were plentifully supplied with corn. Hanno accordingly marched into Campania and, carefully avoiding the consuls who were both en amped in Samnium, he selected a position for his camp on some rising ground about three miles from Beneventum. He then issued orders for the corn which had been stored in the friendly cities round to be carried to his camp, and assigned detachments to guard the convoys. A message was despatched to Capua stating the day on which they were to appear in the camp to receive the corn, bringing with them all the vehicles and beasts they could collect. The Campanians carried out his instructions with the same slackness and carelessness that they showed in everything else.

Hardly more than four hundred country carts were sent and a few draught cattle. Hanno scolded them severely, telling them that even the hunger which rouses the energies of dumb animals failed to stimulate them to exertion. He then fixed another day for them to come for corn provided with much more efficient means of transport.

Everything was reported to the people of Beneventum exactly as it happened. They at once sent a deputation of ten of their principal citizens to the consuls, both of whom were near Bovianum. On hearing what was going on at Capua they arranged that one of them should march into Campania. Fulvius, to whom that province had been assigned, made a night march and entered Beneventum. He was now in Hanno's immediate neighbourhood and was informed that he had left with a portion of his army on a foraging expedition, that corn was supplied to Capua under the superintendence of the head of his commissariat, that two thousand wagons with a disorderly and unarmed crowd had arrived at his camp, that haste and confusion prevailed everywhere, and that the rustics had invaded the camp from all the country round and destroyed all semblance of military order and all chance of military discipline. When he had satisfied himself that this information was correct, he issued an order for his men to get ready their standards and arms against nightfall—and nothing else—as they would have to attack the Carthaginian camp. Leaving their kits and all their baggage in Beneventum, they started at the fourth watch and reached the camp just before dawn. Their appearance created such alarm that, had the camp been on level ground, it could undoubtedly have been carried at the first assault. Its elevated position and its entrenchments saved it; in no direction could it be approached except by steep and difficult climbing. When day broke a hot fight commenced; the Carthaginians did not confine themselves to defending their lines; but being on more even ground themselves they threw down the enemy who were struggling up the heights.

XIV. Courage and resolution, however, overcame all difficulties, and in some places the Romans had forced their way to the breastwork and fosse, but with heavy loss in killed and wounded, when the consul, calling round him the superior officers, told them that they must desist from the hazardous attempt. He thought it would be wiser to march back to Beneventum for that day, and on the next day to bring their camp close up to the enemy's camp, so that the Campanians could not quit it and Hanno would be unable to return to it. To make more certain of this, he prepared to send for his colleague and his army and direct their joint operations against Hanno and the Campanians. The " retire " was already being sounded when the general's plans were shattered by the angry shouts of the soldiers who spurned such feeble tactics. The Paelignian cohort happened to be in closest touch with the enemy, and their commanding officer, Vibius Accaus, snatched up a standard and flung it across the enemies' rampart, at the same time invoking a curse on himself and his cohort if the enemy got possession of the standard. He was the first to dash over fosse and rampart into the camp. Now the Paelignians were fighting inside the lines, and Valerius Flaccus, the commanding officer of the third legion, was rating the Romans for their cowardice in letting the allies have the glory of capturing the camp, when T. Pedanius, a centurion in command of the leading maniples, took a standard out of the bearer's hands and shouted, " This standard and this centurion will be inside the rampart in a moment, let those follow who will prevent its capture by the enemy." His own maniples followed him as he sprang across the fosse, then the whole of the legion pressed hard after. By this time even the consul, when he saw them climbing over the rampart, changed his mind, and instead of recalling the troops began to urge them on by pointing to the dangerous position of their gallant allies and their own fellow citizens. Every man did his best to push on; over smooth and rough ground alike, amidst missiles showered upon them from all directions, against the desperate resistance of the enemy who thrust their persons and their weapons in the way, they advanced step by step and broke into the camp. Many who were wounded, even those who were faint from loss of blood, struggled on that they might fall within the enemies' camp. In this way the camp was taken, and taken too as quickly as though it lay on level ground, entirely unfortified. It was no longer a fight but a massacre, for they were all crowded together inside the lines. Over 10,000 of the enemy were killed and over 7000 made prisoners, including the Campanians who had come for corn, and all the wagons and draught animals were captured. There was also an immense quantity of plunder which Hanno, who had been raiding everywhere, had carried off from the fields of the allies of Rome. After totally destroying the enemies' camp they returned to Beneventum. There the two consuls—Appius Claudius had arrived a few days before—sold and distributed the spoil. Those to whose exertions the capture of the camp was due were rewarded, especially Accaus the Paelignian and T. Pedanius the centurion who headed the first legion. Hanno was at Cominium-Ocritum with a small foraging party when he heard of the disaster to his camp, and he retreated to Bruttium in a way which suggested flight rather than an orderly march.

XV. When the Campanians, in their turn, heard of the disaster which had overtaken them and their allies, they sent to Hannibal to inform him that the two consuls were at Beneventum, a day's march from Capua, and that the war had all but reached their walls and gates. If he did not come with all speed to their help Capua would fall into the hands of the enemy more rapidly than Arpi had done. Not even Tarentum, much less its citadel, ought to be of so much importance in his eyes as to make him give up to Rome, abandoned and defenceless, the Capua which he always used to say was as great as Carthage. Hannibal promised that he would take care of Capua, and sent a force of 2000 cavalry by whose aid they would be able to keep their fields from being devastated.

Metapontum and Thurii go over to Hannibal.—The Romans, meanwhile, amongst their other cares, had not lost sight of the citadel of Tarentum and its beleaguered garrison. P. Cornelius, one of the praetors, had, acting on the instructions of the senate, sent his lieutenant, C. Servilius, to purchase corn in Etruria, and after loading some ships sailed to Tarentum and made his way through the enemies' guard ships into the harbour. His arrival produced such a change that the very men who, having lost almost all hope, had been frequently invited by the enemy in their colloquies with them to go over to them, now actually invited and tried to persuade the enemy to come over to them. Soldiers, too, had been sent from Metapontum, so the garrison was now strong enough for the defence of the citadel. The Metapontines, on the other hand, relieved from their fears by the departure of the Romans, promptly went over to Hannibal. The people of Thurii, on the same part of the coast, took the same step. Their action was due in some measure to the defection of Tarentum and Metapontum, but it was due quite as much to their feeling of exasperation against the Romans at the recent massacre of their hostages. It was the relations and friends of these who sent messengers with despatches to Hannibal and Mago, who were in the neighbourhood, promising to put the city in their power if they would march up to the walls. M.

Atinius was in command at Thurii with a small garrison, and they thought that he would easily be drawn into a precipitate engagement, not because he trusted to his own small garrison, but because he relied upon the soldiery of Thurii, whom he had carefully drilled and armed against such an emergency.

After the Carthaginian generals had entered the country of Thurii they divided their forces: Hanno proceeded with the infantry in battle order up to the city; Mago and his cavalry halted and took up a position behind some hills admirably adapted for concealing his movements. Atinius understood from his scouts that the hostile force consisted entirely of infantry, accordingly he went into battle quite unaware of the treachery of the citizens or the manœuvre of the enemy. The contest was a very spiritless one, only a few Romans were in the fighting line, and the Thurians were awaiting the issue rather than helping to decide it. The Carthaginian line purposely fell back in order to draw their unsuspecting enemy behind the hill where the cavalry were waiting. No sooner had they reached the place than the cavalry dashed forward with their battle cry. The Thurians, an ill-disciplined crowd, disloyal to the side on which they fought, were at once put to flight; the Romans kept up the fight for some time in spite of their being attacked on one side by the infantry and on the other by the cavalry, but at last they, too, turned and fled to the city. There a body of the traitors admitted the stream of their fellow townsmen through the open gate, but when they saw the Romans routed and running towards the city they shouted that the Carthaginians were at their heels and the enemy would enter the city pell mell with the Romans unless they instantly closed the gates. The Romans accordingly were shut out for slaughter by the enemy, Atinius and a few others being alone allowed to enter. A heated discussion thereupon arose amongst the townsmen; some were for maintaining their loyalty to Rome, others thought they ought to yield to fate and surrender the city to the victors. As usual, evil counsels and the desire to be on the winning side carried the day. Atinius and his men were conducted down to the sea and placed on board ship, not because they were Romans, but because, after Atinius' mild and impartial administration, they wished to provide for his safety.

Then the Carthaginians were admitted into the city.

The consuls left Beneventum and marched their legions into the territory of Capua, partly to destroy the crops of corn which were now in the blade, and partly with the view of making an attack upon the city. They thought that they would make their consulship illustrious by the destruction of so wealthy and prosperous a city and at the same time they would wipe out a great stain from the republic which had allowed the defection of so close a neighbour to go for three years unpunished. They could not, however, leave Beneventum unguarded. If, as they felt certain would be the case, Hannibal came to Capua to help his friends, it would be necessary, in view of the sudden emergency, to provide against the attacks of his cavalry. They sent orders, therefore, to Tiberius Gracchus, who was in Lucania, to come to Beneventum with his cavalry and light infantry, and to leave some one in command of the legions in the standing camp who were protecting Lucania.

XVI. *The Death of Tiberius Gracchus.*—Before he left Lucania a most ill-omened portent happened to Gracchus whilst he was offering sacrifice. The sacrifice itself was just finished when two snakes glided unobserved up to the reserved parts of the victim and devoured the liver; as soon as they were seen they suddenly disappeared. On the advice of the augurs a fresh sacrifice was offered and the parts reserved with greater care, but according to the tradition the same thing happened a second and even a third time; the snakes glided up and after tasting the liver slipped away untouched. The augurs warned the commander that the portent concerned him and they bade him be on his guard against secret foes and secret plots. But no foresight could avert the impending doom. There was a Lucanian named Flavus, the head of that section of the Lucanians who stood by Rome—one section had gone over to Hannibal—and they elected him praetor. He had already been a year in office when suddenly he changed his mind and began to look out for an opportunity of ingratiating himself with the Carthaginians. He did not think it enough to go over himself and draw the Lucanians with him into revolt, unless he could make his league with the enemy sure by the life-blood of the very man who was his guest-friend, and betray the Roman commander. He had a secret interview with Mago, who was commanding in Bruttium, and obtained his solemn pledge that if he would betray the Roman commander to the Carthaginians the Lucanians should be taken into friendship and allowed to live as a free people under their own laws. He then took Mago to the spot where he said he would bring Gracchus with a small escort. Mago was to bring foot and horse fully armed to the place and place a large force in concealment. After the spot had been thoroughly examined and an investigation made of every part, a day was fixed for carrying out the project.

Flavus went to the Roman commander and told him that he had an important enterprise on hand and required Gracchus' help for its accomplishment. He had persuaded the chief magistrates of all the communities which in the general disturbance of Italy had seceded to the Carthaginians to return to friendship with Rome, since the cause of Rome which had been all but ruined at Cannae was every day becoming stronger and more popular, whilst the strength of Hannibal was waning and had almost reached the vanishing point. The Romans, he knew, would not be implacable to those who had formerly offended, there had never been a nation more ready to listen to prayers and more quick to grant forgiveness. How often had they pardoned even their own ancestors after their repeated renewal of hostilities! This was the language he had addressed to them. " But," he went on, " they would rather hear all this from Gracchus himself in person, and touch his right hand, and carry away with them that pledge of good faith." He explained that he had mentioned a place to those whom he had taken into confidence not far from the Roman camp, and only a few words would be needed so to arrange matters there that the entire Lucanian nation would become faithful allies of Rome.

Gracchus, impressed by the apparent sincerity of the man's language and the proposal he made, and carried away by his smooth and plausible address, started from camp with his lictors and a troop of cavalry under the guidance of his guest-friend. He rode straight into the snare; suddenly enemies showed themselves on all sides, and to take away all doubt as to his being betrayed Flavus joined them. Missiles were hurled from every quarter upon Gracchus and his cavalry. He sprung from his horse, and ordered the rest to do the same, and called upon them to make the one thing which Fortune had left them glorious by their courage. " For what is left," he cried, " to a little band surrounded by an enormous host in a valley shut in by forest and mountain, except death? The one question is, are you going to offer yourselves like cattle to be butchered without striking a blow, or are you going to turn all your thoughts from passively awaiting the end and make a fierce and furious onslaught, doing and daring, until you fall, covered with your enemies' blood, amidst the heaped-up bodies and arms of your dying foes? Make, every one of you, for the Lucanian traitor and renegade! The man who sends him beforehand as a victim

to the gods below will find in his own death a glorious honour
and unspeakable consolation." Whilst saying this he wound
his *paludamentum* [8] round his left arm—for they had not even
brought their shields with them—and charged the enemy.
There was more fighting than might have been expected from
the number of the combatants. The Romans were most
exposed to the darts, and as they were hurled from the higher
ground all round they were pierced by them. Gracchus was
now left without any defence and the Carthaginians tried to
take him alive, but catching sight of his Lucanian guest-friend
amongst the enemy, he made such a furious onslaught on their
serried ranks that it became impossible to save his life without
incurring heavy loss. Mago sent his dead body to Hannibal
and ordered it and the captured *fasces* to be placed before the
general's tribunal.

If this is the true story, Gracchus perished in Lucania at the
place called the " Old Fields."

XVII. There are some who point to a place in the neighbourhood of Beneventum, near the river Calor, as the scene of his
death. He had left the camp with his lictors and three attendants to bathe in the river, whilst the enemy were concealed in
osier beds on the bank, and whilst naked and defenceless was
killed, after vainly endeavouring to drive off the enemy by
stones from the bed of the river. Others say that, acting on the
advice of the augurs, he had gone about half a mile from the
camp for the purpose of averting the above-mentioned portents
in a place free from defilement, when he was surrounded by two
squadrons of Numidians who happened to have taken up their
position there. So little agreement is there as to the place and
circumstances of the death of this brilliant and famous man.
And there are different versions of the account of his funeral.
Some say that his men buried him in his own camp; others say
that he was buried by Hannibal, and this is the more generally
accepted account. According to this version, a funeral pyre
was erected on the open space in front of the camp and the whole
army fully accoutred went through various evolutions with
Spanish dances and the movements of limbs and weapons
peculiar to each tribe, Hannibal doing honour to the dead in
every way by his acts and words. This is the account given by
those who say that his death took place in Lucania. If you
choose to believe those who place it at the river Calor, it would
appear that the enemy only got possession of the head; this
was sent to Hannibal, and he at once despatched Carthalo to

carry it to Cn. Cornelius, the quaestor, who carried out the obsequies in the Roman camp, the people of Beneventum taking their part in the ceremony as well as the soldiers.

XVIII. *Renewal of the Fighting round Capua.*—The consuls had invaded the territory of Capua and were devastating it far and wide when great alarm and confusion were caused by a sudden sortie of the townsmen supported by Mago and his troopers. They hurriedly recalled to the standards the men who were scattered in all directions, but they had hardly time to form their line before they were routed and lost more than 1500 men. The self-confidence and arrogance of the people of Capua were immensely strengthened by this success and they were continually challenging the Romans to fight. But that one engagement brought about by want of caution and foresight put the consuls much more on their guard. An incident occurred, however, which put heart into the Romans and lessened the confidence of the other side, an insignificant one it is true, but in war nothing is so insignificant as not sometimes to involve serious consequences.

T. Quinctius Crispinus had a friend in Capua called Badius, and their friendship was a very close and intimate one. The intimacy had been formed before the defection of Capua when Badius was lying ill in Rome at Crispinus' house and received the kindest and most careful attention from his host. One day this Badius walked up to the sentinels on duty before the camp gate and asked them to call Crispinus. Crispinus, on receiving the message, imagined that he had not forgotten the old ties of friendship even though public treaties were torn up, and that he wanted a friendly and familiar talk, and accordingly he went on a short distance from his comrades. As soon as they came in sight of one another Badius called out: " I, Badius, challenge you, Crispinus, to battle. Let us mount our horses and, when the others have withdrawn, decide who of us is the better fighter." Crispinus replied that neither he nor his challenger lacked enemies upon whom they could display their courage, but as for himself, even if he met Badius on the field of battle, he would avoid him sooner than pollute his right hand with a friend's blood. Then he turned round and was in the act of departing when Badius became more insolent and began to taunt him with effeminacy and cowardice and hurled at him abusive epithets which he himself more properly deserved. He said that he was an enemy masquerading as a friend and pretending to spare a man for whom he knew he was no match. If he were under the impression that when the bonds which held states together were broken the bonds of private friendship were not broken at the same time, then he, Badius of Capua, openly renounced in the hearing of both armies the friendship of T. Quinctius Crispinus the Roman. "There is," he went on, "no fellowship, no bond of alliance between foe and foe, between me and the man who has come to attack my home, my country, and my country's gods. If you are a man, meet me!"

For a long time Crispinus hesitated, but the men of his troop at last prevailed upon him not to let the Campanian insult him with impunity, and so, only waiting till he could ask his commanders if they would allow him, against regulations, to fight an enemy who challenged him, he mounted his horse with their permission and called upon Badius by name to come out and fight. The Campanian showed no hesitation; they spurred their horses against each other and met. Crispinus with his lance wounded Badius in his left shoulder above his shield. He fell from his horse and Crispinus leaped down from the saddle to despatch him as he lay. Badius, before he was overpowered, escaped to his comrades, leaving shield and horse behind. Crispinus, proudly displaying his spoils, the horse and shield which he had taken, was conducted amid the cheers and congratulations of the soldiers to the consuls. Here he was addressed in terms of high praise and loaded with gifts.

XIX. Hannibal left the neighbourhood of Beneventum and encamped close to Capua. Three days afterwards he led out his force to battle, feeling quite certain that as the Campanians had fought a successful action a short time before in his absence, the Romans would be far less able to withstand him and the army which had been so often victorious. As soon as the battle commenced the Roman line was in difficulties, chiefly owing to the attack of cavalry, as they were almost overwhelmed by their darts. The signal was given for the Roman cavalry to charge the enemy at full gallop, and now it had become simply a cavalry engagement when the sight of Sempronius' army in the distance commanded by Cn. Cornelius created equal alarm on both sides, as each feared that a fresh enemy was coming on. The signal to retire was given in both armies as if by mutual consent, and the combatants separated on almost equal terms and returned to camp.[9] The loss on the Roman side was, however, somewhat the greater owing to the cavalry attack at the beginning.

In order to draw Hannibal away from Capua the consuls left

in the night after the battle for different destinations; Fulvius went into the neighbourhood of Cumae and Claudius into Lucania. On being informed the next day that the Roman camp was evacuated, and that they had gone in two divisions by different routes, Hannibal was at first undecided which he should follow; he decided to follow Appius. After leading his enemy about just as he pleased, Appius returned by a circuitous route to Capua.

Another chance of achieving success in this country presented itself to Hannibal. There was a certain M. Centenius, surnamed Paenula, who was conspicuous among the centurions of the first rank for his physical stature and his courage. After completing his period of service he was introduced by P. Cornelius Sulla, the praetor, to the senate. He requested the senators to allow him 5000 men; he was well acquainted with the enemy and the country where he was operating and would very soon do something worth the doing; the tactics by which our generals and their armies had been outwitted up to that time he would employ against the man who invented them. Stupid as the promise was it was quite as stupidly given credence to, as though the qualifications of a soldier were the same as those of a general. Instead of 5000 he was given 8000 men, half of them Romans and half troops furnished by the allies. He himself, too, picked up a considerable number of volunteers in the country through which he was marching, and he arrived in Lucania with double the army he started with. Here Hannibal had come to a halt after his fruitless pursuit of Claudius. The result could not be doubtful, seeing it was a contest between armies one of which consisted of veterans habituated to victory, the other a hastily raised and half-armed force. As soon as they caught sight of each other, neither side declined battle and they at once got into fighting order. For more than two hours, however, in spite of the utterly unequal conditions, the Roman army kept up the fighting as long as their leader stood his ground. At last, out of regard for his former reputation and also fearing the disgrace he would incur if he survived a defeat brought on by his own headlong folly, he rushed upon the weapons of the foe and fell, and the Roman army was instantly routed. But even when they fled they found no way of escape, for all avenues were closed by the cavalry, so that out of that multitude of men only a thousand escaped, all the rest perished in one way or another.

XX. *Investment of Capua.*—The consuls now resumed the

siege of Capua in earnest, and everything necessary for the task was brought together and got into readiness. Corn was stored at Casilinum; at the mouth of the Vulturnus, where the town of Vulturnum now stands, a fort was constructed and a garrison was placed in it and in Puteoli also, which Fabius had previously fortified, so that they might command both the river and the adjacent sea. The corn which had lately been sent from Sardinia as well as that which M. Junius had purchased in Etruria was conveyed from Ostia into these two maritime fortresses, that the army might have a supply throughout the winter.

Meantime the disaster which had overtaken Centenius in Lucania was aggravated by another which resulted from the death of Gracchus. The volunteer slaves who had done excellent service when he was alive to lead them, looked upon his death as discharging them from further military duties and accordingly disbanded themselves.

Hannibal was anxious not to neglect Capua or desert friends who were in such a critical position, but after his easy victory through the foolhardiness of one Roman general he was watching for an opportunity of crushing another. Envoys from Apulia had informed him that Cn. Fulvius, who was attacking some of their cities which had seceded to him, had at first conducted his operations with care and prudence, but afterwards, intoxicated with success and loaded with plunder, he and his men had given themselves up to such idleness and self-indulgence that all military discipline had disappeared. Hannibal knew by repeated experience, and especially within the last few days, what state an army gets into under an incompetent commander and he at once moved into Apulia.

XXI. Fulvius and his legions were in the neighbourhood of Heraclea. When they heard that the enemy were approaching they were almost on the point of dragging up the standards and going into battle without waiting for orders. In fact the one thing that restrained them more than anything else was the confidence they felt of being able to choose their own time for fighting. The following night, when Hannibal became aware that the camp was in a state of tumult and that most of the men were defying their commander and insisting that he should give the signal, and that there was a general cry, "To arms!" he was quite certain that the opportunity was presented of a successful battle. He quietly disposed some three thousand of his light infantry in the surrounding homesteads and in the woods and copses. They were all to spring from their concealment at the same moment when the signal was given, and Mago had orders to place about two thousand cavalry along all the roads which he thought the direction of the flight might take. After making these dispositions during the night, he marched out to battle at dawn.

Fulvius did not hesitate, though he was not drawn on so much by any hopes of success on his own part as by the blind impetuosity of his men. The same recklessness which sent them on to the field appeared in the formation of their line. They went forward in a haphazard way and took their places in the ranks just where they chose, and left them again as their caprices or fears dictated. The first legion and the left wing of the allies were drawn up in front and the line was extended far beyond its proper length. The officers called out that it possessed neither strength nor depth and wherever the enemy made their attack they would break through, but the men would not even listen to, much less attend to anything that was for their good. And now Hannibal was upon them; a general so different from their own, with an army so different and in such different order! As might be expected, the Romans were unable to withstand the very first attack; their general, quite as foolish and reckless as Centenius, though not to be compared with him in courage, no sooner saw the day going against him and his men in confusion than he seized a horse and made his escape with about two hundred of his cavalry. The rest of the army, repulsed in front and then surrounded in rear and flanks, was so completely cut up that out of 12,000 men not more than 2000 escaped. The camp was taken.

XXII. The news of these disasters, one after another, created very great grief and alarm amongst the citizens in Rome, still, as they knew that the consuls were so far successful where success was most important, they were not so much disturbed by the tidings as they might have been. The senate despatched C. Laetorius and M. Metilius with instructions to the consuls, telling them to carefully get together the remains of the two armies and to see to it that the survivors were not driven by fear and despair to surrender to the enemy, as had happened after the disaster at Cannae. They were also to find out who had deserted amongst the volunteer slaves. Publius Cornelius also was charged with this latter task, as he was with the raising of fresh troops, and he caused notices to be published through the market-towns and boroughs, ordering that search should be made for the volunteer slaves, and that they should be brought

back to their standards. These instructions were all most
carefully carried out.

Appius Claudius placed D. Junius in command at the mouth
of the Vulturnus, and M. Aurelius Cotta at Puteoli; whenever
the vessels arrived from Etruria and Sardinia they were at once
to have the corn sent on to the camp. Claudius then returned
to Capua and found his colleague Q. Fulvius bringing everything
from Casilinum and making preparations to attack the city.
Both of them now commenced the investment of the place, and
they summoned the praetor, Claudius Nero, who was in Claudius'
old camp at Suessula. He, too, leaving a small force to hold
the position, came down with the rest of his army to Capua. So
three commanders had their headquarters now established round
Capua, and three armies working on different sides were preparing to ring the city round with fosse and dyke. They erected
blockhouses at certain intervals, and battles took place in
several places at once with the Campanians as they tried to stop
the work, the result being that at last the Campanians kept
within their walls and gates.

Before, however, the circle of investment was completed,
envoys were despatched to Hannibal to remonstrate with him
for having abandoned Capua which was now almost restored to
the Romans, and to implore him to bring them succour now, at
all events, as they were no longer merely besieged but completely blockaded. A despatch was sent to the consuls by
P. Cornelius bidding them give an opportunity to the inhabitants, before they completed the investment, of leaving the
place and carrying away their property with them. Those who
left before the 15th of March would be free and remain in possession of all their property; after that date those who left and
those who remained would be alike treated as enemies. When
this offer was announced to the Campanians they treated it
not only with scorn but with gratuitous insults and threats
as well.

Shortly before this Hannibal had left Herdonea for Tarentum
in the hope of acquiring the place either by treachery or by
force, and as he failed to do so he bent his course towards
Brundisium, under the impression that the town would surrender. It was whilst he was spending time here to no purpose
that the envoys from Capua came to him with their remonstrances and appeals. Hannibal answered them in high-
sounding words; " he had raised the siege of Capua once
already, and the consuls would not wait for his approach even

now." Dismissed with this hope the envoys had considerable difficulty in getting back to Capua, surrounded as it now was with a double fosse and rampart.

XXIII. *The Conquest of Syracuse.*—Just when the circumvallation of Capua was being completed the siege of Syracuse came to an end. This result was due in a large measure to the energy and courage of the general and his army, but it had been helped on by domestic treachery.

At the commencement of the spring Marcellus was undecided whether to turn the stress of war to Agrigentum against Himilco and Hippocrates, or whether he should press the siege of Syracuse. He saw that this place could not be carried by assault, as it was unassailable by sea or land owing to its position, nor could it be reduced by famine, since it was nourished by a free supply of provisions from Carthage. However, he determined to leave nothing untried. There were with the Romans some leading members of the Syracusan nobility who had been expelled when the defection took place, and Marcellus told these refugees to sound the feelings of the men of their own party, and give them an assurance that if Syracuse were surrendered they should be free and live under their own laws. It was impossible to get any chance of interviews, for the fact of many being suspected made all more careful and watchful, so that no attempt of the kind should escape detection. A slave belonging to the exiles was admitted into the city as a deserter, and after getting a few men together, broached the subject in conversation. Subsequently some were hidden under the nets in a fishing boat and in that way taken round to the Roman camp where they had conversations with the refugees. Different people, one after another, did the same thing, until at last there were as many as eighty concerned in the matter. When all the arrangements for surrender had been made, information was given to Epicydes by a certain Attalus who resented not having been intrusted with the secret, and they were all tortured to death.

This hope, which had proved so illusory, was soon succeeded by another. A certain Damippus, a Lacedaemonian, had been sent from Syracuse on a mission to King Philip and was captured by some Roman ships. Epicydes was particularly anxious to ransom this man, and Marcellus raised no objection, as just at that time the Romans were bidding for the friendship of the Ætolians with whom the Lacedaemonians were in alliance. Those who were sent to discuss the terms of the ransom thought that the most central place for the conference, and the one most convenient to both sides, was a spot near the tower called Galeagra, at the Trogilian port.[10] As they went to and fro there several times, one of the Romans took a near view of the wall, counted the stones and formed an estimate in his mind of the thickness of each stone. Having thus calculated the height of the wall as well as he could by conjecture, and finding it lower than he or any one else had supposed and capable of being scaled by a ladder of even moderate length, he made a report to the consul. Marcellus attached considerable importance to his suggestion, but as that part of the wall, being lower, was for that very reason more carefully guarded, it was impossible to approach it and they had to watch their opportunity, which soon came. A deserter brought word that the townspeople were keeping the festival of Diana which lasted three days, and that, through lack of other things, owing to the siege, they were celebrating the feast mostly with wine, which Epicydes had distributed amongst the populace, and the leading citizens amongst the tribes. On hearing this, Marcellus talked the matter over with a few of the military tribunes, and through them selected the centurions and private soldiers who were fittest for such a daring enterprise. Scaling ladders were quietly got ready, and then all the rest of the men were ordered to seek refreshment and rest as soon as they could, as a nocturnal expedition was in front of them.

As soon as he thought the time had come when, after feasting all day, the men would have their fill of wine and be in their first sleep, the consul ordered one maniple to carry scaling ladders, and about a thousand men were silently marched in a narrow column up to the spot. They got up on to the wall without any confusion or noise and others at once followed in order; even those who felt nervous were reassured by the daring of those in front.

XXIV. By this time a thousand men had got possession of that section of the wall. They went on as far as the Hexapylon without meeting a soul, as the majority of those on guard in the bastions were either stupid with wine after their revels or were drinking themselves drunk. They killed a few, however, whom they surprised in their beds. When they reached the Hexapylon they gave the signal, and the rest of the troops marched up to the walls bringing more scaling ladders with them. The postern gate near the Hexapylon was giving way to the violence of the blows, and the agreed signal was given from the wall. They no longer attempted to conceal their movements, but commenced an open attack, as they had now reached Epipolae, where there was a large force on guard, and their object was now to frighten rather than elude the enemy. They succeeded perfectly. For no sooner were the notes of the trumpets heard and the shouts of those who held the wall and a part of the city, than the men on guard thought that every part was taken, and some fled along the wall, others leaped from it, and a crowd of panic-struck citizens took to headlong flight. A great many, however, were ignorant of the great disaster that had befallen them, for everybody was heavy with wine and sleep, and in a city of such vast extent what was happening in one part was not known to the population generally.

At daybreak Marcellus forced the gates of the Hexapylon and entered the city with his entire force, rousing the citizens who all betook themselves to arms, prepared to render what help they could to a city which was all but captured. Epicydes made a hurried march from the Island—its local name is Nasos—under the impression that a few men had succeeded in scaling the walls owing to the negligence of the guards and that he would soon drive them out. He told the terrified fugitives whom he met that they were adding to the confusion and making things out to be more serious and alarming than they really were. When, however, he saw every place round Epipolae full of armed men, he simply discharged a few missiles at the enemy and marched back to the Achradina, not so much through fear of the strength and numbers of the enemy as of some opening for treason from within, which might close the gates of Achradina and the Island against him in the confusion.

When Marcellus mounted the fortifications and saw from his higher ground the city below him, the fairest city of the time, he is said to have shed tears at the sight, partly through joy at his great achievement, partly at the memory of its ancient glories. He thought of the Athenian fleets which had been sunk in that harbour, of the two great armies with their famous generals which had been annihilated there, of all of its many powerful kings and tyrants, above all, of Hiero, whose memory was so fresh, and who, in addition to all his endowments of fortune and character, had distinguished himself by his services to Rome.[11] As all this passed through his mind and with it the thought that in one short hour all he saw round him would be burnt and reduced to ashes, he decided, before advancing against Achradina, to send the Syracusans, who, as already stated, were with the Roman troops, into the city to try if kind words could induce the enemy to surrender the place.

XXV. The gates and walls of Achradina were mostly held by the deserters who were hopeless of obtaining mercy on any terms, and they allowed no one to approach the walls or to speak to them. So Marcellus, finding that his project had failed, ordered the troops to return to Euryalus. This was a hill in the furthest part of the city, away from the sea, and over-looking the road which leads into the country and the inland part of the island. It was, therefore, admirably adapted for the reception of supplies from the interior. The command of the citadel here had been entrusted by Epicydes to Philodemus an Argive. Sosis, one of the regicides, had been sent by Mar-cellus to open up negotiations, but after a long conversation in which he found himself put off with evasive replies he reported to Marcellus that Philodemus was taking time for consideration. He continued to procrastinate from day to day, to allow time for Hippocrates and Himilco to bring up their legions, feeling quite sure that if he had them in his stronghold the Romans would be shut up within the walls and annihilated.

As Marcellus saw that Euryalus could not be taken by either treachery or force, he established his camp between Neapolis and Tycha—parts of the city, and almost cities in themselves—as he was afraid if he entered the more populous parts he would not be able to keep his soldiers from dispersing in their eagerness for plunder. Envoys came to him from these two places with olive branches and woollen fillets, imploring him that they might be spared from fire and sword. Marcellus held a council of war to consider this request, or rather this entreaty, and in accordance with the wish of all present he gave notice to the soldiers that they were not to lay hands on any free citizen; everything else they were at liberty to appropriate. Instead of fosse and rampart the camp was protected by the private houses which served it for walls, and sentinels and pickets were posted at the gates of the houses which stood open to the street to secure the camp against attack while the soldiers were dispersed in the city. After this the signal was given and the soldiers ran in all directions, breaking open the house doors and filling everything with uproar and panic, but they refrained from bloodshed. There was no limit to the work of rapine until they had cleared the houses of all the goods and possessions which had been accumulating during the long spell of prosperity. Whilst this was going on, Philodemus saw that there was no hope of succour, and after getting the promise of a safe conduct for him to return to Epicydes, he withdrew his garrison and handed the position over to the Romans.

Whilst everybody was preoccupied with the tumult in the captured part of the city, Bomilcar seized the opportunity to escape. The night was a tempestuous one, and the Roman fleet were unable to keep their anchorage off the harbour, so he slipped out with thirty-five ships, and finding the sea clear set sail for Carthage, leaving fifty-five ships for Epicydes and the Syracusans. After making the Carthaginians realise the critical state of affairs at Syracuse he returned with a hundred ships a few days later and was rewarded—so they say—by Epicydes with gifts from Hiero's treasury.

XXVI. The capture of Euryalus and its occupation by a Roman garrison relieved Marcellus of one cause of anxiety; he had no longer to dread an attack from the rear which might have created confusion amongst his men, shut in and hampered as they were by walls. His next move was against Achradina. He established three separate camps in suitable positions and sat down before the place, hoping to reduce it by famine. For some days the outposts were undisturbed, when the sudden arrival of Hippocrates and Himilco led to a general attack upon the Roman lines. Hippocrates had formed an entrenched camp at the Great Harbour, and after giving a signal to the troops in Achradina he made an attack on the old camp of the Romans which Crispinus commanded. Epicydes made a sortie against Marcellus and the Carthaginian fleet which lay between the city and the Roman camp was brought ashore and so prevented Crispinus from sending any help to Marcellus. The excitement which the enemy caused was, however, much more alarming than the fighting, for Crispinus not only drove Hippocrates back from his entrenchments, but actually went in pursuit as he fled hurriedly away, whilst Marcellus drove Epicydes back into the city. And now, apparently, ample provision was made against danger arising from any sudden attacks in the future.

To add to their troubles both sides were visited by pestilence, a calamity almost heavy enough to turn them from all thoughts of war. It was the time of autumn and the locality was naturally unhealthy, more so, however, outside the city than within it, and the insupportable heat affected the constitutions of almost all who were in the two camps. In the beginning people fell ill and died through the effects of the season and the unhealthy locality; later, the nursing of the sick and contact with them spread the disease, so that either those who had caught it died neglected and abandoned, or else they carried off with them those who were waiting on them and nursing them, and who had thus become infected. Deaths and funerals were a daily spectacle; on all sides, day and night, were heard the wailings for the dead. At last familiarity with misery so brutalised men that not only would they not follow the dead with tears and the lamentations which custom demanded, but they actually refused to carry them out for burial, and the lifeless bodies were left lying about before the eyes of those who were awaiting a similar death. So what with fear and the foul and deadly miasma arising from the bodies, the dead proved fatal to the sick and the sick equally fatal to those in health. Men preferred to die by the sword; some, single-handed, attacked the enemies' outposts. The epidemic was much more prevalent in the Carthaginian camp than in that of the Romans, for their long investment of Syracuse had made them more accustomed to the climate and to the water. The Sicilians who were in the hostile ranks deserted as soon as they saw that the disease was spreading through the unhealthiness of the place, and went off to their own cities. The Carthaginians, who had nowhere to go to, perished to a man together with their generals, Hippocrates and Himilco. When the disease assumed such serious proportions Marcellus transferred his men to the city, and those who had been weakened by sickness were restored by shade and shelter. Still, many of the Roman soldiers, too, were carried off by that pestilence.

XXVII. When the land army of the Carthaginians had been thus wiped out, the Sicilians who had been with Hippocrates took possession of two walled towns, not large ones certainly, but made safe by their situation and strong fortifications.[12] One was three miles from Syracuse, the other fifteen. They carried supplies to these towns from their own states and asked for reinforcements. Bomilcar had in the meantime paid a second visit to Carthage with his fleet and had drawn such a picture of the state of things in Syracuse as to lead the government to hope that they might not only render effectual assistance to their friends, but even succeed in capturing the Romans inside that city, which they had in some measure captured. He persuaded them to despatch as many cargo ships as they could, laden with stores of all kinds, and also to augment his force of fighting ships. The result was that he left Carthage with 130 ships of war and 700 transports. The winds were favourable for him whilst sailing for Sicily, but they prevented him from rounding the promontory of Pachinus.

The news of Bomilcar's approach and then his unexpected delay excited first hope and then fear amongst the Syracusans and just the reverse among the Romans. Epicydes was afraid that if the east wind lasted much longer the Carthaginian fleet would return to Africa, and he handed Achradina over to the commanders of the mercenaries and put off to meet Bomilcar. He found him at anchor with his ships headed for the African coast and anxious to avoid a naval engagement, not because he was inferior in the strength or number of his ships—he really had more than the Romans—but because the winds were more favourable to them than to him; Epicydes, however, persuaded him to try his chance in a sea fight. When Marcellus became aware that an army of Sicilians was being raised from the whole of the island, and that a Carthaginian fleet was approaching with vast supplies, he determined, though inferior in the number of ships, to prevent Bomilcar from reaching Syracuse, lest he should be shut in by sea and land whilst he was confined and hampered in a hostile city. The two fleets lay facing each other off the promontory of Pachinus, ready to engage as soon as the sea was calm enough to allow them to sail into deep water. As soon as the east wind, which had been blowing strongly for some days, dropped Bomilcar made the first move. It seemed as though he was making for the open sea in order the better to round the promontory, but when he saw the Roman ships sailing straight for him he crowded on all sail and skirting the coast of Sicily made for Tarentum, having previously sent a message to Heraclea ordering the transports to return to Africa. Finding all his hopes suddenly crushed, Epicydes did not care to go back to a city which was in a state of siege and a large part of which was already taken. He sailed for Agrigentum, to watch events rather than to control them.

XXVIII. When the news of what had happened reached the camp of the Sicilians, viz. that Epicydes had left Syracuse and that the island had been abandoned by the Carthaginians and almost surrendered a second time to the Romans, they sent envoys to Marcellus to treat for the surrender of the city, having previously sounded in frequent interviews the feelings of those who were undergoing the siege. They were practically united on these two points, that all that had been included in the king's dominions should belong to Rome, and that all else was to be retained by the Sicilians together with their liberty and their

laws. They then invited those who had been left in charge by
Epicydes to a conference, the envoys telling them that the army
of the Sicilians had sent them to them as well as to Marcellus,
so that those who were within and those who were outside of the
beleaguered city might share the same fortune, and neither should
make separate terms for themselves. Admission was granted
to them that they might converse with their friends and relatives.
After explaining the nature of their understanding with Marcellus
and holding out a prospect of safety, they persuaded them to
join in an attack upon those to whom Epicydes had committed
the government—Polyclitus, Philistio, and Epicydes, surnamed
Sindon. They were put to death and the citizens were summoned to a public meeting. Here the envoys complained bitterly
of the straits they were in for food, and the other evils which
they had been in the habit of grumbling about in secret; they said
that although they had so much to distress them, they must not
throw the blame on Fortune; it was in their own power to decide
how long they would endure it. The motives which led the
Romans to attack Syracuse were those of affection, not animosity.
When they heard that the reins of government had been seized
by Hippocrates and Epicydes, who had been first creatures
of Hannibal and then of Hieronymus, they set their armies in
motion and began the siege, not for the purpose of destroying the
city but of crushing those who were tyrannising over it. But
now that Hippocrates was disposed of and Epicydes shut out
from Syracuse and his officers put to death, what was there left
to prevent the Romans from wishing that Syracuse should be
free from all harm, just as they would have wished it had Hiero,
that eminently loyal friend of Rome, been still alive? There
was, then, no danger either to the city or its people other than
what would arise from their own action if they let slip that
chance of reconciliation with Rome. There would never be
another so favourable as the one they had at that moment, just
when it was plain to all that Syracuse had been delivered from
an impotent tyranny.[13]

XXIX. This address was received with universal approval.
It was, however, decided to elect magistrates before sending the
envoys. From amongst the magistrates so elected they selected
the envoys who were to be sent to Marcellus. Their leader
addressed him in the following terms: " It is not we, the people
of Syracuse, who have revolted from you, but Hieronymus,
who acted much more wickedly towards us than towards you.
And when peace had been restored by the tyrant's death it was

no Syracusan, but the king's creatures Hippocrates and Epicydes, who disturbed it, by crushing us on the one hand by fear, on the other by treachery. No man can say that there was ever a time during which we enjoyed liberty when we were not at peace with you. Now, at all events, no sooner have we become our own masters through the death of the oppressors of Syracuse than we come to you to give up our arms, to surrender ourselves, our city and its fortifications, to accept any condition which you may lay upon us. To you, Marcellus, the gods have vouchsafed the glory of capturing the noblest and fairest of Grecian cities. Whatever memorable achievement we have wrought by sea or land enhances the splendour of your triumph. Would you wish that it should be only a glorious tradition how great a city you have captured, rather than that it should be a spectacle for the eyes of posterity to rest upon? That it should exhibit to all who visit it by land or sea the trophies we have won from Athenians and Carthaginians, which are now the trophies you have won from us? That you should hand down to your house an unharmed Syracuse to be kept under the patronage and protection of all who bear the name of Marcellus? Let not the memory of Hieronymus weigh more with you than that of Hiero. He was your friend for a far longer time than the other was your enemy. You found in him a real benefactor; this man's madness only availed to his own destruction."

As far as the Romans were concerned they could have gained all they wanted in perfect security. It was amongst the besieged themselves that war existed with all its perils. The deserters, thinking that they were being betrayed, communicated their fears to the mercenaries; they all flew to arms, and beginning with the murder of the magistrates they commenced a general massacre of the citizens, killing in their desperate madness everybody they met, and plundering all they could lay hands on. Then, that they might not be without officers, they elected six, three to command in Achradina and three in Nasos. When the tumult had somewhat subsided and the mercenaries found out on inquiry what agreement had been come to with the Romans, the truth began to dawn upon them, and they realised that their case was quite distinct from that of the deserters.

XXX. The envoys came back from their interview with Marcellus just at the right moment, and were able to assure them that their suspicions were groundless and that the Romans saw no reason why they should visit them with punishment. One

of the three commanders in Achradina was a Spaniard named
Moericus, and amongst those who accompanied the envoys a
soldier from the Spanish auxiliaries had designedly been introduced. When they had entered Achradina this man obtained
a private interview with Moericus and described to him the state
of affairs in Spain, which he had quite recently left, and how
everything there was under the power of Rome. If Moericus
chose to make himself of use to the Romans, he might be a leading
man among his countrymen, and either take service under the
Roman standard or return to his own country, whichever he
chose. But if on the other hand he preferred to remain under
siege, what hope had he of relief, shut in as he was by sea and
land?

Moericus was impressed by the force of these arguments, and
after it had been decided to send envoys to Marcellus, he
sent his brother as one of them. The same Spanish soldier
conducted him by himself to Marcellus. In this interview the
details were settled and Marcellus pledged himself to observe
the conditions, after which the envoys returned to Achradina.
In order to avoid the least chance of suspicion Moericus made it
known that he disapproved of envoys going to and fro, and gave
orders that none were to be admitted and none sent. Also,
with a view to greater security, he thought that the conduct of
the defence ought to be properly distributed amongst the three
commanders, so that each might be responsible for his own
section of the fortifications. They all agreed. In the division,
his command extended from the fountain of Arethusa to the
mouth of the Great Harbour, and he managed to let the Romans
know that. So Marcellus ordered a cargo ship filled with troops
to be towed by a quadrireme to the Island, and the men to land
near the gate adjoining the fountain. This order was carried
out in the fourth watch, and Moericus, as previously arranged,
admitted the soldiers through the gate. At dawn Marcellus
attacked Achradina with his full strength, and not only those
who were actually holding it, but the troops in Nasos also, left
their posts and ran to defend Achradina from the assault of the
Romans. In the confusion of the attack some swift vessels,
which had previously been brought round to Nasos, landed
troops. These making an unexpected attack upon the half-
manned posts, and rushing through the gates, still open, out
of which the garrison had just sallied to defend Achradina,
had little trouble in capturing a position which had been
abandoned owing to the flight of its defenders.[14] There were

none who did less to defend the place or to maintain their ground with any spirit than the deserters; they did not even trust their own comrades, and fled in the middle of the fighting. When Marcellus learnt that Nasos was captured and one district of Achradina occupied, and that Moericus with his men had joined the Romans, he ordered the retreat to be sounded, for he was afraid that the royal treasure, the fame of which exceeded the reality, might fall into the hands of plunderers.

XXXI. The impetuosity of the soldiers being thus checked and time and opportunity given for the deserters in Achradina to effect their escape, the Syracusans were at last relieved of their apprehensions and opened the gates. They at once sent a deputation to Marcellus with the one request that they and their children might remain unharmed.

He called a council of war, to which he summoned the Syracusan refugees in the Roman camp, and made the following reply to the deputation: " The crimes committed against the people of Rome during these last few years by those who have held Syracuse quite outweigh all the good services which Hiero rendered us during his fifty years' reign. Most of these, it is true, have recoiled on the heads of those who were guilty of them, and they have punished themselves for their breach of treaties far more severely than the Roman people could have wished. I have been for three years investing Syracuse, not that Rome may make the city her slave, but that the leaders of deserters and renegades may not keep it in a state of oppression and bondage. What the Syracusans could have done has been shown by those amongst them who have been living within the Roman lines, by the Spaniard Moericus who brought over his men, and last of all by the belated but courageous resolution which the Syracusans have now taken. After all the toils and dangers which have endured for so long a time round the walls of Syracuse by sea and land, the fact that I have been able to capture the city is nothing like such a reward as I should have received had I been able to save it." After giving this reply he sent the quaestor with an escort to Nasos to receive the royal treasure into his custody. Achradina was given up for plunder to the soldiers, after guards had been placed at the houses of the refugees who were within the Roman lines.

Amongst many horrible instances of fury and rapacity the fate of Archimedes stands out. It is recorded that amidst all the uproar and terror created by the soldiers who were rushing about the captured city in search of plunder, he was quietly absorbed in some geometrical figures which he had drawn on the sand, and was killed by a soldier who did not know who he was. Marcellus was much grieved and took care that his funeral was properly conducted; and after his relations had been discovered they were honoured and protected by the name and memory of Archimedes.

Such, in the main, were the circumstances under which Syracuse was captured, and the amount of plunder was almost greater than if Carthage had been taken, the city which was waging war on equal terms with Rome.

A few days prior to the capture of Syracuse, T. Otacilius crossed over from Lilybaeum to Utica with eighty quinqueremes. He entered the harbour before daylight and captured some transports laden with corn, and then landing his men ravaged a considerable portion of the country round Utica and carried back to his ships every description of plunder. He returned to Lilybaeum three days after he had started with a hundred and thirty transports laden with corn and booty. The corn he at once sent on to Syracuse; had it not been for that timely assistance, victors and vanquished alike would have been in danger of a very serious famine.

XXXII. *Roman Defeats in Spain—The Death of the Scipios.*—For two years nothing very remarkable had happened in Spain; the contest was carried on by diplomacy more than by arms. This summer the Roman commanders on leaving their winter quarters united their forces. A council of war was called and they came to a unanimous decision that as up to that time all they had done was to keep Hasdrubal from marching to Italy, it was now high time to make an effort to finish the war. During the winter they had raised a force of 20,000 Celtiberians, and with this reinforcement they considered themselves strong enough for the task. The enemies' force consisted of three armies. Hasdrubal, the son of Gisgo, had united his army with Mago, and their joint camp was about a five days' march from the Romans. Somewhat nearer to them was Hasdrubal, the son of Hamilcar, an old commander in Spain, who was in camp at a city called Amtorgis. The Roman commanders wanted to dispose of him first, and they believed that they had more than enough strength for the purpose; the only doubt in their minds was whether, after his defeat, the other Hasdrubal and Mago would not retreat into the trackless forest and mountains and keep up a guerilla warfare. The best plan, they thought, would be to form their force into two armies and finish the war in Spain at one stroke. They arranged accordingly that P. Cornelius was to advance against Mago and Hasdrubal with two-thirds of the army of Romans and allied troops, and Cn. Cornelius with the remaining third of the old army and the recently raised Celtiberians was to oppose the Barcine Hasdrubal. Both generals with their armies advanced together as far as the town of Amtorgis where they encamped in full view of the enemy with the river between them. Here Cn. Scipio took his stand with the force above mentioned, while Publius Scipio went on to execute his share of the operations.

XXXIII. When Hasdrubal became aware that the Romans formed only a small portion of the army and that they were depending entirely upon their Celtiberian auxiliaries, he determined to detach the latter from their Roman service. He was quite at home with every form of treachery known to barbarians, and especially those practised by the tribes amongst whom he had for so many years been campaigning. Both camps were full of Spaniards, who had no difficulty in understanding each other's language, and secret interviews were held, in the course of which he made an agreement with the Celtiberian chieftains, by the offer of a large bribe, that they should withdraw their forces. They did not look upon this as very atrocious conduct, for it was not a question of turning their arms against the Romans, and though the money was quite equal to the pay they received in war, it was given them to abstain from war. Then, too, the mere rest from the toils of the campaign, the thought of returning home, the delight of seeing their friends and their possessions were universally welcomed. So the mass of the troops were quite as easily persuaded as their chiefs, and they had nothing to fear from the Romans who were too few in number to keep them back by force. This is a thing against which Roman generals will always have to be on their guard, and instances such as these ought to serve as warnings that they must not depend upon foreign auxiliaries to such an extent as not to have in their camp a preponderance of that solidity and fighting power which native troops can alone supply.

The Celtiberians took up their standards and marched off. The Romans asked them why they were going, and appealed to them to stay where they were, but the only answer they got was that they were called away by a war at home. When Scipio saw that his allies could not be detained by either appeals or force and that without them he was no match for the enemy, whilst a junction with his brother was out of the question, he

determined to retreat as far as he could; this seemed the only
safe measure to adopt. His one object was to avoid an encounter
on open ground with the enemy who had crossed the river and
were pressing closely at his heels.

XXXIV. P. Scipio was at the same time placed in a position
quite as alarming but fraught with much greater danger by the
appearance of a new enemy. This was young Masinissa, at that
time an ally of the Carthaginians, but afterwards raised to fame
and power by his friendship with Rome. He first sought to
check Scipio's advance with a body of Numidian horse, and he
kept up incessant attacks upon him day and night. He not
only cut off all who had wandered too far from camp in search
of wood and fodder, but he actually rode up to the camp and
charged into the middle of the outposts and pickets, creating
alarm and confusion everywhere. In the night he frequently
upset the camp by making a sudden rush at the gates and the
stockade; there was no place and no time at which the Romans
were free from anxiety and fear, and they were compelled to
keep within their lines, unable to obtain anything they wanted.
It was fast becoming a regular siege and would evidently become
a still closer one if Indebilis, who was reported to be approaching
with 7500 Suessetanians, should join the Carthaginians.

Cautious and prudent general though he was, Scipio was
compelled by his position to take the hazardous step of making
a night march to oppose Indebilis' advance and to fight him
wherever he met him. Leaving a small force to guard the
camp and placing Tiberius Fonteius in command, he started at
midnight and encountered the enemy. They fought in order
of march rather than of battle; the Romans, however, had
the advantage, in spite of its being an irregular battle.[15] But
the Numidian horse, whom Scipio thought he had eluded, swept
round both flanks and created the greatest alarm. A fresh
action had now begun against the Numidians when a third
enemy appeared; the Carthaginian generals had come up and
were attacking the rear. The Romans had to face a battle on
both flanks and on their rear, and could not make up their minds
against what enemy to make their main attack or in what direction to close their line and charge. Whilst their commander
was fighting and encouraging his men and exposing himself in
the hottest of the turmoil he was run through by a lance in his
left side. The massed body of the enemy who had charged
the closed ranks round their general, as soon as they saw Scipio
falling lifeless from his horse were wild with joy and ran in

all directions shouting that the Roman commander had fallen. The news spread over the whole field, and the enemy at once regarded themselves as unquestionably victorious, while the Romans equally felt themselves vanquished. With the loss of the general there began at once a flight from the field. It was not difficult to break through the Numidians and other light-armed troops, but it was almost impossible to make one's escape amidst such numbers of cavalry and of foot soldiers who rivalled horses in speed. Almost more were killed in flight than in battle, and not a man would have survived had not the day been rapidly drawing to a close so that night put an end to the carnage.

XXXV. The Carthaginian generals were not slow to take advantage of their success. After allowing their men the needful rest, they proceeded straight from the battle-field by forced marches to Hasdrubal, fully expecting that when they had joined forces the war could be brought to a close. When they reached his camp, the generals and the soldiers, in high spirits over their recent victory, exchanged hearty congratulations at the destruction of so great a commander and his entire army, and looked forward with confidence to winning another victory as complete. The report of the terrible disaster had not reached the Romans, but there was a gloomy silence, a secret foreboding, such as usually happens when men feel a presentiment of coming misfortune. The general, who saw himself deserted by his allies and knew that the forces of the enemy were so largely augmented, was led still further by his own conjectures and inferences to suspect the occurrence of some disaster much sooner than to entertain any hopes of success. " How," he asked himself, " could Hasdrubal and Mago have brought up their army without opposition if they had not brought their own share of the war to a successful close? How could his brother have failed to stop them or to follow them up so that if he could not prevent their forming a junction he could at least have united his own forces with those of his brother? " Filled with these anxieties he believed that the only safe course for him for the time being was to retreat from his present position as far as he could. He accordingly accomplished a considerable march in a single night, unobserved by the enemy and therefore unmolested. When it grew light the enemy became aware of his departure, and sending on the Numidians in advance, commenced the pursuit with the utmost speed of which they were capable. The Numidians came up with them before

time—and short enough it was—in strengthening the defences
of the camp and storing supplies in it, and the soldiers carried
out all his commands with alacrity and in anything but a de-
spondent mood. But when the news arrived that Hasdrubal—
Gisgo's son—had crossed the Ebro and was coming to stamp
out the remains of the war and the soldiers saw the signal for
battle put out by their new general they gave way completely.
The recollection of the men who had so lately commanded them,
the proud confidence which they had always felt in their generals
and their armies when they went into battle quite unnerved
them; they all burst into tears and smote their heads; some
raised their hands to heaven and reproached the gods; others
lay on the ground and invoked the names of their old commanders. Nothing could check these wild outbursts of grief,
though the centurions tried to rouse their men, and Marcius
himself went about calming them and at the same time
reproaching them for their unmanly conduct. " Why," he
asked them, " have you given way to womanish and idle
tears instead of bracing yourselves up to defend yourselves
and the republic and not allowing your commanders' death to
go unavenged? "

Suddenly a shout was heard and the sound of trumpets, for the
enemy was now close up to the rampart. In an instant their
grief changed to fury, they rushed to arms, and racing to the
gates like madmen they dashed upon the enemy who were
coming on carelessly and in disorder. The sudden and unlooked-
for movement created a panic among the Carthaginians. They
wondered whence all these enemies had arisen, after their army
had been all but annihilated, what gave such daring and self-
confidence to men who had been vanquished and put to flight,
who had come forward as their commander now that the two
Scipios were killed, who was over the camp, who had given the
signal for battle. Bewildered and astounded at all these utterly
unlooked-for surprises they at first slowly retired, then as the
attack became heavier and more insistent they turned and fled.
There would have been either a frightful slaughter amongst the
fugitives or a rash and dangerous attack on the part of the pursuers if Marcius had not hurriedly given the signal to retire and
kept back the excited troops by throwing himself in front of the
foremost and even holding some back with his hands. Then he
marched them back to camp still thirsting for blood. When the
Carthaginians saw that none were pursuing them after the first
repulse from the rampart they imagined that they had been

afraid to go any further, their feelings of contempt returned, and they marched at a leisurely pace back to their camp.

They showed as much carelessness in guarding their own camp as they had shown in attacking the Roman, for although their enemy was near them they regarded them as only the wreckage of two armies which had been destroyed a few days before. Whilst they were, in consequence of this, neglectful of everything, Marcius, who had become thoroughly aware of it, thought out a plan, at first glance hazardous rather than bold, which was to assume the aggressive and attack the enemy's camp. He thought it would be easier to storm Hasdrubal's camp whilst he was alone than to defend his own, in case the three commanders united their forces once more. Besides, if he succeeded he would have gone far to retrieve their late disasters; if he failed the enemy could no longer despise him, since he would have been the first to attack.

XXXVIII. His plan seemed a desperate one, considering the position he was in, and might easily be upset by some unforeseen incident creating a panic in the night. To guard against these dangers as far as possible, he thought it well to address some words of encouragement to his men. He called them together and made the following speech to them:

"My loyalty and affection for my old commanders whether living or dead, as well as the situation in which we now find ourselves, ought to convince every one of you, soldiers, that this command, honourable as you rightly deem it to be, is, as a matter of fact, a position of very grave anxiety. For at a moment when I was hardly sufficient master of myself—did not fear dull the sense of pain—to find any comfort in my distress, I saw myself compelled to take thought alone for you all, the hardest thing in the world in a time of grief. Even when I have to consider how I can possibly preserve for my country you who are all that remain out of two armies, it is still a grief to have to divert my thoughts from a sorrow that is ever with me. Bitter memories vex me; the two Scipios haunt me in anxious thoughts by day and in dreams at night; they rouse me from my slumbers and forbid me to suffer them or their soldiers—your own comrades who never for eight years knew defeat in these lands—or the republic, to remain unavenged. They call upon me to follow their example and act on the principles they laid down; as no man obeyed them more faithfully while they lived, so now that they are gone they would have me think that what they would have done on any occasion that arose is the best thing for me also to do. And I would have you, my soldiers, not follow them with tears and laments as though they had ceased to be, for they live and are strong in the glory of all that they have done, but go into battle thinking of them as if they were here to encourage you and give you the signal. Surely it was nothing else than their image before your eyes which brought about that memorable battle yesterday, in which you showed your enemy that the Roman name did not perish with the Scipios, and that a people whose strength and courage even Cannae could not crush will rise superior to the hardest blows of fortune.

"Well, as you showed such daring yesterday on your own account, I want now to see if you will show as much daring at the bidding of your commander. When I gave the signal yesterday to recall you from your hot pursuit of your disordered foe it was from no wish to damp your courage but to reserve it for a greater and more glorious occasion, when you will shortly be able, prepared and armed, to fall upon the enemy when he is off his guard, without his arms and even wrapped in slumbers. And in thus hoping, I am not trusting simply to chance, but have good grounds for what I say. If any one were to ask you how, few as you are, you managed to defend your camp against a mighty host, how after your defeat you were able to repel those who had defeated you from your rampart, you would, I am sure, reply that this was the very danger you feared, and therefore you strengthened your defences in every possible way and held yourselves at your posts in readiness. And such is generally the case; men are least safe when their circumstances give them no cause for fear; what you think of no importance you leave open and unguarded. There is nothing which the enemy are less afraid of than that we who were lately surrounded and attacked should of our own motion attack their camp. Let us venture where no one can believe we will venture. The fact that it is thought too difficult will make it all the easier. I will lead you out in a silent march at the third watch of the night. I have ascertained that they have no proper arrangement of sentinels and pickets. When once our shout is heard in their gates the camp will be carried at the first rush. Then, whilst they are heavy with sleep, panic-struck at the unlooked-for tumult, and surprised defenceless in their beds, that slaughter will take place amongst them from which you were, to your intense disappointment, recalled yesterday.

"I know that the plan seems a daring one, but in difficult circumstances which leave little to hope for the boldest measures are always the safest. If, when the critical moment comes, you hang back ever so little and do not catch the opportunity as it flies past, you will look for it in vain when once you have let it go. There is one army near us, two more are not very far away. If we attack them now, there is some hope for us; you have already tried your strength against theirs. If we put off the day, and after yesterday's sortie are no longer regarded with contempt, there is the danger of all the generals and their armies uniting. In that case, shall we withstand the three generals, the three armies, which Cn. Scipio did not withstand when his army was in its full strength? As our generals perished owing to their forces being divided, so the enemy can be crushed in detail while they are divided. There is no other way of carrying on war; let us, then, wait for nothing beyond the opportunity of the coming night. Now go, trusting to the help of the gods and get food and rest so that, fresh and vigorous, you may break into the enemies' camp in the same courageous spirit in which you defended your own."

They were delighted to hear this new plan from their new general, and the more daring it was the more it pleased them. The rest of the day was spent in getting their arms ready and in looking after themselves. At the fourth watch they began to move.

XXXIX. The other Carthaginian forces were about six miles beyond the camp nearest to the Romans. Between them lay a valley thickly wooded, and on some ground about half-way through the wood a Roman cohort, adopting Punic tactics, concealed themselves with some cavalry. After the road was thus occupied midway, the rest of the force marched in silence to the enemy nearest to them, and as there were no outposts in front of the gates and no guard mounted they penetrated without any opposition into the camp just as if they were entering their own. Then the signals were sounded and the battle shout raised. Some slew the enemy while half asleep, others threw firebrands on to their huts, which were thatched with dry straw, others held the gates to intercept the fugitives. The fire, the shouting, and the slaughter, all combined, bereft the enemy almost of their senses and prevented them from either hearing one another on taking any measures for their safety. Without arms themselves they fell amongst troops of armed men; some rushed to the gates, others, finding the ways blocked, sprang over the rampart, and all who escaped in this way fled at once to the other camp, where they were met by the cohort and the cavalry running out from their concealment and all cut down to a man. Even if any one had escaped from the carnage the Romans, after taking that camp, ran on so swiftly to the other one that no one could get there before them to announce the disaster.

When they got to the second camp they found neglect and disorder everywhere, partly owing to its greater distance from them and partly because some of the defenders had dispersed in quest of fodder and wood and plunder. At the outposts the arms were actually piled, the soldiers, all unarmed, were sitting and lying about on the ground or walking up and down in front of the gates and rampart. In this state of careless disorder they were assailed by the Romans who were tired by their recent fighting and flushed with victory. It was impossible to hold the gates against them, and once within the gates a desperate battle began. At the first alarm there was a rush from all parts of the camp, and there would have been a long and obstinate struggle if the Carthaginians had not seen in the blood-stained shields of the Romans plain traces of the former contest, which filled them with dismay and terror. They all turned and fled wherever they could find the way open to escape, and all but those who had been already killed were driven out of the camp.

So in a night and a day two of the enemies' camps had been carried under the leadership of L. Marcius. According to Claudius, who translated the annals of Acilius from Greek into Latin, as many as 37,000 of the enemy were slain, 1830 being prisoners, besides an immense amount of plunder. The latter included a silver shield one hundred and thirty-seven pounds in weight, together with a statuette of Hasdrubal. Valerius Antias relates that only Mago's camp was taken, when the enemy lost 7000 killed; in the other battle when the Romans made the sortie and fought with Hasdrubal 10,000 were killed and 4380 made prisoners. Piso says that 5000 men were killed when Mago was ambushed while recklessly pursuing our men. All these authors dwell upon the greatness of Marcius, and they exaggerate the glory he really won by describing a supernatural incident. Whilst he was addressing his troops they say that a flame shot from his head, without his being aware of it, to the great terror of the soldiers standing round. It is also stated that there was in the temple on the Capitol before it was burnt a shield called " the Marcian " with a statuette of Hasdrubal, as memorials of his victory.[17]

For some time after this, matters were quiet in Spain, neither side after the defeats they had suffered being anxious to risk a decisive action.

XL. *The Campaign in Sicily.* — While these events were occurring in Spain, Marcellus, after the capture of Syracuse, settled the affairs of Sicily with so much justice and integrity as to enhance not merely his own reputation but the greatness and dignity of Rome as well. He removed to Rome the ornaments of the city, the statues and pictures in which Syracuse abounded; they were, it is true, spoils taken from the enemy and acquired by the laws of war, but that was the beginning of our admiration for Greek works of art, which has led to the present reckless spoliation of every kind of treasure, sacred and profane alike. This has at last recoiled upon the gods of Rome, upon that temple especially which Marcellus so splendidly adorned. For the shrines near the Capena Gate, which Marcellus dedicated, used to be visited by strangers on account of the very beautiful specimens of that class of ornament; but very few are to be seen to-day.

Whilst Marcellus was settling the affairs of Sicily, deputations from nearly all the communities in the island visited him. The treatment they received varied with their circumstances. Those who had not revolted or had returned to our friendship prior to the capture of Syracuse were welcomed and honoured as loyal allies; those who after its capture had surrendered through fear, had to accept the terms which the victor imposes on the vanquished.

The Romans, however, had considerable remnants of the war still on their hands round Agrigentum. There were still left in the field the generals Epicydes and Hanno who had commanded in the late war, and a fresh general who had been sent in place of Hippocrates by Hannibal, a man of Libyphoenician nationality, called Hippacritanus—his fellow-countrymen called him Muttines—a man of energy and enterprise, who had had a thorough military training under that master of war, Hannibal. He was furnished by Epicydes and Hanno with a force of Numidians, and with these troopers he committed such extensive depredations on the lands of those who were hostile and was so active in keeping his friends loyal by always bringing them help at the right moment, that in a short time all Sicily had heard of him and there was no one from whom the supporters of Carthage expected greater things.

Up to that time Epicydes and Hanno had been compelled to

keep within the fortifications of Agrigentum; now, however, in a spirit of self-confidence quite as much as in compliance with the advice of Muttines, they ventured outside and fixed their camp by the Himera. No sooner was this reported to Marcellus than he promptly moved up and encamped about four miles from the enemy with the intention of waiting for any action he might take. But no time was allowed him for either delay or deliberation; Muttines crossed the river and charged his enemy's outposts, creating the greatest terror and confusion. The next day there was almost a regular battle and he drove the Romans within their lines. Then he was recalled by tidings of a mutiny which had broken out amongst the Numidians in Hanno's camp. Nearly three hundred of them had gone off to Heraclea Minoa. When he left the camp to reason with them and recall them, he is said to have most earnestly advised the generals not to engage the enemy in his absence. They both resented this; more especially Hanno who had long been jealous of Muttines' reputation. "Is Muttines," he exclaimed, "to dictate to me; a low-born African to give orders to a Carthaginian general bearing the commission of the senate and people?" Epicydes wished to wait, but he brought him over to his view, that they should cross the river and offer battle, for, he argued, if they waited for Muttines, and then fought a successful action, he would undoubtedly get all the credit for it.

XLI. Marcellus was of course intensely indignant at the idea of the man who had turned Hannibal, flushed with his victory at Cannae, aside from Nola now giving way before enemies whom he had defeated by sea and land, and he ordered his men to seize their arms at once and march out in order of battle. Whilst he was forming his lines, ten Numidians from the opposing army galloped up to him at full speed with the announcement that their countrymen would take no part in the fighting, first because they sympathised with the three hundred mutineers who had gone to Heraclea, and secondly because they saw that their leader had been got rid of on the very day of battle by generals who wanted to cast a cloud on his reputation. Deceitful as that nation usually is, they kept their promise on that occasion. The news flew quickly through the ranks that the cavalry of whom they stood in greatest fear had left the enemy in the lurch, and their courage rose accordingly. The enemy, on the other hand, were in a great state of alarm because, not only were they losing the support of their strongest arm, but there was a chance of their being attacked by their own cavalry.

So there was not much of a conflict, the action was decided by the first battle shout and charge. When the opposing lines met, the Numidians were standing quietly on the wings; when they saw their own side turn tail they joined them in their flight for a short distance, but when they saw them making in all haste for Agrigentum they dispersed to all the neighbouring cities for fear of having to stand a siege. Several thousand men were killed and eight elephants captured.

This was the last battle Marcellus fought in Sicily. After his victory he returned to Syracuse.

As the year was now almost at an end, the senate decreed that the praetor P. Cornelius should send instructions to the consuls at Capua for one of them, if they approved, to come to Rome to appoint new magistrates while Hannibal was at a distance and no very critical operations were going on at Capua. After receiving the despatch the consuls came to a mutual arrangement that Claudius should conduct the elections and Fulvius remain at Capua. The new consuls were Cn. Fulvius Centimalus and P. Sulpicius Galba, the son of Servius, a man who had never before filled a curule office. The election of praetors followed; those elected were L. Cornelius Lentulus, M. Cornelius Cethegus, C. Sulpicius, and C. Calpurnius Piso. Piso took over the urban jurisdiction, Sicily was allotted to Sulpicius, Apulia to Cethegus, Sardinia to Lentulus. The consuls had their commands extended for another year.

NOTES

BOOK XXI

1 (p. 16). *i.e.*, of course, not the Gaul beyond the Alps, the scene of Julius Caesar's triumphs, but the country between the Alps and the Po, inhabited by Gallic (Celtic) tribes which had been recently conquered (*see* Mommsen, Vol. II. pp. 70-76).

2 (p. 17). The consul who concluded the treaty at the close of the first Punic war.

3 (p. 20). These were the Phoenician towns on the north coast of Africa who enjoyed municipal autonomy but were bound to pay a fixed tribute and furnish contingents of troops.

4 (p. 21). A very doubtful reading.

5 (p. 28). The Campus Martius.

6 (p. 29). Even in Livy's time, as we see a little lower down (p. 35), the route by which Hannibal reached Italy was a controverted question, and it is just as much so to-day. The one main authority accessible to us besides Livy himself is Polybius, who wrote in Greek. He was born during the war and went over the ground himself some fifty years after Hannibal traversed it. His account differs in many respects from Livy's, and would appear on the whole to be the more accurate one. But the descriptions given of localities by the ancient writers were extremely vague, even where they wrote from personal knowledge. We cannot make out even from Caesar's own language for certain where he landed in Kent and where he crossed the Thames. And the difficulty with regard to Hannibal's route is aggravated by the fact that there were no towns or villages with well-known names through which it lay, and by which, therefore, we could fix it. The most probable view appears to be that he followed the Rhone till he reached the spot where the mountains of Savoy (the Mont du Chat) approach the river. Crossing this chain of mountains he marched past the present town of Chambéry in a southern direction until he reached the Isère again at Montmelian, and followed its course to the foot of the Little St. Bernard. Livy's account takes him from the Drôme to the Durance and across Mont Genièvre. The vivid account of this march in Mommsen (II. pp. 99-103) should be carefully studied.

7 (p. 30). " This resolution of Scipio to send his own army on to Spain and to meet Hannibal with the army of the two praetors appears to show that he possessed the highest qualities of a general, which involve the wisdom of a statesman no less than of a soldier. As a mere military question his calculation, though baffled by the event, was sound; but if we view it in a higher light, the importance to the Romans of retaining their hold on Spain would have justified a far greater hazard; for if the Carthaginians were suffered to consolidate their dominion in Spain and to avail themselves of its immense resources not in money only but in men, the hardiest and steadiest of barbarians, and under the training of such generals as Hannibal and his brother, equal to the best soldiers in the world, the Romans would hardly have been able to maintain the contest. Had not P. Scipio then despatched his army to Spain at this critical moment, instead of carrying it home to Italy, his son in all probability would never have won the battle of Zama " (Arnold, *Hist. Rome*, III. 81).

8 (p. 31). Whilst the infantry had halted to repel the rear attack the cavalry and baggage had gone on, leaving a gap into which the barbarians rushed, thus isolating the infantry.

9 (p. 34). This famous story has, of course, received scant courtesy from modern critics. The difficulty of felling " tall trees " in such a barren snow-bound region was perhaps not greater than that of finding a sufficient quantity of vinegar for the purpose, unless it were what the soldiers had to drink, but they could hardly have spared much of this. Still Livy could not simply have invented it, he must have found something of the sort in his authorities.

10 (p. 35). This is in all probability the correct number. Polybius quotes the numbers from the tablet which Hannibal had caused to be fixed up at Lacinium, viz. 12,000 Africans, 8000 Spaniards, and 6000 cavalry. Thus his march from the Pyrenees to the plains of Northern Italy must have cost him 33,000 men, or more than half the number he started with. Cincius' recollection of what Hannibal told him was, therefore, fairly accurate.

11 (p. 35). I have followed Madvig's text here in spite of the boldness of his conjecture. The other suggested readings give an obscure sense. A note of Strabo's would seem to imply that the Taurini were a mixed race of Gauls and Ligurians.

12 (p. 35). The portion of the Graian Alps which extends from the Little St. Bernard to Mont Blanc.

13 (p. 35). " This was the pass of the Great St. Bernard. The name Poenine has been traced to the Celtic deity Penn. Jupiter Poeninus was worshipped on the summit, and the name has been found on thirty *ex voto* tablets which have been discovered near the top. The range was also called *Mons Jovis*, which survives in the names Mont-Joux, Plan-de-Joux, which are still localised on the height " (W. Capes, in a note on the passage).

14 (p. 43). He was in his seventeenth year.

15 (p. 47). The Carthaginians had in the previous war been vastly superior in handling their ships; the object was to ram and run down the enemy's ships. The Romans always tried to board, when their superior soldiership told.

16 (p. 47). The Liparae.

17 (p. 58). The list of portents here and in the next book were no doubt taken from the records of the pontifical college (*see* Introduction, p. xii). They are a vivid witness of the nervous terror which had seized the whole population; we find their counterpart again and again in later history. These oracular tablets were slips of wood—probably oak, as the sacred tree—inscribed with archaic characters, and used for purposes of divination.

18 (p. 59). As tribune of the plebs (228 B.C.) he proposed settlements on an extensive scale in the country round Ariminum and Picenum, where the land was lying waste and depopulated since the war of extermination against the Senones. It was held probably as pasture by some of the Roman aristocracy, and his proposal was therefore strenuously resisted by the senate. Ultimately the measure was passed by the Assembly without the sanction of the senate, a breach of the existing usage from which Polybius dates a change for the worse in the Roman constitution. His first consulship was in 223 B.C., and was won in spite of the opposition of the patricians. He at once took command of the war against the Insubres, and on the eve of a decisive battle a despatch was handed to him from the senate informing him that a flaw had been discovered in his election. Possibly suspecting the nature of its contents, he did not open it till after the battle, which was won by the bravery of the soldiers in spite

of his bad generalship. Then he declared that as the gods had fought for him they had clearly ratified his election. His subsequent triumph was refused by the senate but allowed by the people.

19 (p. 59). This measure was intended to restrict the growing foreign trade carried on by the great houses, who enriched themselves and their friends by commercial speculations supported by the whole power of the government. This was especially the case with regard to corn, which was probably becoming a monopoly and so raised the price of food. The *amphora*, a two-handled jar with a narrow neck and holding a little more than five and a half gallons, was the unit of the Roman measures of capacity, and was used to denote the size of ships like our ton. This law soon became obsolete, as the aristocracy of birth became supplanted by an aristocracy of wealth.

BOOK XXII

1 (p. 68). The Romans regarded all hostility to Rome as more or less criminal, and the more dangerous the hostility the more criminal they held it to be. Hannibal, therefore, is generally painted in the blackest colours, and his " Punic faith " is a stock accusation. As a matter of fact, as we learn from Polybius, in the present instance he decided that Maharbal had no authority to grant such terms, therefore they were cancelled. This is almost precisely what the Romans did in the affair of the Caudine Forks, and in the case of Lutatius in the last book.

2 (p. 70). *i.e.* he was a pro-dictator. The MS. text is unintelligible. Madvig's conjectural interpolation rather explains than amends the text. Weissenborn's suggestion seems the simplest, and is followed in the translation. It is supported by Livy's description of the office in chap. xxxii.

3 (p. 71). *Mens* = Intelligence. She was the goddess of reason and sound sense, which were certainly needed at this critical time. Many years later, in the equally disastrous days of the Cimbric war, M. Æmilius Scaurus is said to have founded a temple to her. Mr. Dowdall in his note on this passage says, " This worship of ' Intellect ' found its counterpart in that of ' Reason ' during the French Revolution." The underlying motives, however, were widely different in the two nations.

4 (p. 74). The translation follows the MSS. reading, the numerous attempts of modern editors to improve the text miss the point. The contrast is between the wariness of Fabius and the impetuosity of his predecessors.

5 (p. 75). The town took its name from the gulf on which it stood. A short distance from the town were the warm baths to which Tacitus tells us the Emperor Claudius resorted in his last illness, and which, like those of Baiae, were a favourite watering-place for Roman invalids. They still exist under the name of I Bagni.

6 (p. 87). The Porta Decumana, marked R in the plan of the Roman camp in the *Class. Dict.*

7 (p. 90). Ihne comments upon this innovation thus: " In the Assembly of the tribes the foolish proposal was made to equalise Minucius and Fabius in the command of the army; that is to say, to destroy that unity of direction and authority which gave its chief value to the dictatorship in comparison with the divided command of the consuls. In the old time, when the office of Dictator was better understood as an embodiment of the majesty and authority of the whole State, it would have been impossible thus to curtail the dictatorial power. Now, however, the terrible disasters of the war had produced the effect which may be observed in the case of sick persons who have tried several remedies in vain and

are almost given up for lost. The usual and regular treatment is abandoned and the chance remedy of some impudent quack is adopted in sheer despair. The Roman people, generally so sober, self-composed, and self-collected, so conservative and so full of confidence in their ancient institutions, suddenly became reckless innovators and undid their own work " (*Hist. of Rome*, II. 223).

8 (p. 98). The secrecy imposed upon the hierophants is supposed to be imposed upon the aristocracy generally, so that the wealthy plebeians, leagued with the patricians in a conspiracy of silence, were doing their part in checking the aspirations of the plebs.

9 (p. 98). Paulus had three years before commanded in Illyria with considerable success, but had afterwards been indicted on suspicion of appropriating some of the spoils. He was acquitted, but he had not forgiven the plebs whose tribunes had tried to blast his reputation. Varro's solitary success in the first election was due to the entire plebs supporting him, whilst the patrician votes were divided amongst the three patrician candidates.

10 (p. 102). In the bitter contempt which Fabius shows for the " man from the ranks " we see the feelings with which the old families of Rome watched the steadily growing power of the plebs. Mommsen formed pretty nearly the same estimate of his character (*see* his remarks in Vol. II. p. 149). A much less biassed view is taken by Dr. Arnold when he says, " Varro, his enemies said, was a butcher's son, nay, it was added that he himself had been a butcher's boy, and had only been enabled by the fortune which his father left him to throw aside his ignoble calling and to aspire to public offices. So Cromwell was called a brewer; but Varro had been successively elected quaestor, plebeian and curule ædile, and praetor, while we are not told that he was ever tribune; and it is without example in Roman history that a mere demagogue, of no family, with no other merits, civil or military, should be raised to such nobility. Varro was eloquent, it is true, but eloquence alone would scarcely have so recommended him; and if in his praetorship, as is probable, he had been one of the two home praetors, he must have possessed a competent knowledge of law. Besides, even after his defeat at Cannae, he was employed for several years in various important offices, civil and military, which would never have been the case had he been the mere factious braggart that historians have painted him."

11 (p. 107). Undisturbed possession and unbroken user for two years constituted a legal claim to ownership, according to the law of the Twelve Tables. Hannibal had practically fulfilled this condition with regard to Italy.

12 (p. 111). This remark has been variously understood. The simplest explanation seems to be that Hannibal saw that once dismounted their escape was hopeless, and they would perish to a man; whereas had they been given up as prisoners they might have been exchanged or ransomed, and so Hannibal might have gained. As *equites* they belonged to the upper classes of Roman society.

13 (p. 112). " Less than six thousand men of Hannibal's army had fallen: no greater price had he paid for the total destruction of more than eighty thousand of the enemy, for the capture of their two camps, for the utter annihilation, as it seemed, of all their means for offensive warfare. It is no wonder that the spirits of the Carthaginian officers were elated by this unequalled victory. Maharbal, seeing what his cavalry had done, said to Hannibal, ' Let me advance instantly with the horse, and do thou follow to support me; in four days from this time thou shalt sup in the Capitol.' There are moments when rashness is wisdom, it may be that this was one of them. The statue of the goddess Victory in the Capitol may well have trembled in every limb and have dropped her wings as if

for ever. But Hannibal came not; and if panic had for one moment unnerved the iron courage of the Roman aristocracy, on the next their inborn spirit revived; and their resolute will, striving beyond its present power, created, as is the law of our nature, the power which it required " (Arnold, Vol. II. p. 143).

14 (p. 114). This was the silver *denarius*, and derived its name from the stamp it bore of a chariot with four horses. It was worth about 8¾d.

15 (p. 118). But repulsive as Livy declares them to be, and to him they must have been repulsive, they appear in later times. The Christian apologist, Justin Martyr, charges the Romans with these horrible practices as late as 150 A.D. They were undoubtedly due to Greek influences. At Athens there was an annual sacrificing of two persons during the Thargelia.

16 (p. 126). " It is a convincing proof of the political wisdom of the Romans and their fitness to rule the world that even now the great majority of their Italian subjects remained faithful in their allegiance. . . . Not only all the colonies, Roman as well as Latin, but also the whole of Etruria, Umbria, Picenum, and the genuine Sabellian races of the Sabines . . . as well as all the Greek cities, remained faithful to Rome. . . . It was due mainly to the political unity under the supremacy of Rome which, in spite of isolated defections, bound the various races of Italy into indissoluble union, and in the end prevailed even over the genius of Hannibal " (Ihne, Vol. II. p. 255. *See also* Mommsen, Vol. II. pp. 124-125).

BOOK XXIII

1 (p. 138). The *modius* was very nearly equal to our peck.

2 (p. 140). I have ventured to take for granted Weissenborn's conjectural reading. His arguments against the ordinary text are conclusive.

3 (p. 141). It would appear that a resolution of both the Senate and the Assembly was necessary to allow the Dictator to appear mounted in the City. Plutarch tells us that the Master of the People—the old title of the Dictator—was forbidden by an ancient law to ride on horseback, either because as the infantry formed their main strength they thought he ought to be on foot with them, or because, in this way, the terrible powers wielded by that office were shown to depend upon the will of the people. But the matter is obscure.

4 (p. 143). The *denarius, see* note 14, above.

5 (p. 145). The MSS. text is hopeless here.

6 (p. 149). This is the emendation adopted by most editors. All the MSS. read " to Cumae," which is meaningless, as they did not come from Cumae and do not appear to be in any way connected with it, and Livy says just below that they returned to Praeneste.

7 (p. 149). The Fortuna Primigenia of Praeneste was a widely honoured deity. She was worshipped as the mother of Jupiter and Juno, hence her epithet of Primigenia, the firstborn and mother of all. The three statues were those of Fortuna and her two divine children.

8 (p. 151). The one mentioned in Book VIII. chap. v. (vol. ii. p. 112).

9 (p. 153). *i.e.* M. Junius, whose nomination is mentioned in the last book, chap. lvii. (p. 119).

10 (p. 160). The appointment of the people was necessary in the case of a magistrate who had made a vow of this character whilst in office and had gone back into private life before he could discharge it.

11 (p. 163). *See* the map of Rome in the *Classical Dictionary*. It is marked No. XII., and lay between the Caelian, the Aventine, and the Circus Maximus. Festus says of it, " The name of the Piscina Publica still survives, but the thing itself has disappeared. The people used to frequent it for swimming and other exercise."

12 (p. 163). " The Punic government had made ready a force to support Hannibal: 12,000 foot, 1500 horse, 20 elephants, 1000 talents of silver; the transports were to be convoyed by 60 ships of war. All was ready, Mago, Hannibal's brother, in command, when news came of the disaster in Spain. This caused alarm and hesitation; and it was soon followed by an appeal from Sardinia, where the leading chiefs, weary of Roman rule, were ready to rise in revolt. The rulers of Carthage lost their balance under the stress of fear and hope. To save Spain, they despatched Mago and his forces, not to Italy but to Spain. To gain Sardinia they fell to preparing another armament of about the same strength. Hannibal had to wait. It is hardly too much to say that the blind folly of this decision marks the turning point of the war " (Heitland, *Rom. Republic*, I. p. 267).

13 (p. 167). For the nature of this purification, *see* Vol. I. p. 51.

14 (p. 171). These were the earlier inhabitants of the island, who had fled before the Carthaginians into the mountain districts. They were called " Pelliti," from their dressing in goatskins (*pelles*).

15 (p. 174). I have followed Weissenborn's text. The usual emendation seems pointless. The garrison at Nola were, from the speaker's point of view, keeping the town in an unwilling subjection, and were at the same time the plunderers of Samnium.

16 (p. 179). For the *spolia opima*, see Vol. I. p. 14. The words are used here in a much looser sense, suitable to the braggadocio tone in which Taurea addresses his opponent.

17 (p. 179). This is the sense given by most interpreters. The point of the skit is in the meaning of the word *asellus*, which means a young ass. It is quite possible that Taurea only suggested the hollow lane as a joke, not for a moment thinking that Claudius would take him seriously, in which case his meaning would rather be, " Do not put your horse where it can do nothing, I certainly shall not follow you." The proverbial expression was used of any one in a hopeless quandary.

18 (p. 181). Livy's phrase is unusual, and is generally taken to mean " furnish a temporary loan," but the Latin hardly bears this meaning, and the context would imply that the contractors were not asked to lend money to the government, but to abstain from pressing the government for payment when they had completed their contract. " In tendering for the supply of the army in Spain contractors were invited to accept a promise of cash payment to be made as soon as the treasury could meet its liabilities and not to insist on payment by a fixed date. That the companies agreed to these terms is represented by the rhetorical moralists of later times as an act of the purest patriotism. But the men of money had a keen eye for a bargain. They stipulated for their own exemption from military service during the continuance of the contract, and also that any losses at sea through storms or act of the enemy should be made good to them by the state. We shall see later to what abuses and frauds this insurance-clause led. Meanwhile, public spirit was in fashion, and credit enabled the senate to feed and clothe the distant armies" (Heitland, I. pp. 270-1).

19 (p. 182). " It is a great pity that we have no more detailed report of these two splendid victories than the dry narrative which Livy gives in half a chapter. But the meagreness of the report might be excused if its truth were beyond suspicion. We shall find in the sequel that all the

statements that have reference to the affairs of Spain, and especially to the exploits of the Scipios in that country, are tainted with laudatory exaggeration on an unusually large scale " (Ihne, Vol. II. p. 275, note 1).

BOOK XXIV

1 (p. 185). Whom they detested most. *See* the beginning of this book.

2 (p. 185). Cicero quotes an interesting story about this column from Coelius, one of Livy's authorities. Hannibal wanted to take it away, and in order to find out whether it was solid gold or only plated he bored a hole in it, and finding it was solid decided to carry it off. That night, however, Juno, the goddess whose temple he was violating, appeared to him in a dream and warned him against his proposed sacrilege; if he persisted, she told him, he would lose the sight of his remaining eye. Like a sensible man he listened to the warning, and made from the gold taken out in the boring a little heifer which he placed on the capital of the column (*De Div.* I. 24).

3 (p. 192). And therefore the consul held the power of life and death, without any right of appeal from his sentence. Once within the *pomoerium* of the City an appeal lay to the people. The Campus Martius was, of course, outside the *pomoerium*.

4 (p. 194). Reading *vicum* instead of the *vocem* of the MSS.

5 (p. 195). In proposing this measure the senators showed their patriotism, as they laid the heaviest burden upon themselves.

6 (p. 195). A lake between Cumae and Puteoli, situated in the midst of gloomy scenery, which was popularly believed to be the entrance to the world of the dead. On its shore stood a chapel devoted to necromantic rites. "That crater of an old volcano, where the very soil still seemed to breathe out fire, while the unbroken rim of its basin was covered with the uncleared masses of the native woods, was the subject of a thousand mysterious stories, and was regarded as one of those spots where the lower world approached most nearly to the light of day, and where offerings paid to the gods of the dead were most surely acceptable. Such worship was a main part of the national religion of the Carthaginians; and Hannibal, whose latest act before he set out on his great expedition had been a journey to Gades to sacrifice to the god of his fathers, the Hercules of Tyre, visited the lake of Avernus, it is probable, quite as much in sincere devotion, as in order to mask his design of attacking Puteoli " (Arnold, III. p. 199).

7 (p. 200). As soon as a slave received his liberty he shaved his head and put on a conical white cap, the right of wearing such a covering being a distinctive mark of a free citizen. Except for this purpose the Romans did not wear anything on their heads. The cap has been an emblem of freedom in ancient and modern times.

8 (p. 201). This is a suspicious account. At the most there may have been a skirmish. Hannibal had left his light cavalry and some of his best infantry at Tifata, and declined a general action with a complete consular army. He probably, as Dr. Arnold suggests, had no thought of attacking the town, but returned to Tifata to take the troops from thence, and having done this and stayed long enough in Campania to allow the Capuans to get in their harvest safely, he set off on his march to Tarentum. None of the Roman armies attempted to stop him or so much as ventured to follow him.

9 (p. 206). As the revolution in Syracuse and its subsequent conquest are given by Livy in considerable detail, the following topographical note may assist the reader in following him. The plan of Syracuse in Everyman's *Classical Atlas* (marked XXIV.) will help to make things clearer. The Phoenicians were the first of whom we have traces, and sometime between 900 and 700 B.C. settled in Ortygia, which Livy generally calls the Island. The Greeks ultimately displaced the earlier settlers and advanced from Ortygia to the mainland. Here they built the town of Achradina, which became the residential and mercantile quarter; Ortygia gradually assuming the character of a fortress, with strong defences all round, especially on the north side, where it was connected by a causeway with the mainland. Subsequently, to the north of it, arose the two suburbs of Tycha and Neapolis, each separately fortified by strong walls. Finally, Dionysius the Elder enlarged the city by taking in the district called Epipolae. The whole formed now a triangle, the base being the eastern shore of Achradina, and the two sides converging to the most westerly point of Epipolae, the fort Euryalus. The walls, it will be noticed, run almost throughout their circuit upon the edge of precipitous rocks, adding thereby immensely to the defensive strength of the place.

10 (p. 206). The Hexapylum, or " Six Gates," appears to have stood in the north wall of Epipolae, close to the wall dividing that suburb from Tycha. The road from the interior of the island passed through it, making it more open to attack than the rest of the fortifications. Hence its exceptional strength, for these six gates appear to have stood behind one another with a continuous wall on either side like an extended barbican. Not till the innermost had been reached and broken down could an entry be effected.

11 (p. 208). The main associations connected with the Island were those of a strongly guarded and strongly entrenched tyranny. The destruction of this wall, as a symbolic act, was akin to the destruction of the Bastille.

12 (p. 227). " *White camp*."—This place and the " Mount of Victory " mentioned just below have not been identified, a remark which applies to many of the Spanish localities Livy mentions.

13 (p. 229). " We cannot read Livy's report here without the conviction that a great portion of it rests on fiction or exaggeration. . . . If we add up the numbers given by Livy, the Carthaginians lost in the two years 215 and 214 B.C. in Spain not less than 80,000 men. The magnificence of such boasting is apt to inspire admiration " (Ihne, II. p. 314, note 2). To the same effect, Dr. Arnold: " The Roman annalists whom Livy has copied here seem to have outdone their usual exaggerations in describing the exploits of the two Scipios, and what is the truth concealed beneath this mass of fiction we are wholly unable to discover " (III. p. 260). *See*, however, Mommsen, II. p. 145.

14 (p. 230). The incident referred to is narrated in Book XXII. (p. 113).

15 (p. 230). Including the army engaged in Spain, the Roman land and sea forces cannot have amounted to less than 200,000 men, that is one-fourth of the whole population of Italy capable of bearing arms.

BOOK XXV

1 (p. 239). It would appear, however, that at this time no minimum age was fixed by law. The restriction first appears in a measure introduced some time afterwards by a tribune of the plebs, L. Villius, in 810 B.C.

2 (p. 239). *i.e.* about three quarts.

3 (p. 240). Those who were burghers of Latin municipalities having the full local franchise and happened to be staying in Rome at the time of the election.

4 (p. 242). " The moral and religious elements of the community must have been deeply tainted, if in the very midst of the Hannibalian war, in the agonising struggle for existence, a great number of men could be found among the influential classes so utterly void of patriotic feeling and conscientiousness, so hardened against public indignation, so careless of just retribution " (Ihne, II. p. 321).

5 (p. 247). The text here seems hopeless. Livy's meaning appears to be that no terms were made for them.

6 (p. 250). Livy is, of course, speaking of it on the landward side; it stood at the western extremity of the town, being very slightly raised above it; on the seaward side it was protected by the high cliffs on which it stood.

7 (p. 253). For these Games, *see* Mommsen, II. p. 324.

8 (p. 260). *See* note 22 in Vol. I. p. 355.

9 (p. 262). It is extremely difficult to understand this account. The addition of Sempronius' army, one would suppose, would have made the Romans eager to renew the fight, instead of which they retired precipitately in the night. In all probability what constantly happened elsewhere happened here; when Hannibal was personally in command the Roman generals kept a respectful distance. The terror of his name was not yet weakened.

10 (p. 268). This is marked in the map of Syracuse at the north-east corner of Tycha.

11 (p. 269). " From this high ground he saw Syracuse at his feet and, he doubted not, in his power. Two quarters, Neapolis (the ' New Town,' as it was called), and Tycha, were open to his first advance; their only fortification being the general enclosure of the lines, which he had already carried. Below, just overhanging the sea, or floating on its waters, lay Achradina and the island of Ortygia, fenced by their own separate walls, which till the time of the first Dionysius had been the limit of Syracuse, the walls which the great Athenian armament had besieged in vain. Nearer on the right, and running so deeply into the land that it seemed almost to reach the foot of the heights on which he stood, lay the still basin of the Great Harbour, its broad surface half hidden by the hulls of a hundred Carthaginian ships; while further on the right was the camp of his lieutenant, T. Crispinus, crowning the rising ground beyond the Anapus, close by the temple of Olympian Jupiter " (Arnold, III. p. 300).

12 (p. 272). A line appears to have dropped out here in the MSS. containing probably the names of the towns.

13 (p. 274). The text is faulty here. Various emendations, some rather violent ones, have been proposed. I have ventured to delete the *si* before *simul* as due to " itacism " on the part of a sleepy copyist, and finish the sentence with *Syracusas*. The fact of their having just been delivered from Carthaginian predominance, of which they had recently had such bitter experience, would make them all the more ready to renew their friendship with Rome.

14 (p. 276). The soldiers were landed from the quadrireme simply to hold the gate on the island leading down to the water. Marcellus' general attack upon the land side of Achradina, *i.e.* upon the wall separating it from Tycha and Neapolis, drew the garrison of the island to its defence, and the swift vessels landed men upon the deserted district, who at once captured it, and pressed through the gates (the Pentapylon) leading into Achradina, which had been left open.

15 (p. 280). And therefore the Romans had not the advantage of their discipline and tactics. It was man against man.

16 (p. 283). Where the fugitives had rallied.

17 (p. 288). *See* Mommsen, II. pp. 146, 147.

THE TEMPLE PRESS, PRINTERS LETCHWORTH